Vulnerable Populations

Volume 1

Vulnerable Populations

*Evaluation and Treatment
of Sexually Abused Children
and Adult Survivors*

Volume 1

Suzanne M. Sgroi, M.D.

Lexington Books
An Imprint of Macmillan, Inc.
New York

Maxwell Macmillan Canada
Toronto

Maxwell Macmillan International
New York   Oxford   Singapore   Sydney

Lexington Books
An Imprint of Macmillan, Inc.
866 Third Avenue, New York, N. Y. 10022

Maxwell Macmillan Canada, Inc.
1200 Eglinton Avenue East
Suite 200
Don Mills, Ontario M3C 3N1

Macmillan, Inc. is part of the Maxwell Communication Group of Companies.

Printed in the United States of America

printing number
5   6   7   8   9   10

Library of Congress Cataloging-in-Publication Data

Vulnerable populations.

   Vol. 2 has subtitle: Treatment of sexual abuse of children, adult survivors, and the mentally retarded.
   Includes index.
   1. Child molesting—Treatment.   2. Sexually abused children—Mental health.   3. Adult child abuse victims—Mental health.   4. Psychotherapy.   I. Sgroi, Suzanne M., 1943–
[DNLM: 1. Child Abuse, Sexual—psychology.   2. Mental Retardation—psychology.
3. Psychotherapy.   4. Sex Offenses. WA 320 V991]
RC560.C46V85   1988   616.85′83   87–29893
ISBN 0–669–16336–8 (alk. paper)
ISBN 0–669–16338–4 (pbk. : alk. paper)

To Margaret Campbell Vasington with admiration, appreciation, and affection.

You have undertaken to lead so many of us along pathways of understanding that few would dare to traverse alone or without your guidance. In your own quest to learn better ways to help children and adults who hurt, you have challenged and enlightened a host of others who work in the field of child sexual abuse treatment. Your courage and fierce determination and generous sharing of yourself are an inspiration and a gift to all. If you cast your eyes around you, Margaret, you will see how your company of fellow-searchers and healers has grown. From trauma to healing, you have shown the rest of us how to proceed.

Contents

Acknowledgments

This book could not have been written without the unfailing support and contributions of many friends and colleagues. I am especially grateful to Jeanette Dille, who has been an inspiration and mainstay to me for many years; to Alma Fitzsimmons, who has been a compassionate and sustaining force in our medical practice; to Barbara Bunk, who has contributed her outstanding clinical skills and ideas to our child sexual abuse practice; and to Norah Sargent, who worked devotedly to edit and organize the manuscript.

Introduction

Suzanne M. Sgroi

This book, originally contemplated as a unity, has rapidly expanded to become the first volume of a two-volume work. In some ways, the rapid expansion of chapters has mirrored the recent explosive growth of awareness and concern about sexual abuse of vulnerable populations. In 1984, the American public had its first exposure to a prime-time network television movie about intrafamily child sexual abuse: "Something About Amelia." Soon thereafter, a series of reports of sexual abuse of children occurring in day-care centers raised fear and ire in parents and most other adults. A U.S. senator revealed that she had been sexually abused when she was five years old and that the single most difficult aspect of her victimization was that the judge did not believe her or the other child because their sixty-year-old abuser was a well-known member of the community.

Since 1984, Americans have become accustomed to seeing features about child sexual abuse on programs such as "60 Minutes" and "20/20." For the first time, childhood sexual abuse has become a household concept—openly discussed in news reports, entertainment features, and conferences, in some public and private schools, and between some parents and their children.

In response, there has been a growing demand by increasingly knowledgeable consumers for comprehensive and compassionate professional services for victims, abusers, and their families. In particular, adult survivors (men and women who were sexually abused in childhood) are becoming a visible and sophisticated consumer group. At the same time, a steady flow of new reports of sexual abuse of contemporary child victims creates a demand for careful and comprehensive investigation of these cases. Meanwhile, mentally retarded adults, a long-overlooked vulnerable population, are finally beginning to be viewed as persons who also deserve to receive protection and empowering interventions such as avoidance training with regard to sexual abuse.

This volume begins with a chapter on children's sexual behavior. Barbara Bunk, Carolyn Wabrek, and I believed it would be worthwhile to pool our knowledge about this topic in an attempt to create a methodology to assist professionals in assessing children as victims and as abusers. The next two chapters by Denise Gelinas on family therapy of intrafamily child sexual abuse are important contributions because they describe an eclectic combination of principles and their applications to a population long ignored by most leaders in the field of family therapy. Four chapters on treatment of adult survivors of child sexual abuse then follow. Lisa McCann, Laurie Pearlman, David Sakheim, and Daniel Abrahamson have provided a thoughtful and elegant formulation of the process by which adult survivors strive to make sense of a world that includes sexual victimization in childhood, and they have pointed out its clinical applications. Michael Johanek has provided us with a cogent perspective on assessing and treating adult male victims of child sexual abuse, another overlooked population. Carolyn Agosta and Mary Loring, two clinicians who work within a private organization dedicated to reducing the incidence of violence, have written a fascinating description of their program for adult survivors—an informed and creative combination of the self-help and therapy models of intervention. Lastly, Barbara Bunk and I have included a chapter that attempts to share a clinical approach to working with adult survivors that is derived from a combined psychodynamic and behavioral perspective.

The last part of this volume includes a comprehensive and thoroughly detailed set of guidelines on criminal investigation of child sexual abuse cases by Detective Richard Cage. A companion chapter by Jan Marie DeLipsey and Sue Kelly James contains ground-breaking material describing their four years of experience in performing videotaped interviews of sexually abused children for courtroom use. Both of these chapters are "must" reading for any investigator; I know of no comparable work.

Connie E. Naitove has contributed a thought-provoking and creative chapter on using the arts therapies as significant clinical interventions to help sexual offenders against children. Finally, Sheila Thompson's chapter on the sexual mores of the Yuit Eskimo in the 1960s and their relationship to child sexual abuse provides a fascinating and enlightening personal historical perspective on conditions that enabled a published study on childhood gonorrhea infections in an obscure Eskimo village to influence the management of thousands of cases in the rest of the United States and Canada.

Volume 2 of the work will address treatment of sexual offenders against children in much greater detail. We will also have chapters on group therapy techniques for adolescent victims and for adult survivors. A chapter on treating sexual functioning problems in adult survivors will also be included along with chapters on several other clinical topics. An entire section of Volume 2 will address evaluation and treatment of the mentally retarded sexual offender as well as sexual abuse avoidance training for mentally re-tarded adults. This section is important simply because so little attention has been paid to this vulnerable population. The current literature on mental retardation reflects a paucity of work on sexual victimization, which is sim-ilar to the dearth of books and articles about interventions for child sexual abuse in the 1950s. We hope that there will be a measurable increase in writings about sexual abuse of mentally retarded citizens in the near future. The very nature of state-of-the-art work is its immediacy and excitement. I am proud to have a small part of this mutual sharing and learning process as we now complete Volume 1 and move to Volume 2.

1

Children's Sexual Behaviors and Their Relationship to Sexual Abuse

Suzanne M. Sgroi
Barbara S. Bunk
Carolyn J. Wabrek

There is a paucity of reliable information about children's sexual behaviors. Most writers have relied on personal observation and opinion about what is normal and what is not. This chapter is no exception. However, we think that it may be helpful to report our own observations, compare them to others', and make some comments about interpreting children's sexual behaviors in relation to the following questions:

1. What are normal and age-appropriate sexual behaviors for children at various developmental stages?
2. When does a child's behavior indicate that she or he has been or is being sexually abused by someone else?
3. When should a child's sexual behavior with others be termed abusive (i.e., under what circumstances might we decide that a child is sexually victimizing another person)?

In addressing the above questions, we have drawn on our combined clinical experiences in working with normal and troubled children and their families and with large numbers of cases involving sexual victimization of children by adults, by older children, and by their peers. Our work has made us acutely aware that the issues we will be discussing are both controversial and conflict-ridden. In the ninth decade of the twentieth century, most adults still do not wish to think about children's sexuality. The topic tends to make us feel uncomfortable and uneasy. Contemporary adults for the most part were neither raised nor trained to regard children's sexual behaviors carefully and calmly. Nevertheless, current social conditions require us to do so. To some degree, our capacity to appreciate what is a sexually victimizing experience is determined by our capacity to define what are and are not normal sexual behaviors for a child.

A Developmental Framework
for Children's Sexual Behaviors

In this section, we will discuss a child's sexuality within an experiential perspective as she or he grows and develops. Unlike some authors who have attempted to catalog changes in children's sexual behaviors from year to year, we believe it is more functional to use broader categories: preschool (0–5 years); early primary school (6–9 years); preadolescent (10–12) years); adolescent (13–17 years). Also, we have attempted to provide a developmental context for the sexual behaviors observed within the different age ranges.

Preschool Age (0–5 years)

Touching Oneself. From infancy to approximately five years of age, young children have the all-consuming task of exploring a universe that expands rapidly as their cognitive capacities enlarge and develop. Before they can see, newborn infants have exquisite sensitivity to tactile stimulation. Unquestionably, a young child's earliest sexual experience is that of masturbation. The baby quickly discovers his or her genital area and notes that it feels good to rub yourself in the crotch. Infants have been observed to self-stimulate many times in a day (Bakwin 1974, 204). The child's opportunity to engage in this pleasurable activity is often inhibited by clothing and diapers. She or he also is likely to experience disapproval from caretakers (especially mothers). Caretakers may scold the infant who masturbates, forcibly pull the baby's hands away from his or her genital area, and perhaps even slap, strike, or restrain the baby who appears to persist in genital exploration or self-stimulation. A young child may be told that she or he is "bad," "dirty," or "wicked" in a manner that conveys anger, rejection, or disgust long before the youngster has the cognitive capacity to understand what she or he has done wrong and why the caretaker is upset. As infants grow into toddlers and begin to comprehend speech, they may be told that masturbation makes people crazy. The caretaker may threaten them with blindness or mutilation ("I'll cut it off!") if they continue the behavior.

By age two to three years, most children have learned that masturbation in front of others is likely to get them into trouble. Accordingly, the child learns by trial and error that privacy is necessary if she or he desires to examine, touch, or rub herself or himself in the genital area. It is unfortunate that the notion that masturbation requires privacy becomes connected in the child's mind with another notion: Masturbation also requires secrecy. This is because many caretakers wish to inhibit children from masturbation entirely; thus they deliberately convey (frequently forcefully and sometimes forcibly) to children that the act of masturbation is wrong. In the absence of some type of physical restraint, however, it is not possible to stop a child from exploring and using his or her own body. Consequently, a child's earliest sexual behavior is likely to be "driven underground."

As children find private opportunities to masturbate (in the bathroom, in bed under the covers, or when they are alone), they inevitably get caught in the act by caretakers and are likely to be scolded or punished. (How many reliable opportunities for privacy does a three-year-old have, after all?) The negative reaction by caretakers when children are found to be masturbating privately reinforces and amplifies the original message that sexual self-stimulation is evil and dirty. As Karpel (1980, 297) has pointed out, secrets are about facts. Thus, the child who continues to masturbate (we believe that most children do, in private) now has a guilty secret: the fact that she or he masturbates from time to time. Nevertheless, masturbation continues. Its frequency may be inhibited by lack of opportunity, but caretakers are unlikely to achieve the goal of extinguishing the behavior.

Looking at Others. As vision and cognition develop, infants learn to recognize faces and gradually to differentiate between human beings. According to Ilg and Ames (1982) by age two and one-half years, children are acutely aware of physical differences between males and females and between persons of different ages. Exploring differences between people is part and parcel of the preschool child's enormous task of exploring his or her universe. Although these youngsters may be intensely curious, they are more likely to take advantage of opportunities to look at others' bodies and to compare themselves to others than they are to create such opportunities. Consequently, preschool children who are old enough to walk are likely to walk through open doors or even open doors themselves. If they view an adult in the act of bathing, using the toilet, undressing, or making love, it is likely that the child will view what he or she sees as part of the larger context of the universe, which is being revealed day by day. In other words, seeing the sexual parts of another's body has the same significance as seeing a mountain, a monument, or an anthill: All are different and have intrinsic interest for the child.

Children also take note of others' reactions. If a child's unexpected presence in the bathroom or bedroom is greeted with horror or anger by adults or if the child is severely admonished or punished for invading adults' privacy, we can expect him or her to infer that nudity, bathing, using the toilet, or making love are shameful and secretive or have other negative connotations. If, on the other hand, the child is quietly redirected to another activity and taught to knock or announce himself before walking through an open door, we can expect and hope that the youngster will learn instead that privacy is important for certain behaviors.

Touching Others. In the preceding discussion of masturbation, we commented that preschool children are likely to take advantage of opportunities to touch others' bodies if circumstances permit (or invite) them to do so. The manner in which a preschool child touches another person's body will be determined both by the child's previous experience and by the second person's response to the child's touching. If an opportunity arises, a child who is not intimidated may touch the sexually significant body parts of someone who is younger, of the same age, or older than himself or herself. Because preschool children tend to be easily intimidated, it should be easy to redirect the youngster who touches others inappropriately.

For example, an adult woman might be visiting in a friend's home and be invited to use a bedroom to change into a bathing suit before swimming. Imagine her sitting down partially undressed to remove her stockings. Suddenly the door opens, and her friend's three-year-old son enters the room, walks up to her, and places his hand on her breast. Should she call the police? Should she knock him down? Is this little boy manifesting prurient interest at an unusually early age?

The answers to the above questions are no, no, and probably not. It would be very appropriate for this woman to say, "Johnny, you surprised me! The door was closed because I was dressing in here." As she ushers him firmly out of the room, she also might say, "Big people like to be by themselves when they are changing clothes. Next time a door is closed, you should knock first before you open it." It is likely that Johnny will accept this redirection without much fuss or back talk.

Primary School Age (6–10 years)

Touching Oneself. The types of sexual behaviors exhibited by primary school children are very similar to those seen in preschool children. Masturbatory activity continues, but the primary school child can be expected to be more discreet and selective about taking advantage of and creating opportunities to masturbate. In other words, the primary school child is likely to take for granted that privacy and secrecy are required to avoid detection and reproof or punishment. Therefore, children in this age range are less likely to get caught masturbating unless they are masturbating as part of some other activity with others.

Looking at Others. Unlike preschool children who take advantage of opportunities to view others' bodies, primary school children are more likely to create opportunities to compare themselves and their own bodies with others. This may take the form of hiding and peeking while other persons are bathing, using the toilet, or undressing. It may also involve initiating direct interactions with others—usually with peers, sometimes with younger children, rarely with an older person. Primary school children may invite their peers or younger children to engage in games that involve sexual exposure (e.g., "playing doctor"). They may also invent games that involve self-exposure and comparison of their own bodies with those of peers (e.g., "Show me your pecker, and I'll show you mine!"). There may also be a competitive element to the games: "Let's pull down our pants and see who can pee the farthest!" or "I bet mine is bigger than yours!" Competition may take the form of one youngster daring another to expose herself: "I dare you to run around the flagpole without your clothes on!" There may also be an initiation component to the sexual exposure: To be admitted to a club, the new member may be required to remove all or some of his or her clothing as part of an initiation process. Lastly, there may be an element of forfeiture associated with the sexual exposure component of the game: A group of children play the equivalent of "strip poker," with the loser being required to remove articles of clothing as a forfeit.

The common threads in all the above activities involving sexual exposure between and among primary school children are the gamelike atmosphere associated with the sexual behavior, accompanied by elements of creativity, competition, forfeiture, and the like. For children in this age range, play is work in the sense that they are constantly learning and practicing social, cognitive, and mechanical skills via their interactive play activities.

Touching Others. As discussed above, primary school children are both taking advantage of and creating opportunities to explore, learn from, and utilize their environment, primarily by interacting with their peers. This also may take the form of sexual touching, again usually within the context of a game or play activity. The type of touching that can be expected would likely involve stroking or rubbing the other person's genital area (or breast area in females). We would not expect to see primary school children engaging in interactive sexual behaviors that involve sexual penetration, open-mouth kissing, or simulated intercourse, unless the children were encouraged or pressured by older persons to do so. Although elements of competition and forfeiture may exist, we would not expect that primary school children would utilize force or coercion (other than peer pressure) to enlist the cooperation of others in games or activities involving sexual touching. For example, an eight-year-old boy might agree to masturbate the genital area of another boy as a forfeit for losing in some type of competition. If the first boy actually carries out the sexual behavior with the other child, he will likely be influenced to do so by peer pressure (not wanting to lose face with others), a very different reason than engaging in sexual behavior because of fear of injury or because another person used physical force to induce his cooperation.

Preadolescent (10–12 years)
and Adolescent (13–18 years)

We have chosen to combine the discussion of usual sexual behaviors of preadolescent and adolescent children for several reasons. First, girls may begin to undergo the physical changes of puberty as early as age ten. Second, strong cultural messages are conveyed by television, radio, records, and tapes, as well as by advertising and merchandising efforts aimed at preadolescent and younger adolescent children, which encourage ten- to fourteen-year-olds to behave as if they are older adolescents or even as if they have reached adulthood. Within this milieu, we are seeing children who have not yet reached adolescence from a chronological, biological, or maturational perspective behaving as if they are indeed adolescents. In addition, we find that what would previously have been labeled adolescent behavior is now being displayed by some children beginning as early as age ten.

Touching Oneself. Masturbation continues as a sexual behavior for preadolescents and adolescents. As children begin to undergo the physical changes of puberty, the quality and amounts of genital secretions produced by masturbatory activity change. Children of both sexes who masturbate purposefully as they reach puberty begin to achieve greater control of their physiological responses to self-stimulation.

Looking at Others. There may be intense interest displayed by preadolescents and adolescents in viewing others' bodies, especially members of the opposite sex. This may take the form of looking at photographs or published material (some of which may be pornographic) as well as films or videotapes. Preadolescents and adolescents are likely to look at others' bodies or to display themselves while bathing, showering, or during sports activities with peers of the same sex. Looking at others may also be accomplished by deliberate peeking and voyeuristic behavior, especially when groups of boys or girls create opportunities to peek at peers of the opposite sex (e.g., peeking in the window of the boys' or girls' locker room at school). Peeking and voyeuristic behavior may also be aimed at viewing the bodies of older persons.

As a general rule, preadolescents and adolescents are socially interested in and drawn toward their peers or older persons. This reflects a developmental stage of individuation, achieving independence, psychological separation from one's family, and focus on peer social activities within certain cultural norms. Preadolescent and adolescent boys and girls are likely to engage in same-sex social activities (sports, games, clubs, sororities, fraternities, and other activities) with friends who are the same age (and in the same class) or perhaps slightly older than themselves. Dating and other heterosexual social activities frequently fall within a cultural norm in which girls are attracted to boys who are slightly older and boys are attracted to girls who are slightly younger than they are. It is particularly unusual for adolescent boys or girls to wish to meet their social needs by befriending or spending large amounts of time with preschool or primary school age children.

Touching Others. The developmental "work" of preadolescence and adolescence involves learning to develop close relationships with others. Success in developing intimate relationships with peers and nonfamily members will require social skills, confidence, decreased self-absorption, and the capacity for the adolescent boy or girl to distance himself or herself from parents (Berkovitz 1985, 36). This does not mean that the adolescent is required to reject his or her parents in order to achieve intimacy with others; it does mean, however, that loosening of one's attachment to parents will be a necessary component for this process. Some children do not engage in any types of interactive sexual behaviors during adolescence. That is, they do not practice intimacy with peers or with older persons in a manner that includes sexual interaction. Most adolescents, however, practice some types of interactive sexual behaviors with others: These may range from open-mouth kissing and fondling or rubbing each other's breasts or genitals to simulate intercourse, to various types of behaviors that involve sexual penetration.

Malmquist has stated that "the most common type of sexual behavior in adolescents, after masturbation, is probably heterosexual contact with another adolescent" (1985, 137). It is also true that many boys and girls have same-sex sexual interactions with peers or with older persons. Alfred Kinsey and his co-workers documented this amply in the late 1940s, reporting that approximately one-half of all boys and one-third of all girls in their samples had engaged in some type of same-sex sexual activities (Kinsey et al. 1948, 1953). The choice of an opposite-sex partner or a same-sex partner does not necessarily reflect an adolescent's sexual identity or preference at that time. Most people identify their sexual preferences in late adolescence or early adulthood, after accomplishing the developmental tasks of establishing relationships and practicing intimacy with peers of both sexes.

Again, it is our observation that it is very unusual for preadolescents and especially for adolescent boys and girls to meet their social needs with younger children. It would be contrary to developmental norms for adolescents to develop close relationships and practice intimacy with children who are preschool or primary school age. Some teenagers (especially girls) are assigned the task of caring for younger siblings; preadolescent and adolescent girls commonly earn money by baby-sitting. It is less common but not unusual for preadolescent and adolescent boys to be assigned the task of caring for younger siblings or to choose to earn money by baby-sitting for younger children. However, we do not consider it to be normal for an adolescent boy or girl to be attracted to a preschool or primary school age child and to wish to develop an intimate relationship that includes interactive sexual behaviors with a younger child. When an adolescent or preadolescent boy or girl initiates interactive sexual behaviors with a younger child, we view this as a form of sexual abuse. The older child's choice to practice intimacy with a child who is younger, less powerful, less knowledgeable, and at an earlier developmental stage may very well reflect the older child's lack of readiness to develop relationships with peers. It is, nonetheless, a serious lapse from normal developmental pathways for the older child and potentially very harmful for the younger child. These issues will be discussed more thoroughly in a later section of this chapter, "Assessing Sexual Abuse Behavior by Children."

Table 1–1 summarizes the sexual behaviors of children that may be anticipated at different ages and developmental stages.

Behavioral Indicators of Child Sexual Abuse

Discussion of this topic requires that we first make some general comments about children's behavior.

As children grow, they change and develop in many ways. Physical size, cognitive capabilities, emotional maturity, and social behaviors all change with time and experience. As was previously described for children's sexual

Table 1–1
Children's Sexual Behaviors

Age Range	Patterns of Activity	Sexual Behaviors
Preschool (0–5 years)	Intense curiosity; taking advantage of opportunities to explore the universe	Masturbation; looking at others' bodies
Primary school (6–10 years)	Game playing with peers and with younger children; creating opportunities to explore the universe	Masturbation; looking at others' bodies; sexual exposure of self to others; sexual fondling of peers or younger children in play or gamelike atmosphere
Preadolescent (10–12 years) Adolescent (13–18 years)	Individuation; separation from family; distancing from parents; developing relationships with peers; practicing intimacy with peers (same sex and opposite sex); "falling in love"	Masturbation: sexual exposure; voyeurism; open-mouth kissing; sexual fondling; simulated intercourse; sexual penetration behaviors and intercourse

behaviors, children of different ages exhibit certain behaviors within a normative range in each area of development.

All behavior is purposeful. We say or do things to achieve a particular end. For example, when a person feels chilled, she or he might walk to a closet, remove a sweater from the shelf, and put the sweater on. Alternatively, the person might say to someone else, "Would you please get my sweater from the closet shelf?" or "Please turn up the thermostat—I'm cold." Each of the behaviors was intended to achieve a particular purpose: to warm the person who felt chilled.

Sometimes behavior, while still purposeful, is unsuccessful in achieving the desired end. If the person who feels chilled is ill and has an elevated body temperature, it is possible that the chilled feeling is a biological response to evaporating perspiration, and the sweater might not eliminate the chill to the ill person's satisfaction. Similarly, the thermostat or the heating system might be malfunctioning, and the ambient temperature may not change in response to the change in thermostat setting. Nonetheless, the behavior (changing the thermostat setting) was intended to meet a particular need of the person who initiated it.

Frequently, unsuccessful behaviors (i.e., behaviors that did not achieve the desired result) are confusing to the observer. That is to say, unsuccessful behaviors may not have a clearly discernible underlying purpose. Children, in particular, often behave in ways that do not clearly indicate the intent or underlying purpose of their behaviors. When an infant cries, we know that he or she is distressed, but we do not necessarily know the direct cause of the distress; it might be that the infant is hungry, needs to have a diaper changed, or simply wants attention. The infant cannot tell us in words what the problem is, and yet we know from the crying that we must look for a problem. We make an interpretation that the crying behavior is sending a message of distress about the current life experience of the child who is crying, and we interpret that message within the context of the child's level of development. That is, our interpretation of the message will take into consideration that an infant does not have the verbal skills to describe a problem.

Appropriate interpretation of the messages that are being sent via an individual's behavior requires that we consider the individual's life experience. The following anecdote illustrates this requirement: A three-year-old boy was crying at bedtime. After searching unsuccessfully for some obvious reason for the crying (e.g., physical discomfort or a missing teddy bear), his father came to the conclusion that he was simply distressed about going to bed. This three-year-old had certainly been known to cry because he preferred not to go to bed at the scheduled bedtime, and that is certainly a behavior that is within developmental norms. As the crying continued, the child said that he had seen a light in the dark sky. His father remarked that it was likely a falling star and that the child should go back to sleep. A few minutes later, the child was again sobbing and said, "You said the sky was falling down. The stars will break, and I'm scared!" The child had interpreted the father's words (falling star) within the context of his own life experience. He knew, for example, that when he fell off a chair, he fell onto the floor and it hurt; that when a glass or plate fell off the table, it crashed to the ground and broke into pieces; and that stars were in the sky and that he did not want the sky to fall down and break around him. The thought of a falling star frightened him. His father, correctly interpreting the initial crying as a message that his son did not want to go to bed, had hoped to distract the child by explaining that the light in the sky was probably a falling star. Unfortunately, the child was frightened instead of comforted and then began to cry for a different reason: He was now scared instead of bored or disappointed about being put to bed. Interpreting the crying behavior thus required a knowledge of child development and an understanding of a three-year-old's life experience.

Through their words and other behaviors, children send messages to adults about themselves and their experience of the world. Behavior is always intended to meet needs, and it is especially intended to meet the needs of the person who is initiating the behavior. Each behavior, in this way, helps the individual to achieve her or his purpose. For example, children can demonstrate to us that they like chocolate ice cream, and, in doing so, they make it more likely that they will eat chocolate ice cream. They can tell us with words ("I like it"), or they can show us by smiling and accepting an offer of some chocolate ice cream. In either case, the child was successful in making the preference known. Similarly, children can tell us about their dislikes ("YUK! Not beets! I won't eat them"), or they can show us via their behavior. All behavior, when viewed in this fashion, is an important communication to others about the way the world is being experienced by the person (child or adult) who is carrying out the behavior.

Dysfunctional or acting-out behaviors are also messages about the individual's experience of the world. Acting-out behaviors help the child in some way and are usually signals that the child is experiencing some type of distress. The dysfunctional behavior does not usually tell us exactly what the problem is, but it does call attention to the fact that a problem exists for the child.

Most acting-out or dysfunctional behaviors in children are not specific indicators of sexual abuse. They may signal that one of a large number of problems might be present, including, but not limited to, sexual abuse. For example, depression or withdrawal from relationships, hyperactivity or an excessive activity level, high anxiety, and fear of people, places, or things are certainly indications that the child is troubled, and one possible source of the distress might be sexual abuse. Anger, hostility, sleep disturbances, or eating disturbances also have been found to be indirect indicators of child sexual abuse on occasion and are always an indication that the child is distressed.

It is interesting to note that many children who have been sexually victimized do not display high levels of emotional distress as a result. A study by Gomez-Schwartz, Horowitz, and Sauzier (1985) compared the severity of emotional distress that was displayed by a group of children who had been sexually abused with the distress displayed by a group of children in a psychiatric outpatient population and that displayed by a group of children from the general population who had no identified history of sexual abuse or psychiatric problems. For three age groups (preschool, school age, and adolescent), the data indicated that sexual abuse victims experienced a greater number of symptoms than the nonabused, nonpsychiatric population but fewer symptoms than the psychiatric outpatient group.

This study points out two important facts about the behavior of the sexually abused child. First, it suggests that children who have been sexually abused do not necessarily appear to be extremely damaged. That is, children who have been sexually abused are likely to be symptomatic, but they are generally less symptomatic than children who are psychiatrically diagnosed. Second, the study suggests that it is important to notice the distress signals that a child is sending via his or her behavior. We should notice especially when a preschool child appears more fretful or anxious than usual or less mature than her or his peers. We should also notice when the school-age child appears to be exceptionally angry or aggressive. These behaviors were frequently seen in children who had been sexually abused. Though these behavioral symptoms are not direct indicators of sexual abuse, we should not fail to consider the possibility that the child who is sending this distress signal has been sexually abused.

Accordingly, we view depression, withdrawal, aggressive behavior, hyperkinetic behavior, anxiety, nightmares, school phobias, and many other symptoms as a signal that the child who exhibits them is disturbed or distressed for some reason. One reason might be sexual victimization. We also believe that there are three direct behavioral indicators that a child has been or is being sexually abused. All involve sexual acting-out behaviors by the child and include excessive masturbation, promiscuity, and sexual abuse of another person. We consider that each behavior is a direct indication that the child is experiencing the emotional distress associated with having been sexually abused. In the following paragraphs, we will describe each of these behaviors in more detail.

Excessive Masturbation

This level of masturbation is obviously not within the norms for masturbation described earlier. Instead, we are talking about a child older than three years of age who continues to masturbate in public even when redirected, scolded, or punished by a caretaker or an authority figure. Some children who fit this description are masturbating compulsively during all their waking hours. When underlying medical reasons (e.g., a pinworm infection) are eliminated, we must ask the question, what needs are met by this behavior?

Since behavior is purposeful, we believe that excessive masturbation may meet the needs of feeling in control and diminishing anxiety for children who have been sexually victimized. It also tends to protect the child from the stress of direct interaction with others, since the masturbating behavior tends to be isolating and to keep others away. When children persist in excessive masturbation despite being punished, warned to stop, or redirected by authority figures, it is necessary to suspect that sexual abuse of the child has occurred and investigate accordingly.

Promiscuity

By this term, we mean to denote a preadolescent or adolescent child who appears to be seeking sexual interaction with peers with a frequency and persistence that is outside the norm. Readers may be quick to note that there are no norms for such behavior, but we believe that there are some imprecise parameters for the amount of consenting interactive sexual behaviors exhibited by a preadolescent and adolescent population. Accordingly, we would suggest that if a youngster's level of engagement in consenting sexual interactions is noticeably greater than that of his or her peers, it is appropriate to raise questions about the purpose of the sexual promiscuity.

What needs are being met for the child who seems constantly to be seeking different sexual partners? One possibility is that he or she has been taught (by an abuser) that offering to engage in sexual activity with another person is a way to initiate a relationship. Another possibility is that he or she is seeking affection and/or affirmation from others, but due to the abuse, he or she lacks the necessary social skills to establish and maintain relationships. A third possibility is that the child sexual abuse victim is now attempting to be in control of himself or herself on an emotional level by being the initiator (rather than the recipient) of sexual advances and by being the person who decides when the sexual relationship will be terminated. Hence the need for multiple consenting sexual partners. We strongly recommend that preadolescent or adolescent children who are promiscuous be evaluated for a history of past or present sexual abuse.

Sexual Abuse

The third direct indicator that a child is or has been a sexual abuse victim is when the child becomes a sexual abuser of others. That is to say, the child uses a strategy to engage someone who is vulnerable by virtue of being surprised, physically weaker, younger, or less experienced than the child who initiates the interactive sexual behavior. In this situation, we believe that the child who is the "abuser" is coping with feelings of powerlessness and loss of control as a result of his or her own victimization by identifying with the aggressor and becoming a more powerful victimizer with a weaker nonconsenting partner. Now the abused child becomes an abuser in order to meet the need to feel less anxious and to be in control. Again, children who abuse other children should be viewed as victims of abuse themselves and should be evaluated accordingly.

In summary, we believe that most dysfunctional behaviors in children are nonspecific indicators of distress. Sexual abuse may be a possible cause of the distress, but it is not directly indicated by most acting-out behaviors exhibited by children. We view sexual acting-out behaviors exhibited by children as a direct indication that the child is or has been a victim of sexual abuse.

Assessing Sexual Abuse Behavior by Children

In this section, we will share a methodology of assessing sexual abuse behavior by children in the hope that it will assist readers in identifying when a child is sexually abusing another person. We will draw heavily on material presented in the preceding sections of this chapter, which form a foundation for the assessment methodology described. This methodology is applicable whenever there is reason to suspect or believe that a child has initiated an abusive sexual behavior with another person. The second person, the "victim" or the person who is the recipient of the sexual advances initiated by the child whose behavior is being assessed, could be a younger child, a peer (same-age child), an older child, or an adult. The following examples are illustrative.

Case 1. A woman jogger complained to the police that a fourteen-year-old boy had thrust his hand inside her shirt and grabbed at her breasts while running alongside her. She stated that she did not know this boy, that she had not spoken to him or invited him to keep pace with her, and that there was no way that his touching of her inside her clothing could have been accidental.

Case 2. Dolores, age fifteen, returned home from a party in a disheveled state. Her clothes were torn, and she was sobbing uncontrollably. She told her parents that her date, a sixteen-year-old boy, had attempted to persuade her to have sexual intercourse with him in the back seat of his car, which he had parked along a riverbank. When she refused, he attempted to force her to cooperate. Dolores broke away from him, left the car, and ran home. Her irate parents called the police, and the family filed a complaint of sexual assault against the boy.

Case 3. A thirteen-year-old girl did weekly Saturday-night baby-sitting for a neighbor's children, a three-year-old girl and a five-year-old boy, for several months. During this time, Judy, the baby-sitter, sexually fondled and masturbated both younger children, engaged in open-mouth kissing with both children, performed oral sex on the little boy, and encouraged him to simulate intercourse with her and with his younger sister. Finally, one night after their parents returned home and Judy had left the house, the boy told them what had been occurring. His parents were initially incredulous and then became increasingly alarmed and angry. The mother of the younger children called Judy's mother and told her that she and her husband were considering a report to the police. Judy's mother asked, "If this has been going on for months, why did your son wait so long to tell you about it?"

Case 4. A child-care worker in a residential care facility, alerted by sounds of a scuffle, walked into a bedroom after "lights out" and discovered that there were six boys in a room designated for two. Five of the boys, all eight to ten years of age, were standing in a circle, facing each other, with their pants pulled down and their genitals exposed. The sixth boy, one of the younger ones in the group, was wearing a blindfold and kneeling in the center of the circle and was observed by the child-care worker to be performing oral sex on one of the boys who was standing. When they realized that they had been caught in the act, several of the boys broke away from the circle and made frantic efforts to pull up their pants. One of the boys cried out, "It was just a game!"

Case 5. Elizabeth, a four-year-old girl, was referred to a pediatrician because she masturbated constantly in nursery school and the staff could not successfully redirect her behavior. As part of a medical evaluation to rule out sexual abuse, the pediatrician obtained cultures for gonorrhea from Elizabeth's pharynx, vulvovaginal area, and anal opening. The cultures showed that Elizabeth had gonorrhea infections in all sites. When questioned, Elizabeth blurted out,

"Jerry makes me suck his pee-pee, you know!" Her older brother, Jerry, age nine, admitted to bribing his younger sister to perform oral sex on him. When tested, Jerry had an asymptomatic gonorrhea infection of his urethra.

Case 6. Anthony, a frail and appealing eight-year-old boy, was admitted to a children's psychiatric facility because of his frequent sexual attacks on other children in the foster home where he had resided for six years. Despite the admitting diagnosis of hypersexual behavior, the staff of the psychiatric facility were unprepared to deal with Anthony's sexual behaviors toward them. He liked to grab at the genitals of male staff members; one of his favorite maneuvers was to slide his hand into a man's pants pocket and then make a thrusting motion inside the pocket toward the startled man's genital area. Alternately, he would thrust his hand inside the female staff members' blouses and grab át their breasts. He also would unexpectedly begin to rub the genital areas of male or female staff members while they were engaged in some activity in which they were using both hands (e.g., carrying a tray of food). Anthony also would frequently hide under desks and tables and grab people from below when they sat down.

Staff members treated Anthony with avoidance during the first month of his hospitalization. No one reported Anthony's sexually aggressive behavior or commented on it in routine meetings. Finally, after a month had elapsed, Anthony's sexual behavior was discussed in a unit meeting. Every staff person, from the cleaning lady to the unit director, disclosed that Anthony had sexually abused him or her on at least one occasion. All acknowledged that they had been shocked, intimidated, and not a little ashamed to find themselves to be the subject of a sexual assault by an eight-year-old boy who weighed less than fifty pounds.

We encourage readers to refer to Table 1–2 as we apply the assessment methodology to the foregoing case examples. All the examples were chosen because they illustrate various common features of cases involving children who sexually abuse others. The assessment methodology provides guidelines for eliciting the facts of the case in a uniform fashion and helps us organize the information that will form the basis for deciding whether we do or do not believe that a child has sexually abused another person.

Complaint Status

In Cases 1, 2, and 3, the persons who were the subjects of sexual behaviors initiated by a child all told third parties about the occurrence. The woman

Table 1–2
Sexual Abuse Behaviors by Children:
Assessment Methodology

1. *Complaint Status*
   Has a complaint of sexual abuse initiated by a child already been
   made? By the victim or the injured party himself or herself? By
   someone else on behalf of the victim? The existence of a
   complaint implies that someone has already objected to sexual
   behavior initiated by a child and deemed it questionable,
   inappropriate, or frankly abusive.

2. *Behavioral Indicators of Sexual Abuse*
   Has one or more children exhibited a behavioral indicator of
   sexual abuse? At least one child will have done so, by definition,
   in the course of initiating an interactive sexual behavior that was
   viewed by others as abusive. If the sexual behavior involved two
   children—an initiator and a recipient, a leader and a follower,
   or an abuser and a victim—the second child may also have
   exhibited a behavioral indicator of sexual abuse (e.g., excessive
   masturbation, promiscuity, or sexual abuse of others).

3. *Developmental Perspective*
   Does the sexual behavior initiated by a child fit into anticipated
   developmental norms with regard to ages of the participants,
   patterns of activity, and sexual behaviors (see also Table 1–1)?
   Specifically, is the pattern of activity and type of sexual behavior
   age-appropriate for the child who initiates the sexual behavior? If
   the other participants are children, is their behavior appropriate
   within a developmental perspective?

4. *Relative Power Positions of Participants*
   What are the relative power positions of the participants? Does
   the child who initiates sexual behavior with another person
   occupy a subordinate position to the other person? Or are they
   peers with regard to their age, size, cognitive abilities, life
   experiences, and the like? Does the child who initiates sexual
   behavior with another child who is apparently a peer occupy a
   less obvious power position over the second child? Or is the
   victim an adult or an older child who is at a disadvantage because
   she or he was not expecting the abuser to initiate sexual activity
   and was taken by surprise?

5. *Force or Intimidation*
   Did the child who initiated the sexual behavior use force or
   intimidation to engage the cooperation of the other party? What

Table 1–2 *continued*

did the victim believe would be the result of noncompliance with the sexual behavior? Was force used or threatened in carrying out the sexual acts? Did the victim fear physical injury to himself or herself or "just" embarrassment?

6. *Ritualistic or Sadistic Behaviors*
Did the sexual behavior have ritualistic or sadistic elements? Did the child who initiated the behavior do so within the context of performing a religious or occult rite? Did the sexual behavior include elements of bondage, sacrifice, torture, or other sadomasochistic elements?

7. *Secrecy*
Did the child who initiated the sexual behavior do so openly or furtively? With concern about discovery or disregard for being detected? Were other participants bribed or threatened? What did the victim think would happen if she or he told others?

in Case 1 made a direct report to the police that a fourteen-year-old boy had assaulted her. The fifteen-year-old girl in Case 2 and the younger children in Case 3 all told their parents; in both these cases, the parents then joined their children in making a complaint. In Case 4, however, four-year-old Elizabeth was not making a complaint against her brother, Jerry. Instead, she merely was explaining to her parents and to others that Jerry had bribed her to perform oral sex on him. Likewise, there is no identified complainant in Case 5 as yet. A staff person in a residential child-care facility has discovered six boys engaging in interactive sexual behavior with each other. Careful investigative interviewing of all the boys, beginning with the boy who was blindfolded, will be necessary to elicit information, which, coupled with the staff person's description of the scene, will provide the data for deciding whether the behavior was an elaborate game or a case of sexual abuse. In Case 6, no one complained of Anthony's sexual aggression for one month, despite its repetitive and intrusive aspects.

It is important to note that people who are sexually victimized by a child frequently fail to make a complaint or delay reporting the incident. If the victim is also a child, he or she may lack the verbal capacity to articulate a complaint or may be too young to understand that the behavior is sexual behavior. We can speculate that the three-year-old girl in Case 2 did not understand that the behavior initiated by Judy, the baby-sitter, was sexual behavior and may not have understood that it was inappropriate. If she had attempted to tell someone about the sexual abuse, her verbal abilities might have been too limited for her complaint to be understood. Her older brother finally did complain to their parents, presumably because his desire for them to intervene outweighed any fears that he may have had about the consequences of disclosure.

When younger children are sexually victimized by another child, they may also fail to complain because they do not recognize that the sexual behavior is inappropriate. We can surmise that Elizabeth, the four-year-old girl in Case 4, may have failed to tell others about performing oral sex on her older brother at his request because she did not herself view the behavior as abusive or inappropriate. Likewise, the blindfolded boy in Case 6 might have viewed the request or demand that he perform oral sex on the other boys as a forfeit, an initiation rite, or an element of a game they were playing. Therefore, he made no report or complaint to the staff before they "got caught." Additional reasons why younger children fail to complain of sexual abuse by another child involve elements of secrecy, which will be discussed later.

When same-age children or older children or adults are sexually victimized by a child, the victims may fail to complain because they fear that no one will believe them or because they are embarrassed or ashamed. Again, the blindfolded boy in Case 5 may have thought that it would be useless to complain to a staff person because "his version" of the situation might be disputed by five of his peers. Alternatively, he might have failed to complain because he was embarrassed to tell about the sexual aspects of the behavior or because he was ashamed of his own inability to protect himself. As noted by Dr. Michael Johanek in Chapter 5, boys are subjected at early ages to strong cultural influences that teach them that "real men" do not turn to others for protection against sexual abuse; they fight off attackers by themselves. A boy who was not able to ward off abuse by his peers might simply be too ashamed to admit his "failure" by making a complaint.

Female children and adolescents or adult women are less likely to be acculturated to keep silent about sexual abuse because of the shame of being overpowered by a younger child. The adult woman jogger in Case 1 had no such barrier to making a complaint, even though her abuser was younger than she. In Case 2, Dolores might have been ashamed to tell her parents that she had "gotten herself into" a situation in which her date demanded a sexual relationship and refused to take "No!" for an answer. However, her parents, perhaps because of her disheveled condition and obvious distress, apparently viewed her as a victim rather than a person who had been inept or injudicious. In Case 6, both male and female staff members failed to complain about eight-year-old Anthony's sexual aggression presumably because they were both embarrassed by the sexual aspects and ashamed of being the object of his attentions. We can speculate that staff members of both sexes wondered whether they had done anything to invite Anthony's sexual advances; at the same time, they were probably embarrassed by their own inability to control his behavior. Thus, they "coped" by avoiding contact with him and by failing to complain to others.

In summary, the complaint status of a case may be a useful starting place for assessment if a complaint has been made by the victim or by another person on behalf of the victim. However, the absence of a complaint by the person who is the object of interactive sexual behaviors initiated by a child is not an indication that abuse has not occurred.

Behavioral Indicators of Sexual Abuse

In Case 4, the decision of at least five (and perhaps six) boys aged eight to ten years to engage in a "game" that involved a type of sexual behavior (oral intercourse) not considered usual for children at their developmental level makes one suspect that at least one or more of them had been sexually victimized by someone else. In contrast, the fourteen-year-old boy in Case 1, the sixteen-year-old boy in Case 2, the thirteen-year-old girl in Case 3, and the eight-year-old boy in Case 6 were all definitely initiating sexual activity with others using elements of force or intimidation. We can speculate that the three adolescents and the eight-year-old were all identifying with an aggressor who had victimized them in the past. This formulation assumes that some victims cope with their own feelings of helplessness and exploitation by identifying with the more powerful aggressor and attempting to feel more in control of themselves by taking control away from someone else. It is easier to make this interpretation when the child who initiates the sexual behavior uses force or intimidation (Cases 1 and 2) or when there is a significant age disparity between the children who are the recipients and the child who is the initiator (Cases 3 and 5) of the sexual behavior. In Case 6, Anthony's identification with an aggressor in his past is more subtle because he utilized the surprise, embarrassment, and shame of his victims to carry out the abuse.

Case 4 is ambiguous because we do not have enough facts to decide whether the "game" represented children engaging in sexual exploration and play with their peers or a behavioral message that some or all of the boys who were standing were themselves past or current victims of sexual abuse by others.

Case 5 is characterized by a child, four-year-old Elizabeth, who sends a behavioral message via excessive masturbation that she is a victim of sexual abuse. Her nine-year-old brother, Jerry, has sent a behavioral message that he is a victim by engaging in the sexual abuse of Elizabeth. An investigator who assesses this case must ask who abused Jerry. Likewise, it is possible that someone else abused Elizabeth (besides Jerry). Lastly, there is a strong possibility that Jerry's abuser also abused Elizabeth and encouraged, taught, or coerced the two children to engage in sexual behavior with each other.

Developmental Perspective

In Case 1, it is appropriate for a fourteen-year-old boy to be interested in exploring intimacy with his peers or even with older persons. It is not, of course, appropriate for him to use force or intimidation to gain access to the body of a stranger of the opposite sex who happens to be older than he. In Case 2, it is expected that a sixteen-year-old boy will seek to initiate an intimate relationship with a girl who is his peer, which may include sexual intercourse. Again, it is not appropriate from a developmental perspective for him to use force or coercion as a means of engaging in an intimate relationship with an age-mate.

Case 3 illustrates a situation in which a thirteen-year-old girl is behaving inappropriately within a developmental perspective by practicing intimate behaviors with very young children instead of choosing a peer for a partner. Although the types of sexual behaviors (open-mouth kissing, sexual fondling, simulated intercourse, and oral sex) are expected for an adolescent, her choice of preschool children as partners is far outside developmental norms. Judy's sexual activity with a three-year-old and a five-year-old is clearly exploitive and abusive because of the absence both of a peer relationship and the capacity for mutuality between the partners.

The patterns of activity described in Case 4 are entirely appropriate for boys in the age range of eight to ten years. As previously discussed, primary school children may be expected to create opportunities to compare their own bodies with those of peers or younger children. The gamelike atmosphere and the possible elements of forfeiture or initiation are likewise appropriate and anticipated. The sexual behavior of oral sex (a form of sexual penetration) is less appropriate from a developmental perspective. Again, more facts would be required to differentiate sexual abuse of the blindfolded boy in Case 4 from normative sexual exploration and play among age-mates.

Case 5, like Case 3, involves an older child who initiates sexual behavior with a much younger child. From a developmental perspective, it is anticipated that Jerry, age nine, may create opportunities to engage in sexual play or exploration with age-mates or, as in this case, with a significantly younger child, his four-year-old sister, Elizabeth. Again, it is far less appropriate for sexual play between preschool children and primary school children to include oral sex. Although the case description does not mention elements of force or intimidation, the age disparity between Jerry and Elizabeth introduces a worrisome potential for Jerry to be exploiting an obvious power position over his younger, smaller, weaker, less sophisticated sister.

Some might speculate that the events in Case 5 may have occurred because one or both of the children observed others (in person, on television, in a film, or in photographs) engaging in interactive sexual behaviors that included oral sex. This speculation would then explain Jerry's and Elizabeth's interactive sexual behavior with each other on the basis that the children selected an opportunity to act out behaviors that they witnessed on another occasion. It is impossible to prove or refute such a speculation. We can say that we believe that it is more likely that children will act out behaviors such as oral sex with each other as a consequence of having participated in oral sex with another person (i.e., the other person performed oral sex on the child or induced the child to perform oral sex on him or her) rather than having witnessed others engaging in oral sex (in person or otherwise). We can also say that we believe that the experience of *active participation* in any type of interactive sexual behavior is more likely to influence a child to initiate such behaviors with others rather than the experience of being a *passive witnesss* to the same interactive sexual behaviors being performed by others. Lastly, we can comment that in a combined experience of working with more than two thousand cases of child sexual abuse, we have yet to encounter a case in which persuasive evidence linked a child's decision to initiate an interactive sexual behavior involving some type of sexual penetration or simulated intercourse to having witnessed such behaviors.

Case 6 involves sexual behavior by an eight-year-old boy that is outside developmental norms because of its extreme frequency and repetitive nature. Anthony was obviously doing more than creating opportunities to explore his universe. His total preoccupation with creating opportunities to engage in sexual behavior with others was distracting and diverting him from age-appropriate play and work and the accomplishment of normal developmental tasks.

Relative Power Positions of Participants

An obvious power imbalance existed in favor of the children who initiated the sexual activity in all of the cases except Case 4. In Cases 1 and 6, the child took advantage of the adult involved by acting quickly and unexpectedly and surprising him or her. In Case 2, the sixteen-year-old boy demonstrated a willingness to use force to overcome his date's resistance to his sexual advances. In Cases 3 and 5, the older child obviously occupied a more powerful position than the younger child(ren) by virtue of age advantage, larger size, superior strength, greater sophistication and experience, superior cognitive ability, and the like. In Case 4, there was the potential for power imbalance in that the boy who was blindfolded and kneeling down was outnumbered by five age-mates who could see and were standing up.

Whenever we consider the relative power positions of participants in a sexual activity initiated by a child, other areas must be reviewed. For example, we teach young children to look to older children and adults for guidance and direction with respect to matters of right versus wrong, appropriate behaviors versus inappropriate behaviors, safety versus danger, and the like. Whenever one child is told by his or her parent or guardian that another person (adolescent or adult) is temporarily in charge as a baby-sitter or caretaker, the younger child has received a parental directive to assume a subordinate position with regard to the baby-sitter or temporary caretaker.

Another area of consideration with regard to interactive sexual behavior is that girls are culturally influenced to expect that boys will take leadership roles and initiate intimacy between the sexes. This cultural expectation places males in the position of being initiators or aggressors and females in the position of being passive recipients of invitations or demands to engage in intimacy or interactive sexual behaviors. Thus, boys have more practice in taking leadership roles and girls have more practice in waiting to be asked. The net result is that many girls view themselves as weaker than boys from a social and physical perspective.

Lastly, in considering relative power positions of participants, we wish to emphasize once again that a younger, smaller, physically weaker person can, under certain circumstances, sexually victimize a larger, older, physically stronger person. The elements of surprise exercised by the initiator and the lack of preparedness by the other party can tip the balance in such a way that a child may sometimes be able to victimize an age-mate or an older person.

Elements of Force or Intimidation

Again, Cases 1 and 2 involved obvious use of force by the adolescent who initiated the sexual activity. In Cases 3 and 5, the older child was clearly in a position to use superior physical force or intimidation to induce cooperation by the younger child(ren). The absence of a history of force or intimidation does not mean that these elements were necessarily absent, especially when the case involves children of obviously disparate ages and size. For example, an adolescent is so much older and larger than a preschool child that use of force or verbalized threats may not be necessary.

In Case 6, a physically frail eight-year-old boy was able to intimidate adult staff members of a residential children's psychiatric facility by virtue of the unexpectedness and personally threatening aspects of his sexually aggressive behavior. In Case 4, it is hard to discount the possibility that the boy who was blindfolded and performing oral sex on an age-mate had been forced or intimidated into doing so.

We believe that whenever elements of force or intimidation are used by a child who initiates sexual behaviors with others, it is appropriate to label the interaction as abusive. Again, we wish to remind readers that it is possible for a younger and smaller person to intimidate an age-mate or older person, under the previously described conditions.

Ritualistic or Sadistic Behaviors

None of the examples above describe obviously sadistic behaviors. Case 4 may or may not have involved some type of ritualistic sexual behavior. Sadistic behaviors or ritualistic sexual behaviors initiated by children are never normative or age appropriate. It is imperative that children who initiate such behaviors be viewed as individuals who are being victimized by someone else. It is hard to overemphasize the potential danger of sadistic or ritualistic sexual behaviors initiated by children.

Secrecy

Cases 1 and 6 did not involve secrecy; all of the others did. In Case 2, the sixteen-year-old boy chose a private place, away from others, in which to initiate sexual interaction with his date. In Case 3, Judy, the baby-sitter, selected times when she was the sole caretaker of the younger children to engage them in sexual activity. Case 4 involved interactive sexual behavior between boys in a dormitory setting after "lights out" with obvious elements of secrecy. In Case 5, it is noteworthy that neither child told about repeated episodes of interactive sexual behavior until specifically questioned by others.

When present, the element of secrecy is important. When a child initiates sexual behavior with another person in the context of secrecy, we infer that she or he does not wish to be interrupted, discovered, or held accountable by others. In turn, we may conclude that the child has some reason to fear discovery or disclosure of the sexual behavior. This, in turn, implies that the child is aware that others may view his or her behavior as wrong or inappropriate. Sometimes the child who initiates sexual behaviors with younger children or with age-mates may use secrecy strategies (rewards, bribes, intimidation) to persuade the other child not to tell others. In Cases 1 and 6, the children did not bother to select a private place or opportunity to initiate sexually abusive behavior directed against adults. One may speculate that the absence of secrecy in these cases implies a wish to be discovered or contained or a lack of concern or appreciation for the consequences of being discovered. This is unlike sexual abuse initiated by an adult, in which there is nearly always an attempt to avoid getting caught by others or to avoid being held accountable for the abusive behavior.

References

Bakwin, H. 1974. "Erotic Feelings in Infants and Young Children." *Medical Aspects of Human Sexuality* 8(no. 10): 200–15.

Berkovitz, Irving. 1985. "Healthy Development of Sexuality in Adolescents: The School's Contribution." *Medical Aspects of Human Sexuality* 19(no. 10): 34–49.

Ilg, Francis, and Louise Ames. 1982. *Child Behavior*. New York: Harper & Row.

Gomez-Schwartz, B., J.M. Horowitz, and M. Sauzier. 1985. "Severity of Emotional Distress Among Sexually Abused Preschool, School-Age and Adolescent Children." *Hospital and Community Psychiatry* 36 (no. 5).

Karpel, Mark A. 1980. "Family Secrets: I. Conceptual and Ethical Issues in the Relational Context; II. Ethical and Practical Considerations in Therapeutic Management." *Family Process* 19: 295–306.

Kinsey, Alfred C., W.B. Pomeroy, and C.E. Martin. 1948. *Sexual Behavior in the Human Male*. Philadelphia: W.B. Saunders.

Kinsey, Alfred C., W.B. Pomeroy, C.E. Martin, and P.H. Gebhard. 1953. *Sexual Behaviour in the Human Female*. Philadelphia: W.B. Saunders.

Malmquist, Carl P. 1985. "Sexual Offenses Among Adolescents." *Medical Aspects of Human Sexuality* 19(no. 9):134–39.

2
Family Therapy: Characteristic Family Constellation and Basic Therapeutic Stance

Denise J. Gelinas

T rauma work is necessary but not sufficient to resolve the negative effects of incest on the victim's life. It is also therapeutically essential to work with the particular relational issues surrounding incestuous child sexual abuse.[1] This is the case for two specific reasons: Particular relational imbalances characteristically precede incest, and they are then perpetuated, and new abuses are introduced, by the sexual abuse itself. Both sets of relational imbalances are an inherent part of the incest and are, therefore, part of the victim's experience of incestuous child abuse. As such, they need to be addressed directly in therapy.

Relational Imbalances Precede Incest

Incestuous sexual abuse of a child cannot develop in a family unless there are pervasive relational imbalances. Relational distortions necessarily precede incest. For one or more members of a family to be thus exploited by another family member requires preexisting, long-standing relational patterns of unfairness, which progressively converge and focus on the child who becomes the primary victim. These patterns of relational unfairness are then reinforced and perpetuated by the onset of the actual sexual abuse, so that a child victim of incest is caught in a progressively more destructive system of unfairness, abusiveness, and isolation. It is perhaps important to emphasize that incest is not "simply" the sexual abuse of a child. It is a particular relationally based form of sexual abuse in which a child is sexually abused within her family, by a member of that family. She experiences not only the significant traumatic effects of sexual abuse, but also confusion and fear from being abused by one of the few people she knows, trusts, and must depend on. To make the matter even more relationally distorted, the abuser not only betrays the relationship, he exploits the child's appropriate dependency, vulnerability, trust, and love and uses them against her.[2]

In therapy, working with the traumatic aspects of the sexual abusiveness is necessary, but this aspect of the therapeutic work usually has little impact on the victim's continuing experiences of relational unfairness. Whether the incest victim is still a child or adolescent living in the home at the time of the disclosure or discovery, or is an adult living outside the family of origin, that family of origin will continue to treat her unfairly, and the forms of unfairness will be consistent through time. Any current adult relationships will tend to follow suit.

Cessation of the sexual abuse does not stop the patterns of relational unfairness; these will continue in the victim's family and in her adult relationships. For these relational imbalances to change, they must be addressed and dealt with directly in the therapy.

These relational imbalances in the family of origin are characteristic of incest and constitute an inherent part of the picture. But where do these patterns come from, and how do they occur? Usually, they are not an expression of malevolence or intent but of complementary individual needs and weaknesses developing over time into a systematically exploitive family system over which no single person has control.

Characteristic Family Constellation

First, it will be helpful to examine the characteristic developmental structure of most families in which incestuous child sexual abuse has occurred. While exceptions can be found for every generalization, there are particular patterns repeatedly evident in families in which paternal incest has developed, and we can use these to provide a working conceptual framework.[3] These characteristic patterns include bilateral marital estrangement, significant parentification of children, and relational imbalances among family members. Understanding how the relational imbalances both necessarily precede the incestuous abuse and then are perpetuated by it is the key to effective treatment.

Parentification of children is particularly important here. In this process, a child is induced to assume, and does assume, premature and excessive caretaking responsibilities in her family. Not only does she perform certain tasks (e.g., cooking, laundry, house or yard work, child care), she also has the responsibility for these functions. That is, she is not expected to *help* with the cooking—she is expected to *do* the cooking; if she does not do the cooking, it does not get done. The parentified child internalizes her role of responsibility and gradually develops her identity around taking care of others. Over time, she begins to meet the needs of other family members to the exclusion of her own. This occurs because she is internalizing the role of a parent, which is nearly unilateral in caring for young children. That is, the parent has an obligation to care for an infant, but the infant has no reciprocal obligation to care for the parent. Hence, the parentified child is gradually taught to put everyone's needs before her own and does, in fact, do so. She forms a self-identity around the notion that she has responsibility for taking care of people and that they have no responsibility to care for her in return. Essentially, she has no right to reciprocity. As an adult, the par-entified child will continue the unilateral caretaking style and self-identity.

In families where incest has developed, the mothers have usually been parentified children. In young adulthood, they are attracted by, and tend to attract, men for whom caretaking is important. Many of these men have experienced early maternal deprivation through death, depression, or di-vorce; they tend to be relatively dependent, needy, and insecure, and they respond to the caretaking of the parentified woman they marry. Although each partner has carried family-of-origin relational imbalances into the new relationship, things go smoothly for a while because of the complementarity involved: He values, or at any rate needs, caretaking, and she is a good caretaker.

A bilateral estrangement often begins with the arrival of the first child. Having already been a surrogate parent (to siblings, parents, and spouse), the wife may feel depleted and somewhat ambivalent about having a child. Nevertheless, at the birth of the infant, she typically shifts her caretaking toward the infant; while this is obviously appropriate, to some extent it also decreases the caretaking she can provide her husband. Also because of the stresses involved during this time, she usually attempts to lean on her hus-band for support, only to find that he is unavailable. He, too, is in some difficulty. His wife is attempting to lean on him for support, and she is expecting him to assume responsibilities for a child, all this while she is withdrawing some of her caretaking of him. Not only is she "abandoning" him and placing new demands on him, but she is essentially producing his rival. Under these circumstances, it is nearly impossible for him to provide his wife with the support she genuinely needs, and the bilateral estrangement progresses.

As she tries to meet the growing demands of a child with her limited emotional supplies and little or no shared caretaking responsibilities for their child, he becomes more demanding. For him, relationships "give," and he is relationally pursuant of her to give him what he needs from this relationship. She, on the other hand, becomes progressively relationally avoidant because her relationships "take" and do not give anything back. As a formerly par-entified child, she is accustomed to relational structures in which she is re-sponsible for taking care of people without any implied reciprocity that they will, in turn, take care of her. She may feel overwhelmed and resentful, but she probably cannot analyze what is happening and thus cannot deal with it directly. Instead, she usually continues to avoid her husband and relation-ships in general, and thereby avoids some of the demands that relationships impose on her. As she increasingly avoids her husband, he escalates his demands for attention, affection, and nurturance. With time, and especially with subsequent births and family demands, this systemic pattern progresses, and the estrangement worsens.

The wife meets only the most pressing needs of the family. Depleted and unable to gain either assistance or emotional nurturance from her husband, she will attempt to gain assistance from a child as soon as possible, and that child (usually the eldest daughter) will respond as best she can out of loyalty to her mother. Mother usually begins to parentify daughter around tasks. She needs help with child care and other family matters, in large part because the husband does not contribute his share in the family. Thus, mother turns to daughter to get some of these tasks done. Daughter responds in part because it is an expectation in the family and in part out of loyalty to her mother, who is usually rather obviously overwhelmed by demands.

Father, on the other hand, will tend to parentify daughter not to get tasks done, but to meet his own emotional needs. To have these needs met, father is relationally pursuant. His wife is no longer available, so he may turn outside the family or he may turn inside the family to someone besides his wife—usually his eldest daughter. He will relationally pursue her to meet his needs, usually for attention, affection, and especially nurturance. Thus begins a second generation of parentification by both parents.

A family with this pattern is at significant risk for the gradual development of incest, which occurs in the context of a father's pursuing his emotional needs, a mother's emotional depletion and relational avoidance, and a daughter's parentification. In this situation, the daughter helps her mother with task functions (and often some emotional caretaking) and helps her father, primarily, with emotional caretaking (perhaps by listening to his day, tending to his emotional or physical complaints, or sitting around with him after dinner watching television or talking). These are all appropriate, within bounds. But in families where father is needy and shows poor judgment, impulsivity, alcohol abuse, or a heightened sense of entitlement, his pursuit of attention, affection, and nurturance puts him at risk to progress gradually from appropriate emotional and physical contact, through sexually tinged contact, to unmistakable sexual contact, and thus to abuse of his parentified daughter.

Mother's relationally avoidant stance and emotional depletion may mitigate against her pursuing information to uncover the incest. Father is rarely willing to disclose the sexual abuse and usually actively works to maintain the secrecy surrounding it, often by further splitting daughter from mother.

When a daughter is sexually victimized by her father in this way, confusion is inevitable. Even if she is old enough to recognize that what is going on is sexual behavior, her right as a child not to be abused by a parent is obscured by her parentified "lack of rights," to say nothing of her fear and confusion. She has an avoidant and depleted mother and an abusive but needy father, and she is typically isolated from her siblings because her parentification is usually viewed by them as favoritism. Altogether, the family members occupy unenviable positions, and the incest victim has the worst lot of all.

Because of the particular family constellation and her parentified role in this constellation, the incest victim usually finds it very difficult to disclose the sexual abuse. She recognizes her mother's depletion and may not want to aggravate it. She is relatively isolated from her siblings because of their interpretation of her parentification as favoritism, so she is not likely to go to them. If she does disclose it to her siblings, she is not likely to be believed or to receive assistance from them. It is especially ironic that her closest ally in the family is usually her father, but in this case, he is the abuser. Reinforcing these coalitional discouragements to disclosure, the family and the victim continue to regard her as obligated to provide caretaking but see her as having no rights of her own. Thus, it is very difficult for the victim to disclose. (It is unusual that the victim has enough self-esteem to feel justified outrage at her predicament. If she does, it is usually because of a positive relational resource outside the nuclear family, such as a grandmother, an aunt, a friend's mother, or sometimes a boyfriend.)

Disclosure or discovery change none of these relational patterns.[4] If anything, they may be reinforced, and the various family members can be extremely unsupportive of the victim. This unfairness tends to continue through time, well into the victim's adulthood, and the specific relational imbalances—that is, the tendency toward obligation to take care of others without any reciprocal rights for caretaking—are characteristically repeated in her adult relationships.

Relational Imbalances Are Perpetuated, and Initiated, by Incest

Continuing Problems with the Family of Origin. Incest occurs in the presence of long-standing relational imbalances, but it also perpetuates them and starts new ones. This is the second reason why it is therapeutically essential to deal with the victim's distorted familial relationships. She learns about relationships from her family, as we all do, and will also repeat these types of relationships later in life, also a universal tendency. But this has especially unfortunate implications for the incest victim because the patterns she learns tend to lead her to expect and demand very little in relationships with others; this pattern is reinforced by the damaged self-esteem that usually follows from sexual abuse. The result is often a troubled pattern of relationships throughout life, in which the incest survivor has few friends and poor relationships with her husband and children. She usually also finds that as an adult, she is relationally exploited by her family of origin in the same old ways, as though nothing had changed, because, in fact, nothing has changed from a relational perspective.

The victim's family of origin usually continues to treat her unfairly; she is induced to be overly responsible for them and is chronically devalued. One obvious example of this is that sometimes the offender may continue in his old ways by persisting in attempts at sexual contact. Many patients have voiced anger and outrage about this facet of offender behavior after they have achieved some personal developmental landmark, such as attaining adulthood, graduating from high school or college, or getting married and having children. The obvious and understandable presumption by the victim is that once one or another of these developmental hurdles signaling adulthood has been achieved, the offender will desist from his attempts at sexual contact. Unfortunately, this is usually not the case. The offender, like the rest of the family, continues to treat the incest survivor in the old ways, as if she were still a child.

The incest survivor usually attempts to deal with the continuing sexual advances by using some variation of her childhood coping mechanisms (for example, she may try to avoid the offender), for she, too, is trapped in the old relational framework and continues to function in the same relational pattern of the parentified child. Although she has more resources, power, and personal freedom than she had as a child, the incest victim usually has difficulty using them because she continues to feel and act as though she is obligated to take care of people but no one is obligated to take care of her. She is responsible, but no one else must be responsible. For most incest survivors, it is as if they do not have access to alternative coping methods or these methods do not exist. In fact, very little has changed with regard to the family structure and respective roles, and the incest survivor, now an adult, does not usually behave as an empowered adult with her family of origin.

Even if the victim receives individual therapy, these relational structures rarely change. Because the victim is usually living outside the home as an adult, the personal changes she is making in her individual therapy are not very apparent to her family of origin. Even if they wanted to see the changes (which they usually do not), they have an investment in maintaining the relational imbalances, and they usually ignore or discount positive changes in the survivor. Thus, change by the adult survivor is actively hampered and limited when her parents and siblings maintain their previous attitudes and relational imbalances with her. By continually experiencing these imbalances, the survivor's usually impaired self-esteem is certainly not helped, nor is her tendency toward depression and social isolation likely to be lessened.

For example, one young woman, a junior in college, received guilt-inducing pressure from her mother to return home every weekend. Invariably, however, this incest survivor would spend Saturdays waiting around the house for her mother to be finished with her meetings, her shower, a nap, and phone calls, and they would not, in fact, have the anticipated time together. During the first year of treatment, this young woman made the long-distance drive to her parents' home approximately 50 percent of her weekends, and never did the promised time together actually occur. Yet mother would continue to call, berating her daughter for not spending time with her. If the daughter attempted to bring up the past weekend, her mother would not agree with her description of it and would simply change the subject. This was a characteristic pattern in the daughter's childhood, and it continued through her first year of treatment, after which time the patient could begin discussing the pattern more directly with her mother. The invitations continued, but the patient declined them or secured clear promises to which she could refer when they were, almost invariably, broken.

Similarly, she could usually remonstrate when her father searched her car and luggage and inspected her phone bills and when one brother broke a bottle on the kitchen floor and laughed when she cut her bare feet on the glass. She did not protest, however, when another brother visited with his wife for the weekend and criticized and belittled her the whole time, nor when the family redecorated her bedroom and gave it to one of her brother's friends.

The patient took a leave of absence from school because of severe problems in thinking and learning and because of difficulty working on and finishing anxiety-producing projects. Although she viewed her return to school with marked trepidation, her parents insisted, ostensibly for financial reasons, that she finish her three remaining semesters in two. These instructions were conveyed the same week her parents presented her with several thousand dollars' worth of trousseau items, even though she was not planning to be married soon and was neither dating nor in any kind of romantic relationship. Juxtaposing these ways of spending money on the patient strongly suggests deep, if perhaps unwitting, ambivalence on the parents' part concerning their daughter's growing up and establishing any independence for herself (i.e., graduating from college with a financially useful degree). Instead, they appear prepared to ignore reality and begin preempting choices on her part by steering her toward marriage, when, in fact, no marriage is in the offing. All this occurred in a context in which several brothers had been supported in lavish style through postgraduate training. The patterns of giving less to the victim of incestuous child sexual abuse, inducing an obligated stance in relationships with no reciprocity forthcoming, and manipulating the victim to remain in a vulnerable, powerless, childlike position are characteristic relational distortions in incestuous abuse.

These situations are not introduced to imply that incestuous families are actively malevolent. The fact that one member of the family has been so exploited, relationally and sexually, however, enables other family members to grow accustomed to exploiting and allowing exploitation of the incest victim. Parents and siblings may not know how to change these relational imbalances, and they may not want to change them because they serve certain functions for the family in general. Worse, they may justify these imbalances by character assassination of the victim, or they may not even notice them anymore. Thus, personal change in the victim through individual therapy rarely has any impact on her family of origin. Even the adult survivor's relationships with her parents and siblings are unlikely to change unless these relationships are addressed directly within the treatment, usually in family therapy.

Characteristic Problems with Current Relationships. The incest victim is usually relationally exploited or devalued by current relationships with others, such as a spouse or partner, children, co-workers, and her few friends. Furthermore, the current form of exploitation is likely to resemble the previous exploitation in her family of origin. Characteristically, the husband is demanding, devaluing, and dominating, and he may be physically abusive as well. Children tend to be poorly disciplined and contemptuous of their mother, who has usually experienced lowered self-esteem because of the sexual abuse and relational distortions. The adult victim usually has very few friends, as incest survivors tend to be emotionally depleted and relationally avoidant— hardly a combination that will initiate, attract, or maintain friendships.

Incest has betrayed and contaminated both the victim's childhood and her adult relationships. Because of this, relational issues are important in therapy, and the place to begin is with her family of origin, the context in which the incest victim formed her "relational templates." It has become increasingly apparent that the best way to do this is by working not only with current relational problems, but also with the particular relational imbalances the incest victim experienced with her family of origin. The family of origin must receive direct attention, both in the material considered and in relation to the patient's current life.

Treatment of Choice

As described elsewhere (Gelinas 1983), incestuous sexual abuse can be conceptualized as having major negative effects. These include the following:

1. A traumatic neurosis, or "post-traumatic stress disorder" (with secondary elaborations arising from lack of treatment).
2. Continuing relational imbalances, with secondary elaborations arising from lack of treatment.

3. Increased intergenerational risk of incest. This effect is especially likely to occur with the female adult survivor of paternal incest, who is at increased risk of participating in establishing a family structure in which her husband will have an increased probability of sexually abusing her eldest daughter.

Unless incest victims receive specific treatment or, through fortuitous life circumstances, have opportunities to work through these problems (an uncommon occurrence), these characteristic negative effects persist. Both the traumatic neurosis and the continuing relational imbalances must be dealt with actively in the therapy. If both are adequately resolved, the intergenerational risk is significantly reduced.

Trauma work is necessary but not sufficient for victims to work through and resolve the impact of incestuous sexual abuse. Working through the traumatic aspects of the incest can allow the therapist and client to begin working on the relational issues, but the trauma work per se does not by itself change the victim's relational structures, either in her head or in the world. These must be addressed directly and explicitly, both in the therapy and in the world.

For adult survivors, this implies dealing with past and current familial imbalances, usually in the context of individual or group therapy. It also implies that toward the end of treatment, the adult survivor usually finds it enormously productive, if understandably anxiety provoking, to confront the offender and other relevant family members about the incest. This confrontation, which receives careful preparation in the therapy, is remarkably effective in removing the residual aspect of the relational imbalance.

For children and adolescents, the treatment of choice is family therapy if it can be provided—that is, if there are family therapists willing to treat incestuous sexual abuse or specialists working with incest who are willing to learn how to do family therapy. Family therapists have the most direct impact on the actual relational structures in which the incest occurs. The impact on those relational structures can be more direct than the one-step-removed work necessarily implied by individual or group work with a child. A family therapist's agenda is family change, and the focus of treatment is on changing relational structures. Also, he or she can have actual contact with those family members needed for that change. Given issues of directness of impact, specificity, and focus of change (the relational structures), along with contact with multiple members of a family, family therapy is preferable.

Even if family therapy is not possible because of a lack of family therapists willing to do sexual abuse work, there is another more compelling reason for changing the relational structures of the child's family, using whatever treatment modality is available. It is important to work with familial relational imbalances as directly and powerfully as possible because the family is currently constituting that child's relational developmental context and will continue to do so. Even if the child and family are separated, the relationships are maintained psychologically and remain in the child's head. Most interventions, including actual physical separation from the family, do not change that. The child will continue to function as before in the old relational patterns and will tend to re-create her familial relational patterns in future relationships.

Individual and group therapy can rarely change this unless the relational imbalances are addressed and worked through directly. If that occurs, these modalities, especially group therapy, can be effective. In these circumstances (as with the individual or group therapy of an adult survivor), an end-phase series of confrontations with the offender and relevant family members is also a very productive intervention. But family therapy is still the best option for the child.

The following material will provide a basic approach for doing therapy with families in which incestuous sexual abuse of a child has been discovered or disclosed. (It will not teach basic family therapy skills, as that is not the focus of this chapter.) The rest of this chapter will focus on the characteristic requirements for working with incest families, while the next chapter will address the critical early structuring of family therapy.

Basic Therapeutic Stance

As mentioned previously, relational problems persist in both the family of origin and current relationships. It is usually most productive to concentrate the therapeutic work on the family of origin imbalances. If current relational crises exist, obviously these also must be addressed in the therapy. It is usually not productive to focus on current relational problems, however, because the same types of problems arise repeatedly. The incest victim often has difficulty changing her role or her contributions to the current difficulty until the relational imbalances in her family of origin have been addressed. Only then will the incest victim be able to become a "survivor," by working on her current relationships and shifting from being a lifelong unilateral caretaker to requiring and getting reciprocal caretaking when appropriate.

Effecting this change is not as difficult as it may seem. Almost invariably, the incest victim has persistently been treated unfairly by others. Being treated unfairly is something a person of almost any age can recognize and, to some extent, describe. Beginning to discuss her family of origin and the members' relationships with each other opens this area for therapeutic work. But because these are family members and family relationships that are being considered, particular attention must be paid to the issue of family loyalty.

Particularly when talking to victims of incest, it can be too easily forgotten that the abuser is the child's father. Family loyalty is a powerful force, and incest victims do feel loyalty to their families and to the offender despite the abuse. Individuals who are inexperienced in working with incest victims sometimes find it difficult to believe that the victim can feel loyalty toward the offender. Not uncommonly, this loyalty is misinterpreted as a passionate sexual bond with the offender, as the victim's desire for the continuation of incest, or, at the very least, as collusion with the offender.

The victim's loyalty is none of these. It is the invariably found regard, affection, and valued tie between all family members and especially between parents and their children. Whether initially visible or invisible, acknowledged or repudiated, manifest or disguised, the loyalty is there, and at some point it will emerge. The success or failure of the therapy often depends on how the therapist has dealt with this issue.

Victims may initially appear to have no loyalty for an offender. Particularly among adolescents, the predominant stance may be anger, bitterness, accusativeness, or repudiation. Underneath all those legitimately angry statements lies loyalty, and heaven help the therapist who, in a mistaken attempt to gain rapport or to ignite an accusation from a depressed, dispirited victim, has sided with the victim's anger toward, or repudiation of, the offender. The inevitable result will be that the victim will rush to defend the abuser and will lose confidence in the therapist. This holds whether the victim is a child, an adolescent, or an adult, and also whether the victim is in individual, group, or family therapy.

Issues of loyalty and accountability must be handled carefully; both have an obvious role in any family in which the child has been incestuously abused. They are the key to the successful resolution of the sexual abuse.

Three Orienting Premises

The following three premises provide a working theoretical framework within which to negotiate the often complicated emotional, relational, and ethical issues inevitably involved with incest (Gelinas 1981, 1983). They have, over the years, demonstrated their usefulness, not only in family therapy, but also in individual and group therapy of victims. They provide a major component of the basic therapeutic stance.

1. *Any time there is sexual contact between an adult and a child, it is always the adult's responsibility.* Stating this may appear needless, but it is not. The issue of who bears responsibility for the occurrence of sexual abuse is sometimes confusing, particularly for people who may be inexperienced in dealing with this. It is certainly confusing for many incest families, where responsibility for the occurrence of sexual abuse

is often assigned to the victim. The above premise is indispensible for a family in treatment, for law enforcement and child protective services personnel, for attorneys representing the offender, and in one's own mind. Simply stated, the adult and not the child brings superior knowledge, experience, and power to adult-child relationships; the child has little knowledge, experience, and power but brings trust and dependency to the relationship. If anything in therapy can be said to be nonnegotiable, it is the premise that the adult bears all the responsibility for an adult-child sexual relationship. (For a discussion of the fundamental asymmetry in the adult-child relationship as it relates to sexual abuse, see Finkelhor 1979.)

The second two premises operate in tandem.

2. *A child is intensely loyal to his or her parents, and that loyalty must be explicitly supported in therapy.*
3. *The adult is held accountable for the incestuous sexual abuse, but the therapist must never scapegoat or allow scapegoating* (Gelinas 1983).

These two premises address the loyalty dynamics in families, while at the same time holding the offender accountable without allowing the accountability process to degenerate into scapegoating or character assassination. Thus, the offender is held responsible for the incest but is not held responsible for other unrelated problems or misfortunes, such as a son's business failure or a family member's auto accident. Holding him responsible only for the problems of his own making begins to demonstrate to the family and to the offender that holding him accountable for the sexual abuse does not necessarily imply he is responsible for all possible family problems. It also indicates that the family's love for him does not undo his responsibility for the sexual abuse of the child victim. These theoretical premises make it possible to differentiate the complicated and confusing issues of love, abuse, loyalty, and accountability without allowing one to nullify the other.

Technique of Multilaterality

This basic therapeutic stance is usually best accomplished by using the family therapy technique of multilaterality (also known as multidirectional partiality).[5] Multilaterality is a process in which the therapist takes into account every family member's needs and interests, lifting up people's sides if they are themselves unable to do so. Rather than being the agent of only one person exclusively, perhaps in these cases the victim, the therapist persistently attempts to deal with every family member's needs and rights and acts responsibly toward all members of the family. Because of family members' loyalty to each other, the therapist must deal fairly with everyone or risk inciting their protectiveness of each other, which would exclude or expel the therapist.

For example, the strongest claim for the therapist's attention is obviously the victim's claim, and in many ways she is the most deserving of therapeutic attention. Yet paying exclusive attention to her and her interests, to the exclusion of the other family members, is not only unfair, it is unproductive. It simply does not work as well as taking a multilateral stance, because the victim's loyalty to the other family members will eventually surface and she will begin to react to the therapist's unilateral alliance with her. Typically the victim will begin defending other family members from the very accusations she made earlier. If the therapist has unilaterally sided with the victim in the family therapy sessions, the victim will now be in the position of defending the family member from the therapist, a difficult and unproductive situation.

The victim's loyalty toward her father is a particularly delicate area. Despite initial appearances, incest victims do have a great deal of loyalty toward the offender, and there are some good reasons for this. During the family's development, the father is usually the primary relational resource for the daughter. The mother often appears distant, unavailable, and depleted. The father, on the other hand, is relationally pursuant, and although he does sexually abuse his daughter, whatever attention and affection she receives usually originates with him. Also, she is tacitly taught by the family to take care of her father in many ways, and this sense of responsibility usually adds to her loyalty toward him.

The issue of fairness is also important. All clinicians have had to work with situations in which a spouse may feel the therapist is paying too much attention to the concerns of the other spouse and, therefore, becomes progressively resistant to influence or change. Conversely, individuals may feel that the therapist is picking on another family member and join with that member to defend him or her against the therapist, thereby again blocking therapeutic change. The technique of multilaterality allows a therapist to avoid these impasses by attempting to deal with everyone in the family fairly and to recognize that all members have a legitimate interest in the family.

The therapist's attempts to take into account everyone's interests and treat them all fairly over time begins to demonstrate his or her trustworthiness. When working with clients in a clinical capacity, it is unrealistic to expect that they can trust a therapist beyond the usual superficial level necessary to begin therapy. The initial level of trust has more to do with professional credentials or perhaps remarks by someone making the referral; it has very little to do with how the therapist will actually act—how he or she will treat clients and whether he or she will eventually deserve and even earn the family's abiding trust. By acting in a trustworthy manner over time, therapists begin to earn that trust and build an invaluable reservoir of credibility.

Acting multilaterally may not be a popular stance with certain family members early in treatment, particularly those who want the therapist to be unilaterally theirs. They may balk or fight an evenhanded and balanced approach. But when the therapist succumbs to the blandishments or demands of one family member for unilaterality, it simply demonstrates to that particular individual that the therapist can be had. In other words, the message is sent to all family members that the therapist can be seduced into an illegitimate relationship with one person that ignores the rights and interests of the other members of the family—clearly a highly undesirable role for a therapist working with an incestuous family.

A multilateral stance requires that the therapist hold each family member accountable for his or her actions, attend to each member's investments and rights, and balance these issues among individuals. For example, issues involving the father might include (1) holding him accountable for the incest, (2) denying his allegations that his daughter or his wife was responsible for the incest, (3) supporting him in the difficulty he faces in living temporarily apart from his family, (4) supporting him in the problem of facing prosecution and public stigma, and (5) supporting his rights as a father to visit his children. If supervision is required to meet protective concerns, then the therapist can assist in setting up such supervision. But the father's rights, as well as his obligations, must be upheld by the therapist, despite the father's admittedly "one-down" position as an incest offender. This stance toward the father acknowledges and works with his accountability as well as his rights.

When using multilaterality, this stance is taken with each family member; each person's rights and interests are tended to, as are his or her legitimate responsibilities. Thus, for instance, the mother of the victim needs and deserves considerable attention from the therapist. The discovery or disclosure of incest is usually a shocking experience for her. Obviously, there are occasional cases in which the mother is an active co-offender or a knowledgeable, collusive silent partner, yet these are in the minority. Usually, the mother of the victim does not know about the incestuous abuse, although she may be able to explain some odd patterns or events after disclosure. Characteristically, the mother will need support simply to assimilate this information. She may well have difficulty believing it, and she is faced with the awful dilemma of having to choose between believing her husband and believing her child. A multilateral approach would recognize and acknowledge her pain and distress, her feelings of betrayal by both husband and daughter, and her depletion.

Multilaterality also would require that the therapist, with the mother and the rest of the family, look at the mother's areas of accountability. Responses to disclosure and discovery vary greatly, and mothers are responsible for their behavior at the disclosure or discovery. One mother discovered the incestuous abuse herself, by walking into an episode when her husband was performing vaginal intercourse on her six-year-old daughter. She walked out without a word and four years later abandoned the family, knowing full well that the sexual abuse had continued and would presumably worsen in her absence. On the other end of this spectrum, a mother discovered bruises on her three-year-old daughter's upper thigh area and labia; she immediately took her daughter to her pediatrician, actively cooperated with the subsequent investigation by the statutory children's protective agency, changed attorneys, and reactivated her plans for a divorce from the child's father. She then spent the following two years in and out of court to maintain her custody of the child, to maintain adequate supervision during visits with the father, and to obtain a divorce. The differences in culpability at the discovery could not be more obvious.

Yet these differences are not always so clear. For instance, if a daughter disclosed on one or two prior occasions and the mother did not believe her and did nothing about it, then clearly she bears some responsibility for her lack of responsiveness. Presumably, whether she believed her daughter or not, such an allegation should prompt some inquiry into why her daughter was saying these things. If the mother did believe the daughter and did nothing, then her degree of culpability clearly increases. Conversely, if there were unusual or confusing circumstances present that could easily obscure the issue, then the mother's culpability could be somewhat decreased. Such obscuring events might include a death in the family, sudden unemployment, or a major geographical move.

The issue of mother's accountability prior to disclosure is especially important. Daughters in these situations are typically protective of their fathers and are angry and accusatory toward their mothers. In addition, husbands often blame their wives for their own abuse of a daughter. Husbands typically accuse their wives of being emotionally cold and unavailable, sexually "frigid" and unavailable, or critical and demanding. They are often portrayed by their daughters as being withholding, uninterested, cold, critical, and neglectful. In a unilateral intervention, it would be very easy for a therapist to attempt to defend a mother to her daughter (often while attempting to defend the daughter to her mother) and assign all culpability for the family problems to the father. This can all too easily develop into a situation in which the therapist is defending everyone against everyone else, people become locked into rigid positions, and the crucial issues of accountability for incest become blurred.

Multilaterality requires the therapist *not* to support one family member over another for a prolonged period of time, but rather to support each person's rights and hold each person accountable for areas of his or her own reponsibility. With regard to culpability about the incest, if a clear picture emerges of a mother who has become increasingly avoidant and isolated over the years, who now knows very little about her children (their activities, friends, experiences, likes, and dislikes), and who has chosen a work schedule in large part to help her avoid contact with the family, then she clearly has responsibility for her own participation in unwittingly establishing a family constellation that is at high risk for incest. This accountability must be described and gradually accepted by that particular individual, and she has a responsibility in the therapy to work toward changing her contribution to the family structure. This does not imply that she is responsible for the sexual abuse of her daughter. Only the person who has the actual sexual contact with the child is responsible for the sexual abuse—not a relationally avoidant wife, a friendly, beautiful child, the economy, or the late-night news.

A point to emphasize here is that holding mother accountable for her part in establishing a high-risk family constellation does not imply that she is responsible for the sexual abuse, but it does hold her responsible for some part of the picture. In turn, this makes it easier in the therapy to hold the father accountable for the sexual abuse itself and for his role in the family structure. The roles of daughter and father have been taken into consideration, but mother was in there somewhere, and because of this, they can begin to ascribe responsibility for the incest to the offender. Mother's own sense of guilt might, in fact, be an expression of her realization that, in some way unperceived and certainly unplanned, she had a role in these events, but that she is not responsible for the actual abuse.

The siblings' positions are also important. They deserve support in dealing with issues, such as shock and dismay at finding out about the incest; anger and embarrassment if the information becomes common knowledge in their school or community; discomfort with the professional intervention with the family and the disruption of family life. They should, however, be held accountable for their behavior. For example, perhaps they knew about the sexual abuse but did not assist the victim, are scapegoating the victim by saying that the problem was all her fault, or wish that she be expelled from the family altogether. Holding the siblings accountable must be handled sensitively and with an appreciation for their differing ages, difficult circumstances, and family dynamics. Nevertheless, it also must be done with some firmness if multilaterality is to be established.

Obviously, multilaterality includes attending to the victim. In incest cases, this usually includes paying explicit attention to, and making interventions that unequivocally endorse, the victim's right to make disclosures, to be free of sexual abuse, to receive whatever treatment is necessary, and to have the opportunity to begin participating in relationships where there is reciprocity.

Her responsibilities might include things such as her behavior during the postdisclosure phase or her active participation in treatment to assist the therapist in reducing her parentification. The victim's rights and obligations are addressed in considerable detail in the following sections.

Some Examples of Establishing Multilaterality

To establish his or her multilaterality, a therapist must work explicitly on attending to and representing every family member's interests in each session, yet be steady enough to let the trustworthiness of his or her position emerge only gradually. Genuine trustworthiness and the response to this, the family's trust, do not occur suddenly, and in the interim the therapist is likely to feel anxious. Examples of some ways to begin establishing multilaterality follow.

Stance Following Disclosures

One obviously common occurrence when working with incest families is that there is a discovery or a disclosure of incest. At this discovery or disclosure, everyone in the family is usually in crisis and needs support, especially the victim. They are all in difficult positions, but the victim is in the worst position of all because everyone in the family is usually angry at her. Yet it would be a major error for the therapist to provide support only to the victim. Although the victim deserves (by virtue of her victimization, her minority status, and the difficulty of being the focus of subsequent investigations) the most support, the other members of the family need and deserve it as well. The father is in an unenviable position personally, socially, legally, and usually maritally. The wife is also in a difficult position. The siblings are suddenly presented with professionals intruding into the family, law enforcement often bringing charges against the father, usually some type of family separation, and nearly always significant disruption. This is the high-risk time for depression, suicide attempts, running away, alcohol abuse, and any number of less-than-desirable events. Each family member needs support, and it is encumbent on the therapist to supply some of that support.

Ironically, although the victim of the incest is a child or adolescent, the characteristic structure of incest families generates a high probability that everyone will blame the victim, including the victim herself. Consequently, although each family member should receive support from the therapist, the victim needs the most support.

The father is usually angry at her if she disclosed and often acts as if his daughter's disclosure was a betrayal. The mother may blame the daughter for the abuse, or may at least be undecided about whom to blame, and is angry at both her husband and her daughter. Often in a direct expression of the unconscious family ethos that the victim had only obligations and no rights, the siblings are angry at the victim for the occurrence of the incest itself. They may regard her as the responsible party or be angry at her disclosure, feeling that she should have remained silent and that the disclosure has "ruined the family name."

For the victim's part, she is usually ambivalent about discovery or disclosure. She usually feels (for specific dynamic reasons) that she is responsible for some elements of the incest and has betrayed her father by disclosing. Although all need and deserve support, the victim is in the worst position because she is also suffering the traumatic effects of sexual abuse. The amount of explicit support she receives should reflect all these considerations.

The therapist can acknowledge each person's distress by recognizing its existence. He or she can gently but firmly, for instance, acknowledge the siblings' anger that the information about the incest has embarrassed them at school but also clearly differentiate that anger from any attempt to blame their sister for the occurrence of the incest or for her disclosure. The news may be socially embarrassing, but their sister had a right not to be sexually abused within her own family. The therapist can explicitly demonstrate understanding of the siblings' embarrassment but also hold them accountable for recognizing their sister's right to protect herself from abuse. The particular way the therapist chooses to do this will be influenced by his or her own orientation and style, but multilateral interventions must be explicit and concrete to be recognized by the family.

Another example might include supporting the father by acknowledging how difficult it is for him to be faced with these allegations and to be living, albeit temporarily perhaps, outside the home. But the therapist must also insist that the father remain outside the home until the victim's safety is resolved and therapeutic changes have occurred. Another facet of this situation is the father's right to see his children (with supervision if necessary). The therapist must simultaneously hold father accountable for remaining outside the home during this time, while explicitly supporting his right to visitation with the children.

Issue of Visitation

When the father and children have been at least temporarily separated for protective reasons, the father's expressed wish to visit his children should be supported by the therapist, but in such a way that the victim's interests are not violated. Specifically, the father should be allowed to visit his children, but these visits should be clearly bounded in time and place and should be monitored if there is any concern that the children might be further abused or coerced. This policy should be advocated to the family and to law enforcement and social service personnel.

Intervenors are often made anxious by the thought of visitation between a father and his children, especially by visits with the incest victim. Anxieties about allowing the father to visit with the victim might be voiced in terms of the victim's unwillingness to see her father because of fear, anger, or hatred. Certainly, allowing visitation, even supervised visitation, runs counter to the punitive feelings that can develop toward incest offenders, particularly if violence was part of the picture.

If the child is fearful of the offender, the therapist must work in liaison with the other intervenors to allow regular visitation but see to it that these visits are adequately structured and monitored. Visits are advisable, because if the child has no further contact with the offender, or only negative, violence-prone contact, her fear cannot abate, and this can have an unfortunate effect on her psychiatric status and later object relations. If, on the other hand, the child has regular visits with the offender under circumstances that are obviously safe and protective, her fear of her father can gradually abate, and she can begin to work through some parts of the trauma attached to her father. This obviously bodes well for her future relational life.

This is not to argue that the visits should be directed at reducing a victim's caution in risky situations. An argument is being made, however, that it is in the child's best interests to have opportunities to begin working through some of the traumatic aftereffects of the incestuous abuse, and the best way to reduce the traumatic aspects of the attachment with her father is to allow regular visits within an obviously protective environment. This teaches a child that there is efficacy rather than helplessness in relationships, and it allows a reorientation of the paternal relationship away from abusiveness.

Under certain circumstances (a very young child and a father with a history of violence, for instance), the therapist might feel comfortable only if visitations occur with a supervisor appointed by the court or a statutory child protective agency. Furthermore, the visit can occur in someone's office rather than in a more informal setting such as a home, a restaurant, or a playground. Alternatively, visits with a sixteen-year-old victim who is making progress in therapy might be supervised by a relative who knows about the abuse and believes it. The degree of protection required depends on the circumstances, including the age of the victim, the presence of any violence, whether the offender has admitted culpability, the presence of current alcohol or other drug problems, the psychological strength or fragility of the child, and the stance taken by the mother and the rest of the family.

Finally, it is not unusual for a child, and particularly for an adolescent, to be reluctant to visit the father. While this reluctance should be handled with respect and sensitivity, it should not dictate the course of therapy.

Almost invariably, behind the anger, rejection, or fear lies profound loyalty. If the therapist allows the child to dictate that there shall be no visits, he or she is reinforcing the child's parentified posture and allowing a situation to develop in which the traumatic affects of the child cannot be worked through. Moreover, at some point, the loyalty will emerge, and the child will begin to blame the intervenors for separating her and her father, and she will eventually begin to defend and idealize him.

Multilaterality and supporting even the offender's rights are necessary for two reasons. First, to be fair and balanced in dealing with the father, the therapist must respect some of his rights as a father; the fact of the sexual abuse does not necessarily abrogate these rights because, presumably, in some or many other ways, he was a good father. He may have provided the financial underpinnings for the family, or he may have been the focus of warmth and relationship in the family. He most likely was the emotionally available parent, who could be approached or who provided vehicles for interacting (e.g., games, errands, shared chores). He may have set limits, helped out with homework, or protected the family from a hostile environment. These behaviors earned him credit, or "earned entitlement," that must be respected, as the children's loyalty to their father is an expression of *their* recognition of his entitlement. Within this context, the fact of the sexual abuse does mean that the father must be held accountable for its occurrence and its effects on everyone concerned, especially the victim. He is responsible for participating in treatment, making the personal changes necessary to help alleviate the pain he has caused, and actively facilitating family changes during treatment. But certain of his rights must be recognized and explicitly supported by the therapist.

The second reason for multilaterality is the well-being of the daughter. Her progress in treatment is in large part dependent on the therapist's being multilateral. If the father's legitimate, as opposed to illegitimate, rights and interests are not upheld, if they are violated by the therapist, the daughter's loyalty will surface with ferocity, and she will begin to defend the offender against the therapist, the public prosecutor, and all others concerned. If this reaction is triggered, the possibility for therapeutic change is essentially nil. Conversely, if the therapist can assign accountability without scapegoating, and if he or she can support everyone's legitimate interests while holding them responsible for their behavior, the incest victim is psychologically free to provide information about the sexual abuse, and the offender can be held responsible. The victim is now free to feel both love and anger toward her father and to participate actively in a family therapy in which she does not have to defend her family from the therapist or fear an illegitimate unilateral alliance with a relationally naive therapist.

Being denied all contact with her father almost invariably feels like punishment to the victim. Many victims begin to regret their disclosure as they (correctly) perceive that the disclosure has cost them their father. They may even retract their allegations. Also, the daughter usually perceives the father's being restricted from visiting as a punishment of the father, which it often is. This only reinforces her loyalty to him and is likely to stimulate a protective response for this poor, unhappy fellow, beleaguered by the punitive forces of society. If this reaction is stimulated, the therapist will find it considerably more difficult to hold the father rather than the daughter accountable for the incest in the eyes of all family members. The victim's sympathy for her father, precipitated by punitive behavior by one or another intervenor, precludes her allowing herself to see the father as responsible, and, therefore, she cannot divest herself of responsibility for the sexual abuse. Her ability to do this work depends on fair treatment of the father.

Also, victims of incest almost invariably need to work through several layers of emotion regarding their fathers: sympathy and caretaking, anger, guilt, affection, contempt, and hatred. This working through is made significantly more difficult if they cannot see their father. If the therapist allows, or supports in a unilateral fashion, what he or she may perceive as the right of the victim not to see her abusive father, that therapist is violating the father's rights and the daughter's loyalty to her father. This makes it significantly more difficult, if not actually impossible, for the victim to divest herself of responsibility for the incest, assign responsibility where it belongs, and work through the relationship with her father. Ironically, paying attention to the father's legitimate rights as a parent helps his daughter work through the negative effects of his illegitimate assumption of "parental rights"—that is, the incestuous sexual abuse of his daughter.

The therapeutic stance of multilaterality is fundamental to incest work, not because of some notion that fairness is nice or that a family should be held together no matter what the cost. Put simply, it is necessary because of the loyalty of family members to each other and the fact that incestuous sexual abuse occurs between and among family members who retain that loyalty to each other before, during, and after disclosure.

Because of this, visitation should continue, especially for very young children, even if legal proceedings are scheduled. There is no surer way to induce a child to retract her statement than having her lose her father because of that statement. Sexually abused children remain loyal to their fathers not only through disclosure but also through police statements, contacts with attorneys, and court testimony. Taking the father away will very likely prompt retraction and denial, and this serves neither legal nor therapeutic ends. If legal proceedings are pending, the visits must be supervised by a neutral or outside party, and no discussions of the sexual abuse, disclosure, or legal matters should be permitted. Admittedly, there is an inherent tension in that the child's love for her father and his presence during visits might prompt her to deny her allegations or make it impossible for her to testify. But the alternative is much worse.

As the date for trial draws near (e.g., next week), visits may be temporarily suspended. The child should be told specifically that it is a temporary suspension because of the court date and that the visits will be resumed as soon as possible. Resumption of visits may in some cases depend on the outcome of this civil or criminal hearing, but neither the therapist nor the mother should move to discontinue the visits. They should explicitly support the child's loyalty and argue for visits with whatever continuing safeguards may be needed. Implementation of this approach must be tailored to the particular circumstances, but the essential elements are maintaining contact with the father in a visitation structure that facilitates the legal proceedings rather than impedes them.

Therapists' Experience of Multilaterality

Multilaterality can be an initially uncomfortable position for the therapist, as all family members demand a unilateral alliance in their distress. Each of them at some point early in treatment will be angry at the therapist if he or she is succeeding in establishing multilaterality. That, in fact, is a sign that the therapist is successfully establishing a multilateral stance. When the father's rights are upheld, the mother or daughter might become angry at the therapist, and when the father is held accountable, he might become angry. When the siblings' distress is recognized, the incest victim might become offended, but when their sister is supported and the notion suggested that she might have some rights, too, the siblings will usually become angry. When the wife's anger at her husband for the sexual abuse is supported, the husband might become incensed, but when the wife is held accountable for continuing to maintain relational distance, she in turn may become angry. If every family member has been angry with the therapist at some point or another for reasons such as these, the therapist has succeeded in being multilateral.

Although family members temporarily experience anger at the therapist, they also gradually appreciate that this person is attempting to be fair and evenhanded. Not only will the therapist prevent a family member from being treated unfairly in the session, but he or she also will prevent a family member from treating other members unfairly, and this, too, is deeply reassuring. Basically, no one is allowed to get away with anything. Establishing multilaterality is a very productive continuing technique that produces relational change as it is itself being established.

Stated quite simply, multilaterality helps to change the family, and as is the case with all of us, family members may not be happy with every aspect of these necessary changes. But if the therapist has behaved multilaterally, he or she has, over time, demonstrated trustworthiness, and the trust earned by this will give the therapist a great deal of influence in the family. Multilaterality is a trust-building technique, and the dearly won resources of trustworthiness and trust will serve the therapist in good stead when working with families in which relational betrayal and exploitation are central problems.

In summary, the basic therapeutic stance for the family therapy of incestuous child sexual abuse includes heightened awareness of the issue of loyalty; the three orienting premises relating to issues of accountability, scapegoating, power, and loyalty; and the techniques of multilaterality. We have described the conceptual framework and mind-set for a therapist, something to inform his or her underlying approach to treating a family in which a child has been incestuously abused. The next chapter describes a specific intervention framework that translates the therapeutic stance into intervention strategy.

Notes

1. When the term *incest* is used, it denotes the incestuous sexual abuse of a child (a clinical definition) and not merely sexual intercourse between persons not permitted to marry by reasons of consanguinity (a legal definition). All present references to incest refer to intrafamilial child sexual abuse.

2. Although 10 to 20 percent of reported incest victims are males, females continue to constitute 80 to 90 percent of the known child victims, so the feminine pronoun will be used throughout to designate incest victims. The framework provided in the chapter is applicable to male victims as well, with appropriate modifications for male victims' tendencies to react with anger rather than depression and the issues raised for many male victims if, as is statistically probable, they were sexually abused by male offenders. The present framework was developed around the treatment of paternal incest (i.e., sexual abuse by father, stepfather, foster father, or surrogate father), but with modifications it is also applicable to other types of incest.

3. This developmental pattern is characteristic of paternal incest, but with modifications it is applicable to other types of incest as well. Paternal incest is described because it is paradigmatic of incest in general.

4. This family constellation is very characteristic. The abuser fits the description of what A. Nicholas Groth and his co-workers have termed the regressed offender (Groth 1982), a man whose usual sexual orientation is toward adult females and who, often after a precipitant (usually something that constitutes a narcissistic injury), may begin having sexual contact with a child. The regressed offender "fits" into the characteristic family structure very well. Groth has also characterized a different group of abusers as "fixated offenders": men whose preferred sexual choice is children. They tend to show a lifelong identification with, and attraction to, children.

These individuals are occasionally found in families as incest offenders, but their victims usually include children outside the family as well. (It is not unusual to find that a fixated offender has married a woman with children, in part to gain access to her children.) Individuals who can be characterized as fixated offenders present a more difficult treatment problem than the more usual incest abuser, the regressed offender. If a fixated offender is identified, the following family therapy framework can be applied, but it should definitely be complemented by work with a specialist in treating offenders, or at least by an offenders' group, and considerable long-term attention paid by the therapist to monitoring behavior and controlling and assisting the offender in learning to control his impulses. The family therapy framework provided here is not sufficient in and of itself for treating the fixated offender.

Occasionally, another type of incest abuser will be a hyperdominant, physically aggressive individual. The following framework is applicable to the family treatment therapy of these cases, as long as the therapist is willing to rely on the legal and police powers available to seek temporary restraining orders and to use the powers of the statutory child protective services when necessary. But the family therapy provisions regarding loyalty must be attended to by the therapist, as victims of hyperdominant, physically assaultive fathers are usually extremely loyal to them, and that loyalty must be handled with considerable delicacy.

5. Multilaterality as a technique and the issues of loyalty, accountability, entitlement, obligation, and fairness in relationships are based on contextual family therapy originated by Ivan Boszormenyi-Nagy and developed by him and his co-workers (Boszormenyi-Nagy and Spark 1973; Boszormenyi-Nagy and Krasner 1980; Boszormenyi-Nagy and Ulrich 1980; also Gelinas 1983; Karpel and Strauss 1983; and Ulrich and Dunne 1986; see especially Boszormenyi-Nagy and Krasner 1986).

References

Boszormenyi-Nagy, I., and B.R. Krasner. 1980. "Trust-Based Therapy: A Contextual Approach." *American Journal of Psychiatry* 1937:767–75.

Boszormenyi-Nagy, I., and B.R. Krasner. 1986. *Between Give and Take: A Clinical Guide to Contextual Therapy*. New York: Brunner/Mazel.

Boszormenyi-Nagy, I., and G. Spark. 1973. *Invisible Loyalties: Reciprocity in Intergenerational Family Therapy*. New York: Harper & Row.

Boszormenyi-Nagi, I., and D. Ulrich. 1980. "Contextual Family Therapy." In A.S. Gurman and D.P. Kniskern, eds. *Handbook of Family Therapy*. New York: Brunner/Mazel, 159–86.

Finkelhor, D. 1979. "What's Wrong with Sex between Adults and Children? Ethics and the Problem of Sexual Abuse." *American Journal of Orthopsychiatry* 49:692–97.

Gelinas, D.J. 1981. "Identification and Treatment of Incest Victims." In M. Bayes and E. Howell, eds. *Women and Mental Health*. New York: Basic Books, 481–96.

Gelinas, D.J. 1983. "The Persisting Negative Effects of Incest." *Psychiatry* 46:312–32.

Groth, A.N. 1982. "The Incest Offender." In S.M. Sgroi, ed. *Handbook of Clinical Intervention in Child Sexual Abuse.* Lexington, MA: Lexington Books, 215–18.

Karpel, M.A., and E.S. Strauss. 1983. *Family Evaluation.* New York: Gardner Press.

Ulrich, D., and H. Dunne. 1986. *To Love and Work: A Systemic Interlocking of Family, Workplace, and Career.* New York: Brunner/Mazel.

3
Family Therapy:
Critical Early Structuring

Denise J. Gelinas

Effective family therapy of incestuous child sexual abuse calls for a combination of general family therapy skills acquired with training and experience and an approach that takes into account some special considerations that arise because of the sexual abuse of a child from within her family. These considerations—protective, legal, and sometimes medical—and the interventions they require will be addressed in the family therapy treatment framework to follow.

This intervention framework is an expression of the premises of the basic therapeutic stance from the previous chapter and is not meant to be used in a rote or mechanical fashion. When treating a family in a situation where emotions can run high, countertransference and multiple agency involvement are the norm, legal proceedings are expected, and a child victim is present, a family therapist can be under enormous pressure. He or she is expected to produce change; protect and treat everyone; reduce symptomatology; "make" it possible for a child to testify in court; control violence, acting out, and suicidal behavior; produce reports for all concerned; and keep cool while doing it. An understandable impulse would be to adopt an intervention framework and apply it as best one could. While this impulse can be regarded with a certain amount of sympathy, it should, of course, be resisted. Any intervention framework is only as good as the ideas on which it is based and the judgment of the person using it. The intervention framework provided here is informed by, and is an expression of, the basic therapeutic stance in the previous chapter, and if in certain circumstances a specific intervention described runs counter to the premises of the basic therapeutic stance, the stance should take precedence over the technique and the intervention should be modified to meet the concerns delineated in the therapeutic stance. If an intervention is made and is not related to the therapeutic stance, it has essentially become an empty ritual, a talisman for change without the power to induce that change. The intervention framework described in this chapter is an expression of the therapeutic stance and should be used by a therapist only after having read the previous chapter.

As with most family work, therapy for incest[1] does not follow an invariable course. If, for instance, preexisting psychiatric disorders, substance abuse, or physical violence are present, the therapist will have to deal with these early in treatment, adding to the complexity of the therapeutic process.[2] Family therapy of incest does, however, follow a usual if not invariable course and can be described as progressing in four phases:

1. Establishing the therapeutic framework.
2. Changing the family structure.
3. Offering marital therapy.
4. Effecting a confrontation between the victim and the offender and family.

Establishing the Therapeutic Framework

In many ways, this first phase of the therapy can be considered the most important. If the therapist handles certain considerations associated with incestuous child sexual abuse early and well, the prospects of initiating therapeutic change are maximized; conversely, if these considerations are mishandled or ignored altogether, the therapy is structured right from the beginning to go nowhere. The combined individual, relational, and systemic elements responsible for the occurrence of the abuse also tend homeostatically to maintain the incestuous abuse. Even after disclosure or discovery, these contributing elements persist and have a continued effect. Altering such a tightly structured system is not easy and requires carefully planned inital interventions.

The therapy framework should be structured from the beginning to facilitate the needed changes. If the changes are not dealt with in this first phase, they will tend to intrude repeatedly during later phases, disrupting the therapy or precluding change altogether. The following specific recommendations are designed to assist the therapist and family in avoiding these pitfalls and to make the changes necessary to avoid recidivism, treat the effects of the abuse, and change the combined individual, relational, and systemic elements that produced and maintained the abuse.

Be Very Active

Particularly at the outset of the therapy (if the family is defined as an incest family) or immediately at the disclosure or discovery (if the family is already in treatment for other reasons), the therapist must be very active. The family is in crisis, there is a great deal going on, and the therapist needs to be directing, not simply reacting to, events. If the therapist is not very active, various family members or other intervenors will direct events, and more often than not, a structure will result that mitigates against therapeutic change. This issue will become clearer in later sections of the chapter as more specific recommendations are made. For now, the general recommendation to be very active is meant to provide an overall set regarding the level of therapist activity and intervention at the time he or she begins to work with the family. If the therapist is very active and directs and influences events, he or she can help establish the treatment-facilitating structure.

Another rationale for an active approach very early in treatment is that it makes a good deal of sense in light of what we know about people in crisis. People are frequently amenable to therapeutic influence, and most motivated and able to make significant changes in their lives, when in crisis. A recent discovery or disclosure of incestuous child sexual abuse tips most families into crisis. Parenthetically, if a family does not go into crisis at the time of disclosure, the therapist should be alerted to the probability that a serious degree of pathology exists within the family and should plan accordingly.

Finally, the period immediately following discovery or disclosure usually includes some risk of suicide or suicide attempts by the offender, victim, offender's spouse, or, more rarely, a sibling of the victim. This period also holds increased risk for problems such as running away, abandonment, sudden emergence of significant psychiatric disorders, substance abuse, or violence. If the therapist is very active and takes charge early, he or she is better able to evaluate these risks and intervene when necessary. When the family comes to treatment soon after discovery or disclosure, meetings usually must be scheduled more frequently than once a week, with two or three meetings a week preferable. Boundaries regarding access to the therapist must be made clear, and some appropriate access route must be delineated in case of emergencies. Finally, the therapist must be seen by the family as an active but deliberate clinician.

Find Out the Referral Route

Whether the first contact on a case is from the family itself, a statutory child protective agency, another therapist, the school, a pediatrician, or a law enforcement official, it is highly advisable for the therapist to learn from that inital contact the specific route by which a particular family has been referred. Since the initial discovery or disclosure of child sexual abuse, what has happened, how has the family been dealt with, and by whom? At what stage are the protective, legal, and medical proceedings? Have family members been treated professionally and with firmness coupled with respect? Or have they been vilified, fragmented, and threatened? Have they been treated in such a way that they have developed the notion that all therapists (or child protective workers, law enforcement officers, physicians, or attorneys) are punitive or, worse, incompetent and impotent?

Depending on how a family has been treated by the time they first see the therapist, they can be amenable to treatment and ready to get to work or, more commonly, threatened, wary, and impervious to influence. Finding out the referral route can avert problems before a family ever steps into the office. The following case example is a useful illustration.

A therapist accepted a family with a history of incestuous child sexual abuse into family therapy but sought consultation after eight months because of a lack of progress in the case. During the discussion, it emerged that the therapist had accepted this referral from a therapist at another agency, who (to cajole the family into family therapy) had promised the parents that their six- and eight-year-old daughters would not be required by the new therapist to attend sessions. The new therapist was then in the position of attempting to provide family therapy to a family that had taken control by setting preconditions negotiated with the previous therapist. For eight months, the therapist was dependent on their accounts of family events and relationships to monitor whether any abuse was occurring. The therapist had no access to the children and obviously very little reliable information about family processes. He had neglected to ascertain the conditions of the referral and had then considered himself bound to comply with a promise he had known nothing about. This therapist had an obviously unworkable structure that blocked effective therapy. All this could have been avoided if he had inquired of the referring therapist what contacts this family had with whom, and what had been done.

One might ask, what if the family refused to come into treatment if their conditions were not met? This is not an unusual problem with incest families, yet it is handled fairly simply. A family should never be taken into treatment if they will attend only under unworkable conditions; instead, the therapist should make clear the necessary conditions. These might include being able to see the children, or perhaps insisting on weekly as opposed to random sessions, the attendance of the father, or the family's coming to the office rather than the therapist's going to their home. If the family refuses treatment under these conditions, the therapist should notify the statutory child protective agency. This will alert (or realert) them to a new risk situation, and the family will have to deal with another set of contacts, another investigation and round of interventions directed at getting them to participate in therapy. If the family is sufficiently intransigent as to refuse to comply with treatment conditions, it is highly probable that they are sufficiently intransigent to obstruct any therapeutic change, particularly when operating under the conditions they have dictated. They should not be taken into family therapy. The therapist's time will be better used in treating those families that do not preclude their own change. Instead of therapy, legal proceedings might be indicated for intransigent families.

Accepting a family into treatment without checking the referral route with all concerned is signing a blank check. This has negative ramifications for the therapist, who now has clinical responsibility for a case that he or she cannot control and that is not progressing. Unfortunately, when treating incestuous child sexual abuse, a case that is not progressing is usually falling apart, because of the increased risks of recidivism and because of the other legal and protective interventions that provide a momentum of their own. There is no neutral gear in family therapy. For the families, the ramifications are even worse: They are in an ineffective treatment program, problems are getting worse, and they cannot get help elsewhere for these problems because they are already in treatment. What sometimes happens is that someone, family member or therapist, provokes a crisis, and the family either leaves treatment or the nature of the crisis removes their care from that particular therapist. Such a crisis might be a serious suicide attempt requiring hospitalization in another part of the state. Alternatively, the sexual abuse could resume, the statutory protective agency would become reinvolved, and law enforcement involvement probably would disrupt the family sufficiently that family therapy would be precluded. Whatever the actual crisis, it is likely to occur if the therapy is at an impasse too long because of an unworkable early structure.

Support Everyone, Especially the Victim

During the early phase—after discovery or disclosure, when the family is in crisis—everyone needs support from the therapist, especially the victim. As mentioned in the previous chapter, all family members are in difficult positions, and all require assistance, but the victim is in the worst position, and the amount of support she receives from the therapist should reflect this. Therapist support can include the explicit verbal support for each family member enabled by a multilateral stance. It also can be provided by seeing people in family sessions, as contact with the therapist and the opportunity to be seen and heard can be supportive in its own right.

Finally, specific interventions can be supportive. For example, if the father continues to return to the home after he has been ordered to stay away and his wife is troubled by this behavior but is also ambivalent, it is often supportive to give her the opportunity to meet alone with the therapist for part of a session to discuss her concerns about the father's visits and her ambivalence about stopping them. If this level of support is insufficient to resolve the problem, the therapist can see the couple together or perhaps recommend to the wife that she seek a temporary restraining order. This will lend substantial legal support to her resolve if she is able to request and obtain the order.

The father can be verbally supported about the loneliness he is experiencing while living away from his family, but the need for this temporary arrangement can also be reinforced. This simultaneously holds him accountable and supports him. A supportive intervention might be to meet with the father, mother, and caseworker from the child protective agency to arrange for the father to have regular visits with his family. If supervised visits will be required, this also can be dealt with in that meeting. Supporting everyone is closely related to the basic therapeutic stance of multilaterality. In this example, for instance, the father's right to see his family is being upheld, but so is the children's right not to be abused or be fearful of abuse, as well as the mother's right to have input regarding her husband's access to herself and the children.

Support for the victim can include meeting with her and her siblings to reiterate her absolute right to disclose the abuse and to stop it, and also to assign explicit responsibility for the occurrence of the abuse to the offender, not the child. Support also includes meeting with her individually to get the information regarding the details of the abuse rather than eliciting this information in a family session.

Believe the Victim and Temporize with the Offender

Believing the victim may seem obvious, but often it is not, in part because incest offenders usually deny the allegations, at least initially, and are often quite convincing in their denials. It is not unusual for a clinician or legal professional to be convinced by an offender that nothing untoward has occurred. This is a particularly interesting point because incest is the only crime of which the author is aware in which professionals approach the accused rather than the victim to ask whether anything happened. It would be unthinkable to ask the person who is accused of robbery, larceny, murder, or assault if he or she did it, yet this routinely occurs in cases of incestuous child sexual abuse. Clearly, this makes very little sense, and the clinician should rely on the victim's account of what transpired.

The therapist's general demeanor and interventions should indicate that he or she believes the victim's report that the abuse did occur. It is not advisable to argue or engage the offender concerning his denials. Instead, it is better to listen briefly to his protestations and accounts, then block them gently but firmly in each session. If the offender is allowed to continue and elaborate his denials, it will be nearly impossible for him to change his position later and accept responsibility for the abuse. In the meantime, the therapist should proceed in a vein consistent with belief of the victim's account. The offender's denials usually will begin to decrease markedly by approximately the sixth to eighth week of treatment, often with statements such as, "Well, even if something did happen . . ." or "I may have done some things, but not what my daughter alleges." Again, it is best to note the shift from outright denial to partial admission and to continue behaving in a manner that is consistent with total belief in the victim's account.

The therapist should see the victim alone to get her account of the abuse. This account should include the details of the actual physical and sexual contact; whatever force, coercion, or secret keeping that might have been involved; information about any other offenders or any other victims; and any attempts, appeals, or threats after disclosure to get her to retract her statement. Although this review of the abuse is usually difficult for the victim, it is supportive and therapeutic, as it allows her to unburden herself of painful information that usually only she and the offender know. Eliminating that degree of dyadic secrecy is important in the family therapy of incest. The process of obtaining the details from the victim can occur over several sessions to make it easier on her. Sometimes it is useful to use the first quarter hour of each session to gain further information in this regard, then use the remaining time to pursue different aspects of family work.

This sharing of information confirms the reality of the abuse for the victim—an issue for many children and adolescents. They know that these things occurred, can give detailed accounts, and suffer from all the characteristic sequelae, but at the same time they doubt the reality of their own memories. This problem occurs in part because of the relational confusion intrinsic to incestuous abuse and also probably because of the dissociative defense mechanisms that are usual in sexual abuse (see Gelinas 1983). For most victims, telling a therapist about what actually happened seems to affirm their own sanity. It also signifies that the therapist is taking the abuse itself seriously and is not merely regarding it as yet another trivial epiphenomenon of disturbed family systems. Finally, the victim's account provides information to the therapist that allows him or her to decide that the abuse did in fact take place. This is a delicate point, but sometimes the denials of the offender are so convincing that the therapist may waver or doubt; if this wavering persists, the therapy is seriously compromised. Hearing the victim's account provides that needed balance to the offender's denials and usually allows the therapist to wholeheartedly believe the victim—and that is the deepest form of support.

It is usually best to see the victim alone to obtain this account, especially if she is an adolescent. She should not be embarrassed by having to give her account in a full family session, nor should she have to give it in the presence of the offender or her mother. Neither parent is usually very supportive of disclosure this early in treatment, and their presence will significantly inhibit her account. If the victim is quite young (three years or younger), however, the presence of a reassuring adult is often helpful. This adult can be the mother, if she is clearly supportive of the child and reasonably steady. If she visibly reacts to the details of the sexual abuse, however, she may inhibit the account because the child, out of loyalty, will tend to protect the mother from distress. If the mother is not the best person in these circumstances, perhaps the protective worker or someone else who has a preexisting supportive relationship with the child and knows about the abuse may provide that necessary presence. But usually the victims, even the young ones, prefer to see the therapist alone.

Meet Protective Concerns

The issue here is for the therapist to meet protective concerns without tying his or her hands in treatment. Protecting the victim usually requires that the offender and victim live apart. Unfortunately, these protective concerns are often addressed by moving the victim from the home. This has several negative ramifications and results in a structure that drastically mitigates against therapeutic change in the family. If the victim is removed from the home, positive change in the family is extremely difficult, if not impossible, to achieve.

Removing the victim from the home does address some of the protective concerns but not others. First, the victim's mother and siblings are still at risk of physical abuse, and the siblings are at risk of sexual abuse. Second, removing the victim reinforces the victim's and often the family's conviction that she is responsible for the incest. The therapist can talk at great length about the father's bearing responsibility for the incest, but if the daughter is removed, neither she nor her family can really believe that. Actions do indeed speak louder than words. Third, removing the victim also reinforces the family structure that parentifies the daughter, assigning her responsibilities but no rights. She is the victim, but she must also bear the burden of separation from the family. The fourth problem in removing the victim is that it decreases the family's motivation for treatment. Usually the victim is seen as the focus of the problem or as the problem itself. When she is removed, the family will tend to close ranks and expel her, thereby expelling the problem as well. Thus, they do not really have to deal with the thorny issue of incestuous sexual abuse. They can continue to deny, rationalize, and project. Any therapist who attempts to help a family begin to deal with incest and to reintegrate a daughter who has been removed from the home is facing an uphill battle.

In addition, the daughter's motivation to participate in family therapy is decreased if she is removed. The removal reinforces her notions of guilt yet simultaneously angers her because of its inherent, if poorly understood, unfairness; the victim is ambivalent, at least, about wanting to rejoin a family that has so unfairly expelled her. Yet her loyalty and parentification impel her to want to rejoin them. Because of the difficulties of her position—familially, psychiatrically, and legally—a victim removed from her family usually shows an increase in symptoms. This is the fifth major problem in removing the incest victim. This increase in symptomatology may include depressive symptoms, running away, suicidal gestures or attempts, or substance abuse. Naturally, these complicate matters considerably for the therapist and the family therapy. Sixth, and finally, finding placement for a child or adolescent is difficult enough. If and when that child or adolescent begins to show an increase in symptoms (particularly running away or suicidal gestures or attempts), it is going to be very hard to maintain her in that placement, and the therapist will need to spend valuable time addressing related crises.

A better course of action is removing the offender from the home. His removal satisfies the same protective concerns, initiates some positive therapeutic processes, and avoids many of the problems inherent in removing the victim.

Removing the offender promotes therapeutic change in a number of ways. First, in addition to addressing the protective concerns regarding the victim, it also protects the other siblings and the mother from sexual or physical abuse in a way that removing the victim cannot. Second, removing the father rather than the daughter assigns responsibility for the incest in a very powerful way. This is supportive of the victim, constructive, and often surprising to the offender, and it serves notice to the family that the issue of accountability is a very real one and the father, not the daughter, bears that accountability. Third, removing the father actually begins to change the structure of the family. It redefines the victim as a child and as someone with an inherent entitlement (as a child or adolescent) to receive some measure of caretaking. Simultaneously, the father is redefined as an adult, who needs in some measure to take care of his own needs and provide for the needs of his children. If someone must go through the onerous process of living apart from the family for a while, it should be the adult, not the child. In families where the father is very powerful and the victim's and the family's perceptions are that they cannot exert any controls on him, it is a valuable and salutary experience to see the father rather than the child leave the home temporarily. (Issues of paternal resistance will be reviewed later.)

Fourth, removing the father almost invariably increases the family's motivation for treatment. Usually the offender wants to return to living with his family; when it becomes clear that his return is contingent on the victim's safety and the progress of family therapy and that this will be an issue discussed and decided upon by the child protective agency in collaboration with the family therapist, the motivation for family therapy increases. Similarly (although there are exceptions to this), once the shock of discovery/

disclosure wears off, the wife usually wants the husband back in the home. Family therapy is linked to this return process (by either his participation or some notion that the risk of further abuse is diminished), and the motivation to participate increases.

Having the daughter in the home is often uncomfortable for the mother. She may have mixed feelings toward the daughter or be concerned that the daughter is having problems or is the focus of hostility from siblings. With her husband out of the house, the mother often needs assistance to handle all this. If she perceives the therapist as someone who can assist her in dealing with the children (especially her daughter, who is the identified patient), this is likely to increase her motivation for treatment. The victim is usually encouraged by the intervention that held her father accountable and required him to leave the home. Although she may have some loyalty issues to deal with, her feeling that she is believed and that the abuse is being taken seriously usually engages at least some temporary cooperation from the victim.

Clearly, removing the offender initiates a number of positive processes. It also avoids all the problems associated with removing the victim.

Establish Good Boundaries and Be Careful about Secrets

Incestuous child sexual abuse occurs in part because of poorly defined boundaries within families. The differences between the generations are blurred, as are the differences between affection and sexual behavior and between privacy and secrecy. At the same time, the boundaries surrounding the family, separating them from the outside world, are often quite rigid and impermeable.

In treatment the therapist should immediately begin to demonstrate clear boundaries regarding the family and himself or herself. For instance, it is advisable to begin and end sessions on time, to have regularly scheduled sessions, and to make it clear that people are, in fact, expected to come for their appointments. Payment should be prompt, regular, and according to the billing procedure for that clinician. Special arrangements regarding either procedure or fee should be avoided.

No special sessions should be given to individuals outside the usual treatment times, although seeing subsystems of the family (and therefore individuals) is legitimate and necessary. This is not really a problem as long as everyone in the family knows who is being seen when and also knows that it is part of the therapist's routine to see subsystems within the family. If a family member telephones with a crisis, the therapist should attempt, if at all possible, to deal with it at the next regularly scheduled session. This is usually not too difficult, as the family is being seen twice weekly for family therapy sessions, at this point, entailing a delay of at most several days. If that is not advisable given the circumstances, the therapist should schedule a special family session and invite all members of the family to attend. If the crisis concerns situations with other agencies or professionals, representatives from those agencies or the other professionals should be invited to the family session, again depending on the particular circumstances of the crisis. Emergency sessions in which the therapist meets alone with just one family member should be assiduously avoided, since working in isolation from the rest of the family is likely to establish either a special relationship or a secret with that person. If the therapist should unwittingly allow a special relationship with one or more family members to develop, it will violate the principle of multilaterality. Secret sharing and special relationships recapitulate, in the family therapy, the relational structure of the family, which contributed to the incestuous sexual abuse in the first place. (See also Chapter 2 for a discussion of multilaterality.)

Special meetings also are conducive to the inappropriate divulging and sharing of family secrets. Matrices of awareness (who knows what and who knows who knows what) are interesting in any family, but they are dangerous in incest families. (Because secrets are so prevalent in incest families, and because the therapist needs to adopt a certain stance regarding secrets early in the treatment, these issues are dealt with more thoroughly later in this chapter.)

It is helpful for the therapist to establish a formal, rather than an informal, route by which family members can gain access to him or her. An office telephone number with a backup answering service for emergencies is appropriate for the family; a home telephone number is not. If the family needs to telephone during the night, they should go through the answering service. Similarly, meetings should be held in a business office or agency, not in the therapist's home, and only under formalized circumstances in the family's home. The therapist needs to be a therapist, not a personal friend; private, personal, or family information about the therapist is inappropriate. Incest families can "pull" for the inappropriate and unproductive blurring of boundaries in therapy that confuses issues and can, if severe enough, entangle the therapist in the family structure, nullifying his or her effectiveness.

Notify the Statutory Child Protection Agency and Establish Liaison with the Necessary Personnel

The therapist must ensure that the appropriate notification has been made in writing to the relevant state agency protecting children. If a report of suspected child abuse has not yet been filed, the therapist must do so. There are two reasons for this. First, in most states, therapists are mandated reporters and are required by law to file for children at risk of abuse or neglect. To protect the child and obey the law, therapists must file. Second, the therapist places himself or herself in an unworkable position vis-à-vis the family if he or she does not file.

Necessity of Reporting. If a family has been referred for treatment by the courts or by a social agency empowered to monitor the welfare of children, then that agency should have been notified of the possibility of sexual abuse within the family and should have investigated that possibility. Presumably, they and/or law enforcement officials have substantiated the allegations. Under these conditions, the statutory child protective agency has obviously received, from somewhere or someone, a report of child sexual abuse. In this case, the therapist does not have to notify the agency of information they already have (particularly if it has made the referral to the therapist). But if the clinician should hear of previously unknown elements of the sexual abuse or of previously unknown physical abuse or neglect, then he or she must report the new information to the child protective services.

Often a therapist does not initially know that a particular case involves incestuous child sexual abuse, and sometimes a case may be referred for treatment of this problem but no one along the referral route has filed a report to child protective services. If child sexual abuse did occur within the family, even if it has demonstrably stopped at present, the therapist must report to child protective services as soon as he or she suspects that the abuse occurred. The family should be notified by the therapist very early in treatment (in the first or second session) that he or she is going to report the problem to child protective services. This is difficult information to convey and very anxiety-provoking for both the family and the therapist. Nevertheless, it must be done, and the family must be informed as soon as possible, not only because they have a right to know, but also because it establishes the therapist's position vis-à-vis the secrecy element of incest. The actual reporting and filing should be accomplished as rapidly as possible.

Clinical Consequences of Not Reporting. Usually a family that hears about the necessity of reporting to child protective services will attempt to dissuade the therapist from taking this action. Some of the more common arguments that families might introduce include the notions that the abuse is now known (so presumably it will not continue), the mother is now alerted to protect the children (so, again, presumably, the abuse cannot continue), and the father's secret is out and he regrets his past behavior (so, again, the abuse will not recur). Alternatively, the family may attempt to expel the victim, their assumption being that if she is not in the home, the father will no longer abuse her—i.e., the incest has stopped. Expulsion of the victim does not ensure that the father will not pursue her or that she will not tell him of her whereabouts; neither does it protect her from further victimization by other individuals or the victim's siblings from their father. Most of the family's arguments against reporting address the notion of stopping further abuse. Unfortunately, these arguments are all specious. The incestuous abuse cannot be stopped simply by disclosing to a therapist. These arguments also ignore the fact that sexual abuse of a child has already occurred, and that, in itself, must be addressed.

If the therapist allows himself or herself to be persuaded to keep silent, he or she has essentially been shifted by the family from the role of therapist to that of family member. At that point, the therapist's effectiveness dwindles rapidly. If the therapist had reported the family's secretive incestuous child sexual abuse, it would no longer be a secret. The thick, rigid boundary around the family (usually imposed by the offender) would have been broken, and information and contacts could flow in and out of the family, allowing change to commence. But if the therapist has not reported to the child protective services, it is not enough that he or she knows about the abuse and that the therapist's knowledge will help stop it; it will not. All that has happened is that the thick, rigid boundary around the family has looped itself over the therapist, to include the therapist as a member of the family and a sharer of the family's secret. The therapist is now colluding with the incestuous family. A family cannot be changed by a therapist in this position because he or she has no foot outside the system—no leverage or credibility—and the family's homeostatic mechanisms support incest at several levels. The individual psychologies of the parents, the dyadic patterns between them, the systemic forces exacerbating the marital estrangement and the daughter's parentification, the possible role of substance abuse, intergenerational sexual abuse and depression—all these contribute to maintaining the incestuous child sexual abuse as part of the family's continuing functional structure. The therapist attempting to change this kind of interlocking situation while standing squarely inside it has embarked on what can only be a fool's errand.

Therapeutic Benefits of Reporting. Despite the anxiety and acting out it can generate in both the family and sometimes in the inexperienced therapist, notifying the statutory child protective agency accomplishes a number of positive things. First, the necessity of reporting often introduces some needed reality testing for the family about the societal view toward incestuous child sexual abuse. For some families, it is quite a surprise that incest is frowned upon. The notions that laws and societal mores forbidding incest are taken seriously by others, that incest involving a child is a form of child abuse and that it will not be tolerated by society, are often real revelations to families and victims alike. There is nothing quite so effective in engendering this response as filing a report of child sexual abuse. Reporting also helps protect the child victim because the assigned caseworker joins the therapist in attempting to protect that child. The therapist and protective worker can be of mutual assistance to each other. For instance, the protective worker must address immediate protective concerns and may or may not want to remove the victim from the home; if the therapist knows and has reported something about the family, he or she can make the argument for removing the offender instead of the victim, an argument that is quite powerful and usually fully understood by the protective worker, who appreciates the problem of finding appropriate placements for children. With both protective worker and therapist cooperating to get the offender rather than the victim removed, this intervention is much more likely to be effective than if either were working alone.

The protective worker also can help protect the child and change the family structure by providing vital information to the therapist. The assigned protective worker is in a better position to make home visits, for instance, than the therapist and has access to sources of information not always available to a clinician. In one case, a situation in which the father had not been removed from the home, after about eight weeks of treatment, the therapist began to feel that there was more going on at home than was being discussed in the sessions and notified the protective worker assigned to the family. She, too, was uncomfortable about the situation without knowing why. The next day she and a colleague paid an unannounced home visit and found that the father had locked all the toilet paper, soap, and light bulbs in his bedroom closet and that if family members wanted to use these items, they had to be "nice" to him. "Nice" no longer involved sexual contact, but this information certainly made clear the degree of the father's continuing control over the family—and the degree to which the family was allowing this to continue by not alluding to it during the family sessions. This kind of information is obviously invaluable, and liaison work by the therapist and protective service workers can help the family therapy a great deal.

The clinician, however, is also in a position to assist the protective workers. First, the therapist may have a good deal of experience in working with incestuous child sexual abuse, and if the particular child protective worker assigned to the family has a lot of general social service experience but relatively little with incest, the therapist can provide an informal educative function.

Also, the protective worker is often in the position of having to make important decisions; these might include issues such as whether visitation between victim and offender should be allowed; when the offender should be permitted to move back into the home; whether the mother is capable of being adequately protective of the children; or whether one or more family members are showing current psychiatric problems to a degree that the children are endangered. On all these issues, the therapist is in a position to provide information and sometimes to make recommendations that the protective worker can use in the decision-making process.

Another obvious area of assistance to the protective worker emerges as the family structure begins to change. As this occurs, the family gradually develops healthier structures and patterns, and the risk of abuse diminishes. This helps the protective worker, who is in the position of providing services to the family and monitoring the situation with respect to the reemergence of the sexual abuse.

Importance of Liaison Work. Good liaison work with the protective worker is a necessity when working with incest involving a child. Together, the therapist and protective worker can operate synergistically to intensify the impact of their interventions for the family. Working cooperatively means that interventions can be timed to be most effective; for instance, both therapist and worker can insist at the same time that the offender leave the home temporarily. Similarly, one person's intervention can reinforce the other's; for instance, the worker's insistence on monitoring visitation can reinforce the therapist's work in sessions with the issue of father's accountability. Good liaison work often makes it possible to avoid working at cross-purposes, and it helps avoid splitting among agencies. In short, there is no substitute for reporting and for developing a good relationship with the protective worker.

Watch for Acting Out

During this early phase of family treatment, when the family is in crisis and the therapist and other professionals providing services are not yet thoroughly familiar with, or in control of, the situation, there is the potential for various people to act out their distress rather than to bring it into the sessions. During this time, it is necessary to watch for signs that someone is approaching the threshold of acting out.

Some common forms of acting out by the victim include running away, suicide attempts, seductive behavior with surrogate caretakers, truancy from school, and sometimes pregnancy. Certain times are more risky than others; particularly risky intervals include when parents are being informed of a recent disclosure, if the father is arrested, and if the father is denied visitation or is in some way "punished" (because this would increase the victim's guilt and therefore her risk of self-destructive behavior).

Acting out by the offender might include suicide attempts or attempts to harm his family. These latter attempts can range from the relatively controlled (verbal, legal, or financial manipulation) to the uncontrolled and sometimes violent (physical assaultiveness and occasionally homicidal behavior). Particularly if the offender operates within a very patriarchal context, he may feel betrayed, shamed, and enraged by any disclosure, and the consequences may be that he feels further entitled to exact revenge or to reestablish what he considers his rightful degree of control over "his" family. The potential for acting out is increased with patriarchal, controlling individuals, and the therapist must watch for this. For offenders of other personality types and histories, the therapist may need to watch for acting out in the form of alcohol abuse or refusal to adhere to previously agreed-upon arrangements regarding visitation, staying away from the home, child support, or attending therapy.

Particularly problematic times are immediately upon disclosure/discovery and immediately after moving into temporary housing. These familial and residential changes more often seem to be triggering events for acting out than the more purely legal events such as arrest, arraignment, and so forth. Although some acting out does occur around these events, it is not as frequent as around the earlier familial and residential events; this appears partly attributable to the effects of time. Legal procedures usually are not the first inkling the offender has about the discovery/disclosure; when they are, they also can provoke acting out, but usually the offender is notified of disclosure by some method other than arrest. The relatively infrequent acting out that occurs around the legal procedures is also attributable to the decidedly repressive attitude that the legal system takes with regard to such behavior. Because it is not usually tolerated, it tends to occur somewhat less frequently than might be expected. Conversely, some degree of acting out in the family often has been tolerated, and this tends to encourage its occurrence. In treatment, the author takes a decidedly repressive stance toward acting out and firmly encourages that all the material be addressed within therapy sessions and verbally, with the therapist and other professionals. While this by no means precludes all acting out, the combination of watching for it and diverting some of it into more workable forms does decrease the overall amount of acting out by family members.

Acting out by the mother may take the form of suicide attempts, but more usually it will be some behavior that provokes acting out by the husband or daughter. Thus, mother may give mixed messages to father about the necessity of his staying away or may actively encourage him to spend the night. She may buy him liquor if he has a drinking problem or phone him with some inflammatory message if he has a history of impulsivity. (The motivation for this is usually unconscious on the part of the mother.) Alternatively, maternal acting out may take the form of dealing with the daughter in such a way that the daughter is practically impelled to act out. One mother in such a situation would lock her fourteen-year-old daughter in her bedroom after school, virtually forcing the girl to run away. The higher risk times for mothers are less clearly circumscribed by time or event, and they appear to be motivated more by anger and hopelessness that things are so bad that they cannot be changed. Thus, it is important that the mother's hopefulness be continually monitored.

Finally, acting out by the therapist should be mentioned here because it can and does occur. This occasionally takes the form of identifying with one member of the family to such an extent that multilaterality is sacrificed. If the therapist overidentifies with the victim, he or she can very easily slide into a punitive position toward both parents, which has implications regarding the victim's loyalties to her parents. Overly identifying with the mother appears to occur less frequently, but when it does happen, it is not unusual for the family therapy to degenerate into supportive individual therapy for the mother with token stabs at family involvement.

Identification with the offender is very common, and particularly if it remains unconscious, it can make it impossible for a therapist to treat incestuous child sexual abuse. Identification with the offender is often unconscious on the part of the therapist. Since identification is easiest with individuals who share a gender and an approximate age with the therapist, it is usually easier for therapists to identify with an adult of the same gender rather than a child or an adult of a different gender. Since incest offenders tend overwhelmingly to be male, adult male therapists are the most likely to experience an unconscious, and unwilling, identification with an offender. Since even unconscious identification with an offender is uncomfortable at best, there will be a tendency on the part of the therapist in this position to distance himself from the situation altogether. A frequent outcome of this distancing is to ignore the signs of incest or to trivialize allegations in the first place so that the disclosure process is never really begun.

Identification with a young offender also can occur; this can sometimes lead to behavior on the part of the therapist that one might expect from a much younger person. One therapist, ostensibly to increase rapport with an offending older adolescent brother, watched pornographic videotapes with this young man for some thirty minutes in the family home while the victimized sister was in another room, fully cognizant of what her brother and the therapist were doing. This may have been attributed to ignorance on the part of an inexperienced therapist, but this individual had had quite a bit of experience. Instead, it appears to have been a problem with blurred boundaries and with identification with the offender. Boundary problems included agreeing to meet in the home, not setting a clear beginning and ending time to the meetings, not setting a particular place to meet in the home, and not expressing clear expectations of who was to attend these meetings. It was also a problem with overidentification with the young offender's problems, interests, and role in the family.

Another more usual form of acting out by therapists occurs when the therapist, because of growing anxiety, fear, or hopelessness about change, does something that essentially forces the family to leave treatment. The reality is that there are moments of doubt, anxiety, and frustration for the clinician in working with any incest family. It can be difficult to change these family structures, which are reinforced by so many individual, dyadic, and systemic elements. In particularly difficult or frightening cases, it can be all too easy to provoke premature termination. Simply bouncing the family around in one's schedule, treating them with disrespect, scapegoating someone, not believing the victim, provoking the daughter to act out so that she requires hospitalization, or provoking the offender to act out so that he is incarcerated or otherwise taken over by law enforcement officials will usually suffice to get the family out of treatment. Consultation with a colleague can restore the therapist's equanimity or help him or her decide to transfer the case to another therapist if necessary.

Be Careful of Family Secrets

The issue of secrets has already been addressed briefly, but since secrets and secret keeping are especially prevalent in families with incest, the subject is worth more detailed consideration. Three areas relating to secrets are of particular concern to the therapist: content, coalitions, and entrapment.

In families where incest has persisted over an appreciable length of time (weeks or months), some major secrets have evolved, and there is a secrecy structure to understand and contend with. Before the disclosure, for instance, the existence of the sexual abuse itself is usually kept secret, at least from some people in the family. The offender and victim know about the abuse, and each typically keeps it a secret from the wife/mother. Alternatively, mother may know about the abuse, but neither father nor daughter knows that she knows, so that is mother's secret. Sometimes one or more siblings know about it but cannot or will not tell the victim they know, so she is not aware that she is keeping a secret that has already been breached to some extent.

Another common secrecy structure occurs in families where the offender promises the eldest daughter that, as long as she tolerates the sexual abuse and does not tell her mother (i.e., keeps the secret), he will refrain from abusing her younger siblings. Out of loyalty and parentification, the victim will usually agree to this "bargain" and will, therefore, be keeping two secrets: one that she is being sexually abused by her father and the other that she is protecting her siblings. Unfortunately, the offender usually does not keep his side of the agreement and is in fact abusing one or more of the younger children. In this case, the younger children know that they are being sexually abused, but the older child does not know this. The younger children may or may not know that the elder sister is being abused and therefore may wonder why she is not. Alternatively, they may know that she also is being abused but may not know about her attempts to protect them (and may then seriously misinterpret her "allowing" the abuse to continue). Finally, they may know both "secrets" of their elder sister, which may of course be secrets to no one in the family, except the elder sister (who knows of her own abuse and thinks it is a secret) and the mother (who may know nothing). There is no denying that the secrecy structure in incest families can be quite complicated.

Incest cannot occur or continue without someone keeping secrets, and in families where sexual abuse has been carried out for long periods of time, the tendencies of family members toward keeping secrets and creating alliances with each other with secrets as the medium of exchange and control can be persistent and very powerful. The existence and sharing of secrets is not merely an exercise involving the withholding or the exchange of information; it is a relational process. Secrets can be the hidden bond in some relationships, and the therapist must understand these for him or her to be effective in the treatment. Coalitions are made and people are controlled by these relational processes, and there is, of course, no reason to think that family members regard the therapist as off-limits to these ways of relating. If anything, in an unconscious attempt to control the therapist (i.e., to render the therapist ineffectual and therefore safe vis-à-vis the upset being caused in the family), incestuous families often include or attempt to include the therapist in their family network of secrets and secret keeping.

The best safeguard against becoming entangled in this relational process is to watch for its occurrence, to be able to sidestep the process, or to address it directly when the process begins to impinge on the therapist.

Another helpful basic position is never to agree to keep a secret without first knowing its content (Karpel 1980). Making such an agreement is too much like signing a blank check. If a patient alludes to what seems to be a tempting secret while asking for such a promise from the therapist, the therapist should simply say no to the offer of the secret and explain the basic stance regarding secrets. If this secret is so important that the family member needs to tell it, then he or she cannot tie the therapist's hands. After all, the therapist has clinical responsibility for the case and for the entire family. Conversely, if the therapist cannot be allowed to act on the secret, the family member should keep it to himself or herself. Occasionally, family members will choose to keep the secret from the therapist but almost invariably the information is disclosed in the context of the basic secrets agreement—that is, that the therapist will not agree to keep the secret or to refrain from acting on it. At times the family member may decide to retain the information rather than agree to this basic secrets arrangement. What often occurs, however, is that the therapist is informed of information at a later date. In this way, the therapist has obtained the information without having been placed in a difficult position. For a particularly good discussion of handling secrets in family therapy, see Karpel 1980.

Finally, the network of secrets is one of the primary indicators of alliances or coalitions in the family. These also point directly to those relational issues that must be dealt with within the sessions. The secrets, and the relationships to which they allude, along with the balance of obligation, entitlement, vulnerability, and caring or callousness, must be dealt with directly in these sessions. For example, if someone knew about the sexual abuse (i.e., knew the secret) and did nothing to assist the victim, and the victim knows this, one can assume she will have some therapeutic issues with that individual. If father and victim successfully kept the secret from mother for several years, does that suggest that mother was, in fact, interested in not knowing, or does it suggest that for whatever reasons, there existed a sufficiently strong alliance between father and victim that this alliance operated against mother?

The therapist must not become entangled in the secrets network, but it can provide information about relationships and often the emotional force to assist people in working with the relational issues that the secrets represent.

Arrange for Medical Treatment of the Victim

In incest cases, as in other sexual abuse cases, the victim should be medically evaluated by someone experienced in examining victims of sexual abuse or by someone who will handle the situation sensitively but nontrivially. Sometimes people feel that this is unnecessary, but usually it is a wise intervention for two specific reasons. First, the child or adolescent may require some medical treatment. It is not unusual for venereal diseases and other infections to be transmitted to children by abusing parents, and occasionally there may be traumatic injuries as well. Medical intervention and documentation are required (cf., *Pediatric Annals* 1979, the entire issue of which is devoted to medical management of sexually abused children).

The second reason for medical evaluation is to reassure the victim. Often the child or adolescent will harbor a fear that the abuse has "damaged" her and has negatively changed her in some physical way. A sensitive medical practitioner is in the best position to notice this fear and to reassure the child that no physical change has occurred or that treatment will be initiated in those rare cases where physical injury was sustained.

Assist Mother in Establishing a Social Support Network

If the mother of an incest victim is asked about her social support network, it usually becomes apparent that she has none. She may be so isolated that she does not even realize how few people she can talk to or how lonely she really is. Often the victim's mother will indicate that she does have friends and confidantes, but when the depth of the relationship, the frequency of contact, and the degree to which mother herself discloses and shares is examined, these relationships are usually found to be shallow, tenuous, or one-sided, with the mother of the victim doing all the listening and caretaking.

As the caretaking and depleted adult of the family, mother is usually still in a relationally avoidant stance derived from her history of being a parentified child, and because relationships for her still take but do not give back, she will tend to avoid them.

This is a lifelong pattern, but it must be modified, in part so that mother is no longer the relationally avoidant member of a high-risk family constellation for incest, but also to help her improve the quality of her relationships and her emotional life. She also will need increased levels of support later in the family therapy, which the therapist will not be able to provide. When that stressful period arrives, it is much better if the therapist has seen to it that a structure for increased support is already in place and ready to be tapped. This stressful period usually begins at the middle or end of the second phase, which is devoted to changing the family structure. That is why the work of establishing the social support network commences near the end of the first phase.

When this work commences, as part of each session with the family, several processes are initiated. First, of course, the extent of mother's isolation and the difficulty of her position become apparent. Taking the issue of establishing a social support network seriously and persisting with mother to help her identify and then cultivate people in her environment who have some potential as supportive friends gives mother the clear message that this way of relating is an expectation in the therapy, and it signals her family that she has the right to have friends. Gentle but persistent pressure from the therapist begins shifting mother toward behaviors where she has to initiate relationships and simultaneously exposes her lack of assertiveness and skill in these areas. The probabilities are that she will continue to be exploited in whatever relationships she does have and will participate to some extent in her own exploitation. With time and attention to the topic in the sessions, most mothers begin to notice, often for the first time, the ways in which they are being exploited.

This expectation and pressure by the therapist has pushed mother into the relational ring in a fairly intense way, and this allows, or precipitates, the emergence of all her resistances to relationships, along with all her deficits; this obviously makes them available to therapeutic work. This also helps mother to notice and identify where, when, and by whom she is being relationally exploited. Very simply put, mother begins to get angry at her relational life. Her anger is a needed resource in the transition from unilateral caretaking toward expecting and demanding some degree of reciprocity in relationships with people outside the family and with her children and husband. This developing ability to demand some kinds of relational reciprocity begins to take her out of her own position of unilateral caretaking with no reciprocal entitlement and enables her to begin changing the marital relationship in the third phase of family work.

Conduct Full Family Evaluation

It may seem obvious, but just as no case should be accepted for treatment until the referral route is known, no family should receive treatment until they have been evaluated. At some point during this early crisis phase of treatment, a family should receive a thorough evaluation. This evaluation should provide information about the structure of the family, relationships, roles, and routines. (How to do such an evaluation is beyond the scope of this paper, but there are several models of family evaluation from which to choose. The reader is directed to methods described in Karpel and Strauss 1983.)

The family evaluation should give the therapist a working understanding of the family and provide material suggesting not only what structures or roles need changing, but also how to do that. For instance, Karpel and Strauss use what they refer to as "probe questions." Probe questions might include asking someone to sketch the layout of the house or to describe a typical day in the family. What does it suggest to a therapist when a probe question about layout of the house reveals that the seventeen-year-old daughter, incestuously abused for fourteen years, must pass through the parental bedroom to get from her bedroom to the nearest hallway? This piece of information was provided by a family in a completely matter-of-fact manner during the evaluation, as they saw nothing unusual about it. This spoke volumes about the father's need for control and his success at gaining it within the family. It also spoke to the family's clearly inappropriate attitude toward the sexual abuse and the mother's collusion in this particular case. Finally, it suggested that because of the extent and duration of the abuse, and the family's attitude toward it, the seventeen-year-old daughter might have become so severely impaired that she, too, in some ways colluded with the continuance of the abuse. She was, after all, seventeen years old; she theoretically could leave her home or could have insisted on a change in bedroom. She had, however, been sexually abused for a very long time by more than one offender. The case could certainly be made that the severity of the abuse had incapacitated her and that her continuing attempts to protect the offenders in the family were an expression of the extent of her impairment. All this was opened up because of an odd outcropping on a sketch of the layout of their house.

Similarly, when the family is asked about a typical day, it often becomes apparent how the daughter is parentified. She may, for example, be the person who gets up first in the morning or wakens the other children, gives them breakfast, supervises their dressing, and gets them off to school on time. Alternatively, she may take care of other household responsibilities, but the detailed description of a typical day is usually revealing of both the structure of the family and where it might be changed.

During this family evaluation, it is advisable to see each member individually for a brief part of a session to evaluate them as individuals, with alcohol abuse, depression, suicidal ideation, and potential for acting out receiving specific scrutiny. This does not violate the proviso about avoiding individual meetings. Individual meetings that are outside the usual treatment schedule and are not balanced by some sort of individual contact with other family members are a problem, as they have the potential for setting up special relationships and for conveying and keeping secrets. These individual meetings during the evaluation occur with each member, are in the regularly scheduled treatment framework, and are public information in the family. Individual meetings with the victim to hear her account of the sexual abuse also provide public information to the family and are part of the treatment context, so these also are regarded as regular and not special meetings.

Usually this extensive family evaluation begins at about the fifth or sixth contact with the family, and sometimes even later, depending on the degree of crisis and the degree of legal involvement. Because of the crisis mode that initiates many such therapies, these crisis elements must be dealt with to some extent before sessions can be devoted to a thorough family evaluation. But this evaluation should not be put off too long; the information and orientation it provides the therapist are important and help him or her avoid mistakes as well as move toward therapeutic change.

Focus on Family Processes

During the early crisis phase of therapy, when the therapist ascertains the referral route, contacts other agencies, and sees members of the family, he or she is essentially doing a rapid evaluation of the situation to be able to provide crisis management and to structure the therapy situation. The subsequent family evaluation several sessions later provides different information. It gives the therapist a working understanding of the family structure and roles and some notions about systemic patterns. The evaluation provides the information needed to begin the more general family therapy work of changing the family itself. Beginning this work in the second phase (changing the family structure) would, in itself, provide the therapist with further systemic information and shift the emphasis from case management to therapy.

The customary proviso is that some therapy does occur during the first phase and some crisis management will continue to be needed during the second, third, and fourth phases of therapy. Some structural and role changes are in fact occurring during phase one. Witness the already described effect on family structure of removing the offender rather than the victim or the effect that maintaining good contact with other agencies has on a family's propensity to induce splitting among helpers. Similarly, crises requiring considerable case management skill can occur at any time during therapy. But there are recognizable phases of therapy, and there is a shift in focus to a more thorough concern with the internal workings of the family. This shift occurs when the situation has been structured well enough that the therapist can, temporarily, not deal with crises and can shift attention to an evaluation of the family itself.

Usually family evaluations of this type require two or three sessions to complete. Since the evaluation cannot really begin until the fifth or sixth session, by the time it is completed the family and therapist may be in their ninth session. The completion of the family evaluation usually signals the end of that early, crisis phase and the transition into the second phase.

In this second phase, the primary task is to change the structure of the family, shifting it away from that high-risk constellation. One of the obvious tasks is to shift the daughter out of her parentified position. As this occurs, the daughter is taking care of her parents less and also performing less work and fewer functions around the house; the mother will usually reassume many of these tasks, so she will be feeling more demands on her. In addition, the daughter will usually drop back into a daughter's position and begin to make child or adolescent demands on her mother, the adult. This adds to the demands on mother. Finally, as the husband shifts his relational pursuit from his daughter to his wife, the wife will usually feel overwhelmed by demands. This is a temporary point in the therapy, where mother feels that everyone is making increased demands on her. This is the time when mother needs to tap into that support network previously described.

As she feels the increasing demands, mother is usually more likely and more able to begin making some demands on her husband, in some cases for the first time. This signals the shift into the third phase, changing the marital relationship, and a gradual decrease in mother's feeling unilaterally demanded upon while receiving little in return. The support network can be invaluable at this juncture. Helping mother establish this network in the first phase can make it possible for her to begin making demands on her husband late in the second phase, and this developing ability on her part signals the onset of the marital work. While the therapist is providing marital treatment, he or she also should be seeing the identified child patient and begin working with her to confront the offender. Confrontations with the offender and other members of the family (the fourth phase) should occur only after careful preparation, but doing so changes the former victim's actual relational life and corrects the residual relational imbalances.

As noted at the beginning of this chapter, family therapy for incest calls for both general family therapy skills and attention to special considerations because incest was involved. Once that first phase is over, the family therapy is more dependent on the clinician's general family therapy skills than on the special considerations relating to incest.

The successful outcome of treatment is usually measured by four criteria. First, the incestuous abuse (of all the victims by all the offenders) has definitely terminated and has not resumed. Second, there is a healthier family structure, as evaluated by the usual family therapy criteria in combination with the particular structures with which the family began treatment. Third, the marital relationship has significantly improved, especially with regard to that rigid, earlier pattern of a relationally pursuant husband and a depleted, relationally avoidant wife. Family therapy will not change these basic personality types, but it should loosen this pattern considerably and help each partner be less extremely pursuant or avoidant as a regular stance. Fourth, the daughter should be very significantly less parentified, and her self-esteem and assertiveness should have markedly increased. With her decreased parentification, the daughter will be out of the high-risk constellation (or put another way, the high-risk constellation for incestuous child sexual abuse cannot exist without a parentified child within the family). Also, with decreased parentification, she is more likely to want and expect some degree of reciprocity in her relationships and be able to assert herself to gain this reciprocity.

Given all four criteria, the family therapy can be said to have succeeded. A final recommendation at that point would be to continue to monitor the family. Incest is supported and reinforced by all the factors reviewed in this chapter, and more that were not mentioned (e.g., certain societal norms, child-rearing practices, certain implications of some religious teachings, and economic factors). It is unwise simply to terminate with a family when these four criteria have been achieved. Instead, it is advisable to monitor the family at increasing intervals. Before termination, therapy sessions are gradually shifted from once a week to biweekly, then monthly. After termination of active treatment, the family should come in every three months for the next one or two years, and then every six months, until either all the children are grown or the therapeutic changes are well ingrained. Recurrence of incestuous child sexual abuse is always a risk, but an experienced therapist can treat some families so that the risk is perceived to be low after three years of treatment.

Notes

1. When the term *incest* is used, it denotes the incestuous sexual abuse of a child (a clinical definition) and not merely sexual intercourse between persons not permitted to marry by reasons of consanguinity (a legal definition). All present references to incest refer to intrafamilial child sexual abuse.

2. This intervention framework is applicable to families in which the abuser, to

use Groth's terminology, is "regressed" rather than "fixated" (Groth 1982). See Chapter 2 for a discussion of the applicability of this family therapy framework.

References

Gelinas, D.J. 1983. "The Persisting Negative Effects of Incest." *Psychiatry* 46:312–32.

Groth, A.N. 1982. "The Incest Offender." In S.M. Sgroi, ed. *Handbook of Clinical Intervention in Child Sexual Abuse*. Lexington, MA: Lexington Books, 215–18.

Karpel, M. 1980. "Family Secrets: I. Conceptual and Ethical Issues in the Relational Context; II. Ethical and Practical Considerations in Therapeutic Management." *Family Process* 19:295–306.

Karpel, M.A., and E.S. Strauss. 1983. *Family Evaluation*. New York: Gardner Press.

Pediatric Annals 1979. 8(no. 5).

4

Assessment and Treatment of the Adult Survivor of Childhood Sexual Abuse within a Schema Framework

Lisa McCann,
Laurie Anne Pearlman,
David K. Sakheim,
Daniel J. Abrahamson

The growing awareness of the prevalence of childhood sexual abuse and the concurrent increase in the number of adult women seeking psychotherapy to deal with their sexual abuse experiences have motivated mental health professionals to develop more effective ways of helping women to disclose, discuss, and integrate this experience into their lives. Some recent models of adaptation to this trauma (see, for example, Finkelhor and Browne 1985: Gelinas 1983; Herman 1981) have provided important insights into the dynamics of childhood sexual abuse. The work we present here integrates knowledge about these dynamics into a more general model of the individual's unique experience of traumatic events.

Our model describes the relation among life experiences, cognitive schemata (or systems of meaning) and their associated emotions, and psychological functioning. The practical purpose of this work is to provide a framework for assessing individual response patterns, which can serve as a basis for treatment planning. The theoretical value is to provide a framework that can be used to investigate and integrate knowledge about the experience of the adult survivor of childhood sexual abuse.

Many writers have stressed the importance of individual differences in response to the trauma of childhood sexual abuse (see, for example, Courtois 1979; Herman 1981; Silver, Boon, and Stones 1983). Yet the factors that determine the differences between individuals are most often viewed as being located outside the individual's system of meaning (i.e., the duration and specific nature of the abuse experience, the relation of the perpetrator to the victim, and so forth). Research on the relation between these external factors and psychological adaptation has, however, yielded few consistent results

(Browne and Finkelhor 1986). In the present model, we focus on the unique meaning of the event for the survivor, as this shapes differential responses to childhood sexual abuse.

Philosophical and Theoretical Background

The philosophical basis for our model is the "critical philosophy" of Immanuel Kant (1724–1804). This philosophy recognizes the individual as actively organizing experience by making judgments and interpretations. The psychological theory in which the model is based is schema theory, with historical roots in the cognitive work of George Kelly (personal construct theory; 1955) and Jean Piaget (structural theory; 1970, 1971). (See Mancuso 1977 for a lively discussion and exposition of these "contextualist" theories.) It is an interactionist model in which person and situation are viewed as continuously interacting, rather than a linear model in which events happen to passive persons who are then altered by the events. Our model is consistent with the information processing theory of Mardi Horowitz and colleagues (1976, 1980) and the symbolization theory of Robert J. Lifton (1976).

The basic tenet of the model is that individuals hold certain beliefs and expectations (schemata) about the self and others, which both shape and are shaped by their experience in the world. Various feelings are attached to these beliefs. The main implication of this notion for understanding childhood sexual abuse victims is that a victim's unique interpretation of the trauma determines his or her reactions (emotional, cognitive, and behavioral) to that trauma, which in turn affect his or her subsequent interactions with others.

We propose that victims of childhood sexual abuse experience disturbances in schemata within one or more of five areas of psychological and interpersonal functioning. These areas, drawn from a review of the literature on trauma and victimization (McCann, Sakheim, and Abrahamson, in press) are those that are consistently cited as salient for victims. The areas are safety, trust, power, esteem, and intimacy.

Schemata develop through one's earliest life experiences (Beck 1967). We hypothesize that the development of schemata in the five areas is sequential, as Erikson (1963) and Piaget (1970, 1971) suggest. The predicted order in which schemata develop is first in the area of safety, followed by trust, power, esteem, and intimacy. It is possible that individuals who are traumatized at a very early age may experience disruptions or arrests in the more fundamental areas, such as safety and trust, while those who experience a relatively safe and supportive early childhood environment may be less likely to hold negative schemata in these more basic areas. It also appears that most individuals, at whatever level of functioning, can experience a sense of vulnerability in any of these areas, perhaps "regressing" to concerns about safety when highly threatened, for example. Within each area, persons have schemata concerning the self and others. Individuals may tend to interpret their experiences more often through schemata in one or two particular areas. Finally, each childhood sexual abuse victim experiences disruptions in areas and ways unique to him or her.

The schemata, then, constitute the individual's organizing framework. Incoming information from the external environment (e.g., the behavior of others) or from within the individual (e.g., feelings or memories) may confirm or disconfirm her schemata. When input from the environment is discrepant with existing schemata, the initial tendency is to respond as though that input were not discrepant. This is most likely when the discrepancy disrupts the complex system which the individual has constructed to protect himself or herself from unacceptable thoughts or feelings. One process the individual may use to minimize the discrepancy (in this case, failing to attend to the input) is denial, repression, dissociation, or other avoidant responses. Those victims of childhood sexual abuse who experience a type of posttraumatic stress disorder in which denial, psychic numbing, and emotional constriction are predominant symptoms (Laufer, Brett, and Gallops, 1985) may be attempting to avoid the uncomfortable emotions associated with a mismatch between schemata and input. For example, the person may be attempting to protect positive esteem, safety, or power schemata by avoiding victimization memories that challenge these beliefs.

While denial may be important and useful for certain individuals in various psychological situations, it is not the most sophisticated process for managing discrepant input. The goal of therapy is usually to help the survivor to use the two other processes, assimilation and accommodation, to manage discrepant input. The adaptive value of these processes depends on the person's system of meaning and his or her current psychological situation.

Assimilation is the process of attempting to integrate input by matching it with existing schemata. For example, a survivor may have assimilated the abuse memories into existing beliefs that he or she is bad and undeserving, that other people are untrustworthy and dangerous, and that he or she has no power to influence events in his or her life. This survivor may experience few symptoms of distress (e.g., intrusive thoughts) but may be chronically depressed, hopeless, and lonely. This pattern has high psychological costs and benefits. A survivor who is able to trust others and who generally feels safe in the world may be helped to transform the meaning of a second victimization (such as a rape) to preserve his or her positive other-trust and safety schemata; this individual may eventually decide that he or she can take certain precautions to prevent future victimizations and that, in general, others are still trustworthy. In this case, assimilation is adaptive in that it enables the person to preserve positive schemata.

Finally, the victim may cope with the abuse by the process of accommodation, or integrating input by modifying schemata. When schemata are flexible or permeable (Kelly 1955), persons may be able to adapt to changing situations by "stretching" their schemata. This capacity may be associated with better psychological adjustment, particularly if this accommodation results in more positive beliefs and expectations. A person who has a rigid construct system may respond to new life events by denying discrepant input or by radically altering his or her system of meaning, which is psychologically traumatic. The process of accommodation may take place in therapy as victims integrate the victimization experience by deriving new meanings and altering nonadaptive schemata in the process. A survivor may gradually come to view himself or herself more positively, for example, as his or her negative self-esteem schemata are gently challenged in therapy.

Schemata and Psychological Experience

An assessment of the adult survivor's schemata in the five areas helps the clinician understand how the trauma affected the client's schemata and how the schemata shape the person's experience of himself or herself and the world. While many schemata seem clearly adaptive or nonadaptive at face value, our approach is based on the belief that people develop schemata in concert with and in response to their environments. Thus, a schema that seems nonadaptive ("I'm bad") may have been adaptive when the victim was young. This may have been his or her only protection against believing that the abuser was bad, a potentially overwhelming thought for a young child. To the extent that the adult survivor is unable to accept the thought that the abuser was at fault, this negative self-esteem schema may continue to be adaptive; to the extent that it inhibits psychological development, it is nonadaptive. *Adaptive* can be understood only in the context of the client's psychological situation. Adult survivors most often come to therapy to deal with schemata that are nonadaptive in the context of their current lives (which we refer to below as negative schemata) or with input that is highly discrepant from their schemata.

Finally, it is important to note that schemata are not independent of one another. Understanding the way they interconnect and overlap for each individual is important to a full understanding of the inner world of each adult survivor. As with any system, a change in one schema will have an effect throughout the system.

Within each area, we describe a proposed constellation of affective, cognitive, and behavioral manifestations of negative schemata. These are based on our clinical observations and are consistent with the literature. Their validity remains to be tested.

Safety: Self

Schemata in this area concern one's belief in the ability to protect oneself from harm, injury, or loss. While the belief that one is invulnerable to harm certainly can have dangerous implications, the belief that one is incapable of protecting oneself from future harm is perhaps more problematic. This belief, most often stemming from the early inability to protect the self, is often supported by repeated exposure to dangerous, uncontrollable situations. It may become manifest in fears about accidents, death of loved ones, or disaster.

Adult survivors with negative self-safety schemata may experience chronic anxiety symptoms, a common pattern among some survivors (Briere 1984; Sedney and Brooks 1984). This response pattern may be associated with intrusive thoughts about danger, irritability, startle responses, psychophysiological arousal, or intense fear of future victimization. The belief that one is unable to protect oneself may lead a person to fail to take self-protective measures, increasing the likelihood of confirmatory life experiences.

Safety: Others

The belief that one is safe from harmful others or that the world is basically a safe place is related to the self-safety area, yet distinct. This refers specifically to the individual's beliefs about his or her ability to protect the self from harmful others, while the self-safety area refers to beliefs about one's safety without reference to others. Childhood sexual abuse victims may develop the belief that other people are basically dangerous. A childhood sexual abuse victim who becomes a battered wife may remain in the situation because she believes that she cannot protect herself from harmful others: The abusive marriage is consistent with her negative self-safety schema. Psychological manifestations of this schema are likely to be fear and anxiety reactions, including phobias, avoidant responses, and intense feelings of vulnerability.

Trust: Self

Schemata in this area concern the belief in one's ability to trust his or her own perceptions and judgments. This belief is essential to making constructive life choices, and it serves an important self-protective function. The perceptions of child sexual abuse victims are especially vulnerable to invalidation by powerful others.

Psychological manifestations of a negative self-trust schema likely include anxiety, confusion, overcaution, or paralysis in the face of life decisions. Persons with such schemata may be unable to protect themselves from harm because they do not make appropriate judgments about potential danger (Finkelhor and Browne 1985). For example, such persons may be exploited by others who invalidate their perceptions that something is wrong.

Trust: Others

The ability to trust others is essential to meaningful interpersonal relationships. Childhood sexual abuse victims can experience a betrayal of trust by someone they depend on, an experience some find devastating (Courtois 1979; Finkelhor and Browne 1985; Gelinas 1983; Meiselman 1978). The belief that others cannot be trusted may develop and may generalize to all people, to men only, to older people, to authority figures, and so forth. Psychological manifestations of a negative other-trust schema include a pervasive sense of disillusionment and disappointment in others, intense fear of betrayal or abandonment, and anger and rage toward past or potential betrayers. These feelings may be particularly intense toward someone with whom the survivor has a dependent relationship.

Power: Self

Self-power schemata comprise one's beliefs about the ability to control oneself—that is, one's behavior, thoughts, and feelings. In moderation, the belief that one can control one's behavior is generally considered to be healthy. The childhood sexual abuse victim may develop negative self-power schemata: the expectation that he or she will be helpless to control forces within himself or herself (such as feelings) or his or her behavior. This belief system may result from the "traumagenic dynamic" of disempowerment within the abusive relationship (Finkelhor and Browne 1985).

Psychological manifestations of a negative self-power schema could include chronic passivity, a sense of futility, and depression. This pattern may be consistent with learned helplessness or the expectation that one cannot control future outcomes (Seligman 1975). In the extreme, persons may seek to confirm the accuracy of these schemata through suicide or other self-destructive life patterns.

Power: Others

This refers to one's belief about others' power vis-à-vis oneself and the world. Childhood sexual abuse victims may develop the belief that others control them or their lives. The female victim may develop the belief that men are powerful and women are powerless. These schemata may manifest themselves in passivity, unassertiveness in interpersonal relations, and vulnerability to future exploitation. This pattern of revictimization has been well documented among some adult survivors (see, for example, Russell 1986). Persons with negative other-power schemata may find others consistently taking advantage of them, thus validating their schemata.

Esteem: Self

Self-esteem refers to the belief in one's worth and value, widely recognized as essential to psychological well-being (Maslow 1970; Sullivan 1940). The common understanding of the development of positive self-esteem includes notions of being understood, respected, and taken seriously (White and Weiner 1986).

Childhood sexual abuse experiences very often result in profoundly negative self-esteem schemata (Bagley and Ramsey 1985; Courtois 1979; Gold 1986). In attempting to integrate the abuse, the victim may develop the belief that he or she is bad, destructive, or evil; that he or she is responsible for destructive or evil acts (one's own or others'); that he or she is damaged or fatally flawed; that he or she is worthless and deserves to suffer. A survivor with negative self-esteem schemata may internalize others' negative attitudes toward him or her; find others unempathic; feel blamed, criticized, or devalued by others; or think that he or she has violated his or her own standards or ideals.

The predominant psychological response pattern likely to be associated with negative self-esteem schemata is depression, a common long-term problem among some adult survivors (Bagley and Ramsey 1985; Briere and Runtz 1985; Sedney and Brooks 1984). Feelings of guilt and shame and self-destructive behaviors are likely to be tied to a damaged sense of self. These clients may experience self-loathing or self-fragmentation, leading to suicide attempts, self-mutilating behavior, or self-destructive life patterns. This latter pattern has been well documented as a possible serious consequence of childhood sexual abuse (Briere 1984; Bryer et al. 1986). Victims may attempt to avoid awareness of these negative schemata through substance abuse or other attempts at numbing and emotional constriction. The increased use of psychoactive medications among adult survivors (Briere 1984; Bryer et al. 1986) may reflect this phenomenon. Extreme examples are childhood sexual abuse victims with multiple personality disorder, where the "bad" self becomes split off as a separate personality (Bliss 1980).

Esteem: Others

One's belief in the value or benevolence of others can be seriously damaged by a deliberate violation by another human being. Sexual abuse experiences in childhood and unsupportive reactions in the posttrauma environment may result in the belief that others are bad, malicious, or uncaring. Individuals with such negative schemata may be unable to experience others as positive, good, or kind. This obviously interferes with one's ability to form relationships.

Adult survivors with negative schemata in this area may experience chronic anger, contempt, bitterness, and cynicism toward others. Genuine acts of caring may be too discrepant with existing schemata and hence may be avoided or rejected. Other manifestations of this schema may be isolation, withdrawal, or antisocial patterns justified by the belief that everyone is out for himself or herself. Extreme outcomes are anomie and existential despair.

Intimacy: Self

Object relations theory is perhaps unique in positing the importance of forming an intimate relationship with one's self. Within this theory, the meaning of such a positive intimate relationship includes the development of the capacity for self-soothing (Kohut 1977), comfort (Horner 1986), and being alone without feeling lonely (Winnicott 1958). A negative schema in this area would be the belief that one does not have the ability to soothe and comfort oneself or maintain (or regain) inner calm. This clinical picture is frequently seen in clients who are diagnosed as having borderline personality disorders. In recent years, this pattern has come to be viewed by some as an extreme manifestation of undisclosed, unresolved childhood sexual abuse experiences rather than representing a distinct diagnosis (Briere 1984; Bryer et al. 1986).

The likely psychological manifestations of this schema are anxiety, despair, a fear of being alone, and a sense of inner emptiness. Persons with this schema may experience periods of anxiety or panic when alone and may seek comfort through spending money, abusing drugs or alcohol, or engaging in promiscuous sex. These behaviors may provide momentary comfort but engender long-term feelings of emptiness. Such persons may be experienced as needy and demanding as they desperately seek calm and comfort from others.

Intimacy: Others

The capacity for connection with others is a fundamental assumption of most models of psychological well-being (see, for example, Erikson 1963; Maslow 1971). It is a very limited or fragile capacity for some childhood sexual abuse victims. Persons who have a negative schema about their ability to engage in meaningful, satisfying, intimate relationships may experience intense fear about loving and may feel alienated from others. Sexual problems, including problems in sexual functioning (Courtois 1979; Meiselman 1978) and dissatisfaction with sexual relations (Langmade 1983), may be manifestations of an impaired capacity to experience intimate connection with others. These persons may be unable to experience intimacy even in relationships with others who genuinely love and care for them. Their partners may feel disappointed and hurt when they are unable to establish an intimate connection. This, in turn, can confirm the person's belief that he or she is unable to form intimate relationships. Lifton (1979) called this the broken connection, resulting in a deep sense of meaninglessness, loneliness, and despair.

Concluding Remarks about Schemata

The purpose of this model is heuristic: Dividing persons' experiences into areas is intended to help clinicians and researchers better understand unique responses to childhood sexual abuse. But ultimately, one's experience is a stream, not a series of discrete ponds. The primary underlying assumption of the model is that one individual's experience differs from everyone else's. This tenet should not be lost in the conceptual framework presented here. We are providing a map; it is not the territory (Korzybski 1958).

Principles of Assessment and Treatment

This model suggests the importance of assessing schemata in each of the areas as an ongoing process in psychotherapy with adult survivors of childhood sexual abuse. As part of this process, it is important to understand the development of schemata in each area, how these were affected by the abuse experience, how they shaped the person's interpretation of that event, and how they may be contributing to problems in current functioning. To clarify these issues and demonstrate the value of this framework for assessment and treatment planning, we present some general principles for assessment, followed by three case examples. Each is a childhood sexual abuse victim, but each responded differently due to the unique system of meaning she constructed to help her understand and cope with this trauma.

Initial Assessment

The relations among the sexual abuse, life experiences, and the development of schemata must be explored thoroughly. A complete assessment includes a detailed history involving the nature of the abuse, the relationship to the perpetrator, the dynamics of the abuse experience (i.e., use of force; perpetrator's approach, whether manipulative, angry, or loving; time span; and family dynamics) (Courtois 1979; Gelinas 1983). It is important to remember, however, that knowledge about the specific nature of the traumatic event does not in itself predict the person's schemata or associated psychological response patterns. Rather, individuals experience and remember victimization experiences very differently through the unique filter of their beliefs and expectations. The reason for such detailed assessment is to help the client recover his or her memory fragments and integrate them into whole memories that he or she can then work through (Horowitz 1976). The timing of this history-taking process must depend on the clinician's assessment of the client's readiness. This process may take months and cannot be rushed. The clinician must take the client's lead, gently picking up on cues that he or she is ready to recover these memories. If the clinician encounters resistance to such exploration, it should be understood as the client's indication that he or she is not ready to do this work. The clinician should tell the client he or she is ready to hear more about the details when the client is ready to talk about them.

In the initial stages of therapy, clinicians must listen carefully for evidence of both positive and negative schemata within the five areas of trust, safety, power, esteem, and intimacy. The centrality of schemata will be revealed as certain themes continue to reemerge in the therapy process. Exploring the client's expectations in both the therapy relationship and other interpersonal relationships will often reveal salient schemata about self and others. The following serve as general guidelines for assessing schemata through listening for recurrent themes and exploring the five areas of personal and interpersonal functioning.

Self-schemata

Safety. Within this area, it is important to listen for themes of unique vulnerability to future harm, anxiety about possible revictimization, and expectations that one will be unable to protect oneself from harm. Exploring the client's fears about therapy may reveal concerns about being unsafe, vulnerable, or revictimized. Often the client with negative self-safety schemata will express the belief that there is something about him or her that attracts trouble or brings about harm. A history of repeated victimizations may indicate negative self-safety schemata.

Trust. Schemata within this area can be assessed through exploring the client's decision-making abilities, including the capacity to form accurate judgments about people or situations and the ability to rely on these judgments to protect himself or herself from future harm. Themes of helplessness and confusion in making life decisions are often indicative of negative self-trust schemata. These schemata also may be revealed within the transference relationship by an overdependence on the therapist for advice or judgments. For example, this client often asks for the therapist's opinions and may express distress and confusion when his or her judgments are not validated by others.

Power. Schemata within this area may be revealed through themes of personal helplessness, a sense of being out of control of oneself and one's life, and a belief that one cannot control future outcomes. Clients with salient self-power schemata will often express fears about losing control of their emotions or becoming weak and helpless within the therapy.

Esteem. Exploration of the client's attributions of causality for the abuse or other harmful life events may reveal negative schemata within this area. For example, questions aimed at exploring beliefs about why bad things happen to him or her may reveal themes of self-blame, unworthiness, or badness. These beliefs should not be challenged prematurely but rather should be followed up by questions about how they developed. These themes also may be revealed in therapy or other interpersonal relationships as clients express fears that they will be rejected when others discover who they "really" are.

Intimacy. Self-intimacy can be assessed through exploring the client's capacity to be alone and/or to comfort or calm himself or herself when distressed or frightened. Themes involving panic when alone, an overreliance on external sources of support, and the use of drugs, alcohol, or sex as a source of comfort are all indicative of negative self-intimacy schemata. These themes also will be revealed in the transference, as the therapist is experienced as a person who can provide calm and soothing. These clients will often require brief, frequent contact with the therapist during times when they cannot regain inner calm on their own.

Schemata: Others

Safety. Anxiety reactions, including hypervigilance, phobias, or avoidant behaviors, should be explored from the perspective of expectations of future harm or danger from others. This can be accomplished by exploring the things the client worries about the most, the specific ways he or she anticipates harm, and the ways in which he or she tries to be self-protective. Clients with negative schemata in this area often fear that the therapist will in some way hurt or revictimize them. This fear may result in premature termination of therapy unless it is addressed directly as an ongoing part of therapy.

Trust. This area can generally be assessed through listening for themes of betrayal, abandonment, being made a fool of, or being continually disappointed or let down by others. These clients will often reveal that they cannot depend on anyone but themselves or that they expect the worst from other people. These expectations will often be evident in the transference relationship, as well as other interpersonal relationships. For example, these issues may emerge around vacations or other disruptions in therapy or when the client is beginning to experience psychological closeness to the therapist.

Power. An assessment of this area should include exploration of the client's expectations for power and powerlessness in relationships, his or her ability to be assertive with others in expressing personal needs, and the capacity for protecting oneself from being dominated or exploited by powerful others. Clients who believe they have less power than others, one type of negative other-power schemata, may be passive or helpless within the therapy relationship and may try to elicit a more active, directive stance from the therapist. Clients with a different potentially maladaptive other-power schema may be very sensitive to any indication that the therapist is domineering or controlling.

Esteem. If clients express contempt, bitterness, or disillusionment about other people or the world at large, beliefs about other people or human nature should be explored. A negative schema in this area will often manifest itself through a devaluation of others and a tendency to interpret care, compassion, or benevolence from others in a cynical light. For example, the client will often find it difficult to imagine that the therapist genuinely cares for him or her and will devalue the relationship by saying things such as, "You're only doing your job."

Intimacy. This area should be thoroughly explored through questions about the quality of the client's interpersonal relationships, as well as his or her internal experience of connection with others. Exploration of sexual relationships will often reveal a sense of disconnectedness or aloneness. It is important to use the transference relationship to explore fears about becoming intimate. It is likely that schemata within this area are interrelated with negative schemata in the areas of trust and safety.

Case Examples: Presenting Information

Sally is a thirty-year-old woman who began psychotherapy after having been a victim of an attempted date rape. During the two months prior to beginning therapy, she had experienced unsupportive and indifferent responses from people within the judicial system and many people in her "support" system. Because her attacker had been her friend and because he did not complete the rape, the prosecutor, police, and her friends told her that criminal prosecution was unlikely and that she should "forget about it and go on with her life." Sally was not able to forget the incident but rather developed severe and disabling symptoms of acute posttraumatic stress disorder, including sleeplessness, flashbacks of being attacked by strange men, nightmares, extreme anxiety, and fearfulness. She vacillated between feeling impotent rage at both her attacker and the people who had failed to support her and experiencing self-destructive impulses culminating in wrist-slashing and suicide plans.

Prior to the assault, she had pursued a successful career as an attorney, a career that had become the focus of her life. She spent little time alone pursuing leisure activities, had few close friendships, and had had a series of relationships with men who exploited her sexually and emotionally. Several episodes of severe depression and suicidal feelings since her early twenties had necessitated psychiatric hospitalizations and treatment with antidepressants. Until the attempted rape, the sexual abuse perpetrated by her uncle from the ages of four through twelve remained completely repressed. Despite chronic feelings of emptiness, loneliness, and alienation, she was able to maintain a fairly high level of functioning and appeared well adjusted to others who knew her superficially.

Paula is a thirty-seven-year-old woman who began psychotherapy for the first time with the presenting complaint of overspending. A single parent with two school-age daughters, Paula had achieved a high degree of success as a stockbroker. She appeared to be an extremely attractive, bright, verbal woman who denied any significant psychological distress except for the problems created in her life by overspending. This problem had led to great difficulty with creditors over the years, forcing her to become overdependent on her parents for financial support. When financial disaster created havoc in her life, she would become self-punitive, guilty, and ashamed. Brief periods of depression and discouragement would follow until she was able to pay her bills. In the initial therapy sessions, she expressed confusion about why she engaged in this pattern when she had "everything going for me—a beautiful home, two good kids, a loving boyfriend, and supportive parents." In describing her confusion, Paula said, "I don't know why I do this to myself. I know I'm a nice person and I like myself too much to cause myself this kind of pain." She did wonder, however, whether the sexual abuse perpetrated by her father, from the ages of seven through thirteen, had any relation to her current problems.

Jean is a thirty-seven-year-old woman who began psychotherapy after finding herself inexplicably depressed, tearful, and sad. She was a single parent who worked in a factory and was recently divorced from an abusive, alcoholic husband. Her chief complaint was that she felt exploited and mistreated at work but was confused about what to do. Jean described her supervisor as an authoritarian man who frequently demeaned her and made her feel "like a little girl." Although Jean frequently fantasized about leaving the job, she vacillated between thinking that it was the right thing to do and wondering whether she was making "'a mountain out of a molehill." She reported having several close women friends but always seemed to pick "the wrong kind of guy." She acknowledged that she allowed other people to push her around and that she had always had difficulty asserting her needs in relationships. There was no history of suicide attempts or psychiatric hospitalizations. The current episode of depression and sadness appeared to be related to reading a newspaper article about childhood sexual abuse survivors. This experience stirred up unbidden images and memories about sexual abuse by her grandfather, which occurred repeatedly from around the time she was in the first grade until she was in the sixth grade.

Case Examples: The Assessment of Core Schemata

In the initial stages of therapy, Sally often ruminated about why she had been victimized. When this question was explored, she revealed the belief that she was repeatedly victimized because she was so physically attractive and "alluring." Furthermore, she expressed the belief that she was uniquely vulnerable to victimization by men and had no sense that she could protect herself. Exploration of how she felt about herself as a woman and how she related to the men in her life revealed the belief that she was either a "virgin" or a "whore." These themes appeared to be indicative of negative schemata in the areas of self-esteem and safety. The self-schema about being a whore was in her mind confirmed through her exploitive and clandestine relationships with older, married men. The virgin self-schema was confirmed through a cool, detached public demeanor toward men. When her relationship history was explored, she described a history of never publicly dating or experiencing an intimate, loving connection with a man. When her relationships with other women were explored, she expressed fears about becoming too close to anyone and felt that other people would only disappoint her if she expected anything from them. The exploration of what she hoped for in therapy confirmed the hypothesis of negative other-trust and intimacy schemata. When the therapist asked her what she hoped for from the therapist, Sally responded, "I don't expect that you'll be any different from the rest. I'll probably keep you at arm's length like all the others."

In exploring her previous coping patterns, Sally revealed that she coped with her uncle's abuse by working very hard to be a "perfect little girl" at home and at school. This involved developing a pattern of overachievement and self-control. She took pride in her schoolwork and developed compulsive work routines. This pattern of overachievement resulted in high expectations for perfection, with corresponding self-punishment when she "slacked off." Her high expectancies for personal control were also revealed in the transference, as she expressed fears that she would lose control of herself and "go crazy" if she allowed herself to experience painful emotions in the presence of the therapist. She also expressed fears that the therapist would reject or abandon her if she revealed the "truth" about herself. Furthermore, as a result of this pattern of overcontrol, she spent virtually no time alone to nurture herself through creative endeavors, play, or relaxation. She experienced little sense of self-connection and in fact felt bored and uneasy when alone. Being the victim of an attempted rape challenged her belief in her personal control and reactivated latent self-devaluation (esteem) and self-danger (safety) schemata. Her suicide attempts were a symbolic attempt to destroy the "bad" parts of herself that were "immoral" and "weak," as well as to punish all those people who had betrayed and violated her.

Paula, on the other hand, appeared to have developed positive schemata in all areas except self-esteem and other-trust. Although she experienced fear and humiliation during the abuse, she was able to establish positive and loving relationships with several relatives and teachers early in life. In contrast to Sally, her self-esteem schemata appeared to be somewhat more permeable in that she was able to experience both negative and positive aspects of herself. This was revealed early in therapy when she was able to describe herself as basically a good, caring person who deserved more happiness than she allowed herself. She appeared to be aware that her overspending was a form of self-punishment, although rationally she knew she did not deserve to be punished. Likewise, her other-trust schemata were flexible enough to include the belief that many people were trustworthy. These positive other-trust schemata were revealed in the transference, as she expressed trust that the therapist would not hurt or betray her. She appeared to have developed intimate relationships with a number of people and lived a balanced life involving work, family, and relaxation. She seemed to take genuine pleasure in being a mother and enjoyed time spent gardening and painting. The pattern of overspending was the one indicator that the trauma of her childhood sexual abuse was not resolved. When asked in one of the early sessions the emotions she experienced after she went on shopping sprees, she said, "pleasure followed by tension, self-hatred, and guilt." When asked whether there were any positive consequences to the overspending, she said, "My parents bail me out and are forced to take care of me. It gives me a chance to be dependent on someone." When this statement was explored, she acknowledged a longing to be nurtured and taken care of by someone and skepticism that these needs could be met. These latter statements appeared to relate to other-trust schemata, centering on themes of dependency and nurturance. The therapist hypothesized that the emotions of self-hate and guilt that followed the overspending reflected latent self-devaluation schemata connected to the repressed victimization memories.

In contrast to Paula and Sally, Jean presented with a very different pattern of psychological adaptation to the trauma of childhood sexual abuse.

A shy, gentle woman, Jean expressed very little confidence in herself, her judgment, or her effectiveness in the world. Despite the fact that she was clearly a capable woman, she agonized about major life decisions and continually questioned her own perceptions. In the initial sessions, this style of relating to others was manifested by asking the therapist for constant reassurance and validation. For example, after describing interactions with her supervisor that were clearly hostile and demeaning, she would ask the therapist, "But how do I know that I'm really seeing this accurately? Maybe I'm just overreacting. What do you think?" Although she was clear about her desire to leave her job, she expressed the belief that she would never be able to escape. When this was explored, she admitted, "I always seem to be stuck in bad situations. Maybe I'm just not strong enough to fight back." The nonadaptive self-trust and power schemata appeared to be central in her life and had been associated with a long history of being "stuck" in less-than-desirable relationships and jobs. Despite the fact that she was able to extricate herself from an abusive marriage, she did not view this as evidence that she possessed good judgment or could exert control in her life. Her current depression and tearfulness seemed to express this fundamental sense of powerlessness and self-doubt.

Treatment Implications

A thorough assessment of the person's system of meaning or salient nonadaptive schemata is the basis for formulating treatment plans and goals. In formulating treatment goals, the therapist must keep in mind that, just as clients' central schemata differ, so must their treatment. The rigidity or permeability of schemata and the degree to which they have resulted in problems in personal and interpersonal functioning have important implications for treatment. In the following section, we describe how the model was helpful in formulating individualized treatment plans and goals for each of the three survivors described above.

Persons who have developed nonadaptive schemata in a number of areas, as in the case of Sally, are likely to present the greatest challenge to clinicians. When the self-devaluation schemata are rigid and entrenched, there may be a history of suicide attempts and other self-destructive acts. Furthermore, if other-schemata in the areas of safety, trust, and intimacy are nonadaptive, the client's support system is likely to be limited, resulting in chronic isolation and loneliness. The process of establishing a positive therapeutic alliance also is likely to be difficult, requiring a high degree of patience on the part of the therapist. In Sally's case, the negative self-intimacy schemata, coupled with the other nonadaptive schemata, resulted in panic attacks when she was alone. This inability to comfort and soothe herself necessitated frequent, brief telephone interventions, most often in the evening when she was alone.

In general, clients who call to be calmed will be satisfied temporarily by a reassuring, brief contact with the therapist. Resolution of this pattern requires long-term therapy aimed at internalizing a self-soothing capacity that is part of building a positive self-intimacy schema.

In Sally's case, the treatment plan included the following: long-term individual therapy to challenge nonadaptive schemata gradually, with particular focus on the central schemata about power, trust, and esteem. Because she was in an acute crisis phase when she first entered therapy, and because of her negative self-intimacy schemata, the therapist contracted with her about management of self-destructive impulses, agreed to be available for brief crisis calls, and helped her to mobilize any other persons who might be available to provide support and nurturance. When the crisis was resolved, through consistent, soothing contacts with others, the therapist recommended that Sally begin group therapy for childhood sexual abuse survivors. The addition of time-limited group therapy was made with the goals of exposing her to persons with whom she had a common bond, experiencing the support of peers, and "normalizing" her current distress. The group modality was believed to be particularly valuable in challenging nonadaptive schemata in the areas of self-esteem, other-trust, and intimacy.

In both Jean's and Paula's cases, the treatment plans were somewhat different. In both cases, the central nonadaptive schemata were more focal, resulting in less overt psychological distress. In Paula's case, a decision was made to begin hypnotherapy very early as a way of uncovering and working through repressed memories of the abuse. This was possible because Paula had so many adaptive schemata and could quickly establish a trusting therapeutic alliance (permeable and positive trust and intimacy schemata) and tolerate intense emotions without being overwhelmed (self-intimacy and self-power). The goal of hypnotherapy was to facilitate understanding of the relationship between the abuse and latent self-devaluation schemata. In Paula's case, combined individual and group therapy was not recommended initially because the memories of the abuse were not consciously accessible. Hypnotherapy was not appropriate for Sally, as she did not possess these same capacities and indeed became overwhelmed after one attempt at hypnosis six months after therapy had begun. Jean, on the other hand, posed a set of contrasting treatment issues. The goals of therapy were to challenge nonadaptive schemata in the areas of self-trust and power, while making the connection between these schemata and memories of the abuse by her grandfather. In her case, hypnosis was not initiated early in treatment because of the danger of the therapist's reinforcing her belief in her lack of personal power. Instead, assertiveness, exerting control, and learning to listen to and trust her "instincts" were seen as focal issues.

These cases provide a brief illustration of how the model provides a framework for formulating treatment plans and goals. This approach builds on a person's strengths, while gently challenging schemata in ways that do not overwhelm the client or force him or her to utilize avoidant defenses. The model provides a way of systematically assessing the client's individual needs, then integrating approaches to meet these needs into the treatment plan.

Tolerable Doses of Discrepancy

A major therapeutic task with the adult survivor is to help him or her change nonadaptive schemata rather than avoid discrepant information. Thus, it is important to design the therapy environment so that accommodation (stretching or changing schemata) rather than denial occurs. If the therapist presents discrepancy prematurely, or if the client feels that is it too dangerous to try to acknowledge it, he or she will then likely use various avoidant defenses (e.g., avoidance, repression, denial, dissociation). A therapeutic environment that addresses these blocks can help the client tolerate the painful aspects of exploring descrepant input. The present model would suggest that what is typically regarded as an empathic environment (e.g., unconditional positive regard) can be a curative element or a destructive element and will not be experienced in the same way by all clients. In other words, what will produce a workable therapeutic alliance or approach for one client may be disastrous for another. For example, one client may need a somewhat confrontational environment to believe that he or she is not being treated like a child or condescended to, but rather is being viewed as an adult with strengths. Another client may experience the same approach as an attack on the self and may shut down or withdraw. On the other hand, a "supportive" or empathic approach may feel very safe to one client, while another may experience this as so alien and discrepant with his or her expectations that he or she feels forced to flee. For example, the childhood sexual abuse victim who equates closeness with hurt can react in this way. What is essential is not to provide a unified "supportive" or "empathic" or even "neutral" approach to all clients, but rather to discover the approach that will provide the necessary balance of safety, trust, esteem, power, and intimacy to allow the client to tolerate the powerful emotions associated with uncovering memories and altering nonadaptive schemata. In the following section, we use the three clinical examples to describe the process of developing a therapeutic alliance and changing nonadaptive schemata through the gradual presentation of tolerable doses of discrepancy.

Sally had developed rigid beliefs in her own badness and firmly believed that the sexual abuse was her fault because she was too beautiful and alluring. Prior to beginning psychotherapy, she had briefly sought treatment at a rape crisis center where she was reassured that the attempted rape and childhood sexual abuse were not her fault. Such reassurance was so discrepant with her negative self-esteem schemata that she fled from therapy at the rape crisis center, feeling that the counselor did not understand. Early in her present therapy, she avoided discussions of fault completely. After several months, the issue reemerged. Instead of directly exploring fault about the early abuse, however, Sally and the therapist explored her tendency to blame herself when angry about issues such as the therapist's going on vacation. The cost of blaming herself instead of expressing her anger was explored and produced some discomfort, but not enough to cause her to flee from the therapy. Both Sally and the therapist began to see that, despite its drawbacks, self-devaluation protected her from intolerable feelings of rage. This was only possible after she experienced a therapeutic alliance within which she was not overwhelmed by acknowledging anger in small doses. In Sally's case, it was important to develop the therapeutic alliance by respecting her need to be in control as well as her need to develop trust and intimacy very slowly. If the therapist had been too challenging, thus threatening her sense of power, or too supportive and caring, thus threatening her trust and intimacy schemata, Sally could have easily fled from treatment. This indeed almost happened in one session when the therapist made the error of prematurely probing into her angry feelings toward the therapist.

Even apparently highly nonadaptive schemata must be understood and appreciated prior to being challenged. It is easy to lose sight of the defensive value of existing schemata. Only when these schemata began to change were Sally and the therapist able to see their adaptive value. The self-blame protected her from significant rage that would have previously been overwhelming. For example, after being in therapy for many months, Sally was able to recognize that the therapist's absences were not her fault. Immediately thereafter, however, she was flooded with confusing and overwhelming feelings about the past. If she didn't cause people to hurt her, why had her uncle hurt and humiliated her? Why had her aunt failed to protect her when she tried to disclose the abuse? Many subsequent sessions focused on coping with her rage and grief. As schemata began to change to match present-day input, she was forced to reevaluate past events from the new perspective as well. This is where a strong therapeutic alliance becomes so important. Without the secure "holding environment," such reevaluation can prove too overwhelming, and flight from the process or other defensive maneuvers will result.

It may be necessary to begin challenging other nonadaptive schemata before it is possible to challenge those that are most affectively laden. For example, with Sally, before challenging self-devaluation schemata, many months were spent gently challenging her rigid belief that she must be in total control of her emotions at all times. As part of this process, the therapist would note her avoidance of any strong emotions within the sessions and would gently ask her questions such as "What do you imagine might happen if you were to allow yourself to experience those feelings in here?" Sally was able to acknowledge fantasies of losing control, going crazy, or being humiliated. This led to a discussion of her intense fear of vulnerability. Respecting Sally's need to be in control, the therapist did not push Sally to express emotions, but rather helped her explore ways she might test out experiencing painful emotions in a controlled way. Sally came up with the idea that she might allow herself to experience her feelings for five minutes a day, after which time she would consciously back away from the feelings through distraction. As she discovered, with much surprise, that she was indeed able to "shut off" the feelings at will, she gradually grew more comfortable with experiencing her emotions directly.

Concurrently, it was important to develop positive self-intimacy schemata, as she continued to experience panic when feelings emerged while she was alone. Her negative self-intimacy schemata were challenged by helping her to see that she could, indeed, develop the capacities to sooth and comfort herself. This involved encouraging use of journal writing, artwork, and soothing self-talk (e.g., "You're going to be okay, Sally") while she was alone. The therapist continued to be available for brief telephone contacts until Sally was able gradually to build the internal resources necessary to tolerate the painful feelings. In her case, directly exploring the abuse memories was possible only after she had developed more adaptive schemata about self-power, safety, and intimacy. Experiencing trust, safety, and intimacy within the therapeutic relationship took many months, as she gradually tested out and disconfirmed her beliefs that the therapist, too, would hurt, humiliate, or abandon her.

In Paula's case, the therapeutic issues were very different. Her permeable and adaptive schemata in the areas of trust, safety, and intimacy allowed her to develop a close, intense therapeutic alliance quickly. In her case, a warm, empathic therapeutic stance was not viewed as threatening, nor was probing into intense emotions experienced as a threat to her self-control. Her adaptive self-power and intimacy schemata also enabled her to tolerate the intense emotions that emerged during the hypnotic sessions. Within months of beginning therapy, she was able to make the connection between the feelings of pleasure followed by tension, self-hatred, and guilt that she experienced after overspending and the feelings she had while her father sexually abused her. A central issue for her was that she could not blame her father for the sexual abuse because he was, in all other ways, a loving father, and because she experienced orgasm during some episodes of oral sex and fondling. At the same time she experienced pleasure and longing, she knew this was wrong and therefore developed a latent self-devaluation schema, the belief that she was a bad little girl. In this way she was able to protect her image of a loving father, something she desperately needed, as her mother was critical and rejecting. She had also developed the belief that, through nurturing and gratifying her father, she would both protect her parents' shaky marriage and receive the nurturance she craved. In this way, her other-trust schemata developed, involving the belief that she could not expect to be taken care of and nurtured without feeling humiliated and ashamed.

As the self-devaluation and other-trust schemata were gradually challenged, it became possible to understand the adaptive purpose these schemata had served over the years. As with Sally, challenging self-devaluation schemata produced powerful emotions. Because Paula was better able to tolerate painful emotions, these schemata were challenged somewhat more directly. For example, in one hypnotic session, Paula struggled with feelings of self-blame for both longing for and feeling pleasure at her father's overtures, while at the same time feeling guilt and self-loathing. The therapist responded empathically to her dilemma by saying, "It's understandable that you would have experienced many conflicting emotions. All little girls long for closeness and nurturance from their fathers. It was not possible for such a little girl to be able to handle such a dilemma. Your father, as the adult, was the responsible party who shouldn't have put you in this dilemma." When this interpretation was made, Paula bolted up in her seat and said, "You sound so sure of yourself when you say that." That therapist calmly said, "I am." At this point, Paula had a flood of powerful and confusing emotions. She was then able to acknowledge her hidden rage at her father and also her mother for betraying and abandoning her, forcing her to seek closeness and dependency by paying the high price of humiliation and self-loathing. In subsequent sessions, she also was able to experience the intense longings she had to be dependent on someone and the sadness and grief she felt at missing out on this normal dependency. The pattern of overspending could then be understood as a symbolic replication of the earlier abuse that served two unconscious motives. First, the overspending forced her parents to take care of her by bailing her out, even though this resulted in shame and humiliation. Second, this pattern was a way of expressing repressed hostility toward them, as they had to make financial sacrifices to do so. As these patterns were fully understood and worked through therapeutically, more adaptive esteem and trust schemata developed and the pattern of overspending was resolved.

Therapy with Jean posed a set of different treatment issues. As Jean's central negative schemata concerned self-trust and power, it was necessary to challenge these schemata by both fully understanding their relation to her past history and gradually introducing discrepancy within the therapy relationship. Not surprisingly, Jean manifested her low self-power and trust schemata through the transference. She experienced the therapist as an all-knowing authority who had the power to make important judgments and interpretations. She manifested a helpless, dependent stance and frequently asked the therapist for her opinions or views. It would have been very easy to assume a more directive and active stance with Jean, as she appeared anxious when advice and direction were not forthcoming. In this case, the major focus of therapy was to challenge her nonadaptive beliefs about her powerlessness and inability to trust her own judgments. When she asked persistently for advice and direction from the therapist, the therapeutic stance was to point out the control Jean had in the therapy process. The basic message was, "I am here to encourage you to develop a sense of your own power and to help you learn to trust your own good judgment." Initially, Jean responded to these messages with helplessness and confusion. When she would ask the therapist for her judgments about relationships that were clearly abusive the therapist would respond, "I would be happy to give you my opinion. However, I'm more interested in how you see things. I'd like to hear how you feel about what's happening."

Gradually, Jean was able to express her own feelings and judgments about what was happening in her life. As she was able to do this, the therapist increasingly validated Jean's perceptions by making supportive statements such as, "It sounds like you have a pretty good handle on what's happening to you." Jean would increasingly leave the sessions feeling clear about where she stood and what she needed (e.g., to mobilize herself to get out of her abusive job situation), but she would come back the following week in a state of self-doubt and confusion. When this process was thoroughly explored, Jean was able to express her fear that she was "making a mountain out of a molehill." The therapist asked her when she last felt like that. Initially she spoke of incidents in her adult life where she felt stuck in bad situations. Gradually she was able to tolerate talking about how these same feelings existed when her grandfather sexually abused her. As the details of the sexual abuse were explored, it became apparent that Jean experienced tremendous confusion about what was happening to her. Apparently her grandfather was a kind and gentle man who in all other respects was good to her. He would take her down to the basement under the pretext of playing with her. The "play" became increasingly sexualized, developing into oral sex, fondling, and mutual masturbation over the years. As the grandfather was abusing her, however, he acted as if nothing unusual were going on. One time she recalled protesting, but he responded by being perplexed, thus invalidating her perceptions. After he abused her, he would resume playing nonsexual games, acting as if nothing had happened. This caused her to doubt her own perceptions that something bad was happening, and at times she even wondered whether she was imagining things.

As Jean recalled these memories, the therapist challenged her self-trust schemata by validating her good judgment about the inappropriateness of her grandfather's behavior. Not surprisingly, this produced powerful emotions of anger at her grandfather and sadness for the little girl who had learned to distrust herself. At this point in the therapy, Jean found these feelings tolerable. As therapy progressed, she was gradually able to develop more adaptive beliefs about her own judgment and power. This enabled her to make the decision to leave her abusive job situation. Her new experience of angry feelings was sometimes uncomfortable and it was important to work through her fears that she would hurt other people in the process of expressing her anger. As she was able to test this out in the therapy relationship, she learned that her anger was legitimate and that nothing terrible would happen if she expressed her needs and feelings for others. Toward the end of therapy, Jean was able to say, "It's funny, but even 'bad' feelings feel good now. I feel more alive inside and much more like an adult than a little girl."

Summary and Conclusions

In the previous sections, we described a schema framework for the assessment and treatment of adult survivors of childhood sexual abuse. The three case examples underscore the point that childhood sexual abuse victims experience the abuse through their own unique filters or systems of meaning. Assessing survivors' central nonadaptive schemata has a number of important implications. First, it can enable the clinician to understand the relation among life experiences, schemata and feelings, and psychological functioning. Second, it provides a theoretical framework for understanding the major processes by which individuals respond to and integrate traumatic life events. An understanding of the adaptive value of what appear to be nonadaptive schemata, such as self-devaluation, can help the clinician to be more empathic and less likely to challenge these belief systems prematurely. Within the social psychology literature, the focus on the attributional correlates of coping and adaptation among victims has been an important step toward understanding the relation between individual factors (e.g., beliefs about causality) and adjustment (see, for example, Gold 1986; Wortman 1983). The meaning and implications of these beliefs differ among individuals. We believe this model has the potential for helping clinicians understand and appreciate the unique phenomenological world of each survivor, leading to better treatment plans. In closing, we share the words of one of our clients: "I want to be thought of as a person, not just another victim."

References

Bagley, C., and R. Ramsey. 1985. *Disrupted Childhood and Vulnerability to Sexual Assault: Long-Term Sequels with Implications for Counseling.* Paper presented at the Conference on Counseling the Sexual Abuse Survivor, Winnepeg, Canada, February.

Beck, A.T. 1967. *Depression: Clinical, Experimental, and Theoretical Aspects*. New York: Harper & Row.

Bliss, E. 1980. "Multiple Personalities: A Report of 14 Cases with Implications for Schizophrenia and Hysteria." *Archives of General Psychiatry* 37:1388–97.

Briere, J. 1984. *The Effects of Childhood Sexual Abuse on Later Psychological Functioning: Defining a Post-Sexual Abuse Syndrome*. Paper presented at the Third National Conference on Sexual Victimization of Children, Washington, D.C., April.

Briere, J., and M. Runtz. 1985. *Symptomatology Associated with Prior Sexual Abuse in a Non-Clinical Sample*. Paper presented at the annual meeting of the American Psychological Association, Los Angeles, CA, August.

Browne, A., and D. Finkelhor. 1986. "Impact of Child Sexual Abuse: A Review of the Research." *Psychological Bulletin* 99:66–77.

Bryer, J.B., J.B. Miller, B.A. Nelson, and P.A. Krol. 1986. *Adult Psychiatric Symptoms, Diagnosis, and Medications as Indicators of Childhood Abuse*. Paper presented at the 94th annual convention of the American Psychological Association, Washington, D.C.

Courtois, C. 1979. "The Incest Experience and Its Aftermath." *Victimology: An International Journal*, 5:322–34.

Erikson, E.H. 1963. *Childhood and Society*. 2d ed. New York: Norton.

Faria, G., and N. Belohlavek. 1984. "Treating Female Adult Survivors of Childhood Incest." *Social Casework: The Journal of Contemporary Social Work*, 65:8, 465–71.

Finkelhor, D., and A. Browne. 1985. "The Traumatic Impact of Child Sexual Abuse: A Conceptualization." *American Journal of Orthopsychiatry* 55:530–41.

Gelinas, D. 1983. "The Persisting Negative Effects of Incest." *Psychiatry* 6:312–32.

Gold, E.R. 1986. "Long-Term Effects of Sexual Victimization in Childhood: An Attributional Approach." *Journal of Consulting and Clinical Psychology* 54:471–75.

Herman, J.L. 1981. *Father-Daughter Incest*. Cambridge, MA: Harvard University Press.

Horner, A. 1986. *Being and Loving*. Northvale, NJ: Jason Aronson.

Horowitz, M.J. 1976. *Stress Response Syndromes*. New York: Jason Aronson.

Horowitz, M.J., N. Wilner, C. Marmar, and J. Krupnick. 1980. "Pathological Grief and the Activation of Latent Self-Images." *American Journal of Psychiatry* 137:1157–62.

Kelly, G.A. 1955. *The Psychology of Personal Constructs*. New York: Norton.

Kohut, H. 1977. *The Restoration of the Self*. New York: International Universities Press.

Korzybski, A. 1958. *Science and Sanity: An Introduction to Non-Aristotelian Systems and General Semantics*. 4th ed. Lakeville, CT: The Institute of General Semantics.

Langmade, C.J. 1983. "The Impact of Pre- and Post-Pubertal Onset of Incest Experiences in Adult Women as Measured by Sex Anxiety, Sex Guilt, Sexual Satisfaction, and Sexual Behavior." *Dissertation Abstracts International* 44:917B (University Microfilms No. 3592).

Laufer, R.S., E. Brett, and M.S. Gallops. 1985. "Dimensions of Post-Traumatic Stress Disorder among Vietnam Veterans." *Journal of Nervous and Mental Disorders* 173:538–45.

Lifton, R.J. 1976. *The Life of the Self.* New York: Simon & Schuster.

Lifton, R.J. 1979. *The Broken Connection.* New York: Simon & Schuster.

Mancuso, J.C. 1977. "Current Motivational Models in the Elaboration of Personal Construct Theory." In A.W. Landfield, ed., *Nebraska Symposium on Motivation.* Lincoln: University of Nebraska Press, 24:43–97.

Maslow, A.H. 1970. *Motivation and Personality.* 2d ed. New York: Harper & Row.

Maslow, A.H. 1971. *The Further Reaches of Human Nature.* New York: Viking Press.

McCann, I.L., D.K. Sakheim, and D.J. Abrahamson. In press. "Trauma and Victimization: A Model of Psychological Adaptation." *The Counseling Psychologist.*

Meiselman, K. 1978. *Incest: A Psychological Study of the Causes and Effects with Treatment Implications.* San Francisco: Jossey-Bass.

Piaget, J. 1970. *Structuralism.* New York: Harper & Row.

Piaget, J. 1971. *Psychology and Epistemology: Toward a Theory of Knowledge.* New York: Viking Press.

Russell, D.E.H. 1986. *The Secret Trauma: Incest in the Lives of Girls and Women.* New York: Basic Books.

Scott, R.L., and D.A. Stone. 1986. "MMPI Measures of Psychological Disturbance in Adolescent and Adult Victims of Father-Daughter Incest." *Journal of Clinical Psychology* 42:251–59.

Sedney, M.A., and B. Brooks. 1984. "Factors Associated with a History of Childhood Sexual Experience in a Non-Clinical Female Population." *Journal of the American Academy of Child Psychiatry* 23:215–18.

Seligman, M.E.P. 1975. *Helplessness: On Depression, Development, and Death.* San Francisco: Freeman.

Silver, R.L., C. Boon, and M.L. Stones. 1983. "Searching for Meaning in Misfortune: Making Sense of Incest." *Journal of Social Issues* 39:83–103.

Sullivan, H.S. 1940. *Conceptions of Modern Psychiatry.* New York: Norton.

White, M.T., and M.B. Weiner. 1986. *The Theory and Practice of Self-Psychology.* New York: Brunner/Mazel.

Winnicott, D.W. 1958. "The Capacity to be Alone." *International Journal of Psychiatry* 39:416–40.

Wortman, C.B. 1983. "Coping with Victimization: Conclusions and Implications for Future Research." *Journal of Social Issues* 39:197–223.

5
Treatment of Male Victims of Child Sexual Abuse in Military Service

Michael F. Johanek

A dult men molested as children have increasingly entered the awareness of today's mental health professionals. A recent telephone poll in the *Los Angeles Times* (dated August 25, 1985) randomly interviewed 2,627 adults nationwide and found that 16 percent of the men had been molested as children.

Men rarely present to the psychiatric clinic or to mental health professionals as identified victims of child sexual abuse. Instead, they generally present with some other complaint. Only a high index of suspicion by the clinician and a thorough exploration of the patient's background and current lifestyle provide the clues that can lead to the history of sexual abuse.

The most common presentations of male victims of child sexual abuse to the psychiatric clinic at the Naval Hospital, Camp Pendleton, California, are:

1. Men sent to the clinic for evaluation after being arrested for a sexual offense.
2. Young men brought to the clinic for evaluation following a suicide attempt or gesture.
3. Men who present with the symptoms of a major depression.
4. Men who present with the symptoms of a generalized anxiety disorder, often with panic attacks or social phobias.
5. Young men who present with concerns about their sexuality, specifically ego-dystonic homosexuality.
6. Young men who present with a diagnosis of alcoholism. (More than 30 percent of the men admitted for treatment of alcoholism to the Alcohol Rehabilitation Department, Camp Pendleton Naval Hospital, admit during treatment to sexual victimization during childhood.)

This psychiatric outpatient clinic is also required to perform clinical evaluations of military personnel prior to court-martial for certain offenses.

Some of the personnel are accused of sexual offenses against other adults; others present with initial charges including rape and molestation of children within or outside the family. Approximately 60 percent of the rapists and more than 90 percent of the child molesters were themselves victims of childhood sexual abuse. A high incidence of sexual victimization appears to be a common early life event for identified sexual offenders. There are no data, however, that indicate that all or most male victims of sexual abuse become sexual offenders themselves.

Although a childhood sexual victimization history is commonly found among sexual offenders presenting to the psychiatric clinic, it may be extremely difficult to obtain this information from the patient. The difficulty arises from our cultural bias toward disbelieving that males can become victims of sexual abuse. Western society has had considerable problems accepting male sexual victimization because of three beliefs:

1. That any "real" man (or male child) would fight to the death rather than become a victim of sexual abuse.

2. That if males are victimized, they certainly would not have a sexual response to the assault.

3. That assaults on male children are performed by male homosexuals and that the young male victims are tainted by this contact.

Such beliefs give rise to thoughts and statements such as "You must have done something to indicate that you were available." The victim may ask himself, "What is wrong with me? Do I look gay? Or act homosexual?" Awareness of these cultural beliefs is essential for clinicians. Such awareness allows the therapist a better understanding of the patient's sense of inadequacy and his need to adhere to accepted masculine roles.

Some Examples

Case 1. J.H. was a married, thirty-eight-year-old Hispanic man who was referred to the psychiatric clinic for evaluation after being accused of sexually molesting his sixteen-year-old daughter. Evaluation of available information indicated that this was the second such charge against him for the same offense. He had been under court order not to be alone with his daughter and, in fact, approached her with a witness present. After considerable time, including three years of court-ordered counseling with Parents United (a self-help organization utilizing professional volunteer counselors that offers treatment for incest families), J.H. admitted to having a sexual relationship with his daughter for more than eleven years. It took extensive individual counseling and a long period of trust development to learn about his early victimization.

J.H. was the oldest of four children from a poor Mexican family. He had a difficult relationship with his father, who apparently was a cruel and physically abusive man, although he never abused any of the children sexually. When J.H. was nine years old, his mother left the family and illegally entered the United States to obtain work. J.H. found that being alone with his siblings and his father was intolerable, and he attempted to cross the border and join his mother. He was apprehended at the border and placed in a jail cell, where he was assaulted and repeatedly sodomized by three adult men. The sexual assaults did not stop until he was released from the prison. He never told anyone about the assaults but soon adopted a hypermasculine lifestyle that included fighting, excessive drinking, and multiple random heterosexual relationships.

Years later, he again crossed the border and enlisted in the U.S. Marine Corps, where he distinguished himself professionally. He remained emotionally distant from all the other men. He viewed himself as a short, unattractive man, when, in fact, he was considered by others to be handsome and charming.

This example of a man dealing with his sexual victimization by exhibiting hypermasculine behavior has not been the most common presentation to the psychiatric clinic. Instead, we are more likely to see a confused, frightened young man exhibiting a bewildering combination of guilt and rage and presenting with suicidal behavior. He is often intolerant of the all-male military living situation.

The military barracks can present a uniquely stressful situation for a young man, especially one who was the victim of a past sexual assault by another man. Minimal privacy is provided; sleeping arrangements are likely to involve sleeping either in open squad bays, with twenty-five to fifty men in one large room, or in a four-man room. Nudity, communal showers, and communal bathroom facilities are commonly encountered.

Wisecracking and teasing are universal, usually consisting of a constant run of sexual jokes and pretended homosexual advances. To men who were not victims of childhood sexual abuse, the jokes and teasing are humorous, but to the victims, barracks humor and living conditions can be extremely threatening.

Such conditions also are present in nonmilitary environments such as college dormitories and high-school and college locker rooms. Thus, if a boy or a young man has a history of unwillingness to participate in athletics or a reluctance to change clothing for gym, it would be appropriate to inquire gently about prior sexual victimization.

The young man who encounters the living conditions of the military barracks may experience ego-dystonic dreams or fantasies about having sexual contact with another man. This, in turn, may lead to a panic reaction, and he may flee or leave the base without permission. Presentation to the psychiatrist in the naval hospital is often to explain an unexcused absence.

The patient often will demand release from military service, stating that his enlistment was made under false pretenses and that he should not be held responsible for his contractual obligations. Further evaluation generally indicates a paucity of mature behaviors and relationships. Most commonly, we find that the male victim of child sexual abuse has experienced an arrest of emotional and social development, which began around the time of the original assault.

Case 2. G.W. was a twenty-year-old single black man with approximately one year of active military service who was sent for psychiatric evaluation by his commander because of an unexplained period of absence, his apparent anger toward others in his unit, and a recent suicidal gesture involving ingestion of fifty aspirin tablets.

At the first interview, he appeared frightened yet hostile. He sat on the edge of his chair, literally wringing his hands. He often became tearful but made minimal eye contact with the interviewer. He would not make any kind of commitment or agreement not to harm himself and so was admitted to the inpatient psychiatric ward for evaluation. On the ward, he demanded a single room, and when this was denied, he became actively hostile, threatening the staff.

Eventually, with group and individual support, G.W. became more able to discuss his feelings. He stated that he was afraid of sexual assault in the barracks. Although no one had directly confronted him, he felt that the conditions were dangerous. His unhappiness was increased by recent developments in his personal life. While on unauthorized leave, G.W. had returned to the home of his mother and stepfather. He attempted to remain in hiding in a bedroom, but when his parents demanded that he return to duty, he left, taking a family car. He was then promptly arrested for car theft, at the request of his parents. After he was released, G.W. went to the home of his fifteen-year-old girlfriend, where he observed arguing between her parents. He found that this intensified his unhappy feelings about his own family. Feeling helpless and hopeless about his situation, G.W. decided to kill himself.

On the ward, it was apparent that G.W.'s social skills were underdeveloped. He was demanding and quarrelsome, acting much like an adolescent. His suicidal ideation diminished after a few days, however, and he was discharged with outpatient follow-up. As an outpatient, the following history was revealed.

G.W. was the third of four children from a chaotic family. His parents were divorced when he was eight years old, following the disclosure of his father's homosexuality. After the divorce, G.W. became a difficult child who resented the presence of a new step-father. At age twelve years, he was sent to live with his father and his father's male lover. Over the next two years, he was seduced by his father's male lover, first involving attention, companionship, and small gifts. The sexual advances initially seemed accidental, with intrusions while showering and bathing. This gradually advanced to physical acts, including the demonstration of masturbation and fi-nally anal intercourse, under the guise of teaching the boy about sex. It was most difficult for G.W. to talk about this relationship, as his feelings toward this man were a confusing mixture of loathing and love. It seemed that a secret sexual relationship was a small price for the attention that he craved. He finally complained to his father, who did not believe him but instead sent him back to live with his mother and stepfather. At his mother's house, he was called a sissy by his siblings, partially because he had lived with his father and partially because he now moved and acted in an effeminate manner.

G.W., now thoroughly confused about his own sexual identity, handled rejection by his siblings by hiding in his room. He associ-ated with them as little as possible. The social isolation continued outside the home. He engaged in no sports or social activities at school, but he did manage to meet a thirteen-year-old girl in his neighborhood when he was sixteen. He began a romantic relation-ship with her.

G.W. graduated from high school with his class but had missed out on a normal peer socialization process. He found it difficult to find any type of employment. With a need to prove his masculinity, he enlisted in the Marine Corps. He did well in recruit training and in his initial schools because of long working hours and extremely limited opportunity for socialization. After reporting to his first command, his anxiety began to increase, as he found himself fan-tasizing about one of his roommates.

This roommate had attempted to befriend G.W. and engage him in activities such as going to the enlisted men's club and to the beach. As his only previous close relationship with a man had de-veloped into a sexual relationship, it is not surprising that the room-mate's overtures of friendship stimulated sexual thoughts and fantasies in G.W. When he became aware of these sexual images, he became extremely frightened and attempted to flee, thus coming to the attention of the psychiatric department.

As stated earlier, our society has considerable difficulty accepting male victims, since most people believe that a man cannot be made to respond sexually against his will. Careful evaluation, however, reveals that most male victims are made to respond physically by their abusers, which, in turn, becomes a very sensitive issue in their sexual identity.

Even less accepted is the reality that young boys are sometimes molested by women. In most discussions of child molestation, the victim identified is a "she" and the perpetrator a "he." In our experience in this psychiatric clinic and in Parents United, it is rare that a female offender is ordered into treatment. In interviewing adult men with a history of child sexual abuse, however, we found that more than 20 percent had been abused by women.

Unlike the concerns over homosexuality for boys who are victimized by male abusers, the boy who is molested or abused by a woman is often unaware that he is being victimized. Popular literature is replete with stories of boys who are introduced to adult sexuality by older women. If a boy discusses such events with his peers, he is often congratulated for his luck, with no one paying any attention to his uneasiness or feelings of being used or exploited. The following case examples are illustrative.

Case 3. R.R. was a single white man who was arrested after fondling a nine-year-old boy at a public swimming pool. He readily admitted to the offense and was court-martialed and referred to the sexual offenders program. He admitted to having molested thirty-seven other children, most of them boys, prior to his recent arrest.

R.R. was the oldest of two children from a family broken by divorce when he was nine years old. His first remembered sexual experience was at age eight years, when a fourteen-year-old female baby-sitter took him into the bathroom and fondled him; she then performed fellatio on him and asked him to attempt vaginal intercourse with her. She then had him suck his younger brother's penis. From that point on, he had sexual contact with as many neighborhood children as he could.

At first these children were about his own age, but as he got older, R.R. found that younger boys, age eight or nine, were most attractive to him. He described the lengthy efforts he made to engage these other children in sexual play, often taking weeks or months to convince them to participate.

When he was eleven, his mother found him engaging in sexual play with a nine-year-old neighbor boy. She took him to an outpatient psychiatric clinic for evaluation. At that time, he was considered to be suffering from an "adjustment reaction to childhood," and his mother was advised to improve her child management techniques.

R.R. continued his sexual behavior with other children, however, and at age sixteen was again found engaging in sexual play with a child. This time it was his younger brother. He was again evaluated at the outpatient psychiatric clinic and diagnosed as a pedophile. Continued outpatient follow-up was recommended but did not take place because of family conflict. From then until his enlistment in the Marine Corps, he continued to engage in relationships with boys.

During his evaluation, he admitted to being very shy and never being able to approach girls his own age or older. He stated that when he was frustrated about his shyness, he turned to younger children. During the interviews, R.R. sat upright in his chair, making limited eye contact with the interviewer. He spoke in a monotone, with a limited vocabulary, and appeared eager to please. He did not hesitate to discuss any of his behaviors. During his therapy, he was treated as if he were a child by the other group members. They simplified their language, spoke softly, and were never hesitant to place a hand on his shoulder.

Most of the male victims we have identified who were molested by women were molested by nonfamily members such as baby-sitters. Men who were sexually abused by mothers or stepmothers have been less commonly encountered in our clinic.

Case 4. R.D. was a thirty-seven-year-old divorced father of two grown children. He was referred to the psychiatric clinic by his commander because of an apparent inability to perform his duties. On initial examination, he had many of the vegetative signs of depression and suicidal ideation. He was admitted to the inpatient service and placed on tricyclic antidepressants. Review of his history revealed an unwillingness to discuss his mother, who was recently deceased. After considerable resistance, he admitted that his mother had been a severe alcoholic. From the time that R.D. was twelve years old, his mother had engaged him in sexual play when she had been drinking. This included mutual fondling and masturbation but not intercourse. These memories had returned to haunt R.D.'s dreams after he had gone to visit his mother in the hospital when she was very ill. During that visit, his mother had grabbed his hand and placed it on her breast. This so unnerved R.D. that he immediately left the hospital, entered a bar, and began to drink alcohol, thereby ending fours years of sobriety with Alcoholics Anonymous (AA).

For years, prior to beginning an AA program, R.D. had used alcohol to get to sleep and "to forget" the sexual relationship with his mother. Despite his marriage, he had always felt uncomfortable with women and was terrified of any close relationship. R.D. found himself distancing himself from any woman, including his own daughter, as soon as any close emotional relationship began to develop.

Identifying Male Victims

Identification of an adult male victim of child sexual abuse requires one to suspect that the abuse may have occurred. Besides the intuitive sense one develops after repeated exposure to these clients, the following strategies have proved useful in our clinic:

1. A question on a routine biographical section of the intake questionnaire. (A surprising number of patients answer such a question honestly, without hesitation, when they are involved in answering a series of questions.)

2. A high index of suspicion of a child sexual abuse history in men who present with demands for an environmental change, especially when they are unable to cite conflicts with authority figures. (Here, careful questioning about the exact nature of the problems encountered with the living conditions may reveal high anxiety when discussing sleeping and bathing arrangements.)

3. Careful evaluation of responses to questions about running away from home, especially when combined with information about nonparticipation in social and athletic activities in high school.

4. While discussing the developmental and sexual histories of suspected victims, suggesting that sexual abuse is a relatively common event in many boys' lives.

5. Recognizing the presence of hypermasculine behavior in the past and present history. (Such behavior may represent a reaction formation to appearing feminine to others.)

6. Recognizing the presence of overt effeminate behavior. This is most notable in occupations such as military service, where such behavior may cause real conflicts in living.

7. Recognizing psychosexual confusion and ego-dystonic homosexuality.

Our index of suspicion for a history of childhood sexual abuse is extremely high for men who present as perpetrators of sexual crimes, especially child molestation. More than 90 percent of the men who are admitted to our prison program for sexual offenses against children admit to having been molested themselves in childhood. The other sexual offenders, such as rapists and exhibitionists, have a nearly 50 percent incidence of child sexual abuse in their past.

Treatment

The initial problem in dealing with adult male victims is one of identification. Identifying sexual victimization often takes considerable time, care, and empathy. A surprising number of adult male victims are themselves unaware of their own abuse history. They are not in a state of repression but simply do not realize that some of the events that took place in childhood were sexual molestation. This confusion is especially apparent in men abused by women.

Taking a clear, complete, and accurate sexual history is often the only route to uncovering the history of child sexual abuse. For example, when one young man was asked about his first sexual experience with another person, he remembered being stroked and introduced to sexual intercourse at age six by his fourteen-year-old sister when he turned to her for comfort. On previous occasions, she had held him close and talked to him in her bedroom when their parents were fighting. Over time, this gradually changed to sexual fondling and finally to persuading him to attempt to perform vaginal intercourse with her. He thought that the sexual relationship with his sister could not be a molestation experience because she was female. He stated that he was uncomfortable with what she was doing and felt that it was not appropriate. He also realized, however, that to stop her meant being completely alone. When interviewed, he was aware only of distrusting and antagonistic relationships with large numbers of female sexual partners, combined with a keen sense of emotional emptiness when he was not attempting to engage in sexual relationships with others.

Although sexual abuse by a female perpetrator is unlikely to be viewed by the male victim as a victimization experience, sexual abuse by a male abuser is apt to be regarded as something to hide. Adult men who were victims of molestation by male abusers are likely to have primary concerns about their sexual identity, especially when the men are in the irrationally homophobic environment of military service. The military tends to view any history of sexual contact between males, at any age, as an admission of homosexuality. The reality is that male-male sexual contact is an extremely common experience in the development of most men. In no way does this indicate a homosexual orientation. Since male victims are apt to be in crisis regarding their capacity to relate to other men, we have found that peer group therapy is critical immediately following disclosure.

Our experience in treating adults who were sexually victimized in childhood has included both group therapy with male patients only and group therapy with men and women together. The immediate effect of the group therapy experience for the male victims is a sense of relief when faced with the universal victimization experienced by all the group members. This phenomenon is present in both the all-male and mixed male-female groups, unless there is only one male victim present in a "coed" therapy group.

Following this initial period of relief, the male victim is likely to begin an outpouring of information concerning his victimization. Unlike female victims who tend to display more affect, however, the male victim's outpouring of details is almost devoid of an accompanying display of associated emotions. The story unfolds in a robotlike monotone, with the victim's eyes fixed on the floor. Initially, even when asked, the man rarely is able to describe how he felt at the time of the abuse. Nevertheless, the importance of these feelings is so great that they become the focus of his therapy.

Most of the men with whom we deal have learned to avoid experiencing and displaying emotions at all costs. They tend to describe events and their reactions to those events without using emotional terms. They withdraw deep into themselves as protection against being hurt by others and, even more significantly, as protection from their own poor self-image.

As group therapy continues, bonding takes place between group members. The therapists take an active role in promoting the bonding by encouraging the clients to share phone numbers and to talk with each other before and after sessions. For many of the men, this is likely to be the first time they have allowed themselves to experience a close emotional relationship with other men, especially if they were sexually abused in childhood by a male abuser. To avoid panic, the bonding process must be monitored closely by the therapists and discussed in the sessions. Otherwise, male group members may take flight from the group when emotional closeness and friendship with other men becomes confused with sexual interest. Many of them have already had the life experience of confusing affectionate feelings, intimacy, and trust with sexual feelings, especially during their adolescence. The therapists must create opportunities for complete discussion of the bonding and friendship processes. Group members need acceptance and reassurance by others, as well as clarification of their mixed emotions. It can be enormously helpful to the men to learn that others are also experiencing fear and discomfort with intimacy.

Individual therapy also is helpful, especially in conjunction with group therapy. The individual sessions are generally utilized to help them disclose and process past life experiences, especially adult homosexual behaviors, which are too threatening for the individual to discuss in the group. In addition, individual therapy sessions help the patient by giving him more attention and the opportunity to discuss his reactions to the group process than is possible in a 90- to 120-minute group therapy session. Long-term individual therapy is not usually available in military service due to a chronic shortage of personnel. In addition, patients in psychiatric treatment often are transferred from one location to another as their work requires. Since a large number of adult male victims exists in the military population, it is fortuitous that a treatment plan for peer group therapy with occasional individual therapy sessions is successful for most clients. The major step in treatment—i.e., improving one's social skills and increasing one's capacity to initiate and maintain satisfactory social relationships with others—can be practiced in group therapy. Again, the therapists must identify the deficits in the male victim's social skills and plan opportunities for him to learn how to relate more effectively to others, initially within the milieu of peer group therapy.

In summary, a large number of male victims of childhood sexual abuse is identified in military service. The challenge is to identify these men as early as possible so that much-needed therapy can begin. Despite other drawbacks, the authoritarian environment of the military base can facilitate victim treatment in that it provides external incentives and controls to participating in therapy, which might otherwise be avoided by voluntary clients in civilian life. We have seen our patients make significant strides toward emotional well-being with the therapy interventions described in this chapter.

6
Understanding and Treating the Adult Retrospective Victim of Child Sexual Abuse

Carolyn Agosta
Mary Loring

T he purpose of this chapter is to discuss specific treatment issues of victims of intrafamily and extrafamily child sexual abuse. As co-founders of Ending Violence Effectively (EVE), a private Denver treatment center for victims of violence (especially rape, child sexual abuse, and other forms of family violence), we have used our own experiences as victims of sexual assault to aid others who have been victimized. Since 1981, we have treated more than twelve hundred victims, ranging in age from three to eighty-four years. The agency has grown from a staff limited to two clinician cofounders and one office to ten staff persons who now work in six offices. Most of the work with victims involved group treatment, including preschoolers (3–5 years), children (6–8 years and 9–10 years), preadolescents, teenagers, and adults. The three youngest groups and the parents' groups include males and females, but all the other groups have been comprised of female victims only. We have treated many male victims, but have had more trouble helping them see the need for treatment, especially in accepting long-term help in a group format.

Since the bulk of our clinical experience has been in helping adult women recover from the impact of childhood sexual abuse, we focus on that population in this chapter. In addition, we refer to the victim as "she" and the perpetrator as "he." We want to make it clear, however, that we recognize the large number of male children who are victimized and the fact that there are many female perpetrators, as well as women who have colluded with male perpetrators.

No one as yet has attempted to identify the percentage of the population at risk for victimization. Only in recent years has our society begun to look into the home and recognize the violence that has permeated family life for centuries. Since the mid-1970s, the women's movement has raised our awareness of wife battering, and more recently, trained mental health professionals have begun to ask questions about childhood victimization. We believe that the primary way in which we are going to hear about victimization is by asking more and more questions.

As the media begin to assist us in shedding light on violence in the family, the nonoffending parent or guardian is beginning to take the problem much more seriously. More and more children are being brought to healers who have an expertise in working with victimization. More and more therapists are recognizing the need for treatment, not only for the victim, but also for the family. Specialized treatment has been developed for the perpetrator in the hopes of dramatically changing his attitudes, beliefs, and behaviors. In addition, there has been a major movement toward the development of prevention programs, especially for children.

Despite all our new awareness about victimization, there is a question about who to "treat" and who to "punish." The belief persists that the perpetrator who is a family member is treatable, while the perpetrator who is not a family member should be punished. Until we begin to focus on the victim's trauma rather than the perpetrator's membership or nonmembership in the family, the severity of sexual abuse will continue to be minimized. Until recently, some therapists even said that sexual abuse, molestation, and rape were not damaging to the victim. It will take a conscientious society that believes in the protection of our children to insist that any form of abuse is wrong and should be punished and that all affected parties should have access to effective treatment.

Definitions

Intrafamily violence includes the sexual abuse of a child by a trusted family member—father, brother, grandfather, uncle, mother, stepparent, or adoptive parent. Extrafamily violence includes abuse by individuals who are in a position of authority over the child but are not blood relatives—baby-sitters, teachers, or temporary caretakers. Sexual abuse is any sexual contact with a child for someone else's sexual gratification. This includes, but is not limited to, fondling, oral sex, intercourse, attempts to penetrate, exhibitionism, forcing children to touch each other or the perpetrator, and using children as the subject of pornography. We use the term *violence* to describe all these forms of abuse, even if no force was used, because we consider all abuse to be a violation of the basic integrity of human beings.

Retrospective treatment refers to helping the adult, victimized as a child, to look back on that victimization in terms of the impact it has on her now. It involves a process of grieving for what was lost in childhood and learning to let go of childhood needs or expectations. It involves learning to individuate and to separate from one's parents or primary caretakers. For most adult victims, this is their first attempt at doing so.

Once the abuse begins, the victim shuts down in order to numb herself to the experience. As these violent acts are repeated over time, she anticipates them with more horror, and it becomes easier for her to shut down earlier, as soon as she suspects that abuse is about to happen. As it becomes easier to distance herself from the abuse, numbness takes over. If she consciously remembers these violations, it is almost as if they occurred in a dream. Her affect becomes more and more flat, and over time, she has difficulty experiencing any type of emotion. Whether her awareness is conscious or unconscious, she maintains a distance from her feelings, and she may react in an unexpected way to stimuli that remind her of the abuse.

Imagine how flashbacks, nightmares, hypervigilance, and other coping behaviors that result from victimization might be misunderstood when their cause is a secret. How did families, friends, or physicians respond to inexplicable periods of depression in women who were beginning to remember? What resources did those women have fifteen, ten, or even five years ago?

The following are quotes from former clients. They graphically describe the violence of sexual abuse and assist us in understanding and appreciating these victims.

Sally: He repeatedly beat and raped me. It seems like it was forever. I can't remember a time when it wasn't happening.

Jane: I'd be scared to get up in the morning because, depending on my father's mood, he could immediately take me in the basement and rape me. There weren't many days when he didn't. The thing that mixes me up a lot is that I love my dad and I miss him. Am I crazy? I mean, there were times when he was a real dad. I could sit in his lap and watch TV. He'd be gentle and wouldn't touch me in that other way.

Dixie: I can remember being left alone in my father's care many times. He'd usually go to the bar and leave me at home, alone. I was really little the first time I remember this happening, maybe three years old. He left and I was terrified. I thought no one was going to come home and I would be left there alone forever. I cried for a long, long time. Then I got mad and took one of my crayons and began scribbling on the wall. Well, my father finally got home. He was drunk, I think. He looked at the wall, picked me up, and threw me across the room. Then he grabbed me by the hair and dragged me upstairs to his bedroom. I still had the crayon in my hand. He ripped my clothes off and took the crayon and stuck it inside me. I was screaming and crying. He kept ramming it inside of me telling me to shut up, telling me he'd teach me not to write on the walls with my fucking crayons. Something died inside of me that day. . . . That was the only time I remember him raping me, but he used to make my brother have sex with me. It was only the beginning of some horrible beatings. I never scribbled on the wall again. Sometimes I think it really was my fault. If I hadn't drawn on the wall, he wouldn't have had to hit me.

Josie: I was pretty young when my father took me into his bedroom. He took off my diaper and began to poke inside my vagina. I began to cry, so he called my mom into the room and told her that something was wrong with me because what he was doing shouldn't be hurting me. My mom just shrugged or nodded or something. She didn't do anything. He was my stepfather, and he used to line us up and play Russian roulette with a gun he had. We never knew if it was loaded or not. He beat and raped all of us kids. He beat Mom, too. I don't know if he ever raped her, though. Probably.

Sylvia: I hate my brother. My mother, too. She used to set me up to get raped by him. I think she knew. When I started my period, I had to tell her 'cause I didn't know what to do. She announced it at the dinner table. She knew what that meant. So did I. My brother raped me again that night. I hate my periods. All that blood. It's disgusting.

Anna: I used to have to stay at my uncle's when my mom was working late. It really scared the shit out of me. I don't know how he did it, but he'd manage to get me alone and rape me. It happened lots of times. I began to make sure that I was never left alone and always slept with his kids, when he finally had some. I think he's raping them, too. Even now I think he is. He still scares me to this day! The thing that is confusing is that I miss him, too. He wasn't bad all the time. Anyway, he was the only person who paid any attention to me.

There have been times in our experience as therapists that we thought we had heard it all, then another person would come to us with a horror story unlike any other. Now there are few surprises. This is a fortunate by-product of working with great numbers of survivors, because one reason they have kept silent is to protect the feelings of those around them. If we are truly familiar with this type of violence, we will care without seeming shocked, and it will be safe to tell us more.

A clinical description of the trauma induced by the child sexual abuse experience may be found in the Diagnostic and Statistical Manual of Mental Disorders (American Psychiatric Association 1980), in the discussion of post-traumatic stress disorder. That text delineates observable symptoms, including "re-experiencing the traumatic event; numbing of responsiveness to, or reduced involvement with the external world." It indicates that posttraumatic stress disorder is "apparently more severe and longer lasting when the stressor is of human design" and that many times the person experiences recurrent dreams, nightmares, or intrusive memories that reflect the stress event (236–238).

In summary, child sexual abuse is an act of violence and control by an adult over a child. The child experiences feelings of helplessness, powerlessness, confusion, and guilt. The perpetrator is usually a trusted person, older sibling, or parent figure. The abuse may include anything from the touching of body parts with the hand to oral, anal, or vaginal stimulation and even intercourse. The more we understand about the victim and her trauma, the more we read, listen, and accept, the more we will be able to assist these individuals in their healing process.

Impact of the Abuse

Childhood sexual victimization affects each individual differently, but there are some common phenomena. It is important to ask the victim how she came to be in therapy at this time and what problems or issues are currently occurring in her life. We must also record current stressors, a history of her relationships, a detailed family history, information about how her life has progressed, her dreams and hopes, her strengths and weaknesses, and her coping patterns.

Our culture is slowly becoming sensitized to and enlightened about family violence. Some of the women in our treatment groups come seeking services for their sexually abused children. In evaluation sessions, they report victimization in their own childhoods. For these mothers, the road ahead in treatment is particularly intimidating. They indeed have their work cut out for them because the current family crisis resonates with their own secret terrors. The child's pain and injury collides in the mother's mind with the memory of herself in similar pain. The flood of emotion may leave her feeling helpless, powerless, inadequate, and confused. She wants to do what is best for her child, but the flood of emotions may immobilize her.

Another version of coping in these circumstances is for the mother to remain aloof and matter-of-fact about the molestation and its effects on her child's life. This mother will appear rigid and uncaring and may be unable to comfort her child if she cannot tolerate the child's tears. But the child is dreadfully in need of the mother's comfort. The mother wants to reach out to her child, but she cannot overcome the recollection that no one offered her comfort. She is then distracted by rage at her parents and is herself more and more unable to parent effectively.

The adult retrospective victim has an immense feeling of guilt and responsibility for her behavior as a child. "How could I have let this happen to me?" asked one woman, whose victimization began at the age of five, when her uncle first raped her. Intellectually, survivors are able to see such thinking as ridiculous, but emotionally, they cannot accept their inaction and inability to protect themselves. They have difficulty accepting the total feeling of helplessness they experienced. Further, as children, they were directly or indirectly told that they were responsible for what happened, either by the perpetrator, the person they told, or others around them.

A victim tends to have mixed feelings about the perpetrator. Sometimes he was a monster, but at other times he was gentle and warm. He often paid the most attention to her. She may have experienced physical pleasure from the sexual abuse, which was mixed with anger and physical pain. She is confused and overwhelmed by these contrasting feelings. She may see everything else in her life as black and white, and she asks, "Why is this different?" She experiences shame for her confusion and mixed emotions.

Survivors typically have nightmares about their abusive experiences or in response to a fear of other acts of violence. It is not uncommon for a person victimized as a child to reexperience victimization as an adult. They have not learned the skills that allow most people to say no and to protect themselves. They may even unconsciously set themselves up to be revictimized. For many, all they have known is being controlled, victimized, used, and abused. They feel helpless to change this and are probably not aware that they are setting themselves up.

Many others have never developed intimate relationships and therefore feel unsuccessful and hopeless about their future. "Will I ever get over this?" is a question frequently asked, as if time really does heal all wounds. Jumping in and out of relationships is not uncommon, although many victims recognize this as unhealthy and less than desirable. Experiences of isolation and feeling unloved, unliked, wrong, helpless, and confused clash with the strong desire to be close, warm, and connected to the world. The adult retrospective victim may see others as having the ability to be intimate. She may want intimacy for herself and at the same time be terrified of having it.

Victims may be overwhelmed with these clashing thoughts and feelings. (It is easy for inexperienced therapists to become overwhelmed by them, too.) Victims want someone to take away the pain, end the confusion, and make them better. Or they may be cut off from themselves and terrified. These women realize that there is tremendous pain under that immense block, but they fear it will overwhelm them and they will lose what little control they have if they acknowledge it.

The adult retrospective victim's anger also is immense and, at times, overpowering. She may be thinking, "If I begin to touch my anger, the rage will take over, and I'll destroy this building and everyone in it." She vacillates between that anger and her deep pain and sadness. She fears that if she begins to cry, her tears will take over and again she will lose that delicate, fragile balance within her. Once she is able to acknowledge to herself that she needs help, she has taken the first major step toward healing.

She may describe her life as being on a roller coaster, with dramatic highs and desperate lows. When she is experiencing the "highs," she is also anticipating the lows, which will be close on the heels of those highs. Or she may describe her life as characterized by a constant state of sadness, depression, and upheaval. She may assume that everyone experiences life as she does, so she may have no hope for change.

Victims may perpetrate acts of violence against others or be neglectful and violent toward their children. For the most part, in our experience, victimization of others has occurred during childhood while baby-sitting or when in some caretaker role for other children. This is an area that needs close attention, since the potential to victimize others can be very high.

To summarize the impact of childhood sexual victimization, the adult retrospective victim experiences life in extremes. Her feelings include helplessness, isolation, powerlessness (especially to change), hopelessness, and immense guilt about her behaviors, both in childhood and adulthood. She has strong feelings of love and attachment to the perpetrator, mixed with equally strong feelings of anger and rage toward him. If she is asking for help, she has made a huge first step toward healing, which she and those around her must validate. The relief of taking her first step is accompanied by an equally powerful emotion: terror.

General Treatment Issues

The general treatment approaches that we address in this section are mainly tips that we have learned over the years. They may be helpful to alleviate further trauma to the victim and may increase the understanding of other clinicians. There is no one "right" way to treat victims of child sexual abuse. Providing a sensitive, safe environment in which the individual feels a sense of control is the first step. Knowing yourself and knowing when you are in over your head is an important part of this process. We have discovered that the more we read, attend workshops conducted by recognized experts in the field, and understand our reactions and processes, the better therapists we become.

Sensitivity and Awareness of Therapists

As a therapist of victims of sexual abuse, it is important to be aware of the variety of roles you play in relation to the victim. One of those roles is as facilitator, easing her process and providing a safer, clearer path. Another role is as healer, gently nurturing, supporting, encouraging, and providing the "medicine" for her wounds to begin to heal. Another is as her advocate in cases where the criminal justice system is involved. She may need someone to assist her in interpreting and understanding the system. It also will be important for you to be a spokesperson for her, to help the system understand and support her through the criminal justice process.

As with any kind of treatment, it is essential to be sensitive to your client. This means several things. First, begin where she is, rather than with what interests you or where you believe the beginning is. Second, provide a safe environment in which she can process her treatment issues. This means that she is able to move at her own pace and touch the pain or move away from it as she needs. She did not have control when she was a child; she needs that control now. Third, find out about her world and what her world means to her. Learn not only all about her experiences, but also understand her interpretation of those experiences. We urge that you do not make assumptions but ask her about her feelings and what they mean. This is especially true if your world is different from hers. For instance, if you are Anglo and are treating a person of color, no matter how much you have studied her world and tried to understand it, your interpretation of it will probably be different from hers. If you are a male therapist treating a female client, your understanding and interpretation of events also will differ greatly from hers. Be sensitive to those differences and address them openly and directly. It is imperative that you take responsibility for seeking that understanding. Offer the individual an opportunity to see someone who may understand her world more clearly than you do. Even if your world is similar to hers (same sex, race, and sexual preference), we caution against making assumptions.

If you have biases and strong beliefs that are in opposition to your client's beliefs, you have a responsibility to refer that individual to another therapist. For example, a straight therapist may believe that homosexuality is an illness, wrong, or blasphemous. That therapist must refer a client who is gay to someone who can understand the client's world more empathically.

Therapists who treat victims must also develop another area of self-awareness: an appreciation of their own potential, both to become victims of violence and to become violent and abusive themselves. Each of us has the capacity to hurt and be hurt. To be effective, the therapist must have an ability to empathize closely with the client's feelings, even if what she is describing is entirely outside the therapist's experience. None of us is immune to sexual assault. All of us are potential victims. Take the time to examine your own attitudes about violence and its prevention. Confront your cultural denial surrounding family violence and sexual assault, whether or not your own life experiences include personal and direct victimization.

Identifying the Victim/Survivor

An adult retrospective victim will refer herself to an identified victim service agency when she has concluded on her own that problems in her present life stem from earlier sexual abuse. "Problems" may mean a huge array of disturbances ranging from major depressive episodes to eating disorders, physical illnesses, substance abuse, and suicide attempts.

Many adult survivors have not told anyone of their victimization, or they told someone in childhood who did not believe them. In either case, it is unlikely that these individuals have discussed their victimization fully. For most it is a major risk for them to identify themselves at all. If they were not believed as children, why should they expect a stranger to believe them now? Many of our clients were involved in mental health services previously. When we ask whether the sexual abuse and its effects were addressed in the earlier therapy, we either hear that the client did not bring it up at all or mentioned it only in passing and neither the client nor the therapist pursued it. Many female victims/survivors have reported that they were unable to discuss victimization by male perpetrators with their male therapists. As discussed earlier, you, the therapist, must take the lead in addressing the victimization and its effects.

As mental health professionals, advocates, or volunteers, it is essential that we ask questions about victimization as a standard procedure for every intake. Some ways of asking these questions follow:

1. What kind of punishment did your parents/guardians use on you as a child?
2. Were there any relatives with whom you felt a particular discomfort?
3. Did anyone ever touch you in a way that felt uncomfortable or frightening?
4. Did you ever have sex with someone when you were not sure that you wanted to (or knew for sure that you did not want to)?

Be sure to be alert to date-rape situations as well. If you receive a positive answer to any of these questions, ask for more details. This will require some gentle probing. Look for family histories that include major memory losses or blocks. It is important to understand why someone has no memory from ages three to twelve, for example. Also look for drug and alcohol use among family members, as well as for the victim herself. Ask specific questions related to this.

Lost Memories

You will probably come in contact with women who suspect they were victimized as children but are unsure. Begin where the client is and with what she remembers. As you examine current coping behaviors, help her reflect back on her childhood to see when those behaviors began and in response to what. Other childhood victims may not identify or remember their victimization. It has been our experience that most will remember before treatment is over. It is no surprise that this will typically occur during the period when such clients are terminating their treatment.

A word of caution about "chasing" memories: Don't. The client is often desperate to recover the memories that will verify and validate what she thinks happened to her. She may have that belief because of pieces she does remember, because of vivid dreams, or because of inexplicable depression or terror reactions to certain stimuli, such as physical intimacy, certain times of the day or year, or anniversary dates. Next to a confession by the perpetrator, a vivid memory is the best confirmation a survivor can have. The therapist must be careful not to discount any of the information shared by the client. Deal with your disbelief privately and endorse and support her whenever you can honestly do so.

The memory cues are sometimes so sparse and disconnected that they yield little useful information. Furthering the process of hunting down the truth by direct examination of dreams, vague memories, or dialogue with family members will sometimes backfire. It is most probable that the client's family has long since determined that keeping the family secret is in everyone's best interest. They will not look kindly on a sister's or daughter's probes for information. Family members may also have denied or distorted their memories in order to keep this secret. The adult survivor is seeking validation. She is desperate for a reason, a way to account for the strong feelings that sometimes interfere with and disrupt her forward movement. Her deepest longing is likely to be a wish to confront the perpetrator with what she remembers. In her fantasy, he will acknowledge wrongdoing, provide the missing pieces, and apologize for hurting her.

This expectation is unrealistic. In all our years of working with these individuals, we have seen very few cases in which this fantasy became a reality. What is more likely to occur is that the family secret continues and the victim is labeled as crazy or hostile and is accused of trying to disrupt the family. It is important for the treatment process to assist the client in coming to terms with her family's unwillingness to validate and support her. They will probably never do so. Unless she can accept this and move on, her recovery will be impeded.

Confronting the Perpetrator

Many therapists believe that it is imperative that the victim confront the perpetrator. This is true, but confrontation can occur in a variety of ways. Careful consideration of the manner and timing of the process is essential.

The decision to confront must come from the victim. Typically, in group therapy one member will present a desire to do so, and other members may then express their wish to confront. Several factors must be considered: Why does the survivor want to confront at this time? What does she believe that she has to gain from doing so? What does she have to lose? Is she prepared for any of the range of responses she may experience? Will she be safe (physically and emotionally) while she is confronting? As her therapist, it is important that you recognize the difference between the client's need to confront versus your own wish that she do so. Confrontation can be very powerful, and the survivor can experience a great deal of relief by doing so, but it must be her choice, and she must understand all the potential consequences.

Role-playing can often be used as a preparatory step toward confrontation or in lieu of an actual face-to-face confrontation. The role-playing can be conducted between the survivor and the therapist during an individual therapy session or between group members in a group therapy session. The latter type of role-playing can allow an entire group to become open to new feelings, thoughts, and memories and can provide a great deal of relief for all involved. Remember that the survivor has the control and must be given the opportunity to manage the pace of the process and stop whenever she chooses.

Group Therapy: Pros and Pros

Many clinicians in the Denver community, as well as at national conferences, have criticized group therapy, questioning its importance and effectiveness in the treatment of incest survivors. At times, their criticism may be based on fact and at times on assumption. At other times, it appears to be based on the therapist's own fear of a group process or lack of training in that area. Our experience has shown, however, that group therapy, when conducted correctly, can be an extremely powerful form of treatment for survivors.

There are several reasons for the use of group therapy in addition to or instead of individual therapy. The healing process seems to occur more quickly when adult retrospective victims work with others experiencing similar pain and struggle. Isolation becomes dramatically reduced. As many of our clients have said, "You mean I'm not the only one? What a relief!" When victims are confronted by supportive peers, they begin to make connections and build bonds with one another. For many, it is their first experience doing so. They are able to role-play interactions such as confronting the perpetrator or discussing a problem with their partner. For many it is the first time that someone has been willing to hold and comfort them in a nonsexual, caring, supportive way. It is difficult, if not impossible, for that to happen in individual treatment between therapist and client, as transference issues are likely to interfere. The effects of transference frighten even the most seasoned therapist, let alone someone who is in the fragile and vulnerable state that confronting childhood trauma often produces. The group can provide caring support for victims in a much safer environment.

While it is true that the best vehicle for working through issues with family members is family therapy, the opportunity is rarely available, and family members usually will not even cooperate with the victim's treatment. In group therapy, clients have said that group members begin to represent their family and provide an excellent vehicle for working through issues with those family members. One group therapist becomes the "good" mom, while the other is the "bad" mom. The group members may be her siblings, and perhaps one of them is her father.

The group therapists must remain clear and focused at all times. They must be prepared to intervene if feelings run so high that someone might feel unsafe. They must be prepared to be the object of strong feelings expressed by clients in the group. The facilitators must be prepared to accept and encourage the expression of strong feelings rather than resist or defend against them. Their role is to monitor the process and confront abusive language, put-downs, and threats if necessary. When confrontations occur between clients in the group, the therapists must keep the process safe for everyone. They must communicate with each other, both verbally and nonverbally. As co-therapists, we have even stopped group activity and talked openly with each other about what was going on. This has allowed group members to step back from what is happening and see themselves and their interactions more clearly.

Anger: Expressing It and Using It Therapeutically

Adult retrospective victims need to understand what anger is and that they do not have to express anger in the way their parents or significant others in their childhood did. Anger is not a tool to be used to control others, nor is it there to control the individual. Anger is an emotion that can be experienced and expressed safely.

Women, even when they have not been victims of child sexual abuse, are often intimidated by the expression of anger. In our society, little girls are encouraged to get along with other children, not to assert themselves if doing so creates problems, and never to get angry. We understand and accept that little boys fight and argue, but when little girls get into scrapes with their peers, we call it "unladylike." Our culture simply does not provide boys or girls with good models for expressing rage in nondestructive ways. Boys learn to inflict pain on others as a response to anger. For girls, it becomes safer to disguise rage as hurt and use tears to provide some semblance of release.

The release is incomplete, however, and many angry feelings are supressed, unexpressed, and unidentified. This is terribly confusing for girls and for those who would support them.

Feelings of rage build in intensity when repressed and held back. The fury victims felt (and could not possibly express) each time they clenched their teeth and silently bore the pain of forcible intercourse does not dissipate. It smolders and grows. The level of fury will vary depending on when they were first victimized, for how long, and by how many people.

One eighteen-year-old woman was sexually assaulted by fourteen different family members from ages four to thirteen. She was depressed, hopeless, and desperate for relief. She had been tempted to take her life and came close to doing so several times. Her treatment had to be carefully planned and structured to provide safe opportunities to tap her rage in degrees and to allow her to express it in nondestructive ways. The therapist must spell out the boundaries or ground rules and be responsive to the rules set forth. The clear limits will make it safer for the victim to begin.

Many people have the idea that they must get rid of their anger. They imagine that a process of venting rage will liberate them from the horrible, hostile feelings that they work so hard to hide. Using anger therapeutically is more than finding safe ways to vent it. It also involves accepting strong emotions as part of oneself. Therapy can provide safe opportunities for those feelings to be expressed, validated, organized, and accepted.

In an abusive household, angry voices are literally deadly. Some survivors will numb up as soon as they hear voices raised. They have learned that rage can escalate suddenly and unpredictably, with no relationship to the expressed content. In other words, if Mom is raging because the dishes are not done, doing them will not necessarily be a remedy. They have learned that anger is always expressed explosively rather than in degrees or gradations. For some, those memory cues are so strong that fear is activated even when there is no risk to themselves. Some will freeze, while others will bolt and run. More will manage the situation with apparent calm because fear and anger have retreated so deeply within them. Their horror will not be known to anyone but themselves.

As a therapist, you can begin to make the expression of anger safer for the adult retrospective victim. There will always be occasions when we feel angry or frustrated in the context of a group session. We may come to group angry for reasons unrelated to the group, or we may become angry about something taking place in the sessions. It will be important to be clear about which is going on. In our sessions, we begin with a quick survey of the members, including the therapists, to learn how each is feeling. If something has taken place during the day that is influencing the therapist's mood, she can let the group know about it. They may become tense, expecting that "Mom" will take her feelings out on them somehow. When she does not, a new view of anger begins.

If the therapist becomes angry about something that transpires in the group, the opportunity for learning is even greater. When the therapist expresses her feelings by verbalizing them—"I'm feeling angry because . . ."—and does so without abusive language or put-downs, the client learns a new model for experiencing and expressing anger. This is all the more powerful if the feelings are very strong. The survivor of child sexual abuse will be astonished that you are angry with her and do not wish her harm. She may defend herself mightily or collapse in tears but she probably believes that you are leaving (anger and abandonment are closely intertwined in her experience), and she is bracing herself for the pain of losing you, as well as ruing the day she first trusted you.

Finding the ability to experience and express strong feelings, especially anger, by verbalizing them and still maintaining the relationship is a relief for anyone who has learned to do so. For the adult survivor, it is a minor miracle. When your client sees you express that anger, realizes that you are not going to leave her, and sees you remain supportive of her, she will have learned a powerful lesson.

Unfortunately, when it comes to anger, she may be too defended and detached from herself to be able to see and hear clearly for some time. Thus, she will need plenty of opportunity to see this modeled in group therapy and eventually to experiment with a direct expression of anger herself. When she does get angry in a group session, it will entail an enormous risk for her. It is easy for an individual to be "stuck" in her anger and it is essential that she struggle through it.

Anger, Sadness, and Pain: Struggle for Control

Strong feelings are not safe for adult survivors. All emotions are unreliable because they have the potential of growing and swelling out of control. Strong feelings arise due to an emotional involvement and investment—in oneself or in another person. But survival has always meant that you do not expect much of others, yourself, or life, so you will be less disappointed.

Survivors learned as small children how to deny and disguise their feelings. They may not recognize subtle changes in their defense system in time to prevent someone from becoming important. Thus, a woman may be surprised by the strong feelings of loss evoked one evening at a group session when she hears another member suddenly announce her plans to leave the group. The first woman may suddenly begin to weep or struggle to keep from crying.

Many victims will resist tears to avoid contact with the reservoirs of pain and sadness within them. They deny their own feelings and the importance of the relationship in order to maintain control over their feelings, but sooner or later the defenses will diminish and trust will build. Gradually, a woman will begin to trust others in the group on some levels and will take some risks in expressing feelings. Once she has opened the door, feelings may be experienced in a flood, and she may cry uncontrollably. Hold her if that is her wish, or demonstrate your support and understanding by other means. Let her know that her feelings are valid and acceptable. Much to her surprise, the flood of feeling passes, and she feels calmer. Breathe with her if necessary. Invite other group members to offer feedback. Express your own sorrow and distress over learning more of her pain. Discuss methods of self-nurturing and ways of comforting and soothing oneself. Applaud her willingness to take the risk of trusting the group.

As this process is repeated in group sessions, week after week, the client will sometimes be involved directly and at other times will have a chance to observe others. Both are opportunities rich in learning about herself, her feelings, her coping styles, and the events in her life that gave rise to them.

When a survivor voices emotions and longings that have heretofore gone unexpressed, she gradually develops an altogether different relationship to those feelings. When emotions are no longer secret and hidden, they are less compelling and dangerous. Once disclosed, the survivor's feelings can be validated by the group, and her fear is eventually relieved. She accepts her feelings as just, valid, and necessary. Free of the fear, she is empowered with a new perspective. By understanding herself, her coping patterns, and her needs more clearly, she can begin to choose new responses if she wishes.

She will need to learn other clear, healthy outlets for anger, sadness, and pain. We have developed two adjuncts to therapy at Ending Violence Effectively, which are an integral part of our clients' healing process, as well as a way for them to experience their personal power. These two adjuncts— wilderness therapy and self-defense training—have become important resources and opportunities for our clients.

Wilderness Therapy:
A Powerful Tool for Healing

Since July 1982, when the program was first offered, hundreds of survivors have taken part in a wilderness therapy experience as an adjunct to their ongoing individual or group therapy. The three-day program has proved to be a powerful opportunity, particularly for the expression of strong feelings. Since therapy in the wilderness is a relatively new area about which little has been written, we will discuss it in detail. We have found that by including this program in our clients' treatment process, they are able to move through their process much more quickly.

Our courses have been offered high in the Rocky Mountain wilderness, in the Collegiate Peaks, a two and a half hour drive from Denver. We work in the shadow of Mount Massive, a 14,000-foot beauty, and Mount Elbert, the tallest peak in the state. The setting's breathtaking beauty and its wild, unbridled spirit—audible in wind and water, visible in rocky terrain—may themselves incite one to risk taking. People like to shout from mountaintops and are exhilarated by a powerful sense of possibilities while standing in view of massive snowfields or steep rock faces. This open and wild setting gives a person permission to act out in a way that she might not in a closer, urban environment.

The usual boundaries are broken down further because this therapy does not last one or two hours but three or four days. The limits that time creates are dramatically altered. The client may feel safer to get close to strong feelings if she believes she will have support through the night, for instance. Support and a sense of safety are essential for a meaningful experience in the course.

Participants anticipate this weekend for weeks, maybe months. They feel anxious, fearful, and excited. They are already dealing with the loss of control on a number of levels because they know very little about what to expect. They know that it will be out-of-doors at 10,000 feet and that they will be doing some challenging activities they have never done before. Most participants have not even been camping before.

They probably struggled mightily with the decision to take part in this course. Their therapists encouraged them, and enthusiastic graduates of the course urged them to go. They had a clearer idea of what the course offered them a few weeks earlier, and they set some pretty well developed goals for themselves last week. Those ideas seem far away and unimportant now that the moment of departure has arrived. Right now they feel as if they have been roped into something, and they may be setting up the "you got me into this" escape clause before we even get our gear loaded into the cars.

The lengthy drive affords some opportunity for participants to begin to get to know one another. Anxiety is still high when we reach the parking lot at the base camp and meet the two Colorado Outward Bound staff persons who will be our guides and will provide the technical expertise for each of the activities. The Outward Bound staff takes full responsibility for safety and logistics. EVE sends two therapists on each course. They may or may not be the primary therapists for these clients. The therapists for the weekend will have been thoroughly briefed by the clients' own therapists so that they have a clear understanding of each client and her issues. They will have met the clients beforehand and begun to establish relationships with them.

The primary issues for participants when they arrive are fear for their physical safety and well-being, fear of trusting others, and fear of failure or loss of control. Courses are offered year-round, and most are in winter conditions, so the cold is a major concern for people.

We begin with lunch and issuing gear. Participants are provided with all the gear and clothing they need, along with information about adjustments to high altitude and increasing their comfort in this setting. Their anxiety increases as they are outfitted for the weekend with backpacks, compasses, whistles, cross-country skis and poles, snowshoes, and so on. Some are able to integrate the information provided and feel more prepared and more in control. Many are overwhelmed by it and feel more terrified than ever. Forgetting gear, important information, and sometimes their own names are common occurrences.

The initial activities are light and playful. We take plenty of time playing "getting to know" games to get acquainted with one another and with the setting. Laughter relieves the tension, and some participants are able to let down and enjoy themselves and one another. The initial activities involve physical contact and cooperation, so the process of trusting ourselves and bonding as a group has begun. The activities build progressively on each other. The skills learned in one initiative are applied in the next. Often anxiety will send a client's thoughts rushing to the future: "When do we eat dinner? What happens after this? I'll never be able to sleep tonight." The staff encourages her to stay focused on the moment and activity at hand.

She may already be beginning to feel angry about being "kept in the dark." She has been working in therapy on taking responsibility for herself and in getting her needs met, but this is impossible here. The feeling of being out of control and the high anxiety cause her to associate with other times in her life when she was threatened and in danger. Quiet panic begins, her stomach starts churning, and she has a sudden urge to run. If running or withdrawing have been her coping styles in the past, that is what she is wont to do or try to do at this time. She will probably keep her cool and hide her panic until she is confronted with a task that challenges her physically or emotionally.

The "trust fall" (falling backward into the arms of her partner) is often a catalyst for strong feelings. Observant therapists will have noticed the rising panic before this moment. They also will have an idea about the participant's pattern and style of avoidance and denial, which tend to be ineffective in this environment.

What the survivor is feeling and thinking right now is not unique. In fact, it is all too familiar. This situation is a metaphor as it represents a fairly common experience for the client—feeling intimidated, inadequate, and fearful of some new opportunity or relationship, for example, and letting those feelings build to a panic that renders her immobile. She may then become angry and accuse others of making her feel this way, or she may feel helpless and hopeless and want someone to take care of her.

By staying focused on the specific task—one victim's falling backward into her partner's arms—the group can encourage her to try something different. It is important to everyone that she accomplish this task so that they can go on. If her style has been to get angry and refuse to move, that will be confronted here, because it means none of us can go on. If it is a cold day or the group is getting hungry, her stubbornness probably will be confronted even more directly. A loving and caring confrontation will include offering assistance in variety of forms, such as providing ideas about how to proceed. Breaking the task down into smaller, more manageable steps will diminish the panic. Talking about what she is feeling and what she needs will enlist even further support from the group. Hers becomes a shared problem, one that the whole group works together to solve. If she does not have adequate resources herself, she can take the risk of trusting the group, disclosing her panic, and using the group's pooled resources to deal with it.

Each task or activity is discussed briefly at its conclusion. Each participant is asked to describe her own role and consider whether it is a customary one for her. Each is encouraged to try new roles and experiment with other approaches. As each participant identifies specific goals for herself, she shares them with the group. We will have an opportunity later to remind the group what the goals were and how the present task relates to them. A client also may disclose aspects of the process that is going on internally—the thinking that is behind the defense. She can then ask group members not only to notice, but also to observe out loud, that she is withdrawing, getting quiet, or sounding angry. They will ask her what she is thinking at the time. She may then discover ways that she sets herself up to have similar kinds of experiences. The metaphor is active on so many levels that it always has a usable application. There is always more to learn.

All the tasks are approached in such a way that success is achievable. One reason this works is that completing the task or reaching the end of the trail is never more important than the process of getting there. If I rush through an event because I am terrified of it and do not take time to be with myself and acknowledge what I am feeling, I am not successful and do not feel successful, even if I finish the task. But if I face my fears and use the moment as an opportunity to learn to manage and proceed in spite of them, I am successful whether I complete the task or not. These women have been prisoners of their fear-ridden past all their lives, so such successes are sweet.

The tasks or events become progressively more difficult. For instance, the "trust fall" is first done in pairs, on the ground. Next one person climbs a four-foot ladder attached to a tree and trusts the whole group to catch her when she gently falls back from that height. They do catch her and cradle her gently in their interlocking arms, rock her, and hold her while she rests and weeps. Each participant has an opportunity to take her turn at falling and trusting.

Strong feelings about what is taking place at the time might elicit flashbacks to another time when similar strong feelings were experienced. Therapists and group members support and encourage the victim as she relives, with them, a hidden horror from her past. They ask her questions, ask for more details, tell her to slow down, and allow her to reexperience events of her childhood aloud. They hold her while she cries and support and validate feelings she describes. Strong feelings, often of rage, come forward after the abusive event is recalled. The group invites her to give voice to those feelings. She can curse, yell, kick the ground, beat a sleeping bag. Clients have built snowmen and then demolished them as a vehicle for releasing rage and hatred.

They have growled, roared, screamed their pain and fury into a formerly still night. The stars are unmoved, the mountains are unshaken, and her supporters are with her still. Her "murderous rage" has dissipated and has done no one harm. Maybe she will sleep well tonight after all.

In summary, wilderness therapy is a powerful vehicle for experiencing emotions and eventually being able to express them. It is a path to learning pragmatic ways of changing one's behavior, of testing newly learned skills of stretching, reaching, and growing beyond one's imagination. It seems almost limitless in its possibilities for aiding in the healing process, and it can provide new hope and excitement and expand a person's limits. Therapists must understand the possible results of such a venture. We urge any therapist desiring to use this tool to experience it yourself first. It is our belief that we cannot ask our clients to do something we have not done ourselves.

Self-Defense as Therapy: New Tools for Change

While the importance of a good personal safety program is still considered highly controversial, we strongly favor providing this option to women and girls. The self-defense program that we use was developed by Carolyn Agosta and is being taught by trained instructors with the Self-Protection Instruction Team. The course includes home, car, and street security, as well as relaxation, body awareness, and simple, effective techniques that any woman can learn and use. It aids participants by providing choices and alternatives when in a threatening situation. Women and girls learn that they are not helpless and that they can reduce their vulnerability, thereby reducing their risk of victimization.

For those who have been victimized, self-defense training is another powerful tool toward healing. They can touch their own physical power, learn techniques, and practice them on supportive and willing (well-padded) male participants. They begin to learn that they have choices and that they can let go of the "I am a victim" attitude. They learn that whatever they do in a threatening situation is right, as long as they get out of it alive. Many victims are relieved to know this, and they can relate this knowledge to a past experience. They learn about the limits they have placed on their bodies, and they learn how to extend those limits. They practice exerting their full physical power by punching, kicking, and beating a punching bag.

They learn skills such as assertiveness training, which teaches them to say "no" clearly and reinforces what they are learning in the physical techniques. As they learn to speak more honestly, they begin to feel better about themselves and are more confident and self-assured. Learning how to set limits in relationships and how to teach those skills to their children also builds confidence and trust in themselves, while providing them with an important skill.

This training can, as with wilderness therapy, bring to the surface feelings and emotions that were hidden even from the victim. The instructors are skilled in handling flashbacks and surges of emotions from participants. They can step into a situation and help the women direct those frightening emotions, thereby releasing them.

While we have only provided a thumbnail sketch of the wilderness course and the self-defense program, we hope that you will understand the importance of these pragmatic ways of helping victims feel safe and actually experience the strength and power in their own bodies. As frightening as it is, it is truly exciting and energizing for a woman who has been a victim.

Closing Remarks

Child sexual abuse is painful, sometimes overwhelming, and often immobilizing, but it is an experience that can not only be survived, but also turned around so that the individual can experience a powerful, strong self who feels confident and capable. She can become someone who is able to enjoy relationships and to bond with people as never before.

To the victim, it seems as if the process will go on forever. Sometimes it seems that way to the therapist as well, but you must be aware of the danger of becoming too involved and must remember to take care of yourself. It is exhausting to work with victims of such tremendous, painful trauma and violence. You cannot help but absorb a large amount of that pain, but you must be prepared to let it go. This will require having a strong support system of peers, as well as excellent supervisors who understand the work you are doing. You need a place to go and shed your own tears without being criticized for getting too involved with your clients. Know yourself, and know when the work has become too much for you. If you focus on regular self-care rather than having to deal with burnout, you will be much better equipped to work in this field. There are going to be more victims of violence, not less, but there is hope and we can see it.

References

American Psychiatric Association (APA). 1980. *Diagnostic and Statistical Manual of Mental Disorders.* 3d ed. Washington, D.C.: 236–38, APA.

Burgess, Ann Wolbert, Nicholas Groth, Lynda Holmstrom, and Suzanne Sgroi. 1978. *Sexual Assault of Children and Adolescents.* Lexington, MA: Lexington Books.

Butler, Sandra. 1978. *Conspiracy of Silence: The Trauma of Incest.* San Francisco: New Glide Publications.

Byerly Carolyn M. 1985. *The Mother's Book: How to Survive the Incest of Your Child.* Dubuque, IA: Kendall/Hunt Publishing Company.

Bein, Judith. 1981. *Are You a Target?* Belmont, CA: Wadsworth Publishing Company.

Herman, Judith, and Lisa Hirschman. 1981. *Father-Daughter Incest.* Cambridge, MA: Harvard University Press.

James, Beverly, and Maria Nasjleti. 1983. *Treating Sexually Abused Children and Their Families.* Palo Alto, CA: Consulting Psychologists Press, Inc.

Jewett, Claudia L. 1982. *Helping Children Cope with Separation and Loss.* Harvard, MA: The Harvard Common Press.

Offstein, Jerrold. 1972. *Self-Defense for Women.* Palo Alto, CA: National Press Books.

Rush, Florence. 1980. *The Best Kept Secret.* Englewood Cliffs, NJ: Prentice-Hall.

Sanford, Linda Tischirhart. 1980. *The Silent Children.* New York: McGraw-Hill.

7

A Clinical Approach to Adult Survivors of Child Sexual Abuse

Suzanne M. Sgroi
Barbara S. Bunk

ealth and mental health professionals frequently encounter adults who were sexually abused in childhood: they are a ubiquitous presence in treatment populations. A growing number of these men and women are specifically identifying themselves to treatment providers as *adult survivors:* persons who now, as adults, find that they have problems in functioning, which they think may be connected to, or the result of, early sexual experiences initiated by others (usually a known and trusted authority figure, sometimes another older child). The implicit premise is that these early sexual experiences were emotionally damaging to the individual in some way, hence the notion that the adult has *survived* a traumatic experience of childhood.

Closely tied to the premise of resultant emotional damage is the person's sense that she or he was *victimized* by being the child subject of an older person's sexual attentions. Often the adult survivor remembers that she or he cooperated with the person who initiated the sexual activity. Nevertheless, as a child, cognitive and emotional immaturity, combined with a subordinate position vis-à-vis the other person, precluded consent (Sgroi 1982, 9). Accordingly, by definition, the adult survivor is a person who believes that he or she was exploited or abused by the person who induced him or her to cooperate with interactive sexual behaviors.

Despite the fact that sexual activity between adults and children is proscribed by law in every state in the United States, there is no universal agreement among clinicians that participating in interactive sexual behaviors with an adult is inherently abusive or emotionally traumatic for the child who is involved (Constantine and Martinson 1981, 5). This was especially true in the past, when clinicians were more likely to encounter people seeking help for a variety of complaints (depression, phobias, sexual dysfunctions, eating disorders, and relationship problems, to name a few) who were unlikely to reveal a history of childhood sexual abuse unless specifically asked. Unfortunately, clinicians often did not ask whether the patient, as a child, had ever been tricked, pressured, or forced by someone else to perform a sexual act. In the absence of a specific query, many patients were ashamed or afraid to volunteer the information. Some doubted the validity or the significance of the past incidents of sexual victimization. Accordingly, some adult survivors have had the experience of participating in (and paying for) months or years of psychotherapy that could not address directly the emotional consequences of their sexual abuse in childhood because it was not part of the working agreement between them and the clinician to do so.

Today, clinicians are far more likely to have adult patients who wish to work directly on the possible connections between sexual abuse experiences in childhood and current life problems. Many of these patients will already have identified themselves as adult survivors and come to the clinicians with this specific request. Other patients may come to clinicians with a different complaint and wait to be asked. Fortunately, more and more clinicians are asking about childhood and adult victimization experiences as they explore their patients' presenting complaints. It is still not unusual to discover that some patients do not remember child sexual abuse incidents in their earlier lives until after the session when the question is asked. When they do recall past sexual victimization experiences, it may be with a sense of sudden realization that the coping mechanisms that they used to help themselves survive a previous emotional trauma are now part of a present response pattern to current life experiences.

It is also possible, however, to remember child sexual abuse incidents in one's own life and be certain that there is no connection between one's response to past incidents and one's current problems in today's world. Whereas in previous decades, an adult survivor was likely to discover that the clinician was unable, unwilling, or unready to help him or her address emotional trauma secondary to child sexual abuse experiences, it is equally likely nowadays for the clinician to discover that the patient does not wish to explore the effects of those experiences to see whether there is a relationship to present complaints. We find that many patients have told other clinicians about child sexual abuse experiences with the result that the clinicians urged them to work on this material. Many patients have refused to do so, sometimes because they were not ready, or they doubted its significance, or they assigned it a low priority on their own therapeutic agenda or list of requests.

From a clinical perspective, we are exceedingly hampered by the lack of prospective data on the emotional sequelae of child sexual abuse. All that we know about the epidemiology of this phenomenon is based on retrospective studies of troubled populations. Various studies of chronic alcoholics, drug addicts, teenage prostitutes, sexual offenders, and persons with eating disorders, phobias, and self-injurious behaviors (to name a few) have all shown that a majority of the persons in these troubled populations were sexually abused when they were children.

What does this mean? The answer is that we really do not know what relationships exist between a person's sexual abuse history dating back to childhood and current problems such as alcoholism or sexual offense behavior. An association probably does exist, but we can never trace a direct cause and effect relationship between emotional sexual trauma in childhood and adult behavior disorders or any later problem. We can speculate about causality with adult survivors, but what is ultimately most important clinically is what *they* think are the consequences and connections. It is important to remember, however, that we cannot predict (and should not speculate about) long-term consequences of sexual abuse for contemporary child victims. It is unfortunate that a public perception currently exists that child victims of sexual abuse are damaged for life and will inevitably manifest a serious problem, such as sexual offense behavior or prostitution.

Variables Influencing Impact

None of this is to say that we believe that sexual abuse has no impact on the child victim; quite the contrary. We also believe, however, that adult men and women are amazingly complex and diverse beings who are capable of a staggering array of responses, experiences, and behaviors. Although it is possible to identify patterns of victim response to child sexual abuse and, indeed, to make generalizations that can be usefully applied when trying to make sense of what may have happened, it is always necessary to respect and appreciate the uniqueness of the individual with whom we are working. The crux of clinical intervention is to help the adult survivor examine his or her sexual victimization experiences in order to discover and articulate the following: *What was the sexual abuse experience like for you then?* and *What do you think about it now?*

In other words, many adult survivors require clinical assistance to recapture memories of their childhood sexual victimization in order to examine how they reacted to what was happening to them at the time and how they coped with those emotions then. Many have erected barriers to remembering either the details of their victimization experiences or their emotional reactions to the abuse. These barriers, in turn, may prevent adult survivors from examining their current reactions to those past experiences, especially within the context of their contemporary emotional functioning and the coping mechanisms they now use. The challenge for both clinician and patient is to overcome or circumvent the barriers that may make it difficult for the adult survivor to examine these connections.

How, then, does one determine whether emotional trauma was a consequence of sexual abuse, thereby stimulating the formation of coping mechanisms that become less adaptive or perhaps even dysfunctional in later life? We have identified a number of variables that seem to influence the impact of the sexual abuse experience on the individual. A systematic exploration of these variables has been helpful to us in working with adult survivors. In this section, we discuss how these variables seem to relate to the individual's response at the time the sexual abuse occurred. We also discuss what we speculate are the connections between childhood response and present-day problems in functioning (and complaints) of the adult survivor.

Engagement and Secrecy Strategies

As previously discussed, abusers use strategies to enlist a child's cooperation with sexual acts (Sgroi 1982, 13). The adult survivor, as a child, may have cooperated with nonviolent strategies (enticement or entrapment) or violent strategies (threat of force or use of force) employed by the abuser to induce the child to participate in the sexual behavior and to enlist cooperation in keeping the fact of the sexual behavior a secret from others. It is important for the clinician to discover the type of strategy used by the abuser in order to determine the patient's perception of the meaning to him or her of having cooperated with that strategy. For example, the abuser may have used an *enticement strategy,* promising the child a reward for cooperation. One father would sexually fondle his young daughter while he read the funny papers to her on Sunday mornings. She submitted willingly to the sexual fondling because of the reward of her father's companionship and the attention she was receiving. She also enjoyed the pleasurable sensations evoked by his fondling of her genitals. As an adult, the woman, whose name is Doris, is ashamed of having wanted the reward of her father's attention and also ashamed that she enjoyed the sexual fondling. She remarked, "Well, I feel guilty because I can remember at times enjoying it and trying to please my father. I felt I had to protect my mother and I had to please my father."

Children who succumb to *entrapment strategies* are likely to view themselves as obligated to cooperate with the abuser. Entrapment means that the abuser (usually a parent or adult authority figure) successfully communicated that the child owed him or her cooperation in sexual acts in return for food, clothing, protection, nurturance, safety, and the like. Adult survivors also may feel ashamed that, as children, they wanted to receive love, nurturance, or support from the abuser and in return cooperated by performing sexual acts at the abuser's behest. In the foregoing example, Doris cannot forgive herself for wanting her father's nurturance. This is a serious barrier for many adult survivors. In response to Doris's comment, another woman, Cynthia, replied, "The hardest thing for me now is realizing that the only human contact I had as a child was the sexual contact with my father."

It is clinically important to differentiate guilt from the shame experienced by the adult survivor of sexual abuse by a *child molester* (an abuser who used engagement strategies of enticement or entrapment). If the adult survivor's perception is that it was shameful to want material rewards or support and nurturance from the abuser and to have traded interactive sexual behaviors to gain them, the shame can frequently be dispelled in peer group therapy. It is exceedingly effective for adult survivors to have their shame challenged by their peers, while receiving support for the choice that all victims of molesters did make: that is, as children, they cooperated with the abuser and, in effect, received rewards or basic nurturance in return. We have not found, however, that either individual therapy or peer group therapy has been especially helpful in dispelling the guilt that seems to be a common response, both for victims of molesters and for victims of rapists (abusers who used strategies of threat of force or use of force). Instead, we now tend to view a guilty response by the adult survivor as an elaboration of a coping mechanism used by the child to feel in control, which has likely become dysfunctional by the time the victim becomes an adult. We discuss the therapeutic approach to guilt manifested by the adult survivor in the next section of this chapter. For now, suffice to say that it seems unrealistic to hope that guilt will be dispelled by cognitive challenges or instruction by therapists or peers.

Consequences of Noncompliance

The victim's perception (or fear) of the consequences to him or her for failing to cooperate with the abuser also is important. Adult survivors who cooperated with enticement strategies may have worried about making the abuser angry or hurting his or her feelings if they failed to cooperate (and symbolically rejected the promised reward). Victims who cooperated with entrapment strategies may have feared abandonment by the abuser or feared the direct consequences of lack of nurturance if they failed to comply with the abuser's wish for them to perform sexual acts. Geraldine, a woman in her fifties, put it very simply: "I thought that if I refused my father or got angry at my mother, I would die; I would simply cease to exist. Children are so dependent on their parents. Abandonment seemed like death to me. I couldn't risk it."

By contrast, the adult survivor who remembers that she or he cooperated with a child rapist may also remember that she or he most likely responded to the threat of force or use of force with fear of physical injury or even death. Some children cope with the overwhelming responses of fear and terror by denial or dissociation. They may deny that they were/are afraid and experience another reaction, such as anger, instead. Others may react by dissociation—cutting themselves off from a painful or dysphoric emotional response and experiencing a feeling of calmness or numbness instead. Peer group therapy also may be very helpful for adult survivors who used dissociation as a coping mechanism for child sexual abuse experiences. It usually requires both intense support and prodding from the therapist and other group members for the adult survivor to become reconnected and to remember and reexperience (on an emotional level) the previous responses of fear and terror. By doing so, the patient can have the present-day life experience of emotionally living through what may have loomed in the background as an intolerable life experience of the past. Again, any individual may react differently; it has nonetheless been our experience that dysfunctional coping mechanisms used to combat intense fear are more likely to be found in adult survivors who were victimized by child rapists.

Relationship between Child and Abuser

This variable, although important, does not have the primacy that one might otherwise assume when considering how many government-funded treatment programs for victims of child sexual abuse are restricted to working solely with children who have been sexually abused by family members and exclude children who have been sexually abused by someone outside the family, regardless of the treatment needs of the individual child. It is inevitable that members of the general public might conclude from such program policies that sexual abuse by a family member is serious business that is worthy of attention and remedial intervention and that sexual abuse by a person outside the family is not. This is unfortunate because, in our clinical experience, there are more similarities than differences in the emotional consequences of intrafamily versus extrafamily child abuse.

Few children are victimized by strangers. When the abuser is not a family member, she or he is likely to be a known and trusted person from the child's neighborhood, school, or church. Often the extrafamily abuser is a temporary caretaker for the child who was selected by the parents (Sgroi 1982, 245). Under these circumstances, treatment issues such as the damaged goods syndrome, betrayal of trust, fear, depression, and impaired self-esteem can be anticipated as possible consequences of the sexual exploitation. It is true that blurred role boundaries and familial role confusion are more likely to occur when the abuser occupies a family role relationship vis-à-vis the child. When the extrafamily abuser is a temporary caretaker (such as a baby-sitter) or someone who occupies a special position with regard to the child's parent (such as the mother's boyfriend or father's boss), there is still ample opportunity for blurred role boundaries and family role confusion to occur.

We believe that clinicians who work with adult survivors must explore the psychological importance of the relationship between the victim and the perpetrator, both past and present, without prejudice. By this we mean that the clinician cannot assume ahead of time that sexual abuse by a father was more significant with regard to emotional impact on the victim than sexual abuse by a teacher or by an unrelated friend of the family. The adult survivor's reality with regard to the significance of the relationship between him or her and the abuser is what must be identified and explored. Again, in many cases, the victim's decision to keep the sexual abuse by someone outside the family a secret from her or his parents will also have an effect on family role relationships for that adult survivor.

We frequently recommend family therapy for adult survivors of child sexual abuse, both with their families of origin and with their spouses and children. It is not unusual to encounter a great deal of resistance to family therapy from the identified patient and from other family members (especially from the family of origin). We are likely to persist, nevertheless, because we believe that the unfinished business between the adult survivor and members of her or his family of origin can profoundly influence relationships with spouses and children. Some work can be done on family role relationships in peer group therapy, but we strongly encourage adult survivors (with varying success) to address these matters with family therapy interventions whenever possible.

Age of Onset and Duration of Abuse

As the phenomenon of child sexual abuse has become more widely recognized, cases are reported involving younger and younger children, even preschool children. In past years, it was assumed that sexual abuse rarely occurred to children before they reached adolescence. We now believe that in a milieu when abuse was rarely suspected, there was little likelihood that cases would ever come to our attention unless a child complained to someone outside the family. Adolescents were better equipped, from a developmental perspective, to separate from their families sufficiently to make a complaint. Today's survivors, however, are sometimes able to track memories of sexual abuse as far back as preschool age. Sometimes these memories are facilitated by hypnosis; sometimes they are even corroborated by others.

Obviously, the younger the child at the onset of sexual abuse, the greater the potential that the abuse will continue for years—perhaps until the child reaches adulthood or even after. Even if the period when abuse took place was of short duration, the potential emotional consequences of the child's response, and the coping mechanisms used by the child to deal with the abuse and his or her response to it, could be more potent if the onset of the abuse occurred at a very young age. To put it another way, the younger the child at the onset of sexual abuse, the greater the potential that the sexual victimization experiences will influence the child's capacity to accomplish development tasks effectively and within age-appropriate developmental norms. In Chapter 5, "Treatment of Male Victims of Child Sexual Abuse in Military Service," Dr. Michael Johanek comments that the men he has treated often appear to have stopped maturing emotionally at the age when their sexual victimization began.

We believe that this variable deserves careful examination by clinicians who treat adult survivors because it is so frequently associated with the patient's capacity to develop and maintain satisfactory trust relationships with others. Relationship and intimacy disorders are so important in the treatment of adult survivors that we discuss them in a separate section later in this chapter. We currently recommend to adult survivors who wish to work on their capacity to have satisfying relationships with others that they participate in peer group therapy first, followed by (or in conjunction with) couples therapy or perhaps some other type of subsystem or total family therapy.

Type of Sexual Abuse Behavior

The nature of the sexual acts that constituted the abuse must be determined for the clinician to ascertain the adult survivor's perception of the meaning to him or her of having participated in those sexual acts at the behest of the abuser. In the past, clinicians have sometimes questioned the necessity of learning the "gory details" of the sexual abuse from the adult survivor. We know of no other way to learn what the patient thinks about himself or herself in the here and now within the context of a past history of having cooperated with the abuser in performing certain sexual acts. We are convinced that the capacity to recall and tell others about a sexually victimizing experience helps the individual regain at least some of the control over body and psyche that was taken away at the time the abuse occurred. It is also, we believe, the only practical method by which the person can begin to differentiate childhood reactions to sexual abuse in the past from present-day adult reactions to current stresses and life events.

In the past, clinicians have assumed that the type of sexual interaction constituting the abuse would have a predictable effect on the child victim with regard to severity of response. That is to say, clinicians frequently assumed that abuse involving sexual penetration would be likely to result in greater emotional trauma to the victim than abuse that was limited to sexual exposure or perhaps to sexual fondling. Experience with large numbers of clients has taught us that this was a dangerous assumption. Some victims have apparently sustained severe emotional trauma associated with sexual abuse that did not involve penetration of the child's body; others have emerged from abuse experiences involving extensive sexual penetration with apparently less severe emotional trauma.

Why, then, do we sometimes exert persistent efforts to determine the exact nature of the sexual abuse from the patient? It is because we believe that the victim's perception of the meaning to him or her of having cooperated with the sexual acts initiated by the abuser is of great clinical significance. Some patients seem to have the capacity to be philosophical about sexual abuse that involved extensive sexual penetration. One woman told a group of adult survivors, "We all did what we had to do in order to survive at the time. No child ever has to be ashamed of doing what she had to do in order to say alive." A fellow group member retorted, "That's easy for you to say. I guess it's not a problem for you. Every time I think of what my brother and I did together, I feel so awful I want to throw up!"

It is always necessary to remember that the victim's contemporary perception of the meaning to him or her of having cooperated with the sexual abuse behavior is reflective of a coping mechanism that is helping the victim in some way. It somehow helps one person genuinely to experience nausea when she recalls mutual masturbation and simulated intercourse with her brother, just as it also helps her fellow group member to view her participation in various acts involving sexual penetration with her father as a necessary survival tactic. The challenge to clinicians is to remember that each victim's reaction is unique and individually determined. After assisting patients to identify their past and present perceptions of the sexual abuse, it is the clinician's task to learn how those reactions are helpful to adult survivors and to find ways for them to learn how to substitute more constructive coping mechanisms for the dysfunctional ones currently being used.

Reaction to Disclosure

Not all children who are sexually victimized disclose the abuse while they are still minors; some never tell anyone at all, while others disclose sometime after they reach adulthood. The reaction of the person who receives the disclosure may be an important variable influencing the impact of the sexual abuse on the individual. For instance, we believe that a supportive and believing response from the person who receives the child's disclosure can be very helpful to the victim. Alternatively, a nonsupportive reaction can be devastating. One man said, "I told my best friend when I was thirteen that my mom liked to have me lie in her bed with her while she gave me body rubs. He said to me, 'And you're complaining!' I was so burned up that I never told anyone else while I was still a kid." This man, as an adult, was still outraged by his friend's reaction, which he perceived as a lack of support. For this adult survivor, a body rub by his mother in her bed at age thirteen years was an abusive experience; his friend's attitude that he should feel lucky to have a mother who fondled an adolescent son was undermining and repudiative.

When the person has coped with his or her emotional response to the sexual stimulation by dissociating and becoming detached, a reaction of disbelief to disclosure can be especially problematic because of the threat to one's reality testing. One victim remembered, "She [her mother] just kept looking right through me like I wasn't even in the room after I told her. Her face didn't change expression, and she never said a word. It was like I never even said anything at all. I felt like I was crazy or something, because I told her this terribly important thing, and she acted like she never heard me. I guess she couldn't believe it."

Sometimes children tell adults about sexual abuse in a manner that would be difficult for anyone to understand. The following scenario is a typical one. Jessie, age eight years, selects a time just before her mother is ready to serve supper to the family to tell her about sexual abuse by her father.

Jessie (in a whining tone): Mommy, I wish you didn't have to go to work tonight.

Mother (preoccupied): Well, I do. What's the problem?

Jessie: I don't like it when Daddy has to put me to bed. I wish you could be home every night.

Mother: How come? Please start to set the table!

Jessie: Because Daddy plays games with me when he puts me to bed.

Mother: What an ungrateful child you are! Don't you know there are lots of little girls who don't have fathers at all? You should be glad when your father takes time to pay attention to you. Now get started on that table, for once and for all!

In this typical example, the child is using an indirect method to tell her mother about the abuse. Many abusers refer to the sexual behavior with the child as a game. Jessie is, in effect, telling her mother about sexual abuse by her father, but she is telling her in code. Her busy mother, not understanding the code, reacts in a hurried and nonsupportive fashion. Unfortunately, what Jessie is likely to take away from this attempted disclosure is the perception that her mother did not believe her. In fact, Jessie's mother probably did not understand what her child was attempting to tell her. Many victims are unable to find the confidence and courage to try to disclose the sexual abuse again and to persist until the listener does understand.

It can be equally harmful when the person who receives the child's disclosure reacts by blaming the victim. When one little girl told her mother that the mother's boyfriend was fondling her genitals, putting his finger in her vagina, and engaging in open-mouth kissing with her, the mother's response was extremely punitive. The mother said to her five-year-old daughter, "You shouldn't have let him do that—you're too young! You have to wait 'til you grow up before you can do things like that with men!" This mother apparently viewed her daughter, at age five years, as a rival and a competitor. She gave her youngster a clear message that the child was to blame for the adult's behavior and that it was her responsibility to see to it that the abuse did not happen again.

In general, when the victim is believed and supported by the person who receives the disclosure, she or he feels less isolated and alone. If the person who receives the disclosure in a believing and supportive manner also continues to be an ally, we can usually anticipate that the overall effects of the abuse will be less traumatic for the victim.

Events Following Disclosure

Many child victims of sexual abuse experience marked disruption in their lives following a disclosure that is believed and acted upon. There may be multiple interviews regarding the abuse, separation from the abuser or the family, estrangement or remonstrances from family members who disbelieve the disclosure or are threatened by the disruption to their own lives, a necessity to miss school or even to change schools, a requirement to testify in court, and so forth. The child may react to this disruption with bewilderment, denial, anger, depression, grief, shame, or some combination of the above. Gertrude, a fifteen-year-old girl who was impregnated by her father, had an angry response to the disruption in her life following the disclosure. She said, "When I told people that my dad had got me pregnant, I lost everything! I had to leave home, I had to drop out of school, and I had to have the baby. He got to stay home with my mom and my brothers and sisters. I hope he gets life [imprisonment]!"

Gertrude's angry reaction indicated that at least she was clear about who was responsible for the disruption following disclosure. Some victims, however, assume blame for the disruption to others' lives as well as to their own when the sexual abuse is disclosed. One adult survivor tearfully told her therapist, "I've never stopped blaming myself that my sister and I had to change schools after I told my counselor that our stepfather was having sex with me. She had been getting terrific grades and was in line for a scholarship. After we changed schools, her grades dropped and never came back up. I blame myself that she didn't get to go to college."

In general, the presence of a consistent adult ally tends to minimize the degree of emotional trauma that may be experienced by the child after disclosure. It is interesting, however, to note that there are significant differences between external and outward support and true emotional support for the victim. The following example is illustrative:

Judy, age thirteen, told her mother about sexual fondling and an episode of attempted vaginal intercourse by her father. Judy's mother believed the disclosure and immediately left the home with her daughter and made arrangements for them to stay overnight with relatives. She then confronted her husband with the disclosure, and he admitted to the abuse. Judy's mother subsequently insisted that her husband see a psychiatrist for treatment. She asked the psychiatrist whether Judy should also be seen. The psychiatrist advised her that it would probably be traumatic for Judy to talk about the abuse and said that if the girl seemed to be doing well, it would be better to "let sleeping dogs lie." Judy's mother did not bring up the subject again with her daughter and, following medical advice, rebuffed the girl's attempts to discuss it again during her adolescence. Judy's father never approached her sexually again; neither did he discuss the sexual abuse.

In this case, the mother offered her daughter a great deal of outward support, but the girl did not feel emotionally supported by her mother because they never talked again about the sexual abuse after the initial disclosure. Thus, although her complaint was believed and prompt action was taken, this adolescent girl perceived her mother's unwillingness to discuss the sexual abuse as a lack of emotional support, which profoundly influenced her reaction to the abuse by her father. Despite the fact that there was no recurrence of the abuse and, comparatively speaking, minimal disruption to her life following the disclosure, this girl became an adult survivor who associated repeated difficulties in establishing intimate relationships with others with her childhood sexual abuse by her father and her mother's perceived lack of emotional support following the disclosure.

Life Context of the Sexual Abuse

This last variable may be an amalgam of many variables. Did the adult survivor experience childhood sexual abuse within the context of physical abuse or neglect or emotional abuse? Or was the sexual abuse the only type of child maltreatment experienced by him or her? Did the patient have, in general, consistent parenting or parent figures, especially during the first five years of life? Or did the child experience sexual abuse within the context of being raised by a single parent or have multiple caretakers, multiple placements, and inconsistent caretaking as a life context for the sexual victimization? Did one or both parents or a significant caretaker have a severely disabling mental illness, drug or alcohol dependency, or severe physical illness? Did the child experience the death of one or both parents, a separation from one or both parents due to problems within the marital relationship, or perhaps a divorce? Were there disputes about custody or visitation as a life context for some type of sexual abuse?

In turn, the adult survivor may have experienced severe physical illness or a physical or mental handicap in childhood in addition to the sexual victimization. Was he or she hospitalized or required to undergo surgery one or more times? Did he or she experience poverty as a child, with a variety of hardships and social deprivations? Did the adult survivor undergo emotional trauma secondary to racial or ethnic prejudices as a life context for childhood sexual abuse? Or did the person experience severe social unrest or social injustice during his or her childhood (war, natural disaster, emigration from one country to another) in addition to sexual abuse? Was the adult survivor kidnapped or physically or sexually assaulted by someone outside the family in addition to being sexually abused by a family member or by a known and trusted person?

All of the above variables may form a life context for childhood sexual abuse that might intensify or increase the impact of the sexual victimization by rendering the victim less able to cope with or integrate the abuse experience. On the other hand, a more benign life context (consistent parenting and the absence of illness, death, separation, drug or alcohol abuse, racial or ethnic prejudice, other types of child maltreatment) might tend to be associated with less emotional trauma to the victim. It can be argued that survival skills are generic and that learning to cope with one type of victimizing or traumatizing experience better equips the individual to cope with another. Emotional trauma, however, can be cumulative, especially if a young child begins to employ coping mechanisms such as dissociation to protect himself or herself from experiencing emotional pain. Although highly effective on a short-term basis, dissociation tends to be a highly maladaptive coping mechanism, especially if learned early and applied often during critical periods of growth and development.

In summary, the life context of the sexual abuse may also significantly influence the impact on the child at the time when the abuse is occurring as well as later in adulthood. We examine this issue in the next section when we discuss the ways in which adult survivors come to treatment.

Patterns of Presentation

We have observed two distinct patterns of presentation for adult survivors of child sexual abuse. We hope that these observations may be useful to other clinicians and may stimulate interest in looking for additional patterns in which patients may come to treatment.

Early Presentation

These patients may be older adolescents or young adults, usually between the ages of sixteen and twenty-five. They come to clinical attention because of symptoms associated with drug or alcohol abuse, acute psychotic reactions, self-mutilating behaviors, delinquency, teenage prostitution, running away, eating disorders, or suicide attempts. Sometimes there will be a history of two or more of the above conditions. In nearly all these cases, the individuals have a history of experiencing more than one type of child maltreatment: that is, childhood sexual abuse in combination with physical abuse, neglect, or emotional abuse. It is also usual for the person to have a history of being raised by at least one and sometimes two or more impaired parent figures or caretakers (e.g., parenting by persons with a chemical dependency, thought disorder, criminal lifestyle, or the like). In other words, adult survivors of child sexual abuse who fit this early presentation pattern are persons who have a life context of multiple victimization experiencés, inconsistent parenting, separation or abandonment, severe physical or mental handicaps, poverty, or social injustice.

Clinicians may recognize in adult survivors who have an early presentation pattern many manifestations of the damaged goods syndrome. In other words, these individuals tend to have low self-esteem, impaired body image, and a pervasive sense of damage and unworthiness. Repeated self-destructive behaviors are very common in this population, which comes to clinical attention most often because of some type of acting-out behavior deemed to be injurious to themselves or to others.

As a general rule, the clinical approach to the adult survivor who has this pattern of early presentation must be directed toward stabilizing the acting-out or self-injurious behaviors that brought them to attention in the first place. Thus, the acute psychotic reaction must be treated by drugs, hospitalization, or both; the alcohol or drug abuse must be brought under control; the suicide attempts, life-threatening self-mutilation, or eating disorders must be countered by external controls; and so forth. It is impossible to address or even to sort out the impact of childhood sexual victimization in the context of acting-out or out-of-control behaviors by these individuals. After the acute symptoms are stabilized, the clinician can then explore the possibility of addressing unresolved and symptomatic sequelae of childhood sexual abuse. However, although it would be a mistake to fail to ask about childhood sexual victimization and to neglect to offer the person the opportunity to work clinically on unresolved sexual trauma, it has been our experience that many adult survivors who fit the pattern of early presentation will either deny a history of childhood sexual abuse or refuse to work on unresolved sexual victimization issues soon after disclosure to the clinician.

Instead, we commonly observe that a longer period of stabilization of the presenting symptomatology, sometimes lasting from months to years, will be required. It is usual for female adult survivors who fit the early presentation pattern to have a history of psychiatric hospitalizations, eating disorders, and/or severe chemical dependency in adolescence and to present with a request to the clinician for treatment of childhood sexual abuse issues any time from one to ten years afterward. Years of sobriety or abstinence or years of living in the community without psychiatric hospitalization seem to be required before most survivors who fit the early presentation pattern are ready to work on unresolved emotional trauma secondary to childhood sexual abuse.

As previously mentioned in this chapter, it is extremely difficult to assess the relative contribution of childhood sexual abuse and the resultant emotional trauma that may occur to any adult's contemporary level of functioning and/or complaints. It is obvious that the problem of ascribing degrees of impact of childhood sexual abuse is compounded when the adult survivor happens to be a person who was multiply abused and suffered many of the variables mentioned in the life context area described in the foregoing section. Suffice to say that the question of how much (if any) emotional damage to ascribe to the individual's child sexual abuse history has little relevance in the acute phase of the early presentation pattern for adult survivors.

It would be a mistake to expect that the serious or perhaps even life-threatening symptomatology will abate if the clinician tries to engage the patient in clinical interactions that might address unresolved sexual trauma dating back to childhood while the individual is out of control and a danger to himself or herself or to others. Addressing emotional sequelae of childhood sexual abuse has a relatively low priority on the treatment agenda during a time when the person is under the influence of drugs or is psychotic or otherwise out of control. The presenting symptomatology must be stabilized, and the individual must have demonstrated some capacity to learn (by practice) to impose internal controls as a substitution for external controls, before treatment for childhood sexual abuse sequelae can usefully begin.

Late Presentation

The adult survivor of childhood sexual abuse who fits a pattern of late presentation is likely to be in his or her mid-twenties, thirties, or early forties. This person is likely to appear to others as outwardly well adjusted, competent, and successful. He or she is likely to have pursued a higher education and to be successful in the professional or business world, often holding a very responsible job. Frequently, the person will be married and have children who may also appear to be well adjusted and asymptomatic. The adult survivor who has a late presentation pattern will also commonly have sought psychotherapy in the past, usually for some other complaint. It is not unusual for persons from this population to report that they told their clinicians about their past history of sexual abuse but that there was a unilateral or mutual agreement between them not to pursue the childhood sexual abuse history with psychotherapy at that time.

Instead, previous psychotherapy may have been focused on one or more typical complaints, such as depression, anxiety, multiple somatic complaints, or sexual dysfunction (especially low sexual desire), to name a few. In the late presentation pattern, the adult survivor often experienced temporary relief of his or her presenting complaint after a period of psychotherapy. It is also likely, however, that the symptom or complaint later recurred or that another symptom or complaint replaced it. Nevertheless, it is usual for adult survivors who manifest a late presentation pattern to have a history of intermittent psychotherapy to address complaints that have waxed and waned or come and gone for years. The important thing is that the symptoms or complaints were never so disruptive or disabling that they prevented him or her from functioning with apparent success in a competitive and demanding world.

Typically, all this suddenly changes at a critical point in time for the adult survivor with a late presentation pattern. Despite his or her past history of competence and apparent success in life, he or she may suddenly become symptomatic in a way that can now be perceived to be connected to the past history of childhood sexual abuse. What has frequently occurred is that the survivor has begun to experience flashbacks or disruptive memories accompanied by disturbing emotions such as extreme rage, enormous anxiety, intense shame, or profound depression and an overriding sense of being out of control with regard to the emotions that are being experienced. For many, this is the first time that, as adults, they can recall feeling completely out of control of their thoughts and emotions. Some are highly upset or even in a state of panic when they seek help from a clinician.

What precipitated such a dramatic change in their lives? Why have they become so acutely symptomatic so suddenly? Why do at least some of them realize at this point that it is now time for them to come to terms with unresolved sexual trauma dating back to their childhood? Why has working on childhood sexual abuse now moved to the top of their therapeutic agenda?

The honest answer to the above questions is "We do not know." We have observed this pattern of the dramatic late presentation of the adult survivor again and again. The precipitating factors for some have included the following circumstances:

1. The cooling of the survivor's marital relationship, sometimes accompanied by sexual dysfunction experienced by one or both partners and sometimes not, but always accompanied by distancing behavior and problems with intimacy between the couple.
2. The experience of genuine intimacy in an interpersonal relationship with another adult, sometimes for the first time in the survivor's life. This may be with another person of the same sex or with a person of the

opposite sex and may occur within a marital or an extramarital relationship.

3. The survivor's own child has reached an age or a developmental stage that is particularly threatening to the parent, sometimes because it forces the survivor to recall the age or developmental stage that she or he had reached when the childhood sexual abuse began or was disclosed.

4. A life change for the survivor that involves increased visibility, greater responsibility, or perhaps public praise or recognition.

5. The survivor's experience of personally identifying with a victim of child sexual abuse. This may occur when the survivor learns that his or her own child or perhaps the child of a relative or friend has been victimized. Or it may occur because the survivor watches a movie or attends a workshop that addresses the topic.

Regardless of the precipitating factors, the adult survivor who appeals to a clinician for help because he or she feels emotionally overwhelmed may indeed be unable to control his or her emotions. Some patients report that they have become intensely fearful and unable to drive or to stay alone in a room or in a building. Others have been overcome by an episode of uncontrollable weeping that lasted for days. The sudden loss of emotional control, when experienced by the patient, is likely to be frightening and highly disruptive. The survivor is thus apt to be in severe distress and is therefore very likely to be motivated to cooperate with clinical interventions that he or she hopes will alleviate the disturbing symptomatology. The clinician is, therefore, faced with a highly motivated and anxious patient who is actively seeking symptomatic clinical relief. The clinical interventions at this time are of critical importance.

Initial Clinical Approach

We recommend that clinicians who are working with adult survivors who manifest a late presentation pattern be aware that they are dealing with patients who are alarmed by their recent disturbing symptomatology but generally have a past history of good to excellent functioning in their lives. It will be necessary to verify by careful history taking that the adult survivor who presents with acute symptomatology is actually someone who does not have a past history of psychosis, substance abuse, or suicide attempts and therefore does, in fact, fit the late presentation pattern. This is important because the survivor who honestly tells the clinician, "I feel out of control and overwhelmed!" may not receive the appropriate type of clinical intervention. As a general rule, survivors who manifest a late presentation pattern are unlikely to engage in suicide attempts or to experience psychotic breaks as long as there is no past history of the above. It is always the responsibility of the clinician to identify those patients who really do require external controls, such as psychiatric hospitalization, to protect themselves and others. In general, adult survivors who manifest a late presentation pattern do not require external controls or psychotropic medication. Careful history taking, coupled with a careful mental status examination in the initial interview(s), will be required to make these distinctions and to verify that the patient does or does not require hospitalization and/or psychotropic medication.

When the clinician is convinced that the adult survivor does not require external controls or psychotropic medication, he or she can begin the massive task of convincing a formerly successfully functioning, highly motivated, and frequently sophisticated patient that immediate relief of disturbing symptomatology is not "the answer" or the immediate goal of treatment. This will be time-consuming as well as difficult, and usually only a beginning can be made in the initial session. We recommend that the clinician utilize the "customer approach to patienthood" described by Burgess and Lazare (1976) and attempt, in the initial session, to elicit a request from the patient to help him or her work through these problems. The request should be finite and measurable and, if possible, not contain an implicit promise to relieve symptoms right away. Examples of requests that clinicians might elicit from the patient and comply with include "Help me to understand why I feel this way" or "Tell me I'm not crazy." It would be potentially much more problematic for the clinician to agree to a request such as "Help me to sleep better at night" or "Help me to stop feeling so guilty."

The clinician must walk along an exceedingly narrow path at this point. On the one edge is the peril of promising the patient too much in the area of symptom relief—an unrealistic and undesirable goal. Most adult survivors experience genuine distress from their presenting symptomatology for weeks or even months; it is, therefore, unrealistic to seem to promise rapid alleviation of anxiety, fear, or emotional lability. Also, the loss of emotional control, which is perceived by the survivor as a serious and threatening disability, may, in fact, be a manifestation of psychological health and strength. In this instance, the loss of emotional control may actually be an indication that the survivor can give up dysfunctional mechanisms used to cope with stress and that he or she can substitute more functional coping patterns that do not require emotional distancing or dissociation. Although the clinician can and should tell the survivor that his or her loss of control may be a healthy sign, it is unrealistic to expect that the patient will view his or her emotional lability as anything but a disaster at this stage of treatment. Understanding and accepting that exercising control may involve giving up control and being able to practice giving up control usually do not occur for adult survivors until a much later stage of treatment.

On the other side of the narrow path that the clinician must tread is the danger of seeming not to understand or seeming to minimize the patient's very real distress and fear that the acute symptomatology is a signal that the patient will permanently lose control and become psychotic, nonproductive, or totally helpless. Adult survivors who manifest a late presentation pattern are genuinely terrified of this. The clinician can and should be reassuring and explanatory about his or her clinical impression that the patient is not crazy, not helpless, and only temporarily nonproductive. Again, this process is only beginning. The clinical reassurance can begin in an individual therapy session and be supplemented by patient education (giving the patient articles to read, for example). The most credible reassurance regarding these matters, however, will come not from the clinician in an individual therapy session, but from the survivor's peers in group therapy sessions.

We recommend the following guidelines for the initial clinical interventions with adult survivors who manifest a late presentation pattern.

Encourage the Survivor to Describe the Sexual Abuse

This will be difficult for some patients, but it should be undertaken immediately in all cases. When patients tell the clinician that they cannot remember the abuse clearly or that they are not sure whether it really occurred, or if they made it up, or they dreamed it, it is always helpful to encourage them to begin by describing where (in what location) the abuse (or the fantasy or the dream) occurred. The clinician can then help by offering to draw, at the patient's direction, the scene where the events occurred. If the clinician draws a simple floor plan of the location, the most frightened patient can usually help fill in details such as location of rooms, location of furniture in rooms, the whereabouts of people in the diagram, and so forth.

It is very important for the clinician to demonstrate by gentle persistence and firmness that he or she is determined to help the client to remember and verbalize the facts of the childhood sexual abuse. Reluctance to do so on the part of the clinician will immediately be noted by the patient, and the patient's fear of the consequences of describing the abuse (e.g., going crazy, getting out of control, becoming homicidal or suicidal) will thereby be intensified. Also (see the next section on questions asked by adult survivors), failure to discuss the sexual abuse early in treatment may result in a disastrous power struggle between the clinician and the patient. Again, as stated in a previous section, we believe that learning the facts of the sexual abuse is an essential first step toward determining the survivor's perception of the meaning to him or her of having participated in the sexual abuse behavior. Lastly, the best way to obtain direct control over events that are part of one's own life history is to talk about them with someone else. Most adult survivors need the experience of discovering that they can tell a clinician about the abuse in an individual session before they can speak about it in a group therapy session. One woman survivor who had not been able to remember all the details of her abuse and who was extremely fearful of becoming psychotic asked in a group therapy session, "What if it's too horrible to remember?" The response of one of the therapists was, "It is horrible, I'm sure. I'm also sure that if you're willing to remember it, we will be here to support and help you in whatever way we can. And that it won't literally kill you; the memory won't kill you. As long as you let us help, it also won't make you schizophrenic."

This was a powerful therapeutic intervention because it validated the patient's fear of remembering the abuse and describing her memory, while at the same time reminding her that she had the strength to endure whatever discomfort she might experience in the remembering and the telling. At the same time, the clinician reminded the patient that the group could support and help her this time (unlike her childhood experience of having to endure the abuse alone). Lastly, the therapist affirmed that the patient was in control, even as she was being encouraged to give up control by remembering and verbalizing the memory aloud to her peers. It is noteworthy that the therapist's willingness to articulate the patient's fears that the memory might kill her or make her schizophrenic had the effect of concretizing those fears and making it possible for the patient to address them directly. This is an excellent example of a therapeutic intervention that addresses telling about one's sexual abuse experience because it illustrates the enormous power of the untold secret and the power to be gained by the patient if she chooses to share the secret, especially in a group therapy session. This woman was able to talk much more openly about her sexual victimization in the next session.

Demonstrate Limit Setting and Consistency

The clinician should be a role model for the patient in most ways, but limit setting and consistency are extremely important, especially in the initial sessions. This means that the clinician must demonstrate that she or he will help the patient to maintain limits and boundaries. For example, the clinician, in encouraging the patient to talk about the sexual victimization, must also set limits on how long this material will be discussed. It is wise to avoid encouraging or allowing the patient to tell too many details or about too many incidents in one session. Although the patient who spills out details of the abuse for more than an hour may initially feel relieved, she or he is likely to be frightened later on by how much was disclosed at one time and react by closing down or refusing to return because she or he now fears future loss of control in the clinician's presence. Clinicians who have been trained to believe that a patient who tells all is performing well in psychotherapy may have to practice saying, "I want you to stop now. Don't tell me about any more of this today. We'll work on it again in your next visit." Patients need this structure and limit setting by the clinician.

Likewise, sessions should begin and end on time. Clinicians should adhere to the therapy contract as negotiated (see below), although it is also appropriate to reexamine the therapy contract at regular and preset intervals. Clinicians should allocate time in each individual session for the patient to bring up new or ongoing concerns, but the bulk of each individual session should be allocated to work on a previously agreed upon topic. Again, it is up to the clinician to identify appropriate limits, set them with the patient's agreement and cooperation, and then adhere to them consistently.

Negotiate a Limited Therapy Contract

We tell patients at the outset that we believe long-term individual therapy is of limited value in working on adult survivor issues. Instead, we tell patients that we believe unresolved emotional trauma resulting from childhood sexual abuse is best addressed in sequential time-limited cycles of peer group therapy. Couples therapy, family therapy, or individual therapy can then be valuable adjuncts for the clinician who uses peer group therapy to help adult survivors in their recovery process.

Accordingly, we usually tell adult survivors that we will limit individual therapy to between six and twelve sessions with specific goals, usually including a clinical evaluation and work on an initially negotiated request. After this limited individual therapy contract is fulfilled, we urge adult survivors to join a cycle of peer group therapy. If they do so, we tell them that we will see them for individual and/or family or couples therapy as an adjunct to group therapy, but only if they participate in the group therapy.

We deliberately limit our contract for individual therapy with adult survivors because we believe that there are barriers that prevent these patients from working effectively on unresolved emotional trauma secondary to childhood sexual abuse in long-term individual therapy. The adult survivor is likely to become very attached to and dependent on a clinician who is kind and empathic when she or he is acutely distressed. It is also likely, however, that the patient will soon erect the same type of barrier to intimacy that she or he uses to cope with the threatening aspects of intimacy in his or her interpersonal relationships. This phenomenon and appropriate clinical interventions are more fully described in the next section of this chapter. Suffice to say at this point that in our experience, by the fifth or sixth individual session, most adult survivors are displaying the distancing and withholding behaviors that were helpful to them when they were children but have become dysfunctional in adulthood. The intimacy of the one-on-

one clinical relationship is probably triggering the distancing behaviors at this stage. One clinical approach is simply to continue with individual therapy and utilize conventional methods of coping with resistance. This is risky, however, because many patients flee from therapy soon after reaching this stage, and many other patients develop extreme dependency on the clinician and enter into years of long-term individual therapy. We believe it is more productive and less risky to utilize time-limited peer group therapy as a primary modality, using individual and family therapy as an adjunct to group therapy as previously mentioned. This requires the therapy contracts delineated above.

Elicit (and Negotiate) a Request; Make and Keep Promises

We described the utilization of the "customer approach" with adult survivors earlier in this chapter. This involves having the clinician and client identify a specific task or area on which the patient wishes to work and that the clinician believes she or he can ethically and realistically address with the patient. It should involve a specific and concrete task that the clinician believes is in some way connected to the patient's treatment needs and that the patient views as something he or she wishes to accomplish. A request is thus symbolically made by the patient: He or she is saying to the clinician, "I ask for your help in doing this." The negotiation regarding the identity of the request is also a symbolic interaction: The clinician is creating an opportunity to make a promise that she or he knows will be kept. That is to say, the clinician intends to keep his or her promise to the patient that they will work on this task or area of concern together. In subsequent sessions, they may renegotiate the original request or identify and negotiate additional requests that the patient may wish to address. The clinician's responsibility is very clear, however: He or she must be task-oriented in the overall clinical approach to the adult survivor. It is the clinician's responsibility to see to it that they do, in fact, address the patient's request(s) as negotiated in the therapy sessions and that they stay on task in a consistent and predictable fashion.

The inherent difficulties in adhering to a negotiated plan to address a specific area or task at the request of the patient are obvious. Even when this process genuinely "feels like help" to the patient, the survivor is likely to be anxious or otherwise symptomatic, and it will probably be very difficult for him or her to stay focused on a specific task, especially if they begin to discuss past or present issues that provoke anxiety or are problematic.

Agreeing to work on a specific request carries with it an implicit promise that also relates to limit setting. By agreeing to work on something specific, the clinician is making a promise to focus on certain areas and limit the attention paid to others. Keeping such a promise may seem unnecessary. Suppose, for instance, the patient brings a crisis to the clinician, the apparent importance of which seems to supersede the importance of the original request. This is, of course, a matter of individual clinical judgment. We urge clinicians to remember, however, that breaking any promise, however seemingly innocuous, is a serious matter. We therefore encourage that the negotiated requests and the corresponding promises be finite, realistic, and time-limited; within these limits they should be adhered to as consistently as possible.

A good rule of thumb is to give patients concrete representations of promises that were kept by the clinician, with an explicit verbal reminder of what has transpired. If the clinician promises to make a telephone call for the patient, a brief written memorandum of the call should be given to the patient. If the clinician promises to give the patient a receipt or statement of services or an informational article, it is imperative that she or he keep the promise and remind the patient that the promise is being kept. Likewise, a promise to limit individual therapy to ten sessions or to work on a particular request should be kept as well. The associations between promise keeping, limit setting, and contract negotiation are, we think, obvious. Not so obvious, perhaps, is the slow and steady trust building that occurs as a result of these behaviors.

Be Honest with Adult Survivors and Do Not Require Them to Trust You

It is, perhaps, unnecessary and redundant to state that honesty and openness are essential elements of trust building, which is part of the recovery process. Most clinicians have been trained to look for evidence that they are trusted by clients almost immediately. At the same time, clinicians have often been trained to put the best face possible on unpleasant situations and to withhold or minimize matters that may disturb their patients. We respectfully suggest that it is unrealistic for clinicians to expect adult survivors of child sexual abuse to take care of clinicians by saying early and often, "I trust you." Instead, it is likely to be far more realistic for the clinician to say to the patient, "It will probably be a long time, if ever, before you feel as if you can trust me (or the other people in the group). That's okay. It's even okay if you never trust us. It isn't necessary that you trust us. It is only necessary that we all behave in a trustworthy fashion."

The implicit message is that the clinician will behave responsibly, will be accountable, and will expect the same of the patient. Absolute honesty in conjunction with adhering to limits and contracts and keeping promises are the essential elements of responsibility and accountability, which are, in turn, the key ingredients of trustworthiness. What the clinician is really demonstrating here is that human beings can never completely control another human being's thoughts, emotions, or behaviors. Humans can control only their own thoughts, emotions, and behaviors. It is up to the clinician to create a healing atmosphere in which the patient can acquire enough confidence to be honest and open and to trust others. We believe that the healing atmosphere that permits the patient to accomplish the above is created by clinicians who display the same attributes.

Accordingly, clinicians would be well advised to admit that they do not know the answer to a particular question or that they do not know what the outcome of a given situation or set of circumstances will be. When a patient says, "I'm so sad because I'll never have a chance, now that my mother is dead, to tell her that I love her," the clinician should suppress the inclination to be reassuring. A typical response from a clinician to the above lament might be, "That's okay, Marilyn. You showed your mother that you loved her in lots of other ways before she died." Such a response by the clinician may be factually true, but it would nevertheless be dissonant with the patient's emotion in this context and, therefore, would be challenging the validity of her emotion, as well as challenging the validity of the patient's internal reality. We would recommend that the clinician instead respond with an honest recognition of the patient's internal reality, followed by an empowering observation. For example, the clinician might say, "That's right, Marilyn, you are sad about that right now, and you will know how long it will be necessary for you to feel sad. When you are ready to feel good about some of the aspects of your relationship with your mother, you'll know that also." The latter intervention affirms the patient's sadness and implies that sadness is permissible, tolerable, and under the patient's complete control. It empowers the patient by reminding her that she and she alone can choose to stop feeling sad and that the choice is completely and solely hers to make. If she chooses to be sad forever, she must take responsibility for that choice (and for being sad for the rest of her life) when it is within her control to give up being sad and experience other emotions as well. Long-term responsibility for one's choices and emotions is surprisingly difficult for many adult survivors to assume.

In conclusion, we wish to share the observation that insight-oriented psychotherapy, by itself, is not likely to help many adult survivors. Instead, they need to understand the basis for their confusion, powerlessness, anger, and sense of being overwhelmed and out of control, in the context of also knowing, by experience, that they are capable of different, more functional, less costly, and less destructive responses to problems in their current lives. To be effective, treatment for the adult survivor must include opportunities to practice more functional and effective responses and coping mechanisms. Honesty and accountability require clinicians to tell adult survivors that they can learn and practice more functional responses most effectively in a peer group therapy setting.

In the next section, we will discuss the themes inherent in questions most commonly raised by adult survivors during the course of their treatment, as well as the therapeutic interventions that we believe constitute an effective response.

Common Questions and Themes Raised by Adult Survivors

We find that adult survivors of child sexual abuse who come to treatment within an early or a late presentation pattern present five recurring questions and themes. The therapeutic interventions described in response to these questions are the cornerstones of our clinical approach to adult survivors. The questions are as follows:

1. Why did I go along?
2. What really happened to me?
3. Why did I keep the secret?
4. Am I damaged for life?
5. Why is it so hard for me to stay connected to others?

We plan to address each question and its inherent themes on an individual basis. They are, however, closely interconnected, so the response and therapeutic interventions for each will likely overlap frequently with the others.

Why Did I Go Along?

Inherent in this question are the following underlying questions: Why me? Why was I selected? Did I do something to invite the abuse? Was it really all my fault that it began in the first place? Why didn't I do something to stop it in the beginning? Why didn't I do something to prevent it from happening?

All of the above questions can be answered cognitively. The clinician in individual therapy and the patient's peers in group therapy can make cognitive responses that address the blame, responsibility, and consequences of noncompliance for all of the above queries. They can tell the survivor, "You were selected because you were handy and available—no other reason. It was the abuser's choice to begin the abuse, to continue it, and to repeat it. In adult-child sexual interactions, the adult always bears the total responsibility for what occurred—never the child. The abuse resulted from a problem that was inherent in the abuser, not in you."

A further cognitive response might be: "You cooperated with engagement strategies used by the abuser. You went along because the engagement strategies were as effective as they usually are, and they worked with you as they do with most children. You are not to blame for your cooperation. To cooperate was appropriate and expected under the circumstances. It is normal and usual for a child to want to receive whatever benefits or positive things are offered by the abuser in exchange for sexual favors. Also, you probably had good and sufficient reason to be afraid of what might have occurred if you had not cooperated.

Yet another cognitive response to these questions might be: "It is not a child's responsibility to set limits on adults. If an adult chose to break the law and to exploit you, a child, sexually, that was the adult's choice, not yours. You were not in charge; the adult was. It would not be realistic to expect that you, as a child, could stop or prevent the abuse from occurring. You were not old enough, tall enough, strong enough, wise enough—because you were still a child. And that's okay."

As mentioned earlier in this chapter, a set of cognitive responses to the question "Why did I go along?" is an appropriate intervention to use with the adult survivor. The only difficulty is that these cognitive responses do not seem to assist the adult survivor with his or her dysphoric reactions to the question. Survivors tell us, "I feel ashamed. I feel guilty. I feel as if I were (am) to blame." Cognitive challenges by one's peers in group therapy have sometimes helped the adult survivor to feel less ashamed about his or her cooperation with the abuser. But we have not yet observed that adult survivors have reported that they feel less guilty about their cooperation with the abuser after they have received cognitive challenges about the appropriateness of their guilt from peers or from the clinician.

Accordingly, we have concluded that feeling guilty about the abuse (and about cooperating with the abuser) serves both a protective and a helpful function for the adult survivor. Lamb has pointed out that being told "You are not to blame" is a challenge to the child victim's sense of power and control (Lamb 1986, 305). We agree that, for many adult survivors, feeling guilty about their cooperation with the abuser has appeared to have an integral connection with the coping mechanisms that they used to deal with their emotions at the time the abuse was taking place. For most child victims, some form of denial or dissociation is the internal response while the sexual victimization is taking place. In addition to all the forms of denial and dissociation discussed below ("Why Did I Keep the Secret?"), there is yet another form of denial, which we call *rewriting the script*. This process is likely to be utilized by a child victim of repeated sexual abuse. The process is as follows.

Many child victims react to the sexual behavior by telling themselves, "This is not happening to me; this is happening to someone else." All children pass through a stage of development in which they believe they are omnipotent. Not only are they the center of the universe, but they are in complete control of themselves and their environment. They fantasize that they are big and all-powerful and can do whatever they wish. In these fantasies, they are heroic superfigures who are omnipotent. Invariably, the fantasy of omnipotence is challenged by external reality; for example, the child's mother says, "You can't have your dessert because you didn't eat your vegetables." A child might react to this challenge by telling himself or herself, "I didn't really want dessert tonight; I don't like strawberry shortcake." Thus, the fantasy of being powerful and in control is preserved: The child did not eat strawberry shortcake that day, not as a result of deprivation or punishment by the mother, but because he or she did not want strawberry shortcake. The child can comfort himself or herself by saying, in effect, "I'm not being punished at all. Nothing is being taken away because I didn't want the strawberry shortcake in the first place!" This internal process of rewriting the script may be a frequent reaction to stress or deprivation for some children.

For the child victim of sexual abuse, rewriting the script can have a powerful protective function. Imagine the little girl whose father creeps into her bedroom on some nights and engages in various sexual acts with her under cover of darkness when others in the home are asleep. Perhaps the child can perceive no pattern to the episodes of abuse. The little girl may lie awake, night after night, wondering, "Will he come tonight? Will tonight be the night? Will he want me to do the same things we did the last time? What will happen to me tonight?" Imagine the increasing anxiety that she may experience. How can she comfort herself? One method, described by adult survivors, is for the child to tell herself, "If he *does* come tonight, it will be because I *wanted* him to come. If he comes, it will be because it was *my* idea, not his. I am in charge—not him. If it happens, it must be because I *want* it to happen!"

This process of rewriting the script by fantasizing that you are in charge, that a stressful event occurs because you wanted it to occur, also requires that the person revise his or her experience of the anticipated event itself. This means, in turn, that the person must rewrite the script with regard to his or her experience of a previous event. The child who successfully persuaded himself that he did not want the strawberry shortcake was able to do so by saying, "I don't like strawberry shortcake. The last time I had strawberry shortcake, it didn't taste very good anyway." The little girl who is successful in persuading herself that, if her father abuses her tonight, it was because she wanted the abuse to occur is also required to revise her previous experience of sexual victimization. She also may need to tell herself,

"It didn't feel so bad (scary, uncomfortable, overwhelming). It was okay. It might have felt good."

Such distortions of a previously dysphoric experience are essential to rewriting the script successfully in order to allay anxiety. It would be very difficult for a child to persuade herself that she wants an event (over which in reality she has no control) to occur if she perceives that event or activity in a completely negative fashion. She may comfort herself further by saying to herself, "If he comes into my bedroom tonight, it will be because I *wanted* him to come. I want him to come because sometimes it feels good. Tonight, if he comes, it will feel good. Last time, it didn't feel so bad; some of it felt good last time."

Many of the adult survivors we have seen have described a step-by-step process of rewriting the script very similar to that described above. They have told us that it was a powerful way for them to allay anxiety and to calm and comfort themselves. Unfortunately, this coping mechanism is exceedingly costly because it requires a great deal of psychic energy to distort one's internal and external reality. It is also unfortunate that rewriting the script in this fashion is consonant with a societal bias that victims of sexual abuse really are at fault if they permit the abuse to occur. Thus, this particular coping mechanism, used by many child victims into adulthood, is likely to be reinforced over time by external reality. If a person grows up in a society in which the victims are blamed when abuse occurs, he or she is now receiving external reinforcement of the fantasy that dictated that he or she was really in control all along and that the abuse was wished for or even precipitated by the victim.

If rewriting the script in this fashion occurs frequently (and we believe that it does), then feeling guilty, responsible, and blameworthy as an adult, for being the victim of abuse as a child, may actually reflect a long-established coping mechanism. In this context, it can be devastating for an adult survivor to have his or her guilty feelings about the abuse challenged by others. The adult survivor who receives a message from clinicians and peers that he or she should not feel guilty is, in effect, being told, "You are wrong, bad, and inappropriate. You have to give up your guilt." We find that adult survivors invariably react with alarm and distress when they are challenged in this way. And no wonder! Within this perspective, they are being asked to give up a process that helped them allay anxiety and feel in control for years. It is highly unrealistic to expect an adult survivor to give up any coping mechanism that has helped allay anxiety unless or until she or he has learned that there are other ways to comfort and soothe oneself in situations of stress or anxiety.

We believe that adult survivors who tell us that they feel guilty are telling us the truth. An appropriate clinical intervention is to acknowledge the emotion by saying, "That's right, you do feel guilty. Many people who were abused in childhood tell us that they feel guilty. We think that one way you will know you are better is when you are feeling less troubled by guilt." Again, this intervention is empowering for the patient because he or she receives the message, "You are in control. You are not going to be required to give anything up unless or until you are ready."

As Lamb pointed out, however, clinicians and other intervenors in child sexual abuse cases are likely to do the opposite (Lamb 1986, 304). Child victims and adult survivors are frequently instructed that they were not to blame for the abuse and implicitly or explicitly told that they should not feel guilty. Ironically, many adult survivors report that they are consumed by guilt, not just with regard to the sexual abuse, but also in many other areas of their lives and interpersonal relationships.

One intervention that has been helpful for patients who were burdened by guilt is to encourage them to make a list of everything in their lives dating back to the time of the sexual abuse about which they feel guilty. The survivor is then encouraged to undertake an expiatory exercise for every item on the list that he or she and the clinician (or members of a peer therapy group) would agree is "legitimate guilt." This frequently involves having the survivor identify a direct or symbolic exercise to make up for or pay back the guilt. For example, it is not unusual for a patient to grieve over something that he or she did to hurt another person or a family member. In this exercise, the patient may be encouraged to apologize to the other person, either directly or by letter or telephone. If it would be problematic for the other person to receive the apology (or if the other person is dead), the letter of apology could be written but not sent. Alternatively, the adult survivor could speak to the other person in a role-playing exercise in a peer group therapy session.

How does one decide what (if anything) constitutes "legitimate guilt" for the adult survivor? The patient and his or her peers in group therapy (or the patient and the clinician) can examine together the specific things about which the survivor feels guilty and assign them to one of two categories: *things most people would feel guilty about* (legitimate guilt) and *things most people would not feel guilty about* (inappropriate guilt). Matters such as taking advantage of or hurting another person would be classified as legitimate guilt. For example, the survivor may remember that he or she took unfair advantage of a sibling at the time the sexual abuse was occurring. Or a woman who was sexually abused by her father might remember that she was deliberately spiteful to her mother during the period of sexual abuse. By contrast, a survivor might describe intensely guilty feelings related to disruption of the entire family at the time of the disclosure of the sexual abuse. The latter issue, after negotiation and discussion, would likely be classified by one's peers as inappropriate guilt—i.e., it was not the survivor's fault that family disruption occurred after the sexual abuse was disclosed.

The survivor and his or her peers would likely agree, however, after negotiation and discussion, that most people would feel guilty about planful injury to another person and consign actions such as taking unfair advantage of a sibling or being deliberately spiteful toward one's mother to the category of legitimate guilt.

Careful examination of everything the survivor can remember feeling guilty about during the time the sexual abuse was occurring is a powerful inducement to identify specifics of one's guilty feelings. This process can help the survivor focus as much as possible on the exact components of what is likely to have been a global and dysphoric (some might say neurotic) sense of blameworthiness. Likewise, the process of telling others about specific actions that make one feel guilty and then negotiating with one's peers about whether a particular action belongs in a legitimate guilt category or an inappropriate guilt category is also helpful. The survivor has, thereby, had the experience of telling others about guilty feelings related to specific actions and receiving feedback from others about whether they would feel guilty about similar actions and experiences. Most patients tell us that they react to this entire process by feeling supported rather than blamed. We speculate that receiving affirmation from one's peers that they, too, would probably feel guilty if they themselves had taken similar actions is empowering. It reminds the patient that he or she is not a totally helpless child but is an adult who can take responsibility for his or her own behaviors and accept accountability for past, present, and future actions.

Expiatory exercises for actions or behaviors that the survivor now views as fitting within a legitimate guilt framework can range from apologizing and asking forgiveness (as previously described) to taking action to make up for past transgressions—again, either with the specific individual who was previously involved or symbolically, with or for another person. For example, one survivor chose to give special help and attention to her sister's child (the sister was dead) to make up for having taken unfair advantage of that sibling in connection with the abuse when they were children.

The entire process can be summarized as follows:

1. The survivor is first helped to identify and tell others about specific actions or behaviors about which he or she feels guilty. These behaviors date back to the time the sexual abuse was occurring.

2. The survivor then negotiates with the clinician and/or other survivors in a peer group therapy session about assigning each of the above actions or behaviors into a legitimate guilt or inappropriate guilt category.

3. Lastly, the survivor undertakes some expiatory action to make up for the actions or behaviors that all agree belong in a legitimate guilt category.

It has been our observation that the above process has been exceedingly helpful to adult survivors who are burdened by guilt. In the first place, they report to us that, as time goes by and they accomplish the expiatory exercises, they feel less and less guilty about the legitimate guilt behaviors from the past. Second, without working directly on the inappropriate guilt behaviors, the survivors report a gradual cessation of guilt regarding those matters as well. We speculate that making the guilty feelings concrete in an interactive process and then engaging in expiatory exercises that are also interactive are important for the survivor. The interactive aspects of all the components of the process force the patient to share the burden of guilt that he or she has been experiencing and to demonstrate acceptance of accountability. The net effect seems to be that the survivor eventually is able to forgive himself or herself, not only for real transgressions, but also for going along and cooperating with the sexual abuse behavior. We believe that this approach can be effective, since the essence of the question "Why did I go along?" is "How can I be forgiven (or forgive myself) for cooperating with the abuser?"

What Really Happened to Me?

This is a recurring question and theme for adult survivors of child sexual abuse. The question can be restated in a variety of ways: Was I really abused, or did I just fantasize it, dream it, or make it up? Was the sexual behavior really abuse, or was it something else? Do I remember everything that happened (with regard to the abuse), or are there more underlying memories waiting to be revealed?"

The above questions all relate to the facts of the sexual abuse: the identity of the abuser(s), the place(s) where the abuse occurred, the type of sexual acts that were performed, the number and frequency of the episodes of abuse, when it started, when it stopped, and so forth. But there are other underlying questions: "Could I be crazy? Is it possible that it never occurred at all? What does it mean if the abuse did happen—about me, about the abuser, about people who knew us both and did or did not realize that the abuse was occurring and did or did not protect me?" This latter series of questions addresses the meaning underlying the facts of the memories of the abuse. The survivor is in a no-win situation here. If one concludes that the abuse did not occur or that the sexual behaviors were not, in fact, abusive, then one is in the position of questioning one's own mental competency and the validity and reality of the memories. Alternatively, if one does believe that the abuse occurred and that the memories are real and valid, then the survivor is forced to define himself or herself within the framework of being a person to whom abuse occurred. If the abuser was someone who occupied a family role relationship vis-à-vis the survivor, then the survivor must include that fact in the definition and so adjust his or her perceptions of the meanings of those relationships.

Again, we believe that it is necessary for an adult who was sexually abused in childhood to be able to demonstrate that he or she can recall the details of the sexual abuse and articulate them to others. Patients frequently dread this process. They are likely to tell us that they fear they will be overcome with rage or will become psychotic if they fully remember and talk about their sexual abuse experiences. Other patients tell us that they have fully recalled the details of their sexual abuse experiences but that they have not fully experienced an emotional reaction to the memories of the abuse. Still other patients report that they are unable to recall details of their sexual abuse experiences and that they sometimes doubt that the abuse ever occurred.

All of the above situations represent different elaborations of the same coping mechanisms—denial and dissociation. These coping mechanisms, which were originally utilized by the survivor to avoid being overwhelmed by the frighteningly intense emotions, continue to be used by the survivor as an adult. Unfortunately, denial and dissociation are coping mechanisms that become increasingly costly with regard to the amount of psychic energy they require when utilized over time. Also, denial and dissociation, when overused as coping mechanisms, tend to be triggered by minimal cues or stimuli as time goes by. As a result, a coping mechanism that, in effect, gobbles up psychic energy is frequently being invoked when the survivor is under stress. Not surprisingly, the patient becomes exhausted and emotionally depleted. The coping mechanism that originally protected the child is now undermining and problematic for the adult.

For example, survivors who fear that they will become psychotic or consumed with rage if they recall and talk about the abuse are persons who have invested an enormous amount of energy in suppressing their fear of what really happened to them. Instead, they actively fear what will happen if they remember what really happened to them. It is poignant to consider the facts of this situation: Since the childhood sexual abuse really did occur, it is a fait accompli—over and done with. Yet, paradoxically, the adult survivor has channeled energy into fearing what will happen if he or she remembers the sexual abuse experiences and talks about what really did occur. It is clear that not being able to remember these details meets a need for protection. And yet, we may ask, protection from what, if the abuse really occurred? The obvious answer is that the memory lapse helps the survivor avoid facing what it really means to him or her to be a person who had such experiences in childhood. If the survivor cannot remember the abusive experiences clearly enough to be sure they actually occurred, then he or she cannot be held accountable for them. It is as if, on one level, the sexual abuse had no meaning, as if it were not real.

The essence of the question "What really happened to me?" is "Can I believe that I really was sexually abused and still accept (and love) myself as a person?" We believe that many adult survivors vacillate between being certain that the memories of the childhood sexual abuse experiences are real and rejecting the reality of the memories because they are too threatening. If they embrace the reality of the memories, they must then grapple with their own fear that they were severely damaged by the abuse. One woman said, "For years, I believed that if I really was abused, I must be evil and contaminated." If they doubt the reality of the memories, however, they must somehow cope with the fear that they are not mentally competent. Another survivor remarked, "I feel like I have to choose between being contaminated (if the abuse really occurred) and being crazy (if it did not). I don't like either choice."

Many adult survivors who have a late presentation pattern have suppressed the memories of their sexual abuse for decades. We believe that the appropriate therapeutic intervention is to help the survivor talk to others about the abuse. A simple technique to help the person begin to talk about the sexual victimization is to ask him or her to say where the abuse occurred. If the person responds by saying that he or she is not sure whether the memory is a memory, a dream, or a fantasy, we would recommend that the clinician persist by asking, "Whatever it may be (memory, dream, or fantasy), where are you (in what location)?" As soon as the location is identified, the clinician can then ask the survivor to describe the details of the location (house, apartment, car, backyard, and so forth). It may be helpful for the clinician to assist the patient to draw a floor map of the scene. This technique allows the patient to concretize the memory of the sexual abuse itself in a less threatening manner because she or he is demonstrating a capacity to remember and describe the external details or the context in which the abuse took place.

In a peer group therapy setting, other survivors can help the patient who is telling about his or her abuse experiences by offering support (e.g., "You're doing a good job. It was hard for me to do this also.") and by asking direct questions about the context (e.g., "Where were you in the house? Who else was in the room with you? What were you doing before the abuse began?").

We find that it is usually preferable to apply gentle and persistent pressure, if necessary, to help the patient to begin to describe the abuse very early in individual and group therapy. We find that the process of telling the story is empowering for the patient and that the process of successfully resisting the invitation or opportunity to tell the story is counterproductive. The longer the patient waits to tell about the sexual abuse, the more fearful he or she is likely to become of the process of sharing the information. It also may create an ongoing power struggle between the clinician and the patient or between the patient and his or her peers (see the following section, "Why Did I Keep the Secret?").

We think that the process of telling others about a memory makes the memory more real for the individual who does the telling. This is a necessary stage of giving up denial and dissociation as coping mechanisms. The sexually abused child usually protects himself or herself from fear, anger, disgust, or the overwhelming physiological sensory responses that a child is too young to integrate by some type of denial or dissociation. The denial may take the form of saying, "This isn't abuse; it's just a game" or "This isn't abuse; it's sex education." Or the denial may take the form of saying, "This isn't happening to me; it's happening to somebody else!" Sometimes the denial may take the form of rewriting the script (see the previous section, "Why Did I Go Along?").

Dissociation is part of the continuum of denial. The sexually abused child may separate from his or her emotional response to the abuse by saying, "I'm not here on the bed; I'm in a corner of the room up near the ceiling watching myself on the bed." Or the dissociation may take the form of choosing to turn off the sensory responses to the sexual abuse by causing the affected body parts to become numb. Unfortunately, dissociation tends quickly to become automatic and to be triggered by minimal cues. As Gelinas (1983, 326) pointed out, when dissociation is used frequently as a coping mechanism, it is not unusual for the patient to experience both detachment and depersonalization. When dissociation is used frequently, it is not unusual for the survivor also to experience sensory disturbances that border on hallucinatory experiences. Many adult survivors of child sexual abuse fear that they may be psychotic because of the effects of the dissociation and depersonalization now being triggered by everyday life experiences that remind them of their sexual victimization.

Nevertheless, treatment of the adult survivor who uses dissociation as a contemporary coping mechanism includes clinical interventions that are planned to help the patient "live through" experiencing the fear and dysphoria associated with remembering and talking about their sexual abuse. Accordingly, clinicians must plan, in individual and group therapy, to create opportunities for patients to talk about what happened to them. Techniques to accomplish this goal include diagramming the scene while the patient describes it, role-playing some aspect of the abuse situation, or requesting one group member to be responsible for describing the feelings experienced by another patient while the second patient describes the "facts" of his or her abuse. The second patient often will remain detached as he or she describes the sexual victimization that occurred in his or her own life but still will be able to identify with the feelings of another patient when *that* person's sexual abuse is described. For example, Sheila may describe her own abuse in a calm, emotionless voice. She then may become angry, distraught, or tearful if she is asked to describe the feelings of another group member, Sharon, as Sharon's victimization is related. Taking the step of feeling for another person is often essential to the process of learning to experience your own feelings that are connected to or arise from previous sexual abuse occurrences.

Many patients report that participating in exercises that help them remember details of past sexual abuse also seems to stimulate nightmares, flashbacks, and other frightening experiences. This can be both painful and terrifying. Patients should be informed that flashbacks or nightmares are likely to occur and are not a sign that the person is becoming psychotic or losing control. Instead, these phenomena should alert clinicians to the probability that the patient is making progress and is better able to connect with the disturbing memories.

We believe that talking about what really happened and living through long-suppressed emotions associated with the sexual victimization is an essential early step for the survivor. He or she may then move toward discarding coping mechanisms that also interfere with the person's capacity to establish and maintain intimate relationships with others. The adult survivor may begin to notice an additional benefit as treatment progresses. The survivor is likely to discover that he or she has made an enormous investment of psychic energy in using dissociation and denial as first-line coping mechanisms for the routine stresses of everyday life. It can be a very freeing experience to discover that one does not have to spend a lifetime suppressing memories of childhood sexual victimization. It is also enabling and empowering to discover that the fatiguing business of using the energy-costly coping mechanisms of dissociation and denial is no longer necessary when the survivor discovers that the meaning of being a victim of sexual abuse in childhood is not that one is "damaged for life" (see below). He or she can then summon the courage to engage in more satisfying interpersonal relationships, as well as the energy required to learn and practice the necessary skills to maintain intimate relationships with others.

Why Did I Keep the Secret?

Restatements of the above question would include, "Why did I permit the abuse to continue?" or "Why did I conceal something important from my parents or caretakers?" or "Did I not tell because I really wanted the abuse to continue?" Adult survivors also want to know the following: "Must I tell others now?" and "What will I lose if I do so?"

Most perpetrators enjoin child victims not to tell others about the sexual abuse. Most child victims cooperate with secrecy strategies just as they cooperated with engagement strategies. A usual scenario is that the child victim does not disclose the fact that sexual abuse has occurred, or is occurring, for weeks, months, or years. Some do not tell others until after they have reached adulthood. Some never tell anyone.

We believe that adult survivors are frequently in conflict regarding secret keeping, especially as it refers to their own sexual victimization. On the one hand, telling the secret might assist them in feeling less lonely and in obtaining help for a variety of problems. On the other hand, disclosure of the secret that a person was sexually abused in childhood may leave the survivor feeling vulnerable and out of control. Anticipating feeling vulnerable or out of control can be very problematic for the adult survivor and may be a reason for the indefinite postponement of telling others.

Karpel (1980, 297) points out that secrets are about facts and that a person who knows the facts (the secret holder) that affect someone else who does not know the facts (the unaware) places the secret holder in a power position over the unaware. In other words, knowing that one's father is sexually abusing one puts the secret holder in a dominant power position over one's mother (if she does not know that the abuse is taking place). Karpel also points out that secrets within a family have an internal tension attached to them and that they are inherently unstable: that is, the greater the significance of the facts of the secret (and the greater the power accrued to the secret holder), the more energy is required to keep the secret. This is because the ultimate exercise of this power is to tell the facts of the secret and catch the unaware when he or she is off balance, vulnerable, or simply unprepared to be surprised (or perhaps dismayed).

The clinical perspective on the question "Why did I keep the secret?" is different with regard to disclosing the abuse while one is still a child, as opposed to disclosing after one has become an adult. Children keep the secret of being sexually abused by an adult or by an older child because they cooperate with the secrecy strategies used by the abuser and because they fear the consequences of disclosing. As adults, they tend to feel guilty about keeping their sexual abuse a secret for some of the same reasons they feel guilty about having been selected as victims of sexual abuse in the first place. Clinicians should be aware that keeping the sexual abuse a secret from others may also be part of rewriting the script for the child, and as such is a coping mechanism that helps the patient feel more in control while the abuse is going on. A child might say, "If I tell someone, it will be because I want it to stop. But if the abuse continues, it will be because I wanted it to continue." The wishful or magical thinking that is so characteristic (from a developmental perspective) of young children comes into play once again. Clinical approaches to this aspect of the secret keeping are similar to those previously discussed under "Why did I go along?" Cognitive challenges by one's peers— e.g., "What would have happened to you as a child if you had told and were not believed?"—may be helpful. In addition, treatment also can address the underlying guilt issues by taking into consideration that the survivor who feels guilty about keeping the secret in childhood is, in part, hanging on to the guilt. Such guilt is still closely associated with coping mechanisms utilized to help him or her feel less overwhelmed and more in control at the present time. We suggest that the expiatory exercises that help survivors feel less guilty about things that "others would also feel guilty about" are helpful for guilt associated with keeping the secret as well.

The adult survivor's contemporary decisions regarding disclosure of his or her childhood sexual victimization also are closely related to his or her capacity to have intimate relationships with others. We have noted that survivors who are having difficulty in maintaining close relationships with others tend to be persons who utilize secrets as a barrier to intimacy. The survivor who sincerely believes that he or she is a bad, damaged, or unworthy human being is likely to try to conceal this information from others. If the other person is someone about whom he or she really cares, the survivor is likely to fear that he or she will lose the relationship altogether if the secret of the sexual abuse is known. Less obvious but also important is that the secret keeping helps the survivor feel more in control of himself or herself within the context of the relationship (see the section "Why Is It So Hard for Me to Stay Connected to Others?").

Clinicians must be aware that if they become people about whom adult survivors care, it is likely that their patients will have difficulty disclosing the facts of the childhood sexual abuse to them for all the reasons stated above. Patients fear losing valued relationships with their clinicians. They also wish to prevent their therapists from learning how "bad" and "contaminated" they really are. Most importantly, they wish to remain in control and avoid feeling emotionally overwhelmed. Consequently, it is easy for both the clinician and the patient to fall into the trap of finding other reasons (such as the patient's fear of becoming psychotic or suicidal or the reported difficulties in distinguishing between real memories and dreams) to avoid talking about the sexual victimization during therapy sessions. Once again, we wish to stress that the clinician must convey both willingness and gentle insistence that the facts of the sexual abuse be discussed. We reiterate that using the modality of peer group therapy for adult survivors of child sexual abuse is an excellent way to prevent a one-on-one struggle from occurring within the context of an individual therapy relationship. A cooperative relationship in individual therapy is, in our experience, best achieved when patients and clinicians share each other in peer group therapy, with individual therapy used as an additional resource.

Am I Damaged for Life?

This question can also be restated as "Can others tell that I was sexually abused?" or "Will I ever feel like a whole human being again?" or "Can you or others ever really care about me?" We infer that these questions are asked because the person does, in fact, feel damaged. If an adult who was sexually abused in childhood continues to wonder whether he or she is damaged, it is probably because his or her current life experiences are unsatisfying or problematic. In addition, it is likely that he or she is receiving messages from others that communicate lack of acceptance or affirmation (or so the survivor perceives).

Adult patients who manifest a pervasive and persistent sense of damage associated with unresolved childhood sexual victimization issues are a challenge to the clinician because they are often persons who are still grieving for the nurturance and protection that were not provided for them and for the appropriate play and healthy growth experiences that were denied them in the past. Unfortunately, these survivors may be escaping from a stressful and unsatisfying present-day life by seeking to recapture or even recreate those last childhood experiences. Patients may seek reparenting from clinicians at a level that is both unrealistic and undesirable.

It is, of course, very easy to view one's patient as a child who needs to be nurtured, protected, and encouraged to play. We wish to stress, however, that therapy for the adult survivor will be less risky and problematic if the clinician strives to remember that it is his or her responsibility to teach the patient to nurture, protect, and care for himself or herself. We believe that the interactional skills that can be learned in peer group therapy are essential to this process. At the same time, when peer group therapy is the primary therapy modality used for adult survivors, there is less likelihood that either the patients or clinicians will become confused about the reparenting aspects of the clinical relationship.

Escaping from the one-down position of feeling damaged can best be accomplished by learning better relational skills in one's present life. Although this may be accomplished by focusing on peer relationships (e.g., relationships with one's peers in group therapy, with one's friends, or with one's spouse or sexual partner), it is also important to come to terms with one's family-of-origin relationships. In peer group therapy, one can practice and role-play the interactions with parents and siblings in a safe and therapeutic environment. Family therapy involving one's family of origin also may be desirable. For many adult survivors, however, significant family members may be dead or inaccessible for family therapy sessions.

We hesitate to recommend a formula approach that invariably includes the requirement that adult survivors confront their abusers and/or parents or caretakers who failed to protect them. Instead, we recommend that adult survivors be helped to come to terms with their connections to these persons. Sometimes this will involve face-to-face interactions and sometimes not. We believe, however, that it is the sometimes painful duty of clinicians to remind patients that, as adults, they can never re-create or recapture the experience of receiving the nurturance or protection from their parents, which was so often denied them in childhood. We frequently work with adult survivors who grieve that lost parenting for years and seek fruitlessly to recapture it from their real parents or caretakers or from parent substitutes. Thus, we emphasize helping patients understand why they have difficulty initiating and maintaining close relationships with others in their present lives and helping them acquire and practice the relational skills required to maintain intimate relationships. Ultimately, it is reasonable to expect that patients will stop wondering whether they are damaged for life after they have experienced success in caring for and being cared for by others.

Why Is It So Hard for Me to Stay Connected to Others?

We learn the rules of relationships from our families of origin and the other persons important to us in our childhood experiences. It is these individuals who teach us how to be in this world and how to interact with it. Children learn to interact by modeling the behaviors of others and by attempting new things and noticing the consequences. The consequences for behaviors can be planned and imposed by others—for example, the rewards or punishments that a parent determines. Or consequences might result specifically from the sequence of events, as when the trial-and-error experience of hopping on one leg results in two-year-old Maggie falling face flat to the ground.

It is through the many and varied types of past experiences that we are taught the essentials of relationships. Each and every experience gives the individual information about himself or herself and about the state of the world, so to speak. The former are messages to the person about the person and contribute to the person's developing sense of "self"; the latter are messages about reality (or the external environment). Both the self and the external environment are essential to the development of all relationships, and both are particularly important to the development of intimate relationships. Intimacy requires that, at minimum, there are two individuals, each of whom can give information, nurturance, respect, and caring to the other and each of whom can receive information, nurturance, respect, and caring from the other. Intimacy requires interdependence—that is, two autonomous "selves" who can depend on the other. Therefore, intimacy requires that an individual possess a concept of himself or herself in relation to the world.

The messages received by a child who grows up in a healthy family are generally supportive and are an honest reflection of external reality. Parents in these families praise their children more than they criticize them and encourage them to explore their world with questions and seek answers. The child learns, mostly by trial and error, that "I am able, capable, and worthy. I try, ask, and explore. Sometimes I succeed, and sometimes I fail." The process of learning by trial and error is central to the development of the concept of oneself. The messages that become internalized about oneself, via the process of trying, relate directly to a person's capabilities and sense of worth. This child will grow up knowing that he or she is able in certain areas and certainly capable of trying in others. In addition, this child learns that the internal reality of thoughts, perceptions, and feelings that he or she is experiencing is a process pertinent to his or her relationship to the environment and other people. Maggie, for example, has learned that it is important to notice that the ground is not soft and cushioned. That information or perception about the nature of the ground will become part of Maggie's internal reality, which will help her to avoid future injury when she is playing.

The messages delivered to a child in a healthy family are messages of capability and permission for exploration. This is consistent over time and consistent among the three identified sources of information—internal reality (the self), external reality (the outside world), and relations between internal and external reality. Consistency in messages received from one's internal reality and external reality is required for the child to verify that his or her perceptions are accurate.

Young children are not chronologically or developmentally capable of integrating all the dissonant or discrepant information received during childhood. When a child is constantly confronted with tasks at which he or she cannot succeed, the child will experience a sense of failure and inadequacy about the tasks and about his or her ability to accomplish them. If the impossible tasks involve the child's relationships with other people, then it follows that the child's perception of himself or herself in relation to others will also be riddled with failure and inadequacy. We believe that the adult survivor was asked to perform impossible tasks in his or her childhood with respect to cooperating with interactive sexual behaviors initiated by an adult or an older child. For many, this contributed to a pervasive sense of inadequacy and failure with regard to their perceptions of how they related to others. For some, an apparent consequence has been a lifelong difficulty in tolerating and maintaining intimate relationships with others.

Case Example

Maggie was sexually abused when she was a child. The sexual abuse began when Maggie was two years old, at a time when Maggie's mom and dad argued with one another quite often. During playtime with Maggie, Dad would tumble with her while he touched, tickled, and fondled her genital area. Over the next ten years, Maggie's father engaged her in fondling of his penis, fellatio, cunnilingus, and finally simulated intercourse. At age twelve, during the second incident of simulated intercourse that Maggie can now, as an adult, recall, Maggie began to feel as though she couldn't breathe and then to gasp for air. Her father stopped what he was doing and simply watched Maggie until the gasping ceased and she appeared calm. He said nothing but left the room. Six months later, Maggie's father died in an automobile accident.

When Maggie was two years old, she enjoyed the playtime with her father; she also liked to be helpful by making her daddy smile and laugh after he and her mother had been arguing. When she was eight, Maggie would go to her room and shut the door when she heard her parents arguing. This was because it seemed that Mom would get even more angry when she and Dad laughed and played together after an argument, and though Maggie still liked to have fun with Dad, she had a "bad feeling" in her stomach when they had fun while Mom was angry. Maggie also had that "bad feeling" in her stomach whenever Dad tickled her stomach or tickled be- tween her legs, but he said that it was really a "giggly feeling" that she was experiencing and not a "bad feeling," because tickling felt good. When she was ten, her father initiated oral intercourse with Maggie two or three nights per month, while she pretended to be asleep. She never told him or anyone at the time, but that "bad feeling" sometimes made her vomit her dinner.

When she was a child, Maggie did not understand that whatever her parents were arguing about was something between them. In- stead, she received the message that she was capable of making Dad smile when he seemed unhappy, and she liked doing that. She tried often to make her parents happy, because when they were happy, she felt good inside her stomach. Sometimes she could make Dad smile simply by cooperating, simply by playing with him, by doing what he asked. All that was required was, in fact, that she act her age, which was easy, and sometimes that made Maggie's parents very happy. When her parents were not happy, Maggie did not like it, and she would attempt to make them smile or giggle with her; sometimes when her parents were unhappy, Maggie had even done something wrong, so she would say she was sorry and then try to cheer them up.

Later, when Maggie was older, she noticed that her special re- lationship with Dad was a source of irritation to Mom. Again, she reacted with age-appropriate responses. All young children are ego- centric and believe that they themselves are the center of the uni- verse. This was true for Maggie as well; she believed that it was she (Maggie) who was irritating to Mom and that there must be some- thing about her (Maggie) that needed to be different in order for Mom not to be irritated. She didn't know what exactly needed to be different, but she thought frequently that it must be something about her. She tried very hard to please Mom, but Mom would just get more irritated and tell Maggie that she should try harder.

Maggie grew up believing that she was in charge of cheering her dad when he was unhappy. She also learned that she was to blame when her mom was irritated; therefore, she should do something to make her mom feel better. Maggie also knew that no change that she made seemed to have a positive effect on Mom, and she doubted that she was smart enough to find the correct answer to the problem. After all, she didn't even know the difference between a "bad feeling" in her stomach and a "giggly feeling" (which is what Dad said it was supposed to be), so how could she ever expect to find correct answers to anything if she couldn't be smart enough even to know what she herself was feeling? Nonetheless, Maggie tried very hard.

The rules that Maggie learned about relationships were as follows:

1. Maggie was expected to focus on either her mother or her father, the two people on whom she was entirely dependent as a child. She liked it when they were happy, and when she focused all her attention on them, she could best anticipate what she should do to make them happy rather than irritable or otherwise meet their emotional needs. Thus, Maggie learned to place the focus on others in relationships.

2. Maggie did like to make her parents happy. In fact, Maggie discovered that she herself was happiest when they were happy, and she became preoccupied with the task of pleasing them. Maggie was so busy that she hardly noticed that her mother and her father did not reciprocate or attempt to anticipate Maggie's emotional needs, even though she was a child and they were adults. Maggie learned not to expect reciprocity in relationships.

3. Finally, Maggie learned that she could not trust her own reactions and her own feelings. She learned that her behavior was inadequate to satisfy those two people who were most important to her, and she deduced that she herself was inadequate. Maggie learned to doubt herself at every turn, to be insecure with herself, and to feel enormously inept.

The adult survivor of child sexual abuse was not offered clear messages that were consistent with being a child. Instead, the survivor was required as a child to receive and attempt to integrate messages about self, reality, and relationships that were much too complex and dissonant for a child to integrate. Maggie, like many child victims, was highly unlikely to be successful at understanding or changing the situation because developmentally it was impossible. The child victim's personal reaction at the time of the abuse might have been any combination of emotions and thoughts, including comfort, pleasure, fear, and confusion.

As children are inherently egocentric, each of these personal reactions is important to the child and his or her development. (The questions of "Why did I go along?" and "What really happened to me?" are especially pertinent here.) At least one of the important external messages—i.e., from the abuser—was probably that the sexual abuse behavior was acceptable or required and that the child's personal reaction did not affect the outcome or was unimportant. (If the child told the abuser about personal reactions and the abuse continued, the message was either that the child's perception was wrong or that it was unimportant, as it did not influence change.) At the same time, the child was getting additional messages from the environment; at the very least, those messages included the general expectation of honesty in relationships ("Tell mother when you hit your sister; don't hide it.") and the overt or covert demand by the abuser for secrecy about the sexual abuse. (This, of course, is especially related to the question "Why did I keep the secret?") The problem is that a child of age two, eight, or twelve is, first, cognitively unable to understand and, later, developmentally unable to integrate the meanings of the differing messages.

It is the cognitive response cycle of the child that establishes the child's understanding of (1) internal reality (self), (2) external reality (the environment of other people and things), and (3) relationships between oneself and one's environment. Since the cognitions we hold to be true about our internal and external reality are the basis for defining and establishing our pattern of relating to others, all aspects of this process are necessary as the child grows and develops. Thus, it is likely that the basis of any relational disturbance might be found in the individual's cognitions about himself or herself, about other people in the world in general, and about the connections between the internal and external reality.

The cognitive process of the sexually abused child is, therefore, at the basis of the disturbances in relationships that adult survivors frequently experience. The survivor was, as a child, confused about the thoughts and feelings that he or she had about himself or herself. The survivor also was confused, as a child, by the dissonant messages he or she received from internal and external reality. As a child, the survivor was unable cognitively to integrate or make sense of the confusing messages received about relating to the world. Consequently, the adult survivor of sexual abuse, as a child, established a pattern of relating that was based on confused cognitions.

The cognitive process by which relationship disturbances occur is diagrammed in Figure 7–1. Essentially, the diagram describes the thoughts, feelings, and reactions of the child during the incident of sexual molestation. At the time that the older person sexually abuses the child (1), there are two sources of information, internal (2) and external reality (3) and (4). The child victim's internal process of thoughts and feelings (described by survivors as fear, panic, pleasure, a flooding of physiological sensations, anger, betrayal, and confusion) or some combination of emotions is frequently intense. The external source of information is comprised of the abuser's behavior and its implications and the messages conveyed by others in the child's world: that the sexual behavior is acceptable and must be kept secret and that children should respect adults who are caretakers and be honest in relationships. The child reacts to this dissonant information but is cognitively unable to integrate it with comfort. Instead, the child is likely to experience a deep sense of inadequacy and a feeling of being overwhelmed and out of control (5).

As those feelings arise, they begin to dominate the child's perception of the event, and the child seeks avenues of escape from the feelings of being overwhelmed and out of control (6). There is no physical escape for the child during the sexual abuse, however, as the abuser is older, wiser, or bigger than the child and has, indeed, engaged the child in the sexual behavior. So the child looks for a means of escape that is not physical but rather psychological. The child learns to minimize the physical event and establishes one or a number of psychological reactions or coping mechanisms. Denial (which might be evidenced overtly as "This doesn't happen" or more subtly with memory blocking) and the various levels of dissociation are often utilized as a means of gaining control over the experience.

With repeated sexual abuse experiences or repeated attempts at successful integration (i.e., the child continues for some reason or reasons to make sense of the event), the chain of events becomes an internalized or habitual reaction. (Here is where the fourth question comes into play: "Am I damaged for life?") Whenever the child is sexually abused (touched, fondled, or engaged in intercourse), there follows immediately the confusion of the child's internal thoughts and feelings with the external (and also confusing) messages of the trusted abuser and other adults. Again, immediately following, is the child's sense of inadequacy and of being overwhelmed and out of control. This is immediately followed by a need and effort to escape from the situation, to gain control. At this point in the process, the survivor chooses to minimize the experience via development of one or more psychological coping mechanisms. Clinicians have identified that survivors frequently utilize memory blocking, denial, and dissociation as means of psychological escape from the emotional trauma of the abuse.

Eventually, the particular style of regaining control (i.e., the coping mechanism), which was generated for self-protection regarding a lack of control, becomes so well established that it no longer requires the conscious control of the individual. For the adult survivor of child sexual abuse, it is then the automatic triggering of the coping mechanism itself that seems to

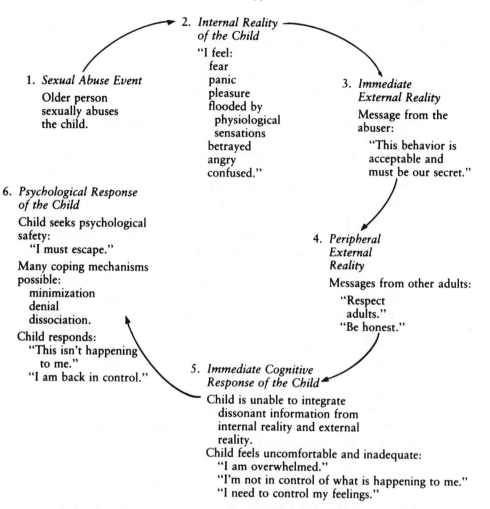

Figure 7–1. The Cognitive Response Cycle of the Sexually Abused Child

create the feeling of being out of control. Remember that the process itself involves a number of feelings and experiences that are common to everyday life, including the existence of pleasure or confusion. Commonplace feelings are likely to be interpreted by the survivor as unusual or extraordinary and are likely to initiate or trigger the entire cognitive process at any time. Sexual contact, fear, sadness, confusion, anger, betrayal, pleasure, and physiological sensations are experiences that any adult human being might have within the course of a given day. For the survivor who has learned to cope with these experiences by triggering the feeling of being overwhelmed and then by denying or dissociating from the event, life itself is likely to become a painful, out-of-control experience.

Case Example Continued

Maggie graduated from high school at the top of her class. She was generally well liked by teachers and peers, as she always seemed to be helpful and quite dependable. She belonged to several organizations during her school years and frequently volunteered herself for committees and extracurricular activities. She received a partial scholarship to a state college, where she continued to receive good grades and to be very popular. Shortly after she began teaching elementary school, Maggie married a man whom she had been dating for the past three years. He worked at a bank and was in line for a promotion, so they decided to begin a family right away. Maggie left her teaching position after one year and had her first daughter six months later. Maggie and her husband had another child (also planned, also a daughter) five years later. Her husband's career had progressed more slowly than they had hoped, but they were both satisfied with his performance and his paycheck.

Maggie was a competent wife and mother and tried always to do what seemed best for her family. In fact, she had little time for her other interests, and her husband often remarked that she had become indispensable. (His colleagues were envious because their wives did not take such good care of them.) Most of Maggie's college friends had either moved out of state or otherwise lost contact with her, but she had become popular with the other mothers in the neighborhood, and she thought they were nice people.

At age thirty-five, during a routine gynecological examination being performed by a physician whom she had known for several years, Maggie had a panic reaction. She found that she was suddenly crying, and she felt as though she could not breathe. The physician (wisely) stopped the examination, waited for Maggie to become calm, and suggested that they reschedule the appointment for another time. Maggie apologized profusely and said she would call to reschedule. She also told the doctor that she had been slightly depressed and nervous lately, and she asked for a referral to a psychotherapist.

Maggie told the therapist in an initial interview that she had been experiencing periodic difficulty with breathing for the last several months but that she had not told anyone about it. She and her husband had been having some minor marital problems for a year or two, and she did not want to worry him. She noticed that she had become increasingly nervous in the past few years, and she felt rather embarrassed by it all. She was fairly certain that the breathing problem was associated with her nervousness and that when she and her husband became close again, she would be fine. In the meantime, she was trying to get more rest so that she could be at her best for her husband. She complained of daily stomach problems and of feeling tired all the time. She also said that she was experiencing some vague and uncomfortable fears on a daily basis. When asked directly, she disclosed that in childhood she had been sexually abused by her father. In fact, she had found herself thinking about this sexual contact quite often lately and had wondered why she was thinking about it.

Maggie had been experiencing a number of symptoms (or evidencing a number of behaviors) that we would consider to be problematic to the development of healthy relationships. The rules for adequate adult-to-adult relationships in general include at minimum (1) some focus on oneself, (2) some focus on the other, and (3) some exchange, mutuality, or reciprocity between the two people who are involved. Even business relationships can be described using these rules. In a business relationship, (1) the first party has a request or a need for some item or service, (2) the second party has the item or can provide the service, and (3) the two parties negotiate some exchange for the provision of the item or the service. The adult survivor, however, has developed an entirely different set of rules for relationships based on his or her experience of being sexually abused in childhood. The adult survivor places little, if any, focus on himself or herself but focuses extreme and inordinate attention on the other person and has no expectation of reciprocity or mutuality in relationships.

Particularly since her marriage, Maggie had focused all her attention on her husband and children. She had become increasingly busy with the tasks of being a wife and mother and taking care of all the physical and emotional needs of her family. She liked it when they were happy, and she was very good at anticipating their needs and making things run smoothly. Maggie knew well how to place the entire focus on others in relationships, which inevitably prevented a focus on herself. She was so preoccupied with pleasing her family that she did not notice that there was little reciprocity in her relationships.

Maggie was a very capable caretaker and competent person, and she rarely needed help of any sort from others. The concerns and self-doubts that she did venture to express to her husband were minimized by him. He was likely to respond as though she were making a mountain out of a molehill, so she further attempted to ignore the doubts and uncertainties. She learned to keep herself busy in spite of her internal insecurity about the quality of her performance. Thus, from all outward appearances, Maggie had relationships with many people.

The truth of the matter is that Maggie extended herself toward other people and that they were the recipients of her care and attention, but they did not focus on her in return. Maggie had an abundance of lopsided relationships with others that lacked reciprocity and mutuality. She was connected to many people because she focused on them and avoided focus on herself. Maggie was not relating intimately to anyone because intimacy requires that both people receive information, nurturance, caring, and respect within a relationship.

Many adult survivors have developed patterns of relating to others that are not conducive to intimacy. In fact, many survivors have established patterns of relating that either avoid intimacy or prevent it. One method of avoiding intimacy that survivors frequently exhibit is utilizing intense emotional reactions to keep others away. For example, persistent anger often has the effect of creating distance in relationships when the other person might be seeking closeness. Depression, intense sadness, aversion, or any persistent expression of intense emotion might have similar effects. Keeping or creating a secret ensures some level of separateness, the point being that there is something important about the survivor that is not known to the other person. Finally, establishing multiple superficial relationships helps survivors avoid intimate contact. We call this "busyness," as the individual has established a pattern of interacting that keeps him or her busy with many tasks (membership in social organizations, parenting, multiple jobs) and gives the illusion that he or she is connected not to tasks, but to people.

We believe that this aspect of the relational disturbance emanates from the survivor's distorted cognitions of himself or herself. The basic issue is that adult survivors do not trust themselves and do not think of themselves as capable, adequate, or worthy of another person's attention. Survivors experience much uncertainty and doubt about all aspects of themselves. They have difficulty identifying their feelings and thoughts and believing in the accuracy or validity of the thoughts and feelings that do surface. The sense of doubt about one's internal reality is heightened by the survivor's negative self-image, which emanates from the cognitive response cycle that was developed when the childhood sexual abuse was occurring. As the survivor thinks of himself or herself as weak, vulnerable, incapable and inadequate, he or she is attempting to avoid developing relationships in which the other person will expect reciprocity. The impaired trust is thus often reflected in a fear of getting close to another person or an anxiety about being seen "as I really am." Feelings of isolation, loneliness, abandonment, separation, loss, unlovability, and unworthiness are reported by the adult survivor with frightening regularity.

Group psychotherapy is the treatment modality of choice for adult survivors of child sexual abuse who present primarily with relational disturbances. We have found that long-term individual therapy is an inefficient and often ineffective method of repairing the relational disruption. It seems likely that this is associated with the one-on-one aspect of individual treatment or, more specifically, with the intense, isolated, and somewhat secretive nature of the format. Many survivors have reported that they could not work on unresolved sexual abuse issues in individual therapy with a therapist who had worked very effectively with them on other issues. It is likely that, as the survivor begins to experience a caring relationship with the therapist, his or her self-doubts and anxieties become enhanced. As in other relationships, the survivor becomes concerned that disclosure about the as yet untold aspects of his or her internal reality will result in abandonment. A survivor might say to himself or herself, "If my therapist really knew me, she would not care so much about me. She would think I am bad and evil. She would think I am crazy." The fears and the lack of trust further increase the survivor's belief that his or her sexual abuse should not be discussed with the therapist. The survivor cannot risk the loss of yet another person on whom he or she is dependent.

The adult survivor's experience of uniqueness or of being different from everyone else in the world is another important factor in the recommendation for group therapy. When the survivor was a child, she or he had the experience of being chosen to engage in a secretive relationship with an adult or an older child. The child victim of sexual abuse frequently asks the question, "Why me? Why was I chosen?" The same question often remains for the adult survivor. In a therapy group, the survivor learns for herself or himself that other people have had similar experiences. The survivor can listen to the experiences of the others in a group and believe that they were abused. He or she also can have the experience of disclosing the abuse or aspects of the abuse that had not previously been disclosed to a number of other individuals who trust that he or she is telling the truth. In group therapy, the adult survivor has the opportunity to relearn the rules of relationships with all the other group members. Knowledgeable peers, with the guidance of clinicians who are experienced in therapy for victimization issues, provide validation for the survivors' internal experience as well as their external reality. They provide consistent messages that the survivor is not unique, is not crazy, is believable, and is worthy of caring and respect. In addition, group members can practice being direct, honest, and caring with each other within the group therapy sessions. We have found this to be the most effective method of counteracting the relational disturbances introduced during the childhood experience of sexual abuse.

Conclusion

In conclusion, we wish to remind our readers that planful therapeutic interventions with adult survivors of child sexual abuse have only recently become a topic of interest and concern to clinicians. Although most clinicians have worked with adult survivors in a variety of practice settings, little attention has been paid to the specific treatment needs of this population. We believe that it is appropriate and necessary to plan strategic clinical interventions for adult survivors who present for treatment. This chapter reflects an effort to incorporate our current ideas about the cognitive response cycle of child victims into treatment approaches that address the most common questions and themes raised by adult survivors with whom we have worked. We are certain that these approaches will be modified and expanded as increased knowledge and experience are shared by all those clinicians who work with this population.

References

Burgess, Ann, and Aaron Lazare, ed. 1976. "The Customer Approach to Patienthood." In *Community Mental Health: Target Populations*. Englewood Cliffs, NJ: Prentice-Hall, 35–54.

Constantine, Larry L., and Floyd M. Martinson. 1981. *Children and Sex*. Boston: Little, Brown.

Gelinas, Denise. 1983. "The Persisting Negative Effects of Incest." *Psychiatry* 46:312–32.

Karpel, Mark A. 1980. "Family Secrets: I. Conceptual and Ethical Issues in the Relational Context; II. Ethical and Practical Considerations in Therapeutic Management." *Family Process* 19:295–306.

Lamb, Sharon. 1986. "Treating Sexually Abused Children: Issues of Blame and Responsibility." *American Journal of Orthopsychiatry* 56(no. 2):April, 303–07.

Sgroi, Suzanne M. 1982. *Handbook of Clinical Intervention in Child Sexual Abuse*. Lexington, MA: Lexington Books.

8
Criminal Investigation of Child Sexual Abuse Cases

Richard L. Cage

This chapter is intended to serve as a guide for law enforcement and social service personnel who investigate child sexual abuse cases. As an investigator of child sexual abuse cases for the past ten years, I am acutely aware of the changes that have taken place and the dire need for further change. With the increase in public awareness in recent years, many police and social service personnel are finding themselves bombarded with these cases. Yet there are not enough qualified personnel to investigate cases adequately and deal sensitively with the families and particularly the children who are in crisis. A few years ago, a suburban police department might have investigated only a dozen child sexual abuse cases in a year; now it might investigate that many in a week. Consequently, we are faced with a severe shortage of investigators with the necessary education and training to deal properly with cases.

By bringing the crime of child sexual abuse into public view, we have made it easier for victims to obtain the help they need to proceed with their lives. We must, however, continue to examine the effectiveness of our treatment on a local departmental level, as well as on a state and federal level. Child sexual abuse is a felony offense in all fifty states. Most people would agree that a more heinous crime could not be committed, but in many areas of the country, an allegation of child sexual abuse does not require that even a single officer respond. We read daily of embezzlements and robberies that have required hundreds of man-hours and thousands of public dollars to bring the perpetrators to justice. Teams of detectives from local, state, and federal agencies are assigned to pore over records that might help in an arrest and the recovery of stolen or misappropriated funds. By comparison, a sexual abuse case might involve a child who has been victimized by a father, stepfather, uncle, or family friend for an extended period of time, sometimes involving thirty, fifty, one hundred, or even more incidents. Each offense is a felony, yet preliminary investigations are frequently carried out by the social service agency and only later, in the most serious cases, does law enforcement become involved.

Where on our priority list do these crimes of child sexual abuse belong?

Although we list child sexual abuse as a felony crime, we are frequently treating it with less importance than shoplifting.

As an investigator, I view this crime as more devastating than murder in the sense that the very essence of the child's being, the intricate feelings of self-worth and self-esteem, are mutilated. He or she is left to struggle with this mutilation, frequently for the rest of his or her life. Our primary responsibility as law enforcement agents and social service workers is the protection of the child, regardless of our initial feelings about the events surrounding the case. The child has disclosed an alleged abuse, and our responsibility is to validate or invalidate that allegation.

Unfortunately, extremely competent investigators find allegations of child sexual abuse very difficult to deal with on a personal level. As in all professions, we must examine our own capabilities and potential for doing a thorough job; the need for a complete, objective, and unbiased investigation is imperative in child sexual abuse cases. An investigator facing his or her first assignment might benefit from asking himself or herself a few questions:

- Can I be sensitive to the issue of child sexual abuse?
- Do I really believe the problem exists?
- Can I be empathic with the alleged victims?
- Can I be empathic with the alleged offender?
- Can I be open-minded in conducting the investigation and avoid making emotional judgments along the way?
- Am I willing to invest the amount of time necessary to do a thorough investigation?

Departments as well should attempt to identify those personnel who are best suited for this type of investigation. Basic characteristics of a good child sexual abuse investigator include the ability to maintain objectivity throughout these emotional investigations, the ability to empathize with both the victim and the offender, a willingness to remain nonjudgmental, and an ability to put aside one's feelings of anger and repulsion to obtain as much information as possible. As in many high-stress occupations, the potential for burnout is high; it is important to recognize the signs and be willing to allow recovery time for investigators when necessary.

From the outset, investigations of child sexual abuse allegations are replete with a unique set of circumstances or conditions that produce a unique set of problems or barriers. These conditions are outlined below.

Barriers Presented by the Victim

1. Children generally do not know that a crime has been committed.

2. Children generally do not report the abuse to police or social services directly. They will usually tell a parent or trusted friend.
3. Children generally care for the offender and do not wish to see harm come to him or her.
4. Children generally are encouraged to keep the sexual behavior a secret.
5. Children generally are afraid to report the abuse. They may have been warned, "If you tell, Mommy won't love us anymore" or "If you tell, Daddy will be sent to jail and you will never see me again." On rare occasions, threats of bodily harm may be the source of the victim's fear.
6. Children do not want to testify.

Due to the above conditions, the investigator is faced with the victim of a crime who does not wish to report or discuss the crime at all. In contrast, in crimes such as robbery, the wronged party solicits help from the police, files a report with all the details of the crime, and openly seeks to aid in the arrest of the offender. In child sexual abuse cases, the investigator must work with a victim who does not report the abuse to the police and does not usually realize that a crime has been committed. The victim of child sexual abuse usually cares deeply for the perpetrator of the crime and may be bound by a code of secrecy or fear the consequences of disclosure. Keep in mind that in most cases of child sexual abuse, there is no threat of bodily harm to the victim. Instead, the art of gentle persuasion is used very effectively; the victim may feel deep emotional ties to the offender, which may worsen feelings of guilt and shame once the disclosure is made, and thereby further impede discussion of the abuse. The result is a child victim who does not want to talk. At this point, the challenge before the investigator is monumental. How does one overcome these barriers to the investigation?

In recent years many allegations of child sexual abuse were dropped at this stage, simply because the investigators could not integrate the fragmented statements made by the victim or could not elicit the necessary information to have probable cause for the arrest of the offender. Frequently we find that added to these barriers are certain qualities of an individual or team of investigators that further detract from the progress of the investigation. These include the points listed below.

Barriers Presented by Investigators

1. Some investigators cannot talk to children or interview them effectively.
2. Some investigators cannot believe a child's statement when it conflicts with an adult's statement.
3. Some investigators cannot piece together the inconsistencies of the report.

4. Some investigators are not able to get past the barriers presented by the victim.

5. Some investigators are overworked and are experiencing burnout.

6. Some investigators are not willing to make an arrest on the word of a child.

The importance of a conscientious investigator with finely tuned interviewing skills is obvious. Without an understanding of the expected barriers or an ability to sort and integrate the information given by all those who are interviewed, even a gifted investigator may have difficulty organizing evidence in a case of child sexual abuse. An investigator who is equipped with the knowledge that barriers are common, even expected, will be less likely to give up on the investigation and will continue to pursue the complaint.

Like the investigators, prosecutors who are trying these cases in court experience a great deal of frustration in working with these cases. Obviously, a child victim who is unwilling to discuss the alleged abuse does not make the prosecutor's work any easier. The inability to talk to the child on his or her own level, the inability to believe the child, the hesitancy to take the case to trial when the information is less than clear-cut, the inability to prepare the child victim adequately for testimony in court, and the drastic increase in the number of these immensely time-consuming cases all add to the prosecutor's dilemma of presenting a child sexual abuse case for trial.

So the question remains: How does the investigator overcome the barriers that threaten the completion of a thorough investigation? Obviously, there is no simple answer; each allegation of child sexual abuse carries its own unique set of barriers that must be dealt with individually. Armed with an awareness that these barriers exist and are to be expected, however, the skilled investigator will not be hesitant to pursue the allegations and will be less willing to drop the investigation as unfounded.

The Investigation

Many states have now mandated that police, child protective services, and the state's attorney's office all work together in a joint investigation of child sexual abuse cases. Through my own experience, I have found a joint investigation to be most advantageous for several reasons. Most importantly, it provides for a multidisciplinary approach, combining the education, experience, and talents of personnel from both law enforcement and social services, and it permits a more supportive atmosphere during the interviews. These interviews are frequently long and demanding. A joint effort can allow different interview approaches to be used during a single interview and will prevent the child victim from undergoing unnecessary sessions. The information obtained also will be consistent on all reports filed, an important issue when the case is presented in court. The joint effort allows police and child protective services to discuss significant details and concerns and to plan together the course of action to be taken.

From the moment of disclosure of a child sexual abuse complaint, the foremost responsibility of the investigator is the protection of the child. Information regarding the accusation must be gathered immediately; it cannot be delayed. The child's safety may be at stake, and removal of the child from the home may be necessary.

It is also the responsibility of law enforcement and child protective services to conduct a thorough and objective investigation, including the gathering of physical evidence related to the alleged abuse (which may include search and seizure) and the procurement of arrest warrants if needed. The experienced investigator will be prepared to report the factual information obtained to either a juvenile or criminal court hearing.

For purposes of simplification, the investigation may be divided into two categories:

1. Interviews
   a. the victim
   b. the nonoffending parent (intrafamily cases)
   c. other interviews (e.g., siblings, other relatives, friends of the victim)
   d. the offender
2. Gathering of evidence
   a. search and seizure
   b. medical evidence

In the following section, a discussion of each interview with its special needs is provided, with specific examples of actual case interviews to provide clarification. For the sake of brevity, the masculine pronoun "he" will be used to denote the offender. This does not mean that there are no cases involving female offenders, but more documented cases involve male offenders.

In general, one may describe any sexual activity that is deemed inappropriate for the child's age and maturational level as child sexual abuse. Many experts working in the field of child sexual abuse find this a simple, workable definition. Statutes specifically defining child sexual abuse may differ somewhat from state to state and from federal statutes. The investigator must be familiar with the statutes and with terminology currently used in the field. The investigator must be careful, however, not to confuse his or her responsibilities with those of clinicians. If investigators spend too much time on attempts to categorize, classify, or otherwise diagnose the offender, it may detract from the investigation of the alleged abuse. The job of the investigator is to validate the complaint, to determine whether probable cause for an arrest exists, to gather evidence, and, ultimately, to protect the child. Comparatively, the purpose of a diagnostic assessment is to identify treatment needs and gather facts to assist in treatment planning. Although interrelated and interdependent, the two functions are separate.

Preparing for the Interview with the Victim

A disclosure of child sexual abuse may come about in a number of ways: The child may tell another person (e.g., a parent, trusted friend, or counselor at school), who then tells the authorities; a child may be observed to behave in a sexually explicit manner (e.g., performing fellatio on a sibling); a younger child may simply reveal the information without realizing that the behavior is abusive (e.g., "Daddy does that to me"); drastic changes in the child's behavior (e.g., bed-wetting, continuous nightmares, declining grades, skipping classes, or runaway episodes) may lead to questioning by parents or teachers, which leads to a disclosure.

Before the actual interview of the victim, the investigator must obtain as much information about the disclosure as possible, attempting to track it to its origin. The statement of disclosure should be exact, clear, and verbatim. One should be aware of the following important factors:

1. To whom did the victim disclose?
2. Was the disclosure accidental? Was it intentional?
3. Who was the first person told? Were others also told?
4. Did that person (persons) attempt to interview the victim?

Of particular interest is the information obtained from the person to whom the victim disclosed. In some cases, this person may unwittingly lead the child, distort the information given, or otherwise influence the content of the disclosure. For these reasons, it is of utmost importance for the investigator to conduct a thorough interview of the person who first heard the child's disclosure, preferably prior to the child victim's interview, in an effort to evaluate and assess the information.

For example, an unskilled interviewer may ask leading questions, eliciting inaccurate information from the victim. When younger children are being questioned by an authority figure, they may give an answer they hope is pleasing to the adult. The following are all leading questions: He hurt you, didn't he? You were afraid, weren't you? Why didn't you tell us? Were you afraid he would hurt you? They elicit "yes" and "no" answers from the victim, and do not leave room for clarification. They also frequently have an emotional impact on the child victim, who for the first time may realize that the behavior in which he or she has been taking part is viewed as "bad" by adults. This occurs when children have been coerced into the abusive relationship without realizing the behavior is criminal or not "normal." In older victims who tend to blame themselves for the abuse, leading questions may elicit answers that help absolve them of the guilt feelings that are inherent in abusive relationships of long duration. By answering "Yes, I was afraid" or "Yes, he hurt me," the guilt may be lessened somewhat and the victim may feel less to blame for the abuse. The problem here is that something probably did occur (current statistics support that children rarely lie about sexual abuse), but responses elicited by leading questions may confuse the child and distort the allegation. The investigator is then presented with a distorted view of what has actually taken place.

The skilled interviewer must keep all this in mind when assessing the information obtained from the reporting person. During the actual interview of the victim, attempts should be made to clarify the information by asking nonleading questions and providing a nonthreatening atmosphere in which the child can talk about what actually happened.

By tracking the disclosure back to the person reporting, the investigator is able to gather specific details of the alleged abuse. For example:

> A child is witnessed performing cunnilingus on her doll. When questioned, the child reports, "Uncle Billy does this to me." The child's mother states that Uncle Billy lives with the family and baby-sits the child while they are out.

This information will give the investigator a framework around which the interview can be conducted. In addition, by interviewing the person to whom the child disclosed, the investigator can attempt to ascertain whether the child has a motive for falsification, an issue that is frequently used by defense attorneys to tear down the testimony of the child during actual hearings.

For example, Uncle Billy states, "Susie made that up because I wouldn't let her play with my Atari game. She's mad at me. I'm never alone with her." Background information about the victim and the offender can help the investigator to see whether there is indeed a motive for the child to get back at Uncle Billy. This is not to say that false reports by children occur commonly, but the investigator who is armed with information before interviewing the victim and offender can be prepared to address the issue of falsification at the outset of the investigation.

To continue with the example, in the subsequent interview the offender said that he did not even own an Atari game and that there had been no disagreement between the child and himself. He also admitted that sometimes he was asked to baby-sit for the child while her parents were out. After a lengthy interview, Uncle Billy, realizing that his veracity was in question because of his prior statements, admitted to abusing the child sexually over a six-month period.

Factors Affecting the Interview

Victims of child sexual abuse range in age from a few months old to the teenage years. Obviously, the investigator must gear the interview to a level of understanding and communication with which the child is comfortable. Certain general factors should be considered before beginning the interview.

Age of the Victim

The interviewer must be able to communicate with the victim on his or her level of understanding. This may vary greatly between children, even in the same age group. The interviewer must be prepared to use the child's own language if needed.

Cognitive Development of the Victim

The interviewer must be aware that each child is a product of his or her own environment and that each child's awareness of his or her surroundings may vary greatly. It is, therefore, important to be aware of the child's level of intellectual understanding. It is also important to keep in mind that some victims may not speak English fluently, if they speak it at all. Some victims also may be deaf, blind, mentally retarded, autistic, or otherwise unable to communicate without special help. Interviewers must be prepared to use bilingual interpreters or sign language interpreters, for example, to complete interviews of some victims. Interpreters or persons who assist the investigator to communicate with the child should never be family members or persons who have a vested interest in the outcome of the investigation.

Location of the Interview

Children usually disclose away from the scene of the occurrence (e.g., children who were abused by a family member frequently disclose to a friend or counselor at school). The site chosen for the interview will depend on where the child feels comfortable and safe enough to talk about the incident (e.g., the intrafamily victim would probably not want to discuss the abuse at her home). The interviewer should provide privacy, as these victims feel an enormous amount of shame, guilt, and embarrassment. Extraneous persons in the room may detract from the trust building between the victim and interviewer. If possible, the interviewer also should allow for a comfortable seating arrangement that provides the victim with lots of space.

Prior Interviews

The interviewer must be informed of information given in prior interviews. This provides a framework for questions to be asked.

Barriers to the Interview

It is important to keep in mind that certain barriers are inherent in this type of investigation. (See the section "Conducting the Interview".) The interviewer should be willing to go forward with the interview, even if he or she encounters these barriers.

Audiotaping and Videotaping

Legislation regarding videotaping of interviews of child victims is now at a crossroads. Much depends on the particular area in which the department is operating and the local and state laws governing that area. Videotaping can be extremely advantageous in the hands of a skilled interviewer. (For more on videotaping, see Chapter 9.) Audiotaping also can be a helpful tool, as taking notes during a session with a child victim can be painstaking at best. Careful note taking during the interview is imperative, however, and having the second person present take notes often works well. An audiotape of the interview serves as an adjunct for the investigator, who may use it to fill in specific details missed in the notes. The audiotape, while not admissible in court proceedings, will allow the interviewer to give full attention to the child and serves as a backup to clarify details.

Age Considerations

Due to the wide range in age of victims, the investigator must be prepared to meet the child at his or her own level of understanding. The interview should be approached in such a way that the child feels comfortable and safe. The following information will help the investigator prepare for interviewing specific age groups.

Preschool Children (1–5 Years)

1. These children may lack the verbal skills necessary to communicate effectively. If so, the interviewer should consider the use of pictures, drawings, or anatomically correct dolls if available. The interviewer should be skillful in the use of these accessory items so that the child is allowed to show what happened without the interviewer's leading (showing) the child.

2. The child and the interviewer may sit on the floor or on pillows. A small table with chairs also may be used. The child should be allowed to move about the interviewing space, from the floor to the table if so desired.

3. Adequate space should be allowed for coloring, drawing, or doll play, thus allowing the child to communicate visually when unable to do so verbally.

4. The interviewer should remain at the child's eye level throughout the interview, facilitating ease of communication and maintaining a nonthreatening environment.

Primary School Children (5–10 Years)

1. These children have more elaborate communication skills with more defined thought processes. Most are capable of distinguishing time frames (e.g., past, present, days, weeks, years, seasons) and concepts (e.g., the truth versus a lie, right versus wrong, good versus bad). Children in this age range are aware of the significance of a secret, are more aware of subtle differences in sexual roles (e.g., Mommy versus Daddy), and are developing a sense of moral values, thus being more likely to feel a sense of shame or guilt over events that have taken place.

2. These children may prefer sitting at a table or in a circle of chairs, on a couch, or on the floor with pillows. The interviewer should make available materials for drawing and coloring, as well as anatomically correct drawings and dolls.

3. The interviewer should maintain good eye contact with the victim, as well as establish and maintain a nonthreatening, nonpunitive attitude throughout the session.

Preadolescents (10–12 Years)
and Adolescents (13–17 Years)

1. These children have excellent communication skills, but they may feel a greater sense of shame, guilt, responsibility for the abuse, or hopelessness and thus have difficulty verbalizing.

2. Some victims in this age group may find pictures or anatomically correct drawings a useful tool, or they may choose to give a written, signed statement about the events that have taken place.

3. Seating arrangements range from table or chair groupings to sofas (essentially those that would accommodate an adult). Privacy is of the utmost importance, especially if the interview is to take place at the victim's school. The interviewer should be aware of rules about the presence of school personnel; this can frequently be detrimental to the interview since the victim may fear that the secret will get out at school or be discussed by teachers.

4. The interviewer should assure the victim that the information obtained will be handled with discretion.

Conducting the Interview

Interviewing the victim is the most important aspect of a thorough investigation. The investigator must use all of his or her communication skills to allow the child to tell about the abuse. The tone set by the investigator will undoubtedly affect the outcome of the interview, so every effort must be made to conduct the interview in a nonthreatening, nonpunitive way. This general approach may be used as a guideline for conducting the interview:

A. Building Rapport
  1. Introduce the interviewer. Identify the interviewer as a police officer, detective, or social worker.
  2. Stress from the beginning that the child has done nothing wrong. Attempt to relieve feelings of shame, guilt, or fear of punishment. The interviewer might say, for example, "Sarah, I want you to know that you haven't done anything wrong. We are not here to punish you. We're here to see that you're protected. We know that none of this was your fault."
  3. Stress that you are there to talk to the child and that this is your job.
  4. Maintain a nonthreatening, nonpunitive attitude. Take time to build rapport; hurrying at this point will detract from the effectiveness of the interview.
  5. Attempt to get to know the child by bringing him or her into a conversation about school, friends, pets, hobbies, siblings, toys, games, sports, family, teachers, and any other topic appropriate for the age group.
  6. During the conversation, begin to assess the child's
     a. verbal and communication skills.

    b. basic comprehension of information. Ask direct questions, such as "Do you watch Sesame Street" on television? Where does Oscar live? What color is Big Bird? Do you go to school? What school do you go to? What is your favorite toy?"

    c. ability to comprehend time and dates. Ask direct questions such as "Which days do you go to school? What time do you get home from school? When does 'Sesame Street' come on television? Which day do you go to the baby-sitter's?" Questions should be asked in relation to when school is in and out of session, seasons, and length of days, weeks, months, or years.

    d. knowledge of family relationships. Ask questions that establish the child's knowledge of Mommy, Daddy, brothers, sisters, aunts, uncles, grandparents, or special friends. For instance, ask who is "Pop-Pop," "Nanna," or "Bubby." These assessments are especially important with younger children.

B. Exploring the disclosure
  1. Note any changes in the child's behavior.
  2. Note any changes in the child's voice level.
  3. Be aware of the child's body language.

Example: Sarah, a five-year-old girl, is fondled by her uncle while he is baby-sitting for her. Sarah tells her mother, who calls child protective services. During the preliminary interview, Sarah answers questions about her school, teachers, friends, favorite television shows, and pets in a comfortable, nonthreatened manner. When the investigator directs his questions to what Sarah told her mother earlier, the talkative, exuberant child stops talking and smiling and crawls beneath the table.

C. Identify barriers
  1. The child withdraws and says he or she does not want to talk.
  2. The child says, "Nothing happened."
  3. The child changes the story out of fear or threats made by the offender.

Example: Sarah, a five-year-old girl, tells a playmate that her daddy touches her private parts. The playmate tells her mother, who notifies child protective services. Sarah is frightened during the interview with police and protective services because her father has told her that if she ever tells, the police will come and take her away and she will never see Mommy and Daddy again.

The child is struggling with a barrier of secrecy and fear imposed by the abuser; the interviewer must understand that adults who molest children will often threaten or otherwise imply that the victim will be blamed, taken away, or not loved.

The interviewer's approach should be supportive and nonjudgmental, while encouraging the victim to talk about the events. The interviewer might say, for example, "Sarah, I help lots of children just like you, who may have had the same thing happen to them. I want to help you, and I want to help your daddy, too. You haven't done anything wrong. This is not your fault. Could you tell me what happened?"

Sometimes children will change their stories when they realize that their parents are upset by the disclosure.

> *Example:* Jimmy, a nine-year-old boy, has been sexually molested repeatedly by a coach while at a playing field. Jimmy tells his mother six months later that he has been sexually abused. Jimmy's mother reacts with hurt and disbelief that the abuse has occurred, along with frustration and anger that Jimmy would allow the abuse to continue. She calls her husband at work and in a panic reports, "Jimmy has been molested. Come home immediately!" The father and mother are both visibly upset. Jimmy overhears their comments, and by the time investigators are on the scene, Jimmy, sensing that he is being blamed for the repeated abuse, changes his story: "It may have been an accident while we were wrestling; it was only outside my clothing." Jimmy insists during the interview that he was not molested.

In this case, the investigator is presented with a child who has disclosed an abuse and due to the reaction of his parents, feels that the only way out is to recant, to say that it was an accident. The victim sees his parents' anger and frustration and feels tremendous shame and guilt. His resulting denial is an attempt to block out the abuse and pretend that it did not happen. As has been discussed earlier, this barrier is not unusual and may actually be expected in cases in which parental reaction is strongly negative toward the victim (Summit 1983).

The approach by the investigator should be nonjudgmental, supportive, and nonpunitive. By being aware that this is not unusual behavior for child victims, the investigator can be prepared to be supportive; these children especially need to be relieved of the guilt they are feeling. For example, the interviewer might respond, "Jimmy, I know it was difficult to tell your mom. But you must realize that this is not your fault; you are not responsible for what happened. The coach was wrong in doing what he did. You did the right thing by telling."

In this case, after a lengthy interview, Jimmy revealed that he was sexually abused by his coach, as were many other boys. Jimmy had been involved in masturbation, oral sex, and digital anal penetration over a period of six months. He finally told the entire story because the interviewer was not discouraged by the barrier of Jimmy's shame and knew how to overcome it.

The skilled investigator must be aware of the barriers and their underlying causes and attempt to make the child comfortable and safe enough to make a disclosure. The interviewer should be particularly careful not to ask leading questions or to answer for the child. He or she should reinforce, repeatedly if necessary, that the child is not to blame for what happened. The victim may find comfort in knowing that she or he is not the only child to whom this has happened and that the interviewer has worked with many other child victims.

The interviewer should assure the child that this is a difficult subject to discuss and perhaps change the direction of the interview (a breather, so to speak) to ease the tension. The interviewer can then approach the subject of the abuse again, encouraging the victim to talk about the events.

One advantage the interviewer has is that a complaint has already been made, either by the child or another source. Exploring the original disclosure can be the bridge across the barriers. For example, the interviewer might say, "Jimmy, I'm a little confused. Could you help me? You told your mom that the coach touched your penis and that this bothered you. But when I talked to you, you told me that it was an accident. You know, Jimmy, I talk to a lot of little boys your age, and they have trouble telling their story, too. You haven't done anything wrong, no matter what happened. And if you're afraid to talk, I understand that, too. But I need your help; this is very important. Can you tell me what happened?" This approach conveys several messages to the victim:

- You believe the story he told his mother.
- You understand that he may be frightened.
- You have talked with other victims his age.
- Many children have trouble talking about this subject.
- This is very important.
- You need his help.

Hopefully, the child will begin to tell you something, providing even a small piece of the puzzle. At this point, many child victims will minimize the abuse. Here is what the children might say at this point in our two case examples:

Sarah: "My Daddy did touch me one time, while I was sleeping."

Jimmy: "Well, he did touch me down there, but only twice."

By minimizing the extent of the abuse, the victim feels less to blame, less ashamed of the part he or she played in the scenario. But this seemingly small bit of information can become the basis for a thorough interview. The investigator should build on this information and continue the interview in a nonjudgmental manner. The child is very capable of judging the interviewer's ability to handle the information given and of perceiving the adult's feelings. Particularly at this point, the victim will be aware of a change in the interviewer's attitude; even the slightest evidence of distaste or any negative feelings on the part of the interviewer may cause the child to withdraw. For example, a change in the interviewer's facial expression from a look of concern to one of distaste (e.g., a frown) could inhibit the child from continuing to describe what happened to him or her. The interviewer must set aside his or her own feelings and concentrate on the victim and the information being revealed.

Two additional barriers may inhibit further disclosure: the child's relationship to the abuser and his or her emotional ties to the abuser. In many cases of child sexual abuse, the child victim feels strong emotional ties to the offender and a need to protect him, even in the face of an ongoing abusive relationship. An incestuous relationship in which a father (or father substitute) is abusing his daughter can give rise to ambivalent feelings: The child may love and revere her father, while at the same time have feelings of disgust and hatred of the things he is forcing her to do. Particularly with younger victims, the adult enjoys an almost godlike reverence, as many children are taught to obey their parents without qualification. An unknowing child who is seduced into a sexual relationship with a parent suffers the ultimate betrayal: "If I can't trust my own father, whom can I trust?" These feelings may give rise to the sense of helplessness and hopelessness so often recognized in child sexual abuse victims. The child feels shame and guilt over the abuse, frequently blames herself for its occurrence, and still tries to remain loyal to the father figure, a terrible burden for anyone, especially a child (Summit 1983).

The skilled interviewer must recognize this conflict and attempt to understand its origin; a show of concern for the offender might help to cross the barrier. For example, the interviewer might say, "Sarah, I know you love your daddy, and I'm sure that he loves you, too. One of the reasons I'm here today is so we can help your daddy. He has a problem, and we really want to help him with it." This show of concern may help the victim feel less as if she is betraying her father and more that her disclosure will lead her father to get help. By understanding the basis for the loyalty-disloyalty conflict the child is facing, the interviewer can be more supportive and objective.

Once the child has revealed that something has indeed happened and has learned that he or she can trust the interviewer with the information without being judged, the door is opened for more in-depth communication. The interviewer can move into this by asking for more exact details about the disclosure. For example, he or she might ask, "Sarah, can you tell me exactly what happened? What exactly did you tell your mom?" Remember that the child may have provided distorted information because of his or her fear and feelings of guilt and shame. It is, therefore, paramount that the interviewer give the child an opportunity to unravel or clarify the details of the incident(s). This should be done without making the child fear that the interviewer might think he or she has lied, which could lead to a defensive stance once again.

In the following example, an unskilled interviewer (the child's mother) leads a child into describing something that did not occur:

Mother: Why didn't you tell me, Jimmy?
Jimmy: I don't know.
Mother: Were you afraid?
Jimmy: Yes.
Mother: Were you afraid he would hurt you?
Jimmy: Yes.
Mother: Did he say he would kill you?
Jimmy: Yes.

The investigator approaching this case initially was met with the information that the child had been molested and that he was threatened with bodily harm (death). The skilled investigator, attempting to sort out the information, must keep in mind that threats of bodily harm are rare in child sexual abuse cases. An examination of the parent's reaction to the disclosure would encourage the investigator to look very closely at its contents. The skilled interviewer might approach the victim at this point with this type of dialogue:

Interviewer: Jimmy, sometimes children say things to their parents because they're afraid they'll be angry. I want to give you an opportunity to start all over. It doesn't matter what you told your mom; we can straighten it all out right now. You told your mom that you thought he was going to kill you. Was that really what happened?
Jimmy: No, I was afraid she'd be mad, so when she asked, I just said yes. But he really did touch me.

By giving the child an opportunity to go over the disclosure without fear and pressure, the investigator is often able to clear up potential distortions.

In many cases of child sexual abuse, the child victim is abused over an extended period of time, frequently involving multiple incidents. The abuse may have started during the preschool years and extended through the adolescent years, with tens or hundreds of incidents. During the interview, it is important to obtain as much factual information and detail as possible, a monumental task in some cases. This condition so often seen in child sexual abuse cases leads to yet another barrier or problem for the investigator: inconsistencies in information given. Should an investigator who finds these inconsistencies in information begin to doubt the veracity of the child or even drop the investigation as unfounded? No. The skilled investigator would realize the improbability of a child victim's ability to recount specific details of, for example, weekly assaults over a four-year-period without inconsistencies. Instead, he or she would try to establish patterns of the abuse and advance to finer details when possible, as the following case example illustrates:

> *Example:* A father begins to fondle his four-year-old daughter while the mother works nights and weekends. This continues until the child is eight years old and tells her mother. At the time of the disclosure, the child is complaining of itching "down there," is bed-wetting, and has frequent nightmares. This little girl would be hard-pressed to recount each specific incident, but could tell you, "Mommy was working; he always came in my room to tuck me in. It started when I was in nursery school. At first I just pretended I was sleeping; he was touching me 'down there.' Then he started taking his pants off, and he made me touch it; then he made me put it in my mouth. I didn't like it."

From this statement, the investigator finds that there was a progression of the abuse from fondling to oral sex, that the abuse took place while the child was in the father's care, and that the child remembers being in nursery school when the abuse began (therefore, approximately three to four years of age). With this information, the interviewer should delve for the details of the abuse but keep in mind that the lack of such details, or even inconsistencies in the disclosure, does not necessarily mean that the child is lying, only that there may have been too many incidents to describe specifically.

Another related issue in interviewing children, which is particularly bothersome to prosecutors and defense attorneys, is the child's inability to be specific about when the abuse started. If this is truly child sexual abuse in which a child is emotionally traumatized, why can't the child tell you when the abuse started (Sgroi 1982, 115)?

We must understand that in many cases of ongoing sexual abuse, the beginning is often very subtle and ingeniously disguised. For example, a father may tuck in his young child and gently rub the child's back in a comforting way. Over a period of time, possibly weeks or months, this may progress to rubbing the stomach, then the legs and thighs, Ultimately, the father may lovingly and gently begin to fondle the child's genital area; by now the child has come to know the father's gentle, loving touch and may not realize that what he is doing would be judged wrong by others. At the same time, the child may enjoy the caressing.

In another example, a soccer coach takes responsibility for getting his team members in shape. After strenuous workouts, he may offer to give certain members a rubdown.

During the rubdown, he may "accidentally" brush his hands over the boys' genital areas. This may occur on many separate occasions, until one day an overt sexual act is played out.

For the victim in either example, describing the exact time the abuse started would be difficult because of the subtle engagement behavior. The incest victim may be able to tell you, "It was after Mommy got her new job," or the victim of the coach may be able to tell you, "It was after we won our first game." Again, this seeming vagueness should not deter the investigation. The information should be corroborated by information obtained during interviews with other family members, siblings, or friends.

In some cases, children can be extremely reticent about the abuse, refusing to confirm or even discuss the occurrence at all. With these victims, special techniques of interviewing can be very useful.

> *Example:* Julie, a nine-year-old girl, describes to her teacher that she was sexually fondled by her Uncle George, age forty-one. Police and child protective services interview the child at her elementary school. On questioning, Julie denies being abused.

Suggested Approach 1

Interviewer: Julie, I believe that what you told your teacher was true. We want to protect you.

Julie: Nothing happened.

Interviewer: Julie, we will be talking to your uncle.

Julie: No! He'll probably lie and say he didn't do it. (The child has indirectly confirmed the disclosure.)

Interviewer: Julie, tell us about your uncle. What kind of a person is he?

Julie: Well, everyone thinks he's really nice, but I don't.

The interviewer has encouraged Julie into a dialogue about her Uncle George and, without asking her a direct question about the abuse, has elicited a confirmation of the disclosure (i.e., Uncle George did it and will probably say he did not do it).

Suggested Approach 2

Interviewer: Julie, what if I ask Uncle George about this; what do you think he might say?

Julie: I don't know what he'll say. Go ask him.

Interviewer: Julie, it's our job to protect you and find out the truth about what has happened. Suppose I ask Uncle George to take a lie detector test. (briefly explain) How do you think he would do?

Julie:

He'd probably fail.

Interviewer: So you don't think he'll tell the truth?

Julie: No, he'll lie and say he didn't do it.

Again the child has indirectly confirmed the disclosure.

Suggested Approach 3

Interviewer: Julie, how about your sister, Patty. Do you think Uncle George might do something to her?

Julie: Maybe.

Interviewer: Did you ever tell anyone else besides your teacher?

Julie: I told my mother, but she didn't believe me.

Interviewer:

Julie, do you sleep over at Uncle George's house?

Julie: No way!

Interviewer: Would you let your sister stay with Uncle George?

Julie: No way!

Interviewer: Julie, if I were to talk to your sister Patty, do you think she would tell me anything?

Julie: No. I don't think he did it to her.

The child has indirectly confirmed the disclosure.

In general, this type of questioning may be adapted for any age victim. Even the most reluctant victim can usually be gently urged to make some kind of statement that will confirm the disclosure, even if indirectly. Once this type of dialogue takes place, the victim frequently feels more comfortable in discussing the abuse.

Gathering Essential Facts
about the Abuse

Once the lines of communication with the child victim are open, the child often feels relieved and becomes more willing to talk. At this time, the investigator should attempt to gather the essential facts of the investigation: who, what, where, how, and when.

Who

Be specific; find out exactly who the perpetrator is. The child may have more than one person whom he or she refers to as "Daddy," including stepfather, father, mother's boyfriend, or grandfather. It will be important to sort this out now.

What

In cases where there are one or two occurrences, the victim can usually be quite specific. But most cases of child sexual abuse involve multiple incidents. Sometimes by starting with the last occurrence and working backward in time, the victim will recall the more recent incidents in greater detail. Note that Dr. Sgroi and her colleagues recommend the opposite approach when interviewing child victims: asking about the first time first, then working forward in time, thus making it easier for the child to describe the less intimate behaviors initially and progress to the more intimate behaviors (Sgroi 1982, 60). The investigator may choose either approach, depending on the degree of difficulty the child is having in discussing the specific details of the abuse.

The progression of events from simple touching to fondling to more explicit sexual contact may be a very slow process, one in which many child victims do not realize that an abusive relationship is evolving. Therefore, the initial phases of the abuse may be difficult for the victim to elaborate on. Once the child realizes that something is wrong, the abuse has frequently progressed to more intimate sexual behaviors, such as masturbation, oral sex, vaginal and anal penetration, and simulated intercourse. Have the child describe the sexual behavior in his or her own words if possible. The use of drawings, pictures, and anatomically correct dolls may help the victim elaborate; this is often the most difficult information for the victim to discuss. The following examples illustrate the subtleness of the engagement behavior, which often makes giving precise answers impossible.

> *Example:* Shelly, a twelve-year-old girl, disclosed that she was sexually abused by her father and that it had been going on for several

years. Shelly's father repeatedly came into her room at night and rubbed her back while she went to sleep. At age four or five, Shelly can't remember exactly, her father's hand began to creep down onto her buttocks. Shelly can say only that it occurred; she is unable to say exactly how it started or when.

Example: Joey, a nine-year-old boy, disclosed that he was sexually abused by his Boy Scout leader. Joey recalls wrestling and playing many games with the leader and remembers seeing sexually explicit magazines and movies. He remembers that the actual abuse started with the leader's touching his genital area while they were swimming nude in the leader's pool. From this, Joey states that the leader introduced him to oral and anal sex.

As has been stated before, this part of the interview is often extremely difficult for the victim to recount. An approach that has proved successful in many cases is to solicit the victim's "help" in clearing up some of the details. The following sentences may be useful:

- I'm a little confused; maybe you can help me with this.
- Let me see if I understand this. . . . Is this correct?
- You know, I really don't quite understand this part. Could you explain it to me?
- This puzzle doesn't quite fit. Maybe you can help me clear this up so that the pieces fit together a little better.

The child also may be invited to make drawings or pictures that provide specific details of the abuse (including the crime scene; location of physical evidence such as magazines, pictures, or Vaseline; and a detailed drawing of the offender). Thus, the attention is transferred to the process of drawing, making this very difficult part of the interview a little easier for some victims. For example, the investigator might say, "Maybe you could draw me a picture of his bedroom. Could you show me exactly where his bed is? Could you show me exactly where the magazines are located?" Or the interviewer might ask, "Would you like to draw a picture of what happened? Could you show me exactly where his hands were? Could you draw me a picture of what he was wearing?" These drawings are often done with great care. The investigator may want to help the child label the parts of the drawing if the child is too young to write.

Where

In most child sexual abuse cases, this information does not present a problem but if the abuse is of long duration with multiple incidents, the child may have difficulty relating very specific details. In general, the victim should be able to relate the various locations (for example, "in my bedroom, in Daddy's bedroom, in the living room, while we were on vacation, at the park).

The investigator should attempt to obtain as much detail as possible but also remember that inconsistencies are not unexpected in cases of multiple contacts. Some areas of confusion about location may be cleared up when the nonoffending parent, the offender, and others are interviewed.

> *Example:* Roselyn, a twelve-year-old girl, has been sexually abused by her stepfather for approximately three years. The sexual abuse began at about age nine when Roselyn began sleeping in her own bedroom. As the abuse progressed, she was abused in the living room, the stepfather's bedroom, and the basement. The victim's mother corroborates the victim's statements by confirming that the family had moved into a new house when Roselyn was about nine years old and that she was given her own bedroom then.

Recording the location of the abuse in as much detail as possible will assist in the interview of the offender and will help explain inconsistencies during the court testimony. In the above example, the victim disclosed that she was abused in her bedroom; during the court proceedings, the child began to explain about the occurrence in the basement. The interviewer's detailed notes offered a quick explanation of the apparent discrepancy.

How

Some of this information will come from the child's explanation of what happened. The specific method used by the adult to engage the child in the sexual behavior is known by police investigators as the *method of operation* (modus operandi), often abbreviated M.O. Various methods have been recognized for engaging a child in a sexual act, including game playing, enticement, rewards, "love," trickery, education (teaching the child about sex), force, blackmail, and persuasion, to name a few. Looking for the method of engagement may be difficult in that the child often does not perceive when the game ends and the sexual abuse begins. The investigator should attempt to discern the method from the detailed information obtained in the interview with the child. In some cases, however, the method of engagement is more cleverly disguised, and the investigator will be forced to deduce from the totality of circumstances. The following is an example of such a case.

Example: Susan, a seven-year-old girl, is observed by her teacher to be masturbating frequently during class, despite repeated warnings. The teacher counsels Susan and her mother on several occasions. Finally, during a talk, Susan discloses that her Daddy touches her vaginal area. Susan loves her father very much and does not view this show of affection as abusive or wrong. Susan explains that she sits on her father's lap and hugs him; he hugs her back and sometimes touches her "down there" (points to genital area). "He said I was his favorite girl, but that I shouldn't tell."

The investigator may deduce that the father has engaged the child by loving, by a show of affection, by making the child "Daddy's special little girl." Other cases may be more straightforward.

Games. A father involves his five-year-old daughter in a game in which the father plays a monster. The child has to tie up the monster and beat him with a belt. The father is nude and has the child whip his genitals.

Rewards. A male child is taken to the movies, and bought expensive clothes, shoes, and toys in return for sexual favors to the man who befriends and seduces him.

Education. A female child is forced into a sexual relationship by her father. The father tells the child it is his responsibility to teach her about sex since he is her father.

Blackmail. A male child is engaged in a sexual relationship with an adult male neighbor. The neighbor tells the boy that if he tells, he will show the child's parents the sexually explicit pictures they have made over the past few months. Occasionally, an adult will use force to engage a child, but these instances seem to be rare. The art of gentle persuasion apparently is used more effectively with child victims.

When

The time frame may be self-explanatory, except in cases of multiple incidents of abuse of long duration. Being specific about the time of the abuse incidents can be particularly troublesome for younger victims, whose cognition of time is not well developed. The investigator should attempt to narrow down the time frame as much as possible, while still trying to obtain specific information. These approaches may be useful:

- Can you tell me about the last time (or first time) it happened?

- Was it near your birthday? A holiday?
- Was it during the summer? The winter? The spring? The fall? Were you in school?
- Was it on a weekday? A weekend?
- Where was your mom (or your dad)?
- Where were your brother and sister?
- Was it during the day? During the night?
- Have you always lived in the same house?
- Have you always had the same bedroom?

Some sample responses might be:

- It happens when we go to Grandma's house every summer. Grandpa says I'm his favorite.
- It started when we moved into our new house. Uncle Jim's bedroom was right next to mine, and sometimes he'd come in my room when Mommy was sleeping.
- It was when Mommy and Daddy went to the beach last summer. I stayed with my girlfriend. Her father did it three times during that two weeks.

After the needed information is gathered, the interview should be concluded by giving the child support and praise for his or her help and for doing the right thing. The investigator should stress that both police and child protective services will continue to be available for further discussion of the abuse if the victim desires or for other assistance if needed.

The Victim Who Will Not Disclose or Confirm

Unlike most other police investigations, child sexual abuse allegations rarely come directly from the victim. Most victims do not want to report the incident to authorities for the various reasons discussed earlier. A child, therefore, will deliberately tell a trusted friend who may then solicit help from authorities, or the child will accidentally disclose the abuse through sexually explicit behavior or language (Kosid 1987). The information given by the victim in its original form is rarely false or distorted, whether it is given in a deliberate or an accidental manner.

For example, Sally tells a playmate, "My Daddy rubs me down there." This unsolicited, deliberate statement given to another child was shared spontaneously without fear of authoritative intervention. Such disclosures are rarely false. Similarly, John, a five-year-old boy, encourages four-year-old Jane to remove her clothing. He then has her perform oral sex on him. Jane's mother discovers the children. When John is confronted, he explains that he learned this from Mr. Jones across the street but that he was not supposed to tell. Again, this accidental disclosure, precipitated by the child's sexual behavior and resulting statement, is likely to lead the investigator to a previously undiscovered case of child sexual abuse.

The reluctance to "tell" may be very strong in some victims, and the investigator may find that he or she is unable to elicit either a disclosure or a confirmation of a prior disclosure from the victim. What does the investigator do at this point? Should the investigation stop? Should the child be pressured by the interviewer?

These victims present a challenging dilemma for the investigator. If progress cannot be made with the interview, alternative approaches must be considered. These might include the following:

1. The child may be interviewed by a trusted person (teacher, pediatrician, minister) with the investigator present.
2. The child may be interviewed by a trusted person, with the interview audiotaped or videotaped. Careful selection of the interviewer is imperative, since the interview must be conducted without leading the child.
3. The investigation may be continued based on the child's disclosure to a responsible person.
4. The case may be monitored, with the child referred for therapeutic evaluation.

All efforts must be made to continue the investigation until a satisfactory conclusion is reached.

Intrafamily Child Sexual Abuse

Interview of the Nonoffending Parent

Intrafamily child sexual abuse cases most often involve a male father figure as the abuser, with a female child as the victim. Therefore, in this text the victim will be referred to as "she," the offender as "he," and the nonoffending parent as "she."

In intrafamily child sexual abuse cases, the interview of the nonoffending parent may give invaluable information to the investigator in that:

1. The information given by the victim may be corroborated.

2. Factual information about the victim and the offender will help build a framework for interviewing the offender.

3. An evaluation of the nonoffending parent's ability and willingness to protect the victim can be made.

Of greatest importance is the assessment of the nonoffending parent's ability to protect the child. It may be necessary to remove the child from the home if the nonoffending parent cannot be an ally to the child. The investigator should take great care in making this evaluation and be very aware of the emotional trauma that the nonoffending parent is facing. Not only has her child been molested, but her spouse is being accused of committing the abuse. Either issue alone would be difficult to face, but both can be devastating. For this reason, the investigator's attitude must be one of diplomacy, empathy, sensitivity, and objectivity.

A common reaction to the disclosure is denial, disbelief, and anger by the nonoffending parent. This woman needs support and understanding and should not be made to feel responsible for the abuse. The investigator must be careful not to come across as accusatory or to imply neglect on the part of the nonoffending parent. This serves only to alienate her and to make her defensive. A far better approach is to help the nonoffending parent be an ally, for she has invaluable information that is vital to the investigation.

Timing of the Interviews. In cases in which the nonoffending parent does not have knowledge of the abuse (or disclosure), the timing of the interview is very important. A frequent scenario involves the victim disclosing to a close friend or teacher, away from the home. Police and child protective services are called, and the victim is interviewed. At this time the nonoffending parent should be notified. An effort should be made to speak with the nonoffending parent away from the alleged offender and before she discusses the events with him. If the mother is at work, a call to her place of employment should be made. The mother should be assured that her child is all right but that there has been a problem of a sensitive nature involving the child and that the investigator wishes to speak with her as soon as possible, preferably at the home, at the police station or child protective services office, or even at her place of employment. Efforts should be made to avoid giving specific details of the abuse over the phone for two reasons: (1) If the mother will be driving to the interview site, she may be too upset to drive safely, and (2) if the mother knows the exact nature of the problem, then she may wish to call her spouse and discuss the charges with him first. The advance notice to the alleged offender prevents the investigator from taking advantage of the element of surprise and may give the offender time to collect and destroy potentially damaging evidence. With nonworking mothers, a visit to the home is preferred if the spouse is not present. This will eliminate the need for her to travel and may allow a search of the premises for evidence if she is willing to sign a consent.

In instances where there is no opportunity to approach the nonoffending parent with the disclosure or to conduct an interview with her without the alleged offender being present, the investigator must use diplomacy and objectivity in dealing with both at once. It is still advisable to ask to interview the nonoffending parent privately and hope that the alleged offender will comply. If not, the investigator must conduct the interview with both present, attempting to corroborate as much information as possible.

Conducting the Interview. The interview should be conducted as soon as possible. The investigator should identify himself or herself as a police officer or child protective service worker. The parent will be eager to know what has happened, where the child is, and the nature of the problem. The investigator should be supportive and understanding during the disclosure. As stated before, many nonoffending parents react with disbelief, denial, and anger. The investigator should emphasize that his or her job is to gather factual information about the allegations, with the ultimate goal of protecting the child victim.

The following guidelines cover areas of information that the investigator should consider:

A. Information about the family dynamics
   1. Marital history. For how long has she been married? How many times has she been married? Are there children from prior marriages?
   2. Sexual relationship between the couple. Have there been problems or changes?
   3. Spouse's relationship with the victim. Is the spouse a birth parent, an adoptive parent, or a stepparent?
   4. Spouse's relationship with all the children. Is the victim singled out as a favorite?
   5. History of violence. Has the spouse ever been arrested?
   6. History of psychiatric problems.
   7. History of substance abuse.
   8. Spouse's background. Was he abused as a child (physically or sexually)?
B. What is the nonoffending parent's knowledge of the abuse?
   1. Is this her first knowledge of the abuse? If not, when were her suspicions aroused? What were the circumstances?
   2. Can she corroborate any of the child's story? (It will help to review the specific facts of the disclosure in as much detail as possible.) For example, is it true that:

      a. Her husband tucks their child into bed every night?
      b. Her husband takes care of their child while she works?
      c. Her husband has a mole above his pubic hair?

3. Has she observed inappropriate behavior on the part of the alleged offender? For example, the nonoffending parent may be able to confirm that:

      a. Her husband often walks in on the victim in the bathroom or engages in tickling or excessive touching of the child.
      b. Her child (especially a young child) displays inappropriate behavior of a sexual nature, such as touching the father in his genital area, or assumes sexually explicit positions or uses sexual language with the father.
      c. Her husband possesses pornographic material, which he leaves in places that are accessible to the child.

C. Has she noticed behavioral changes in the victim?

1. Have there been changes in sleep habits, including bed-wetting, nightmares, excessive sleeping, or insomnia?
2. Have there been changes in school performance, such as a drop in grades, behavior complaints, or reports of skipping school?
3. Have there been complaints of pain, especially vaginal or anal pain, or a burning, itching, or rash in the genital area? Has a venereal disease been identified?
4. Have there been changes in the child's mood, especially mood swings or depression?
5. Has the child displayed inappropriate sexual behavior, such as using explicit sexual language or drawing sexually explicit pictures? Has there been excessive masturbation?
6. Have fearful behaviors been displayed, such as fear of being alone with certain adults or clinging to the nonoffender?
7. Has the child exhibited serious acting-out behaviors such as runaway episodes or drug abuse, physically aggressive behaviors, or criminal behaviors such as theft (especially by older victims)?

The above are guidelines for investigators to explore with the nonoffending parent. It is appropriate to add any questions that are peculiar to the specific cases and might be enlightening to the investigation.

Once the factual knowledge is obtained in the interview, it will be necessary to explain to the mother the importance of gathering potential physical evidence. After obtaining a signed consent search of the house (which abides by the standard operating procedures for the individual department), this can be guided by the information obtained through the interviews and attempt to confiscate any physical evidence that is present. Items to consider include sheets, towels, pajamas, pornographic videos or movies, magazines, sexual paraphernalia, pictures of the victim or offender, cameras, Vaseline, and any other suspect item. All items must be labeled and the evidence preserved according to department policy.

Interview of the Alleged Offender

The content of the interview and the sequence of the investigation vary somewhat in cases of intrafamily abuse versus those involving extrafamily abuse. This does not imply that an offender must be involved in only one type of abusive relationship, as there may be some overlap. For example, an offender who is accused of sexually abusing a child in the neighborhood may also have sexually abused children in his own family.

It is preferable for the investigator to conduct the interview of the alleged intrafamily offender after the interviews of the victim and the nonoffending parent have occurred, thus providing a framework for questioning the alleged offender. It is also preferable for the investigator to interview the alleged offender before he has had time for discussion with the victim, spouse, or other family members. Therefore, the interview should be conducted in sequence without delay. This is particularly important in cases in which physical evidence may exist and in cases with volatile family relationships in which the offender may force the victim to recant the allegations (usually through pressure or threats).

A useful approach is to ascertain from the spouse the time that the alleged offender will be home and attempt to approach him there for the interview. If at all possible, arrangements should be made so that the spouse and other family members are away from the home at the time of the interview. This provides the interviewer the opportunity to be the first to tell the alleged offender of the disclosure and to note his reaction to the accusation. This approach also minimizes the opportunity for him to destroy or remove physical evidence that may be present in the home.

Another approach would be to call the alleged offender at his place of employment, tell him that there has been a problem of a sensitive nature involving his child, and ask him to come to the police station. Again, it is wise not to give specific details over the phone. Another option is to offer to meet the alleged offender at his place of employment. Few offenders choose this option, however, because it may create an embarrassing situation with employers. Regardless of the location, it is important not to delay the interview.

As with all phases of the investigation, the investigator must keep an open mind, appreciating his or her role as a fact finder and resisting the temptation to prejudge the offender. This may be difficult in some cases, for example, when there has been a witness to the abuse or overwhelming physical evidence is present. Nonetheless, it is the responsibility of the investigator to ascertain the alleged offender's version of the events and attempt to establish its truth or falsehood. Obtaining a confession is the ultimate goal of the interview when the accused cannot present information to refute the allegation of child sexual abuse.

Conducting the Interview. Objectivity on the part of the investigator is paramount during the interview; he or she should not come across as accusatory. The alleged offender should not be judged as guilty but should be given the opportunity to provide exculpatory information.

A. The interviewer should present the accused with the nature of the accusation. For example, the investigator might begin by saying, "Mr. Smith, your daughter is alleging that you have made inappropriate sexual contact with her." The investigator can then:
   1. Note his response to the disclosure. If he has more than one daughter, note whether he names the victim or asks which one is accusing him.
   2. Note whether the man asks for details of the inappropriate sexual contact. In my experience, most offenders who are guilty of the abuse will not ask for details and will avoid speaking of the abuse.
   3. Expect denial and allow it at this time. Note the alleged offender's voice, posture, eye contact, and nervous habits as he is denying. There may be a vehement "That's absurd! I'd never do such a thing!" or a subdued "It's not true." Body language also can be a powerful communicator of a person's true feelings; discrepancies between body language and verbal statements may signal that the person is lying or under great stress.
B. The interviewer should establish the alleged offender's view of family dynamics.
   1. Are there problems with the marriage relationship? What is the duration of the problems?
   2. What is his current marital status? Is he married, separated, or divorced? If divorced, does he have visitation rights? If so, the interviewer should make note of specific times of visitation.
   3. What is the alleged offender's view of his relationship with the child victim? With other siblings?
   4. Why does the alleged offender believe the child would accuse him of these charges?

In some cases, information disclosed at this point may redirect the investigation. For example, an alleged offender may reveal that his wife has been married twice before and that each husband has been accused of the same charges. Or an alleged offender may reveal that his daughter's best friend has just accused her father of the same charges after both girls were refused permission to go to the beach alone. Under such circumstances, a different light may be shed on the information given by the victim as the investigation is continued.

C. The investigator should confront the alleged offender with specific information revealed in the interviews of the victim, nonoffending parent, and others. The following approaches may be used.

1. Name the specific offense (e.g., picture taking, games, nudity). For example, the investigator might say, "Mr. Smith, your daughter says that the two of you play a game called 'little man' and that the 'little man' tickles her all over and then rubs her 'down there.'" Or the investigator might say, "Mr. Smith, your daughter says that you take pictures of her with no clothes on and that you keep them in your top dresser drawer."

2. Take detailed (quoted) statements from the alleged offender. These might include statements such as "I'm never alone with her," "I never go into her room," "I was out of town that weekend," or "I don't own any dirty magazines."

3. Compare his responses with the information given by the victim and others.

4. Confront the alleged offender with the existence of (potential) physical evidence, such as sheets, pajamas, pornographic magazines, movies and videos, nude pictures, sexual paraphernalia, and any other items named by the child.

5. Show drawings depicting the abuse made by the victim; show the anatomically correct dolls in the positions the victim used; show the written statement by the victim and ask for his response. At this point, the full extent of the disclosure should be made clear.

6. Note carefully the alleged offender's reaction to this line of questioning. Watch for nervous habits such as sweating, nail biting, twitching, excessive smoking, or nervous tics.

D. The investigator should appeal to the alleged offender's emotions. For example:

1. Attempt to relieve the alleged offender of his guilt.
   a. "Mr. Smith, I don't think you would ever really want to hurt your daughter; I think you really love her."
   b. "Mr. Smith, I know that you love your daughter, and she tells me that she loves you, too."
   c. "Mr. Smith, why would this child who loves you so much say something like this if it wasn't true?"

2. Create a comfortable, nonthreatening environment in which the accused can tell you that he committed the crime.

3. Do not come across as punitive or accusatory.

4. Attempt to make the alleged offender an ally; do not alienate him.

E. If the alleged offender chooses to make a confession, the investigator should take proper action according to his or her department's policy regarding Miranda warning, warrant application, and arrest.

F. If the alleged offender denies the charges, the investigator may offer him the opportunity to take a polygraph examination. The investigator might say, "Mr. Smith, I'm trying to understand your position; maybe we can clear this up right now. I can arrange for a polygraph exam right now. Are you willing?" The alleged offender will usually grant permission at first, then frequently become agitated and nervous and want to discuss it with his wife or an attorney. The investigator should make an effort to have the test done immediately. Many offenders confess before actually undergoing the polygraph examination.

   1. If the alleged offender takes and fails the polygraph, this adds to probable cause for the arrest (but is not sufficient on its own); many offenders will confess at this point.
   2. If the alleged offender takes and passes the polygraph examination, a reexamination of the investigation must be made. This does not, however, conclude the investigation of the allegation.
   3. If the alleged offender refuses the polygraph examination, the investigator should ascertain his reasons for refusal and make a note of them.

G. At the conclusion of the interview, the alleged offender should be informed that the investigation will be ongoing and that the services of police and protective services are available if he needs assistance.

Sample Interview.

Interviewer: Mr. Smith, your daughter is alleging that you have made inappropriate sexual contact with her.
Offender: I'd never do anything to hurt my little girl.
Int: Why do you think she would say something like this?
Off: Maybe she saw it on TV or read it in a magazine or something.
Int: She says you go into her bedroom at night.
Off: Never.
Int: She says you sit on her bed and fondle her.
Off: No, never.
Int: She says you put something on your finger like Vaseline.
Off: No, I don't even have any such thing.
Int: She says you have her masturbate you.
Off: No, never.
Int: She says you ejaculate on her bed.
Off: No, never.
Int: She says that you have a large penis.

Off: Maybe she saw me in the bathroom.

Int: She says that you have brown pubic hair. What color is your pubic hair, Mr. Smith?

Off: Brown, but maybe she saw it in the shower.

Int: She says you showed her a magazine with nude people in it.

Off: No.

Int: Do you subscribe to or have any such magazines?

Off: Yes.

Int: Where do you keep them?

Off: In my bedroom.

Int: May I see them?

Off: Yes.

The victim may have described specific details of a magazine or picture inside a magazine. If magazines are located that corroborate the child's statement, these items should be considered instrumentalities used during the commission of the crime to lower the child's inhibitions and teach the child specific acts. It should be remembered that these items may have already been seized during a consent search of the residence.

Int: Mr. Smith, I have already seized several magazines from your bedroom. We have already conducted a consent search of your house. Would there be any reason for your seminal fluid or sperm to be on your daughter's sheets or pajamas?

Off: No. No.

Int: Would there be any reason for your pubic hair to be on the floor next to your daughter's bed.

Off: No.

Int: Would there be any reason for your fingerprints to be in or on the jar of Vaseline we took from your bathroom?

Off: No.

Int: Mr. Smith, I feel you really care for your daughter. We need to know where your daughter will be safe. We need to know the truth. Would you consider taking a lie detector examination?

The investigator would by now have noted the suspect's response to learning that items had been seized during a consent search of the house. The suspect had previously denied knowledge of any Vaseline but then denied that his fingerprints would be on it. His reaction to the offer of a polygraph examination also should be noted.

Off: Yes.

Int: I can arrange for it right now.

Off: Well, I do have high blood pressure. I'm a nervous person.

Int: Mr. Smith, all those areas are taken into consideration. I'll call for the appointment. We can do it right now.

Off: Well, I don't think I will take it right now.

Int: Mr. Smith, I think we know why you don't want to take the exam. Your daughter is telling the truth, isn't she?

Off: (silence)

Int: Mr. Smith, we have a problem we need to talk about.

Off: (silence)

Int: I know you love your daughter; I don't think you ever wanted to hurt her.

Off: I do love my daughter.

Int: I think you owe it to your daughter. She hasn't done anything wrong. Don't put her through this.

Off: You know I love her. (He starts to cry.) It's true.

The investigator must be patient, sensitive, empathic, and nonjudgmental during this type of interview. The atmosphere must be one in which the offender can tell the interviewer about this most difficult set of circumstances in his life. If the investigator can create such an atmosphere, the likelihood that an intrafamily abuser will confess to the crime is substantially increased.

Extrafamily Child Sexual Abuse

The interview of the alleged offender in suspected extrafamily child sexual abuse cases is usually conducted after interviewing the victim, other potential victims, or others having corroborative information. Frequently, based on information given by the victim and others, a search warrant is obtained and the residence of the alleged offender is searched for physical evidence before he is interviewed. The investigator should keep in mind that a pedophile may molest hundreds of children over his lifetime and that because many pedophiles tend to be "collectors," there is frequently an abundance of physical evidence to be confiscated. The search should focus on items that have been named by the victim and any other items typically collected by pedophiles.

In one case, a child said, "He showed us dirty movies and pictures of naked people. He has a list of other boys in his dresser drawer." Items to be considered in the search for this case would include the following (Dworin 1985):

- Camera equipment, video cameras, VCRs, videotapes, home movies, pictures, slides, Polaroids, undeveloped film.

- Phone registers, address books, correspondence or papers with names that might identify the current victim and others.

- Diaries and any other writings, tape recordings, or letters that may show the identity of victims.

- Magazines, books, movies, or photographs depicting nudity or sexual activity; collections of photographs depicting children in a particular age group in nude poses or engaging in sexual activity.

- Magazines, newspapers, classified advertisements, and other publications that list names, addresses, and phone numbers of individuals with similar interests.

- Sex toys, sex aids, dildos, rubber penises of various sizes, or vibrators.

- Articles of personal property belonging to the child victims, including toys, drawings, crayons, or clothing, or any other item pertinent to the case.

- Safe deposit box keys or bills and checks showing the location and identity of safe deposit boxes and storage facilities.

- Rent receipts, canceled mail, utility bills, or telephone bills showing the identity of the occupant of the residence.

If the search turns out to be productive, the stage is set for the interview of the alleged offender. The investigator's goal is to obtain a confession from this person using information that has already been brought to light (Dworin 1985).

The interview may be conducted at the alleged offender's residence or place of employment or at the police station. Particularly in these cases, with the potential for much physical evidence, any advance warning from the police or child protective services will allow him to remove or destroy potentially incriminating items. If the first contact with the alleged offender must be made by phone, the investigator should avoid giving the specific details of the accusation. It is better simply to state that there have been allegations made of a sensitive nature involving a juvenile and that you will meet him to discuss the allegations immediately. It is wise to forestall his attempts to delay the interview; time is very valuable in these cases.

The investigator must maintain a neutral attitude and avoid a stance of prejudgment, even when the physical evidence and testimony of the victims is extremely incriminating. The responsibility of the investigator is to gather the facts regarding the case and to give the alleged offender an opportunity to tell his version of the story. This is best accomplished when the investigator avoids approaches that will cause the alleged offender to become defensive. The following approach is suggested:

A. Present the alleged offender with the nature of the accusation (e.g., "Mr. Jones, there has been a complaint that you have made inappropriate sexual contact with a juvenile.").
   1. Note his response; does he name the alleged victim or another child?
   2. Expect denial and allow it at this time.
B. Establish the alleged offender's view of his relationship with the victim (e.g., "Mr. Jones, the victim says he has been to your apartment many times.").
   1. Note his response (e.g., "No, I don't even know that child.").
   2. Ask why the child has accused him of this. A typical response might be: "I don't even know the child. I've seen him in the neighborhood. He wanted to ride my moped, but I wouldn't let him. Maybe that's why."
C. Confront the alleged offender with the information revealed during the interviews of the victim and others. The following sample dialogue is illustrative.

Int: Mr. Jones, John states that on several occasions you have invited him to your apartment and that you have shown him X-rated movies and magazines. He says that you also took nude pictures of him and several other boys.

Off: I don't even own X-rated movies and magazines. That kid has never been in my house. (The investigator may have removed evidence of movies and pictures during the search already conducted.)

Int: Mr. Jones, John and his friend Joe state that you took them to King's Dominion and that you got a motel and spent the night near there. He says you introduced them to some friends of yours and that all of you were nude.

Off: I've never even been to King's Dominion. I don't have any friends in Virginia. (The investigator may have removed pictures of the alleged offender and the victims at King's Dominion, as well as motel receipts for that date.)

   1. Take detailed notes of his responses.
   2. Compare the alleged offender's version with the information obtained in prior interviews with the children and others.
   3. Confront the alleged offender with the existence of physical evidence either already gathered or potentially gathered. For example, the investigator may say the following at this point: "Mr. Jones, I have already gotten a search warrant for your apartment; we have in custody the photos and slides you made of John in your apartment." (The alleged offender had denied knowing the victim or having him in his residence.) Or the investigator might say, "Mr. Jones, we have

a list of young boys' names taken from your diary, and John's name is given, along with details of your trip to King's Dominion."
4. Note the alleged offender's reaction to the above information. There may be an increase in nervous habits such as sweating, smoking, twitching, or nervous tics.
D. Appeal to the emotions of the alleged offender. These men frequently care very deeply for their victims.
  1. For example, the investigator might say:
    a. "Mr. Jones, I feel that you care very deeply about John. He tells us that you have been very good to him."
    b. "Mr. Jones, I don't think you really meant to hurt the boys."
    c. "These boys need your help, Mr. Jones."
  2. Create a comfortable, nonpunitive, nonthreatening atmosphere in which the alleged offender can tell you that he committed the abuse.
  3. Allow the alleged offender to talk. Once he has admitted these incidents, he may be willing to cooperate by giving a list of victims.
E. With physical evidence to corroborate the victim's disclosure, many pedophiles will confess. If so, take proper action according to individual departmental policy regarding Miranda warning, application for arrest warrant, and procedures.
F. If the alleged offender denies the allegations and
  1. there is no physical evidence to corroborate the disclosure, offer him an opportunity for a polygraph examination and proceed as with the intrafamily offender.
  2. there is physical evidence that corroborates the victim's disclosure, then probable cause for arrest is established and the investigator can proceed with the arrest according to departmental policy.

Evidence Collection

Evidence as used in law means "that which demonstrates or makes clear or ascertains the truth of the very fact or point in issue, either on the one side or the other" (*Leonard* v. *State* 1919). Physical evidence in child sexual abuse cases has frequently been overlooked. Investigators must be aware of its existence and its importance in corroborating the child victim's disclosure.

Many investigators, upon hearing that the most recent sexual contact with a victim had been three weeks ago, are quick to dismiss the existence of physical evidence. The following case is illustrative.

Example: Jane, a six-year-old girl, is sexually abused by her father. The abuse occurs at night in the child's bed and involves oral sex and masturbation. The last incident occurred approximately three weeks ago.

Should the investigator seize the sheets, pillowcases, and the child's pajamas? Yes. Seminal fluid, sperm, hair, and fibers can be located in these items. The acid phosphatase enzyme test can locate seminal fluid many weeks, months, or sometimes years later. Sperm and seminal fluid, like blood, can seldom, if ever, be washed completely from fabric.

Would a sheet seized from the child's bed be admissible as evidence if it were washed with other clothing, possibly transferring body fluids? Certainly this question would be raised by the defense counsel at a suppression hearing, and the sheet may very well be suppressed as evidence. Even so, the investigator should not be deterred by this possibility. The responsibility of the investigator is to gather any and all evidence and to maintain a chain of custody of the evidence.

For many offenders, the knowledge that police are gathering material evidence can provoke overwhelming anxiety and at times may lead to confession of their guilt. By way of comparison, the gun used to commit a murder is considered an instrumentality in the commission of the crime. Child sexual abuse cases may also involve the use of instrumentalities during the commission of the abuse. These are some items to be considered as potential evidence:

- Vaseline or other lubricants.
- Vibrators, dildos, or other sexual paraphernalia.
- Sexually explicit books, magazines, movies, or videos.
- Cameras or sexually explicit photographs or drawings.
- Any other item described by the victim as being used as an accessory in the abuse.

The following case is illustrative.

> *Example:* Mary, a four-year-old girl, is shown several magazines by her father. The magazines have pictures of adults in bondage. Mary is later engaged in a game called "attack," which involves bondage with rope and handcuffs. As the abuse progresses, Mary is taught to place dildos in her father's anus.

In this case, all the instrumentalities of the abuse, including magazines, ropes, handcuffs, and various dildos, were seized as physical evidence and were crucial in obtaining a conviction.

Some cases, such as those involving exposure or fondling, may not present physical evidence, but the possible existence of evidence should always be considered, especially at the outset of the investigation, to prevent its loss or destruction.

What is physical evidence in child sexual abuse cases? What types of items should the experienced investigator be looking for? The investigator must carefully consider all the child's statements to ascertain what type of evidence may exist. In the following list, statements by children are paired with items seized as evidence after the child's statement was made.

1. "Daddy used a green towel to wipe the yukky off." (The investigator confiscated a semen-stained towel.)

2. "Grandpa got my pajamas all wet. It was sticky." (The female child's pajamas were seized and examined in the laboratory, and semen stains were identified on the pajamas.)

3. "Sometimes it would be wet on my legs, so I used my shirt to wipe it off." (Again, the child's shirt was analyzed, and semen stains were found on the shirt.)

4. "Uncle Bill would stand next to my bed and rub his penis until white came out. It went on my rug." (In this case, the rug in the child's room had semen stains on it, and pubic hair was found, mixed with the carpet fibers.)

5. "He tried to put a stick in my thing." (This child had a urethral injury documented by a medical examination. In a search of the house, the stick used to inflict the injury was found and confiscated.)

6. "Once he tore my underwear off." (In this case, the investigator was able to confiscate the child's panties, which had been torn by the abuser.)

7. "He showed me a magazine and said we should do this." (The magazine was confiscated.)

8. "He took pictures of me with my clothes off." (The photographs were found and confiscated.)

9. "He read me a book about sex." (A search of the alleged offender's room revealed the book described by the child.)

10. "He made me dress up like Mommy and took my picture." (Photographs of the child dressed in her mother's clothes were seized as evidence.)

11. "He made me suck his penis." (On medical examination, cultures for gonorrhea obtained from the child's pharynx revealed that the child had an asymptomatic gonorrhea infection of the pharynx.)

12. "He always wears these green sweatpants." (The green sweatpants were found and analyzed, and semen stains were found on the clothing.)

13. "He has a list of other boys on his computer disk; I saw it once." (A search revealed computer equipment and computer software that contained the incriminating list.)

Each statement about the abuse can lead the investigator to a piece of physical evidence. Once the existence of potential physical evidence is established, proper channels of action must be taken to obtain a search warrant. With this, the search is conducted according to departmental and jurisdictional guidelines.

Conclusion

The investigation of child sexual abuse allegations is often a long and tedious process, which requires an investigator who can be sensitive to the needs of the child. An increase in public knowledge and awareness of child sexual abuse has created a demand for this type of investigator. These guidelines are designed to serve as an aid to those beginning to work with these cases.

Our ultimate goals as investigators are to protect the child victims and to bring abusers to justice. Careful investigative interviewing, comprehensive and complete documentation of facts, and meticulous collection and preservation of physical evidence are all essential. When these processes are carried out carefully and the investigator understands how best to interview the accused, the odds of obtaining a confession from the offender are greatly improved. Child victims enjoy the best protection when their abusers confess to committing the crime and the children are spared the burden of testifying and living through a lengthy trial. Investigators who understand and empathize with victims and abusers, and are willing to conduct investigations with skill and care, can achieve both goals.

References

Dworin, William 1985. Personal Communication. Federal Law Enforcement Training Center, Glynco, GA.

Kosid, Janet E. 1987. "Considerations in Obtaining Expertise Search Warrants in Cases of Preferential Child Molesters." In *Interviewing Child Victims of Sexual Exploitation*. Washington, D.C.: The National Center for Missing and Exploited Children, 33.

Leonard v. State. 1919. 100 0.5 456, 127, N.E. 464.

Sgroi, Suzanne M. 1982. *Handbook of Clinical Intervention in Child Sexual Abuse,* Lexington, MA: Lexington Books.

Summit, Roland C. 1983. "The Child Sexual Abuse Accommodation Syndrome," *Journal of Child Abuse and Neglect* 7: 177–93.

9
Videotaping the Sexually Abused Child: The Texas Experience, 1983–1987

Jan Marie DeLipsey
Sue Kelly James

Case 1. A nine-year-old boy was forced by a twenty-year-old male neighbor to fondle his (the boy's) mother and simulate intercourse with her. The perpetrator then raped the mother at knife point and forced the child to watch. He threatened to kill them both if they reported the crime. The assaults were reported, and the mother and son sought psychotherapy. Immediately after the attack, the boy began failing in school and experiencing nightmares. His grades improved to passing, however, after he began counseling.

In a few months, the mother and son were beginning to return to a normal lifestyle. The criminal assault trial began five months after the rape incident. The child was told that he might have to testify. Although the boy was prepared to testify through visits to the court and procedural explanations of the courtroom process, he again started experiencing problems. Sleep disturbances and violent dreams increased as the trial date drew near, and academic performance declined. The child reported that he was afraid to testify in a public courtroom, the reason being, in his words, "I didn't want everyone to know what I had to do to Mama."

Case 2. A five-year-old girl, who had been sexually abused by an adult male family friend, was given extensive preparation for the courtroom trial process. The child took the witness stand and easily answered questions until the defense attorney asked, "Have you ever taken an oath before?" The child began to cry. The attorney continued the questioning in a gentle, though persistent, manner. As the questioning progressed, the child became hysterical, and a recess was called. When calmed, she whispered to her counselor, "I have never stolen anything." The child communicated that she felt as though she had been accused of doing something wrong and was afraid that she was in court to be punished.

Case 3. A ten-year-old girl refused to enter the courtroom to testify to a violent rape committed by her stepfather. Sobbing, she grabbed her therapist, saying, "Please don't make me go in and tell this." She never regained enough composure to testify. The man was convicted only because the medical evidence was overwhelming.

The Child in the Criminal Justice System

The traumatic effects on the young witness associated with the courtroom experience are well documented in the literature. In a study of these effects, Colao and Hosansky (1983) concluded that "the legal process is arduous and traumatic" (p. 135). These findings support the earlier efforts of Burgess and Holmstrom (1978), who also observed that the courtroom experience was a stressful event for children. This documentation of secondary victimization is consistent with reported clinical experiences of mental health professionals and with anecdotal accounts of courtroom trauma cited in the literature (Gager and Schurr 1979). This body of anecdotal research indicates that numerous cases are dismissed due to either a child's inability to testify or the poor presentation of testimony. The child's fear or confusion is often cited as the primary impetus in such circumstances.

Adult and child witnesses alike experience hardship or trauma as a result of the adversarial nature of our criminal justice system. These unfortunate by-products are tolerated, however, because we believe this process, serving as a crucible, generally protects and ensures the rights of both parties. Although this may be the case for most adults, our contention is that the child witness encounters hardships that infringe on that child's right to safety and protection. Therefore, procedural reforms are in order to balance the rights of both defendant and young witness.

In their 1979 criminal justice system review, Gager and Schurr noted that "few representatives of the judicial process demonstrated expertise in techniques required to interview children" (p. 54). They also observed that a common defense strategy was "putting children on trial" (p. 54). Parker (1982) pointed out that the vulnerability of the child victim has been well defined, but the ability of the criminal justice system to respond appropriately has not been shown. New legislative reforms (Bulkley 1982), such as videotaped or surrogate testimony, are designed to minimize the trauma experienced by the child witness and to "rebalance" her or his rights. However, we still do not adequately understand the specific nature of the problems the child encounters.

Children's Rights: A Historical Perspective

In the United States at the end of the last century, the prevention of cruelty to animals superseded the protection of children. In an effort to provide protection for a severely abused child, a New York lawyer, Elbridge Gerry, resorted to employing a statute that protected animals from abuse. As no laws existed to protect children, the statute was interpreted to mean that "the child should be treated as a 'little animal' of the human race" (Oates 1982, 299). Thus began the American movement to protect children through the justice system.

By the beginning of this century, our country had recognized not only the need for societal protection of abused children, but also the need for differential treatment of the young criminal. Juvenile courts were first established in the early 1900s. The Declaration of the Rights of the Child, adopted nearly thirty years ago by the United Nations General Assembly, was another important milestone:

> The child shall enjoy special protection and shall be given opportunities and facilities, by law and by other means, to enable him to develop physically, mentally, morally, spiritually, and socially in a healthy and normal manner and in a manner in conditions of freedom and dignity. In the enactment of laws for this purpose, the best interest of the child shall be the paramount consideration. (Declaration of the Rights of the Child 1959)

Translating the spirit of the declaration into statutes and practice has been difficult. Although children are theoretically well protected by law, in reality the protection has been in name only. As Parker (1982) writes, "Procedures that operate solely to vindicate a societal intent often fail to take into account the psychological damage that can be done to a young child in the role of the witness" (p. 643).

Problems of the Child Witness

To date, there has been limited empirical investigation into the criminal justice difficulties children encounter, particularly those associated with their cognitive and emotional resources. In an effort to summarize and organize information, we have drawn a distinction between cognitive and social development. Memory and language fall into the cognitive category, while contextual and interpersonal issues fall under social development. This distinction should prove helpful in framing and understanding the problems of the child witness.

Cognitive Development

Melton (1984) writes that children in the criminal justice system "are less likely than adults to have the cognitive skills necessary to organize the experience" (p. 110). This issue takes on increasing importance in the presentation of testimony in an open courtroom setting. Of the many factors that may affect testimony given by any witness, the following three are particularly germane to children: memory retrieval and contamination, effects of the passage of time, and courtroom language.

Literature relating to recall abilities suggests that children have greater difficulty with long-term memory than do adults (Johnson and Foley 1984). Studies indicate that a long lapse between an event and the first recall of the event has an adverse effect on the completeness of recall (Dent and Stephenson 1979; Loftus and Davies 1984). This is especially true for the accurate recall of faces (Chance and Goldstein 1984).

Even though studies show that time lapse has a detrimental effect on completeness of recall, however, it is important to note that they do not show a decline in the accuracy of recall. Given that memory decay is greater for children than for adults, a long delay between reporting the event to police and the final court trial is apt to have a more adverse effect on a child's recall abilities. With the passage of time, the child's testimony, though accurate, is more likely to seem fragmentary or less complete than that of an adult witness. Unfortunately, a sketchy account given by a child may be interpreted as a confused or incompetent rendering of the incident. Although rehearsal of testimony has been associated with more complete recall for children, it also obstructs accuracy.

The traditional criminal justice process cannot avoid this problem of memory decay, which can develop in young children within a few days (Loftus 1979). The problem is even more acute if the perpetrator was unknown to the child and a correct physical description is needed.

Many researchers, when speaking of information retrieval, refer to a principle known as *encoding*. Encoding is a process of organizing and storing information by linking the new material to older, more familiar information. Studies looking at children's memory have found that poor recollection of material is associated with inadequate encoding (Bjorkland and Hock 1982). An interpretive framework for comprehending events and thus storing them is essential for recall. The narrow life experiences of most children limit their organizing abilities, as they generally categorize only familiar material well.

Loftus and Davies (1984) found that children were more open to suggestion and information contamination than adults regarding events that were not efficiently encoded. This is a fundamental issue when examining possible corruption of material. Information given by children who may not have efficiently organized their experience is more subject to contamination from multiple interviews or interviewers than is information given by adults. Traditional criminal justice procedures that require multiple interviews increase the opportunity for contaminating information.

Research regarding information contamination indicates that highly accurate though incomplete recall is more likely to come from a free-style report or narrative statement (Dent and Stephenson 1979). Leading, suggestive, or closed-ended questions (questions that require a yes or no answer) can alter or transform a recollection (Dale, Loftus, and Rathbum 1978; Loftus 1979). Unfortunately, the traditional courtroom setting is not conducive to narrative, free-style reporting.

Trial delays are routine and are frequently accompanied by false starts in which a child is prepared for testimony but the case is continued. Repeated questioning and interviewing during these periods invariably results in a loss of spontaneity or original information. Although many children may generate initial statements of alleged abuse using their own words, repeated interrogation by adults usually spoils the "freshness" of the statement.

A final note regarding the memory retrieval of children relates to actual recall abilities. Children do not become any more confused than adults regarding "who did what" (Johnson and Foley 1984) or in knowing "what they said from what others said" (Foley, Johnson, and Raye 1983). Research suggests, however, that children do become confused in distinguishing what they said from what they thought. Therefore, methods for supplementing a videotaped statement with other evidence may be necessary.

Courtroom language is confusing, even for adults, and it can be even more so for children. One example is Case 3 above, where the girl thought she had been accused of stealing (taking) an oath, but the problems may be as numerous as the children who testify. Clark (1983) provides an excellent summary of the research relating to vocabulary acquisition of children. She points out that a child's meaning and an adult's meaning for the same word may vary. The traditional courtroom setting does not provide an opportunity to explore an idiosyncratic language. Attorneys and judges are not trained to communicate with children of different ages and developmental stages. Thus, an interview setting may be more conducive to exploring the problem of idiosyncratic language used by the child than a courtroom setting.

Social Development

Contextual issues related to the traditional courtroom setting are more problematic for young witnesses than for adults. These problematic issues include frequent and unpredictable distractions, formal and authoritative behavior, and situationally induced distress.

Wellman and Lempers (1977) found that distraction was one of four significant factors relevant to children's ability to perform memory tasks. The activity of the courtroom, with spectators, jury, court reporter, attorneys, bailiffs, and defendant, as well as procedural practices allowing interruption of testimony, are particularly difficult for the young witness to comprehend. A limited attention span and distractibility work together to hinder the child's concentration and recall. Videotaping a child's narrative provides a protective environment without these situational obstructions.

Little is known regarding the child's understanding of the interaction of social and physical environments and their effects (Shantz 1983). The interplay of the authoritative atmosphere and the adversarial context of the traditional courtroom setting may present enormous problems for the child witness.

The authoritarian nature of the courtroom influences children, whose need to cooperate and please leads them to behave in a manner that they believe is expected. Considering Hartup's research on the child's relationship with an adult world, Shantz (1983) writes, "[It] is marked by the fundamental relation of [the] authority of the adult to the child, authority in the sense of greater power physically, socially, mentally, and financially" (p. 529). Few institutions rival the traditional courtroom's austere, authoritative climate. The formal demeanor of its participants can be intimidating, and a child may distort information in response to perceived pressure.

The adversarial context presents a different sort of obstacle for the young witness. A useful framework for viewing this problem would be Piaget's concept of egocentrism. Egocentrism describes a fused state between the self and the nonself (Piaget 1929). Consider a young child participating in a contested trial. This child is less able to "remove" himself or herself from the distressing situation at hand than is an adult. There is a lack of differentiation between the child's own thoughts and feelings and those of others. Conformity and cooperation or fear accompanied by withdrawal may be the repercussions. The adult witness is more likely than the child witness to be able to see beyond the immediacy of her or his own experience and abstractly comprehend that courtroom participants play out roles or functions. This phenomenon is sometimes referred to as *perspective taking,* which is the ability to adopt the view of another person.

In researching perspective taking, Selman and Jacquette (1978) found that somewhere between the ages of six and twelve, a child becomes able to "put [himself] in the other's shoes and to see the self as a subject to the other" (p. 274). Perspective taking enables adults to understand that courtroom animosity is in part a function of role-playing behavior. A defense attorney must play the part of closely scrutinizing testimony, regardless of his or her opinion about the veracity of the information. A child is developmentally unable to execute this higher order processing and is vulnerable to being enveloped in the situational distress and harassment. This vulnerability to distress, coupled with less sophisticated linguistic and communication abilities, limits the child's opportunity to have her say in court. The child lacks the ability to withstand temporary distress in order to accomplish a greater goal or task.

Children also are restricted in their moral judgment, which runs hand-in-hand with social perspective taking. Kohlberg and Elfenbein (1975) assert that perspective-taking abilities allow an understanding of the Golden Rule. A child is less likely than an adult to appreciate the need to endure personal discomfort to advance the welfare or safety of others. The acquisition of this ability is associated with the process of becoming less egocentric (Rest 1983).

Addressing the Problem

Using videotaped statements of a sexually abused child in the courtroom solves many of the problems specific to the child witness. The California Trial Evidence Committee (Joseph 1983) concluded that the use of videotaped evidence could become a viable tool in the presentation of evidence. This alternative to traditional proceedings may afford a greater opportunity for justice to be served for the child victim of a crime.

Lawmakers in a number of states are attempting to legislate alternatives to the live testimony of the child witness by enacting laws that allow videotaped testimony. Bulkley (1982) provided an excellent review of current legislative trends in child sexual abuse cases. She indexed the reforms into categories designed to address three basic issues: "legal procedures to be more sensitive to child victims, to improve prosecution and conviction rates, and to provide treatment in special programs for the offender, child, and family" (p. 645). Bulkley reported that as of May 1985, seventeen states had passed statutes permitting videotaped testimony and/or live closed-circuit television procedures for child witnesses. Similar bills were pending in nine other states. The majority of these legislative efforts require that the child be shown to be at risk, either emotionally or physically, should she or he testify in a public courtroom. We can conclude, therefore, that protecting the child witness from emotional trauma was the key concern in prompting these legislative changes.

What is missing is a concern for the more fundamental issue of due process and the presentation of unprejudiced testimony. Although emotional protection of the child is important, the preservation of the child's fundamental rights must be addressed as well. Young victims should have a fair opportunity to report what happened to them. Judges and juries are duty bound to consider carefully the information given by the young witness. Criminal justice procedures that do not allow for that fair opportunity must be modified, not only to preserve the rights of the child, but also to preserve the rights of the accused.

Texas Videotape Law

The Texas Family Code, enacted in 1984, established general procedures for the evidential admission of videotaped and live closed-circuit interviews of children under twelve years old in child abuse cases. The statute requires that all videotaped interviews of children be conducted outside the presence of the defendant. Only the videotaped testimony of children twelve years of age and younger is admissible. The statute provides for videotaping under three different conditions. The first section of the statute describes general requirements which must be met whenever videotaped testimony is introduced at a trial. Section 2 allows a videotaped or filmed statement of a child to be presented in court if the prosecution is then prepared to make the child available for cross-examination at the trial. The following conditions must also be met:

1. No attorney for either party was present when the statement was made.
2. The recording is both visual and aural and is recorded on film or videotape or by other electronic means.
3. The recording equipment was capable of making an accurate recording, the operator of the equipment was competent, and the recording is accurate and has not been altered.
4. The statement was not made in response to questioning calculated to lead the child to make a particular statement.
5. Every voice on the recording is identified.
6. The person conducting the interview of the child in the recording is present at the proceeding and available to testify or be cross-examined by either party.
7. The defendant or the attorney for the defendant is afforded an opportunity to view the recording before it is offered into evidence.
8. The child is available to testify.

Under Section 3 of the Texas statute, the court may order the testimony of a child witness to be taken in a room other than the courtroom. It is then transmitted into the courtroom and viewed by the court via closed-circuit television equipment. Only the attorneys for the defendant and for the state, persons necessary to operate the equipment, and persons whose presence might contribute to the welfare of the child may be present in the room during the witness's testimony. The defendant is not allowed in the room but can observe and hear the testimony by means of the closed-circuit television.

Section 4 outlines procedures similar to the previous section if the testimony is to be taken outside the courtroom. The videotaped proceedings are then viewed in the courtroom. Under Sections 3 and 4, the child is not required to testify or appear in open court.

Videotaping Program at Dallas County Rape Crisis and Child Sexual Abuse Center

In September 1983, the Dallas County Rape Crisis and Child Sexual Abuse Center began developing a program for interviewing and videotaping children who had made complaints of sexual abuse. Requests for videotaping the child's statement came from the district attorney's office, police departments, child protective services, and private citizens. Although members of the staff participated in two cases that involved a prerecording of a child's testimony with direct examination and cross-examination by attorneys and one case in which a hearing was conducted via closed-circuit television, the principal part of the program relied on Section 2 of the statute. Staff therapists made videotaped recordings of the child's statements to be used in court at the time of the actual proceedings.

Although the Texas videotape statute outlined basic requirements, there were no guidelines for its practical application. In applying the statute, we became aware of many serious problems.

Problems Encountered

A six-year-old boy who alleged molestation by his stepfather was brought by his grandfather to participate in a videotaped interview. The child was unable to make a clear statement when interviewed according to recommended guidelines. No legal action resulted. Three months later, the grandfather brought a videotape to the police department, demanding that an arrest be made. The videotaped interview, conducted by the grandfather, was the last of ten attempts to "get a good one."

Another case involved an interview by a professional who failed to identify herself or the child during the early part of the interview. In addition, the visual field of the camera included the child's face and upper torso but only the upper torso of the interviewer. Realizing her error, the interviewer interrupted the session and momentarily ducked her head horizontally into the camera's view. To make matters worse, the interview contained only leading and suggestive questions.

We also noted numerous examples of bribery and coercion during our review of videotaped interviews. Uncooperative children were frequently offered candy and food or denied access to the lavatory until they completed the interview.

Undoubtedly, the most distressing problems were the use of leading and suggestive questions and coercion to make the child confirm certain information. As professionals, we were challenged to evaluate our own credibility.

In the traditional criminal justice setting, if a child's information became corrupted from multiple or inappropriate interviews, the only evidence of this was the conflict between trial testimony and early reports. In many cases, the conflicting information was not discovered. Our concern was that these inappropriate interviewing practices had been employed for some time but were not exposed until the statute was passed. We soon came to realize that the videotaped interview protected the rights of the accused as well.

Although we encountered many problems, we think that most resulted from the lack of clear guidelines, poor training, and no legislated quality of standards rather than a deliberate attempt to falsify or distort information.

Developing the Videotaping Program

Using a trial-and-error process, procedures and policies for the Dallas County Rape Crisis and Child Sexual Abuse program evolved. First, we sought advice from judges and attorneys, asking for direction in the appropriate application of the law. These experts suggested that the videotaped interviews should approximate, as closely as possible, the live courtroom situation. They also recommended developing the competency of interviewers and establishing formal procedures and policies for videotaping.

Relative to interviewing competency, the experts stated that the most important skill interviewers would need would be the ability to question children without using leading or suggestive questions. They also said interviewers would have to acquire a thorough understanding of the videotape statute and laws governing the presentation of testimony. Submitting videotapes to legal experts for assessment and feedback was recommended as a learning tool.

Consultants agreed that when children were being interviewed, they should demonstrate age-appropriate intellectual competency and be able to discriminate between the truth and a lie. These procedures were to be included in the videotaped interviews. In addition, once the child made this distinction, the experts recommended that the child be sworn to tell the truth. In deference to the language development of children, phrases such as "promise to tell the truth" were considered acceptable. Advisers acknowledged that these elements were not necessarily relevant to the truth of the allegations, but they concluded that having children demonstrate competency and ability to take an oath are currently accepted and valued procedures for allowing the testimony of a child witness and should therefore be included. This also was considered a way to make the child understand the seriousness of the interview.

Procedural recommendations included developing a written protocol that stated the procedures and policies that would be used for videotaping. We were told that we would have to assure the court that videotapes could not be tampered with by establishing a procedure for maintaining the chain of custody of evidence. Also, judges advised us that videotapes had to be made available for viewing by attorneys, other justice officials, and the accused prior to court proceedings. A procedure to provide for these viewings, while still maintaining the security of the videotapes, had to be established. Further procedural recommendations included not allowing persons other than the child and the interviewer in the room during the taping, thus excluding the equipment operator and parents or caretakers. This policy was recommended not only to decrease the number of people who would have to testify to the authenticity of the videotape, but also to minimize the pressure on, or interference with, the child during the interview.

The consultants stated that both the child and the interviewer must be clearly visible. They added that if voices were heard but the speakers were not visible, the content of the interview could be questioned. For example, they mentioned the possibility that the child might be being cued by a person outside the viewing area. We were reminded that in a live courtroom, all activity is visible to the judge.

A final suggestion concerned the use of anatomically correct dolls. Although the legal experts generally agreed that the dolls were effective in helping the child to relate an incident, the dolls also were considered innately suggestive. Therefore, minimal use of the dolls was recommended.

Experts agreed that the atmosphere and demeanor displayed on videotape would have to resemble those of the live courtroom if they were to be effective.

With a view toward incorporating the legal consultation, we carefully reviewed the literature to learn about the use of videotaped evidence involving other types of offenses. In addition, we prepared a setting where we could conduct the interviews and trained counselors in using videotape equipment. We then explored and tested different methods of preparing the child for the interview. After the initial videotaped interviews had been conducted, we asked various professionals, including judges, attorneys, children's therapists, and child development specialists, to review and critique them. Lastly, by trial and error, we determined what information the interviewer would have to obtain from other sources prior to the taping session.

We also used practical experience and research support to define and outline a style of interviewing that seemed to be efficient and appropriate.

The procedures and policies from that program, along with recommendations for improvement and changes, are presented here as guidelines. With more experience, we will continue to improve our procedures and urge that other agencies adapt them to their needs. In addition, laws vary from state to state, so an agency might have to modify our procedures to meet the legal requirements in its area.

Guidelines for Videotaping

The Setting

We installed the videotape equipment in a playroom that included a puppet theater, children's furniture, and numerous toys. A brightly colored mural covered one wall, and children's drawings were displayed on the other three. Although the room provided immediate comfort for the child and greatly facilitated development of rapport, the therapists experienced problems because the setting was too conducive to play. This caused two problems: First and most obvious, the children were easily distracted. Second, the play atmosphere of the setting allowed defense attorneys to attempt to undermine the children's credibility and suggest that their statements were make believe or fantasy.

We decided that the setting must be comfortable for children, with warm colors and child-size furniture, but also have a businesslike atmosphere to communicate that the interview is a serious matter. The interviewer also can help a child feel comfortable. As Sgroi (1982) noted, the success of an interview depends on the ability of the interviewer to establish positive rapport with the child.

Video Equipment and Operation

The following video equipment is needed:

1. Video recorder and playback machine.
2. Video camera with omnidirectional microphone.
3. Monitor for viewing videotaped interviews.
4. Supply of videotapes.

VHS players that use half-inch videotapes are recommended, as this is the most widely used type of player. An omnidirectional microphone attached to the camera will pick up sound from any direction and is preferable to a handheld or lavaliere microphone, which attaches to clothing. Microphones that children can touch or see also tend to be distracting. The camera should have a graphic digital display for recording the date and time elapsed during the interview, which may be needed to verify that the tape has not been edited.

Preferably, the videotape equipment should not be visible to the child. The child's past experiences with being photographed may cue "hamming" for the camera or distract the child. The obvious presence of equipment also may suggest that a performance is expected. A defense attorney may raise this issue in an attempt to challenge the process as prejudiced testimony. Concealing the camera can be accomplished through the use of a screen, taping through a one-way mirror, or mounting the camera on the wall.

The interviewer should be the equipment operator. If an additional person is used to operate the equipment, that person will also have to testify in court regarding the tape content to verify that it has not been altered or changed.

The interviewer/operator should check all the equipment prior to the interview to be sure that it is operating properly. The visual field of the camera should be checked through the monitor to ensure that the interviewer and child are both fully on camera. A brief test tape should be used to verify that the equipment is operating properly.

Assuming that the equipment is operating properly is a common and serious mistake in the interview process. Sometimes children have tampered with the equipment, or the cables between the camera and the recorder have been loosened during cleaning of the room. Redoing an interview is confusing to the child and often results in a loss of "freshness." Such mistakes also set the stage for the defense to suggest that evidence has been "produced" rather than "discovered," as the child has been rehearsed by the first interview.

The visual field of the camera should include the interviewer and the child. Any demonstration, such as the use of anatomically correct dolls or anatomically correct drawings, should be in the viewing area. Focusing on the child and not including the interviewer fully, as well as having obscured demonstrations, can result in confusion about exactly what was happening during the interview.

Dealing with Family Members and Caretakers

Although the statute does not mandate that no one except the child and the interviewer be present during the videotaping, we believed that the presence of parents, caretakers, or even child protective workers might prejudice the interview in some way. Our goal was to accomplish a context in which the child could be free to make an unprejudiced, narrative-style statement.

Preparing the Child for the Interview

Young children are usually not comfortable in new surroundings and should be given the opportunity to become familiar with the interview setting. After the interviewer has introduced herself or himself to the child and accompanying adult, the child should be taken into the room where the interview will occur. The child should be allowed to explore, play, and ask questions about the new surroundings. The parent or caretaker should be present in the room with the child during this orientation process. The time spent with the child and parent will let the child know that her or his caretaker is comfortable with this new adult and process.

When the interviewer believes that the child has adapted to the new surroundings, the caretaker should be taken to another room. Young children need to see exactly where their parent will be waiting while the interview is taking place. The interviewer may want to make a comment such as "Let's go see where your mother will be sitting during the interview." The child should then be taken along to watch the parent be seated and be told that "this is the chair where your mother will be sitting during the interview." Generally, this procedure is effective in relieving the child's anxieties about being separated from the accompanying adult. We have found that most children who were prepared in this manner would willingly leave their parent and go alone to be interviewed.

We found that an effective way for controlling the activity of a small child is to work with a child-size table and chairs. When returning to the videotaping setting, the interviewer should tell the child that each of them will be sitting in his or her own chair during the interviewing process and will get up when the interview is completed. A small chair and table not only provide a comfortable setting for the child, but also provide a work area for demonstrations with anatomically correct drawings or dolls. In addition, a table pulled in front of the chair prohibits the child from easily moving in and out of the chair or leaving the visual field of the camera. It is important to limit the mobility of the child, as not doing so may leave him or her more vulnerable to distraction, frustrate the interviewer, and lengthen the tape with irrelevant material.

Finishing Up

When the videotaped interview is complete, the interviewer should review it to make sure an accurate recording was obtained. As the videotape is considered to be evidence, a special procedure must be followed. The tape should be labeled with the name of the interviewer, the name of the child, and the date of the recording. It should then be stored in a locked area until it becomes the property of the court or authorized officials, guaranteeing secure protection of the evidence.

Interviewing Guidelines

Skills Development of the Interviewer

Beyond basic child sexual abuse interviewing skills as outlined by Sgroi (1982), special training in child development is needed. Target areas of concern are perception, learning, logical reasoning, language, and social/moral development. In addition, the interviewer should be well trained in appropriate interviewing techniques that facilitate narrative reporting. Interviewers should have knowledge about the law and procedures so that the interview can proceed within those parameters. Laws vary from state to state, so each interviewer must be familiar with her or his own state's statutes and procedures. For example, some states do not require child witnesses to show an understanding or appreciation of telling the difference between truth and a lie, while others require the ability to make this distinction. States also vary in the competency requirements of witnesses.

Finally, role-playing, with another adult playing the role of a child, can be helpful in preparing an interviewer. After an interviewer has begun to conduct videotaped interviews, he or she can review them with professionals such as prosecutors, judges, defense attorneys, and mental health specialists. Reviewing your own videotapes and receiving feedback from others will prove to be a valuable experience.

Who, what, when, and where are questions that must be answered in the videotaped interview. The interviewer is responsible for ensuring that all these issues are addressed. When reviewing videotapes from other programs, we noted that many interviewers had taken a list of questions into the interview room to cue their memory. In our opinion, asking questions from a list makes the interview appear staged and distracts from the spontaneous quality that has proven to be an important element in conducting a videotaped interview. A brief pause at the completion of the interview to recall whether all issues were covered thoroughly will solve this problem.

Flexibility and patience are key traits for the individual who conducts a videotaped interview. The interviewer must be prepared to have the child change the subject, point out flaws in the interviewer's appearance, ask to go to the bathroom, or expose private parts of his or her own body. When these unexpected and sometimes startling events occur, the interviewer must respond appropriately and calmly.

The interviewer should focus the conversation on the subject of the interview. Allowing the child's conversation to stray presents difficulties for viewers, who, in the past, have reported problems in following a child's story when his or her statements stray from the topic at hand. Because children typically have short attention spans, allowing a child to engage in too much irrelevant conversation lengthens the interview and limits his or her ability to focus on the complaint. Furthermore, tired children may challenge limits or become distracted, which also may affect their credibility.

Interview Style

We have already covered research that supports the "free report interview" as the method of choice. If important issues are not addressed, however, direct questions should be asked to include necessary details or clarify information. These direct questions should not, under any circumstances, add new information to the statement. A technique that we have found helpful is avoiding asking questions that can be answered "yes" or "no."

We have defined suggestive and leading questions as those that imply or encourage an answer. Here are examples of these sorts of questions, taken directly from videotapes in which the interviews were poorly conducted:

"You told the police about the abuse, didn't you?"

"Your mother said that the person who touched you was your stepfather. It was him, wasn't it?"

"Did she [perpetrator] tell you that she would hurt you if you told anyone?"

By contrast, statements or inquiries that encourage a free report do not imply a particular or expected response. They leave the child free to report the experience without pressure or guidance. We recorded the following statements from videotaped interviews that seemed to encourage a free-report narrative:

"Can you tell me what you feel happened to you?"

"What, if anything, happened next?"

"Is there anything else you remember?"

Examples of appropriate clarifying questions would be:

"You said you were at your uncle's house. Do you know what town his house is in?"

"Can you tell me or do you know how old the baby-sitter is?"

"You said this happened around the end of the summer. Do you know what month it was?"

In summary, feedback from judges, attorneys, and juries clearly indicate that use of the free-report narrative is a key factor in conducting effective videotaped interviews. This interview style facilitates and helps maintain objectivity on the part of the interviewer, and it also elicits contamination-free material from the child.

Information the Interviewer
Should Know Beforehand

We believe that the interviewer should not discuss the case with the referral source or with the child's family prior to the videotaped interview. The minimal amount of information needed is that the family suspects abuse or has noticed a certain behavior pattern. For example, if the child gives a report of the abuse to his or her mother, it is preferable that the interviewer not know the content of that report prior to the videotaped interview. Knowing that the child made a complaint is sufficient information to conduct an interview.

Avoiding assumptions or information given by others seems to allow the interviewer to give the child free rein in reporting. Our experience in reviewing problematic videotaped interviews suggests that interviewers who know particular information about the case tend to close the sessions prematurely once the information is either confirmed or denied, thus losing vital information. Simply put, not knowing where to go requires that the interviewer follow the child.

A previously formed mind-set also increases the likelihood that the interviewer will ask a leading or suggestive question. Lack of prior knowledge can serve as an insurance policy should the interviewer slip and ask a suggestive or leading question. Such a question is not as likely to be framed as a deliberate intent to elicit a particular response if the interviewer has no prior knowledge, and thus doing so does not jeopardize the interview. This blind interview may seem difficult at first, but it becomes less difficult with practice and it elicits more accurate information from the child (James and DeLipsey 1985).

After the interview with the child is completed, the interviewer may choose to question other contacts for additional information. The interviewer should carefully note this information, the source(s), and the time sequence during which it was gathered for future reference or testimony.

When to Conduct a Videotaped Interview

A videotaped interview should be conducted as early as possible for all children who have made allegations of sexual abuse. Conducting the interview soon after the allegations are made helps minimize the contaminating effects of others' verbal interactions with the child. In addition, an interviewer who decides to see the child several times before videotaping risks losing the spontaneity of the narrative.

There are times when it is not possible to videotape the child's statement during the first visit. Some children may take more time to "settle in" and will not interact with the interviewer early on. If the videotaped interview is conducted after the child has had several visits, then reference to that fact should be made in the interview. Also, if the child has already given the interviewer information about the abuse before the videotaped interview is conducted, the interviewer should note the prior disclosure during the interview. Care should be taken not to present this information in a leading or suggestive way. Past discussions should be referenced by making comments such as "Do remember when you told me about what happened to you at school? Could you tell me about that again?" The interviewer is cuing the child but is not cuing content of the response. If the child does not respond to the cue or remember the past discussion, this should be carefully documented.

Because videotaped interviews are conducted outside the presence of attorneys, jury, judge, and defendant, the interviewer must be particularly straightforward, frank, and ethical. Complete neutrality is of paramount importance in this process. The child's statement must stand on its own merit; the interviewer is not an advocate.

Number of Videotapes

Conducting only one videotaped interview is recommended in most instances. Remember that the child can add information to the testimony from the witness stand. An additional videotaped interview may, however, be conducted if further relevant information is discovered or needs clarification. For example, in one videotaped interview, a nine-year-old child identified two strangers as perpetrators. After the interview, the child revealed that the perpetrators had in fact been her mother and her mother's boyfriend. The child stated to the interviewer that she had lied to protect them. Due to the sensitive nature of the revelation, another videotaped interview was conducted, rather than presenting the information from the witness stand. The interviewer was careful to include reference to the previous taped interview and to preserve both videotapes.

Technical difficulties also may require a second videotaped interview. These difficulties may include sound interference, an equipment malfunction, or a power failure. If a second videotaped interview is conducted, the videotape of the first interview should be preserved to document the problem. The existence of the faulty tape also helps account for why the child may not sound or appear to be as spontaneous as in the original interview.

Unfortunately, we have encountered situations in which interviewers conducted several videotaped interviews until they got it "right" or the way they wanted it. This dilutes the child's credibility and creates the appearance of manufacturing evidence. Again, the interviewer's role is one of facilitation, not creation, of testimony.

The videotape should be copied only for backup security. Those who wish to view the videotape should do so within a secure setting where the tape can be protected. Reckless handling of the videotape or the information it contains may pose a threat of serious psychological harm to the child, the accused, or others. The more copies that are made, the more likely that the tape will be seen by an inappropriate viewer. If proper control of a tape is not practiced, the controlling party may be liable for resulting injury. The Dallas County program does not allow viewing or handling of videotapes outside a secured area. The tapes do not leave the custody of the center until they are entered as evidence. Although motions have been filed requesting the court to order videotape copies to be surrendered to various parties, the court has ruled against this practice.

Postinterview Tasks

The videotaped interview may arouse conflict or renew trauma in the child, so he or she should be encouraged to talk about his or her feelings following the interview. Allowing time for the expression of feelings through free-play therapy following the videotaping is helpful for most children. The interviewer also should allow time to debrief the child's family or caretakers.

Family members frequently request and need feedback regarding the child's well-being and emotional state, as well as information about the interview itself. No interview content should be revealed, as the court typically invokes the rule regarding the testimony of witnesses. Exceptions would, of course, include situations requiring medical intervention, reporting of additional incidents, or protective actions. Debriefing statements such as "His statements were clear" or "She seemed to do her best" are appropriate. The interviewer also should explain how the videotape will be used and the procedures used to protect the information. Finally, the future therapy needs of the child and the family should be addressed.

Special Problems

The trial-and-error approach of our early program development has helped to identify problem areas in the videotaping process. These problems, along with those observed in videotapes from other programs, are described below.

Interview Atmosphere

A common practice we observed was for the interviewer to use puppets or stuffed animals to communicate with the child. This seemed to confuse the child, as he or she did not seem to be able to determine whether the interview was a time for play or a time to be serious. Several attorneys have challenged this playtime climate, and judges and juries have questioned its possible effects. Their position was that the use of toys or puppets involves fantasy, and they raised credibility issues regarding the child's statements. This point is illustrated by the case of a four-year-old child who viewed a sexual abuse prevention movie that used mice as characters. After the movie, the child wanted to know why the uncle mouse had harmed the little girl mouse. This child, being in a developmental stage in which concrete thinking is predominant, had not been able to identify her vulnerability as a child with that of the girl mouse. Her conclusion was that girl mice are in danger from uncle mice. Young children are likely to be hindered more than helped when animal puppets or similar props are used in the videotaped interview.

Playtime activities also make it more difficult to command the child's serious attention. If the child is not clear about the nature of the interview, the resulting videotaped interview may be disjointed and lengthy. Not only is the narrative difficult to follow, but it is tiring to the viewer as well. Finally, unless the interviewer clearly controls the proceedings, he or she is at risk for becoming irritated or confused. As a result, the interviewer may lose rapport with the child.

We recommend structuring the interview according to guidelines we have already mapped out. The free-report style of interviewing applies to verbal statements only, not to the structure of the interview. Contrary to popular belief, interviews without clear limits do not help a child feel more comfortable.

Anatomically Correct Dolls

If an interviewer chooses to use anatomically correct dolls during a videotaped interview, he or she should exercise caution.

During reviews of videotapes from other programs, we have frequently viewed tapes in which the interviewer chose particular dolls, initiated removal of the dolls' clothing, and reviewed the dolls' private body parts with the child. In some instances, the interviewer requested a demonstration of sexual activities and then asked the child, "Did that happen to you?" These practices are leading and suggestive. They will be challenged in the courtroom, and they may contaminate the child's information.

If dolls are needed, it is better to introduce them after the child has made reference to the sexually abusive event. The dolls should be used only to clarify the child's statements. The interviewer should not remove the clothing but permit the child to do so if he or she wishes. Many children prefer to demonstrate acts described with the dolls' clothing in place. In these instances, a clarifying question can be asked, for example, "How were your clothes when this happened?" The use of dolls in a videotaped interview should be minimal, and they should be used only as a clarification tool. Research regarding the effects on children of working with dolls is sketchy, and the potential for corruption of information is unknown.

Finally, in reviewing videotaped interviews in which dolls were used, the most common mistake we noted involved the use of the word *pretend.* A statement such as "Pretend this is you and this is your father" will draw a challenge from the defense: "You instructed the child to pretend. How do you know the report was real?"

Current State of the Texas Videotape Law

The constitutionality of the Texas videotape law has been the focus of heated debate. Less than two years after the enactment of the statute, trial court decisions based on Sections 2 and 4 were reversed at the district court level. All these cases are still awaiting final disposition.

The most controversial issue is that Sections 3 and 4 prohibit a face-to-face confrontation between the child witness and the adult defendant. Even though the right to a public trial and confrontation of witnesses has been the cornerstone of the U.S. justice system, technological advances now require that finer distinctions be drawn.

Does confrontation apply only to the right to participate in cross-examination of witnesses? If so, confrontation can be preserved with the use of videotaping and closed-circuit proceedings. Two-way communication microphones between the defendant and the attorney while the defendant views the proceedings in another room on a closed-circuit television can allow the defendant active participation. This technique, which was used in Dallas County in a criminal sexual abuse trial, is one of the issues that has been appealed at the district court level. In that case, *Long v. State of Texas* (1985), the district court ruled in 1987 that Section 4 violated due process as guaranteed by the Sixth and Fourteenth amendments. This ruling would logically extend to Section 3, as the only difference between them is whether the proceedings are live or videotaped.

These cases have raised issues that were not considered in the law itself. As mentioned earlier, special provisions were improvised to provide defendant and attorney adequate communication during the proceedings. These arrangements, though workable, were awkward and allowed for only one-way communication from the defendant to attorney. This system also opened the door to other problems, such as the defendant's talking or becoming upset while the attorney was questioning the witness. The usual procedure of writing notes back and forth during a witness's testimony allows communication but enables the attorney to concentrate on his or her task. We have found that clear and immediate communication between attorney and defendant is not possible within the limits of Sections 3 and 4.

The proceedings themselves also tended to be as confusing to the child as those that occurred in the traditional courtroom setting. This finding is congruous with the previously noted complications associated with the adversarial context. At times, the child was unable to testify clearly as to what he or she believed happened, even though he or she had given a clear statement under more favorable conditions.

The positive aspects of videotaped or live closed-circuit proceedings that prohibit face-to-face confrontation have been limited. This fact, coupled with the violation of fundamental constitutional rights, has led us to question the usefulness of Sections 3 and 4. We believe that they threaten the fundamental constitutional rights of confrontation and due process and offer little or no practical advantage to the young witness.

Our experience with the second section of the statute, allowing for the use of a prerecorded videotaped statement with an interviewer other than an attorney, has been more positive. With these provisions, the child has the opportunity to make a statement without interference or intimidation, and the accused is guaranteed face-to-face confrontation. Differing district court opinions have been rendered regarding Section 2. One court decision (*Jolly* v. *State of Texas* 1984) upheld the constitutionality of the section, while another (*Long* v. *State of Texas* 1985) was struck down. The Texas appellate court's reversal of Long in 1987 addressed a number of issues. In summary, the court found the following:

> Statutory videotaped child testimony procedures used in prosecution for sexual abuse of a child, permitting complainant to be taped in conversation with therapist and forbidding presence of defendant or counsel violated defendant's protection under confrontation and cross-examination, testimony was not under oath and protective no trial, non-adversarial setting may have distorted complainant's credibility, although jury could evaluate demeanor to extent permitted by videotape and complainant had stated she understood difference between truth and falsehood and that a lie would get her into trouble. (p. 185)

The court cited the four core issues of concern. First, the court determined that allowing a protective environment in which the child could make a statement may have prejudiced the videotaped testimony. We have presented research that supports the belief that the nonadversarial interview setting does indeed affect the testimony of the young witness. We contend, however, that our criminal justice system is ethically burdened to provide a setting that does not prohibit a child's free statements and thus deny his or her rights to protection under the law.

Second, the court determined that the interviewer was not authorized by the state to swear a witness to oath. This is a technical difficulty and easily resolved. Court reporters and notaries are frequently imparted this authorization.

Third, the court questioned whether the videotaped interview accurately portrayed the actual event. This issue regarding factual representation of the interview includes control of the viewing field, lighting, color intensity, and similar issues that might "affect the viewer's impressions and attitudes as to what he or she sees in the picture" (p. 189). This same concern prompted our detailed and rigid protocol of defining the visual field and outlining specific recommendations for lighting, microphones, and sound control for videotaping.

Limited evidence (Millerson 1982) suggests that film may indeed distort communication, but the key issue is the nature and extent of the distortion. We need to answer research questions such as "Is the effect of a videotaped interview versus live testimony biased against or in favor of the child witness?" or "Are the child's emotions or facial expressions more obscured on film than live testimony?" or "Does viewing a child's tears or smile in a more remote mode of communication—i.e., a videotaped interview—diminish the empathic response of the jury or judge?" Contrary to what the appellate opinion implied, if videotaped interviews distort communication, the bias may work in favor of the defendant rather than the young witness. Furthermore, the court did not address the issue of whether the traditional courtroom setting distorted or prejudiced the communication of the young witness. There is much more empirical research support for this position than for the argument against videotaped interviews.

Videotaped evidence has been used in various ways in the criminal justice system, including in depositions and driving while intoxicated (DWI) cases. The question of evidence distortion has not yet led to the abandonment of videotaping in these cases.

Finally, the court judged that confrontation was not adequately granted because the defendant and defense counsel were not present during the videotaped interview. This concern goes hand-in-hand with the issue of testimony presented outside an adversarial context. The apprehension is that testimony given in a protected environment without the presence of the defendant may violate the mandate of "trustworthiness of evidence." This, in turn, affects fundamental rights as guaranteed by the Constitution.

Balancing Rights: How Shall We Proceed?

Goodman and Helgelson (1985) point out that the initial interview with child witnesses and the immersion of children in the adversary process are a crucial concern. There are several ways in which current legal practices could be improved so that more accurate and detailed reports are obtained. One change is to ensure trained professionals are the first to interview the child witnesses and that the interviews are conducted quickly and recorded fully on videotape. (p. 56)

Our current understanding of research regarding children's capabilities and our experience in working with young witnesses in the criminal justice system have persuaded us to accept that the child is plainly at a disadvantage in the traditional adult-oriented courtroom. This disadvantage ultimately affects the child's rights to protection and safety. Videotaped testimony seems to be a viable option for resolving this quandry.

Ultimately, our lawmakers and their constituents will have to address the question of permitting the use of videotaped testimony in a courtroom. We, as adults, must consider to what extent we are willing to abridge our own rights to balance the rights of children.

References

Berliner, L., and M. Barbieri. 1984. "The Testimony of the Child Victim of Sexual Assault." *Journal of Social Issues* 40(no. 2):125–27.

Bjorkland, D.F., and H.S. Hock. 1982. "Age Differences in Temporal Locus of Memory Organization in Children's Recall." *Journal of Experimental Psychology* 33:347–62.

Bostor, F.J., G.R. Miller, and N.E. Fontes. 1978. "Videotape in the Courtroom: Effects in Live Trials." *Trial* 14:49–59.

Bulkley, J.A. 1982. "Evidentiary and Procedural Trends in State Legislation and Other Emerging Legal Issues in Child Sexual Abuse Cases." In *Report of the Child Sexual Abuse Law Reform Project.* Washington, DC.

Burgess, A.W., and L.L. Holmstrom. 1978. "The Child and Family in the Court Process." In A.W. Burgess, A.N. Groth, L.L. Holmstrom, and S.M. Sgroi, eds. *Sexual Assault of Children and Adolescents.* Lexington, MA: Lexington Books, 205–30.

Chance, J.G., and A.G. Goldstein. 1984. "Face Recognition Memory: Implications for Children's Eyewitness Testimony." *Journal of Social Issues* 46:69–85.

Clark, E.V. 1983. "Meanings and Concepts." In J.H. Flavell and E.M. Markman, eds. *Child Psychology.* New York: John Wiley & Sons, 787–840.

Colao, F., and T. Hosansky. 1983. *Your Children Should Know: Teach Your Chil-*

dren the Strategies That Will Keep Them Safe from Assault and Crime. New York: Berkley Publishing Co.

Dale, P.S., E.F. Loftus, and E. Rathbum. 1978. "The Influence of the Question in the Eyewitness Testimony of Preschool Children." *Journal of Psycholinguistics* 7:269–77.

Declaration of the Rights of the Child. 1959. United National General Assembly XIV.

Dent, H.R., and G.M. Stephenson. 1978. "Identification Evidence: Experimental Investigations of Factors Affecting the Reliability of Juvenile and Adult Witnesses." In D.P. Farrington, K. Hawkins, and S.M. Lloyd-Bostock, eds. *Psychology, Law and Legal Process.* Atlantic Highlands, NJ: Humanatics Press, 195–206.

Dent, H.R., and G.M. Stephenson. 1979. "An Experimental Study of the Effectiveness of Different Techniques of Questioning the Child Witness." *British Journal of Clinical and Social Psychology* 18:41–51.

Foley, M.A., M.K. Johnson, and C.L. Raye. 1983. "Age Related Changes in Confusion between Memories for Thoughts and Memories for Speech." *Child Development* 54:51–60.

Gager, N., and C. Schurr. 1979. *Sexual Assault: Confronting Rape in America.* New York: Grosset and Dunlap.

Goodman, G., and V. Hegelson. 1985. "Child Sexual Assault: Children's Memory and the Law." In *Report of the ABA Child Sexual Abuse Law Reform Project,* Washington, DC.

Hocking, J.E., G.R. Miller, and N.E. Fontes. 1978. "Videotape in the Courtroom: Witness Deception." *Trial* 15:52–64.

James, S.K., DeLipsey, J.M. 1985. "Guidelines for Interviewing Suspected Cases of Child Sexual Abuse." Unpublished manuscript, Dallas County Rape Crisis Center, Dallas, Texas.

Johnson, M.K., and M.A. Foley, 1984. "Differentiating Fact from Fantasy: The Reliability of Children's Memory." *Journal of Social Issues* 40(no. 2):33–50.

In re *Jolly* v. *State of Texas,* 681 S.W. 2d, 689 (Texas Appellate–Houston, 1984).

Joseph, G.P. 1983. *Videotape Evidence in Courts.* In Report of the Videotape Evidence Subcommittee, Trial Evidence Committee, ABA section on litigation. Washington, DC.

Kohlberg, L.P., and D. Elfenbein. 1975. "The Development of Moral Judgments Concerning Capital Punishments." *American Journal of Orthopsychiatry* 45: 615–40.

Labai, D. 1969. "The Protection of the Child Victim of a Sexual Offense in the Criminal Justice System." *Wayne Law Review* 15:977–84.

Loftus, E.F. 1979. *Eyewitness Testimony.* Cambridge, MA: Harvard University Press.

Loftus, E.F., and G.M. Davies. 1984. "Distortions in the Memory of Children." *Journal of Social Issues* 40(no. 2):51–67.

In re *Long* v. *State of Texas,* 694 S.W. 2d, 185, 186 (Texas Appellate–Dallas, 1985).

In re *Long,* Texas Family Code Annals, Sec. 11.21 (Vernon Suppl. 1987, Texas Appellate 5 Dist., 1985).

McIver, W.F. 1985. "The Case for a Therapeutic Interview in Situations of Alleged Sexual Molestation." *The Oregon Defense Attorney* 4:3–4.

Melton, G.B. 1984. "Child Witnesses and the First Amendment: A Psycholegal Dilemma." *Journal of Social Issues* 40(no. 2):291–305.

Millerson, G. 1982. In opinion by Hon. J. Vance re: *Long v. State of Texas,* 694 S.W. 2d 185,186 (Texas Appellate–Dallas, 1985).

Mussen, P.H., ed. 1983. *Handbook of Child Psychology.* New York: John Wiley & Sons.

Oates, K. 1982. *Child Abuse: A Community Concern.* Boston: Butterworth Publishing Co.

Parker, J.Y. 1982. "The Rights of Child Witnesses: Is the Court a Protector or Perpetrator?" *New England Law Review* 17:643–717.

Piaget, J. 1929. *The Child's Conception of the World.* New York: Harcourt, Brace.

Powell v. *State of Texas.* 1985. 694 S.W. 2d 416 (Texas Appellate–Dallas).

Rest, J.R. 1983. "Morality." In Flavell and Markman, *Child Psychology,* 556–629.

Selman, R.L., and D. Jacquette. 1978. "The Development of Interpersonal Awareness: A Working Draft Manual." Unpublished scoring manual, Harvard–Judge Baker Social Reasoning Project, Cambridge, MA, in Shantz, 1983. "Social Cognition." In Flavell and Markman, *Child Psychology,* 495–55.

Sgroi, S.M. 1982. *Handbook of Clinical Intervention in Child Sexual Abuse.* Lexington, MA: Lexington Books.

Shantz, M., 1983. "Communication." In Flavell and Markman, *Child Psychology,* 841–89.

Texas Family Code Annual, Sec. 11.21, Art. 38.071 (Vernon Suppl. 1984).

Wellman, H.M., and J.D. Lempers. 1977. "The Naturalistic Communicative Abilities of Two-Year-Olds." *Child Development* 48:1052–57.

Appendix 9–A:
Data from Videotaped Interviews

Child Age Range

Age	Number*	Percent
3	3	2
4	34	26
5	50	37
6	15	11
7	6	5
8	5	4
9	6	5
10	11	8
11	3	2

*Total = 133; female = 96; male = 37.

Relationship of Child to Perpetrator

Relationship	Number*	Percent
Relatives	51	38
Acquaintances	53	40
Strangers	29	22

*Total = 133; female = 4; male = 129.

Type of Offense

Type	Number*	Percent
Sexual abuse	90	67
Rape	31	23
Indecency	12	10

*Total = 133.

Case Disposition

Criminal		
Disposition	*Number**	*Percent*
Guilty	35	32
Not guilty	1	1
Case pending	1	1
Plea bargained	29	26
Charges dropped	5	5
Unapprehended or unidentified perpetrator	7	6
Tapes not used	32	29

*Total = 110.

Civil		
Disposition	*Number**	*Percent*
Protective action ordered	10	44
Protective action not ordered	4	17
Tapes not used	5	22
Cases pending	4	17

*Total = 23.

Appendix 9–B:
Dallas County Rape Crisis and Child Sexual Abuse Center Videotaping Protocol

Procedures and Policies for Videotaping Testimony of a Child Who Is a Victim of a Sexual Offense.

I. *Eligibility for Videotaped Interview:*
   Any referred child twelve years and under who is a Dallas County resident or who is allegedly sexually assaulted in Dallas County is eligible.

II. *Referral Procedures:*
   Upon referral the following information must be supplied by the referring party:
   (a) name, address, age of child
   (b) indictment or charge
   (c) the grand jury case number, if case has been filed with the grand jury

III. *Mechanics of the Videotaping (Prerecorded statement):*
   (a) the staff member conducting the interview must be trained and efficient in the use of the recording equipment (No equipment operator other than the interviewer will be used.)
   (b) a blank cassette shall be used in all recordings
   (c) a record of time in seconds shall be displayed on all tapes to facilitate ease in replay and to ensure proof that the recording has not been altered
   (d) the television monitor shall not be on during the recording
   (e) no attorney shall be allowed within 50 feet of the interview room during the actual recording
   (f) after the interview is completed it shall be immediately reviewed by the interviewer to assess whether an accurate recording was made
   (g) if the recording actually represents the interview and the above conditions are met the interviewer shall initial and date the tape cassette

    (h) if the recording does not accurately represent the interview it shall be preserved and information regarding the failure of the recording shall be made

    (i) a log of all recordings shall be maintained including the date and time of the recording, the name of the child and the interviewer, and the name of attorneys or prosecutors involved

IV. *Mechanics of the Videotaping (Closed Circuit):*

    (a) closed circuit videotaping will be conducted upon motion from either party that has been granted by the district court in which the case is filed

    (b) the party requesting proceedings shall notify the Dallas County Rape Crisis Center at least ten days prior to the taping

    (c) closed circuit equipment shall be tested when all parties are present to ensure it is working properly

    (d) the Dallas County Rape Crisis Center will coordinate arrivals of all parties to avoid confrontation between the alleged victim and alleged perpetrator

V. *Interviewing Aids*

The following interviewing aids shall be readily available for use in every recorded interview:

    (a) drawing materials

    (b) body maps/anatomical drawings

    (c) anatomically correct dolls

VI. *Viewings of Recordings*

The Dallas County Rape Crisis and Child Sexual Abuse Center will make videotapes available for viewing by attorneys and defendant; 48 hour notice is requested but viewings can be arranged with less notice on an emergency basis. Defendants viewing tapes must be accompanied by their attorney.

VII. *Notice of Recorded Interviews*

Notice of videotaped interviews will be given by telephone and letter to attorneys involved in the case. The district attorney's office will provide names of attorneys of record when available.

Appendix 9–C:
Partial Transcript
of Blind Videotaped Interview

Interviewer: Mary, you remember that my name is Jane. I would like for you to use a very loud voice because sometimes when we talk it is hard to hear, okay?

Child: Okay.

Interviewer: Mary, can you tell me your complete name?

Child: Mary Davis.

Interviewer: Thank you for using a loud voice. Mary, how old are you?

Child: Six.

Interviewer: Okay, do you know when your birthday is?

Child: April 29.

Interviewer: Do you go to school somewhere?

Child: Yeah.

Interviewer: Where do you go to school?

Child: Smith Elementary.

Interviewer: What grade are you in?

Child: First.

Interviewer: And what is your teacher's name?

Child: Miss Jones.

Interviewer: Mary, I want to ask you some questions. Can you tell me how many legs a cat has?

Child: Four.

Interviewer: Okay, now can you tell me what color grass is?

Child: Green.

Interviewer: Okay, let me see, what color is my shirt that I have on today?

Child: White.

Interviewer: Mary, I have some blocks over here. I use them for counting. Would you count them for me as I lay them out?

Child: All right.
One, two, three, four, five, six, seven, eight, nine.

Interviewer: Mary, can you hand me four blocks?
Okay, Mary, how many blocks are left on the table?

Child: Five.

Interviewer: Now can you hand me a yellow block?
What other color blocks are there?

Child: Pink and orange and green.

Interviewer: Okay.
Can you hand me a pink one?
Okay.
Can you hand me a green one?
Mary, we are getting ready to talk about something very important, and that is what it means to tell the truth and what it means to tell a lie, okay? Have you heard that word?

Child: Yeah.

Interviewer: What is the truth?

Child: The truth means that you don't tell a lie but the truth.

Interviewer: Okay.
What does a lie mean?

Child: When you tell something that is not right.

Interviewer: You said this was green. (Interviewer holds up green block)
If I tell you it is pink, am I telling the truth or a lie?

Child: That's a lie.

Interviewer: If I tell you this block is green (Interviewer holds up green block), is it the truth or a lie?

Child: That's the truth.

Interviewer: What happens if you tell a lie?

Child: You get a spanking.

Interviewer: Should you tell the truth or should you tell a lie?

Child: You should always tell the truth.

Interviewer: Do you promise that everything we talk about today will be the truth?

Child: Uh-huh.

Interviewer: Can you say a word, yes or no, instead of uh-huh?

Child: Yes.

Interviewer: So, do you promise that you will tell the truth?

Child: Yes.

Interviewer: Mary, we are here to talk about something that you said happened to you. Tell me about what you think happened to you.

Child: Tell about Kimberly too?

Interviewer: Let's talk about what you think happened to you first.

Child: He—um—he made us kiss his penis and stuff.

Interviewer: Who is he?

Child: Tom.

Interviewer: Do you know Tom's last name?

Child: No.

Interviewer: Tell me what Tom looks like.

Child: He has blond hair.

Interviewer: Is his skin the color of your skin or is his skin a different color?

Child: My skin.

Interviewer: Okay.
And how do you know Tom?

Child: He is my uncle.

Interviewer: Okay, so is Tom a little child like you or is he a grown-up person?

Child: No, he is a big man.

Interviewer: And you said that Tom made you do something. What was that?

Child: Kiss his penis and stay in his room and kiss my parts and takes pictures of me naked and one day he opened the door when I was taking a bath. He knew I was in the bathtub naked.

Interviewer: I have some dolls here that are just like real people. You said he made you kiss his penis. Can you show me on the man doll where the penis is?

Child: (Child points to the genital area with her finger)

Interviewer: Can you show me on the girl doll where the privates are?

Child: (Child points to genital area)
It's the "gina."

Interviewer: Can you use the dolls to show me how you think it was?

Child: (Demonstrates with dolls)

Interviewer: So, you kissed down here on top of his pants.

Child: No, his pants were off.

Interviewer: How did his pants get off?

Child: He took them off and took my panties off.

Interviewer: Will you show me exactly how you remember it? Including what clothes were on or off?

Child: Okay. (Removes the male doll's pants and girl's panties)

Interviewer: Did anything else happen, besides what you have shown me?

Child: He kissed my "gina."

Interviewer: Can you show me with the dolls what you mean by that.

Child: (Demonstrates with dolls)

Interviewer: Where were you and Tom?

Child: My grandmother's house.

Interviewer: Where were you in the house?

Child: Tom's room. We had to sit on the bed.

Interviewer: Who do you mean by we?

Child: Me and Kimberly.

Interviewer: Who is Kimberly?

Child: She is my cousin.

Interviewer: Are you saying Kimberly was there with you when this happened?

Child: Yes.

Interviewer: How old is Kimberly?

Child: She's a little person like me.

Interviewer: So the three of you were sitting on the bed?

Child: No, not three. He was sitting on the couch.

Interviewer: What room is the couch in?

Child: In the same room with the bed.

Interviewer: And did anything happen while you were in there?

Child: He made us kiss his penis and he kissed our "ginas."

Interviewer: How did he do that when you were on the bed and he was on the couch.

Child: Well, he stood up while we were on the bed.

Interviewer: Show me with the dolls.

Child: (Demonstrates)

Interviewer: Did anything else happen?

Child: He would kiss ours too.

Interviewer: Show me.
How would the kiss be?

Child: He would make it long.

Interviewer: He would make what long?

Child: He would make the kiss long.

Interviewer: Oh, he would make it be a long kiss. Did anything else happen, besides the kissing of the penis and the vaginas?

Child: Well, he touched boobies right here and then he tried to kiss my boobies. (Shows on self)

Interviewer: Okay.
Did anything else happen?

Child: I think so.

Interviewer: If you don't know, or if you don't remember, that's okay. I want you to just tell me what you know for sure and tell me the truth.

Child: Okay.

Interviewer: Did anything else happen?

Child: Well, he sticked his hand way down in there and he sticked his penis in there too and it hurt.

Interviewer: He stuck his penis in where?

Child: Right here. (Shows on self)

Interviewer: Can you show me on the dolls?

Child: (Shows on dolls)

Interviewer: Okay, Mary, other than what you've told me already, did anything else happen?

Child: Well, he did it a lot.

Interviewer: Do you remember the first time?

Child: I think it happened a long time ago.

Interviewer: Were you in school at the time?

Child: Yes.

Interviewer: Who was your teacher?

Child: Ms. Jones.

Interviewer: How about the time with you and Kimberly. When did that happen?

Child: When I was at my grandmother's.

Interviewer: When was that?

Child: I think last week.

10

Using the Arts Therapies in Treatment of Sexual Offenders against Children

Connie E. Naitove

T he decision of the Superior Court of New Jersey, in the case of *Wilkerson* v. *Pearson*, established the precedent for the acceptance of an arts therapist's testimony as "expert testimony" based on the following reasons:

> (1) the interpretation of an individual's drawings as an expression of thoughts stimulated by conflicts and pressures are 'beyond the understanding' of judges and the average juror; (2) the science of art therapy has long been recognized in the fields of psychiatry and psychology and has been taught in several medical schools; and (3) the art therapist in question has extensive experience and training in the field. (Law Alert 200, 1986)

Although it is not the purpose of this chapter to make arts therapists of the readers, I hope not only to demystify the subject, but also to present some tools and techniques to facilitate the assessment and treatment of sexual offenders against children. This chapter was solicited, written, and published in the hope of expanding the diagnostic and treatment capacities of those concerned with understanding and correcting the behaviors of sexual abusers against children. Although treatment of this population is relatively recent and modest at best, we have no sense of the effectiveness of any one approach. It behooves us, therefore, to explore all available techniques that have demonstrated some effectiveness.

Unfortunately, it has been my experience that clinical staff who are trained in the more traditional verbal modes of psychotherapy tend to bypass any opportunities to augment their therapeutic armarium with skills that were not included in their basic training. Ignorance of the relatively new disciplines of expressive therapies is not the only deterrent to their employment by therapists. Few clinicians outside large metropolitan institutions have had contact with trained arts therapists. Most clinical team staffs do not include arts therapists. Preconceived notions related to aesthetics, talent, and skill in the arts have been powerful inhibitors to the development of arts therapy skills by psychiatrists, psychologists, social workers, and others working with sexual abusers and the abused. My hope is to overcome this ignorance and inhibition and to present some simple and useful techniques that can be safely applied in a variety of settings.

The techniques described in this chapter come from the fields of art, movement, poetry, photography, and creative drama. They are not intended to form a comprehensive therapeutic approach to the treatment of sexual offenses. Nor are the techniques presented here the only ones that the clinician could successfully incorporate into his or her assessment and treatment approach. Readers are encouraged to explore some of the literature suggested in the Resources section at the end of this chapter for additional methodologies, tools, and theoretical approaches to expressive verbal and nonverbal therapies.

Definitions and Qualities of the Arts Therapies

As a prelude to discussing the use of arts therapy techniques in the treatment of sexual offenders against children, it is necessary to describe these modalities in some detail. The expressive therapies include art (both graphic and plastic), dance and movement (including yoga and the martial arts), drama (creative and psychodrama, as well as puppetry), music, poetry and literature, photography, and play (including games and sports). These therapeutic modalities use the techniques and media of the arts and the theories and methodologies of psychiatry, psychology, and developmental education to facilitate the resolution of conflict and the enhancement of functional and cognitive skills. In this way, the expressive therapies may assist clients in their desires to achieve a sense of identity, to feel more confident about their own efficacy, and to express themselves in a more socially acceptable manner.

Basic to the use of these modalities is the understanding that all arts expressions are metaphoric. Similarly, development of a symbolic repertoire and the creation of metaphoric expressions are inventive processes akin to problem solving. When the creator of a metaphoric expression is a client, we can (with his or her assistance) untangle the skein of psychodynamic processes that have led to the individual's aberrant behavior and impede his or her ability to function. We may then be able to select, devise, and employ techniques that would facilitate the development of appropriate, realistic, and socially acceptable alternatives for that client. This is made possible by the expressive therapies because the arts engage perceptual and sensory motor functions as well as cognitive skills.

Participation in an arts therapy session involves the individual's functional areas of object relatedness, focus of attention, interpersonal and group social skills, reality testing, impulse control, personal and body awareness, gender awareness, and individuation, while accommodating both the pre-ferred learning and expressive modes. Arts therapy sessions have the addi-tional advantage of being immediate and satisfying. In analytic terms, they offer an opportunity for abreaction and catharsis and an opportunity for the appropriate displacement of fantasy and power issues, as well as a sense of participation and efficacy in the resolution of personal issues.

Theoretical Framework

My original background and training was primarily in the arts and educa-tion, and years of additional training and clinical experience in psychother-apy have led to an eclectic approach toward assessment and treatment. Today most arts therapists have a predominantly psychoanalytical or human de-velopmental training bias, with a strong emphasis on background training in one of the arts. More than one hundred graduate level training programs, which also include hundreds of hours in supervised practicums, are available in colleges, universities, and medical schools around the nation and abroad.

My own bias includes the premise that most disordered behaviors not caused by human biochemical imbalance are the result of coping mechanisms developed in response to psychological or physical trauma. Based on the severity of the trauma and the developmental age at which these coping mechanisms were integrated, it is quite possible that the individual might not have explored other, compensatory conceptual developmental stages. He or she may have been developmentally arrested at a characterological stage that mitigated against the more socially acceptable response to similar situ-ations as they arose. The emerging adult may apply a coping mechanism similar to that used by him or her as a child to other situations. Thus, we find a certain consistency among sexual offenders who perceive their victims either as an extension of themselves at a certain chronological age or as an extension of the circumstance in which they themselves were traumatized.

It is my impression that sexual offenders, not unlike their victims and substance abusers as well, have suffered a developmental arrest at some point in their maturation. My impression is that this arrest corresponds to Piaget's preoperational level of conservation, wherein the individual can focus on only one perceptual dimension at a time and fixates on what is perceived to be the most salient feature of that dimension. Susan Harter infers from this "that when a young child attempts to understand his or her *emotions,* such cognitive limitations might also make it difficult to acknowledge that two feelings can occur simultaneously" (Harter 1983). Harter's work has sug-gested a three-stage process in developing the ability to accept a multiplicity of feelings associated with a given individual or circumstance. This theoret-ical concept is most useful both in establishing the level of developmental arrest in sexual offenders and in planning therapeutic interventions utilizing the expressive therapies.

Beyond the three stages of development in a person's ability to conceptualize simultaneity of emotions, Harter also suggests that there may be four substages involving the positive or negative qualities of these emotions and the targets toward which they are directed. The first stage in the developmental sequence involves a simple denial that more than one feeling can exist simultaneously. In stating "I love my mommy," a child may be saying that he or she cannot accept the possibility of loving *and* hating the parent. The second stage is one of acknowledging the experience of a multiplicity of feelings sequentially. Thus, the child may admit, "I hated mommy when she played with my peepee-er and bottom in the bath, but I loved her when she tucked me into bed and kissed me goodnight." In the third stage, these feelings are acknowledged to occur simultaneously: "I love my mommy even when I'm scared of her."

Within the concept of the simultaneity of emotions lies the additional complication of similar or conflicting emotions being directed at one or more targets. For example, substage 1 may have emotions of similar valence directed toward the same target—i.e., emotions such as love and affection are almost synonymous and therefore of the same valence. Substage 2 would have simultaneous emotions of the same valence directed at more than one target—i.e., love and affection toward both the child and the spouse. Substage 3 would have different or dichotomous feelings directed at different targets—i.e., the offender who loves and is jealous of the relationship between the child against whom the offense was committed and the offender's spouse who did not meet his/her needs. Substage 4, the most difficult to acknowledge and rationalize, directs feelings of different valence toward the same target: "I loved my mother, but she was disgusting."

The ambivalence of suffering from dichotomous feelings toward someone or something leads to frustration, guilt, and anger. Regression to a simpler stage of rationalization can make it easier to cope. In my work, I attempt to have the client first establish the stage at which he or she is currently functioning and then try to discern whether the individual is cognitively limited or arrested at that stage. My optimism concerning the range of therapeutic techniques available and the time line for achievement of goals may be influenced by that conclusion. Developmental arrest can be overcome by offering the client an opportunity to explore succeeding stages.

Another theoretical framework that I have found useful has been that of Eric Berne's transactional analysis (Berne 1975). Simply stated, the theory transforms Freudian elements of ego, id, and superego into a triad of parent, child, and adult attributes. The parent ego state is both the nurturer and the authoritarian in us all, while the child ego state encompasses the hedonist, the idealist, the adventurer, and the compliant characteristics. It is the role of the adult ego to mediate between the other two personality elements in a socially acceptable, ego-syntonic manner. The theory maintains that difficulties arise either when the boundaries between the adult, parent, and child parts of ourselves are poorly defined or one part overwhelms and dominates our thinking and leads to disruptive behaviors. My clients seem to comprehend this concept readily on a superficial level. I find it relatively easy to enhance the client's self-awareness and behavior change by helping him or her recognize that these feeling states serve separate and sometimes conflicting motivational goals. These conflicting motivations also may correlate with conflicting attitudes and dysfunctional behaviors seen in the same person.

To help clarify these issues of apparent conflict, I select arts activities that facilitate the client's objectification. It is my experience that it is easier to talk about an object (a photo collage, drawing, or sculpture) than the constellation of emotions that gives rise to it (Groth 1982). The simple experience of having the client physically enact the cliché of "going around in circles" and then asking him or her what other options might be available (such as going "over there" instead) can then be related to realistic possibilities of altering the behavior. These activities clarify the role of metaphor in our lives and can facilitate the awareness of other operant metaphors for our behaviors. These premises are summed up by the following:

> If a child lives with criticism,
>> He learns to condemn.
> If he lives with hostility,
>> He learns to fight.
> If he lives with ridicule,
>> He learns to be shy.
> If he lives with shame,
>> He learns to be guilty.
>
> If a child lives with tolerance,
>> He learns to be patient.
> If he lives with encouragement,
>> He learns to be confident.
> If he lives with praise,
>> He learns to be appreciative.
> If he lives with fairness,
>> He learns justice.
>
> If a child lives with security,
>> He learns faith.
> If he lives with approval,
>> He learns to like himself.
>
> If a child lives with acceptance and approval,

He learns to give love to the world.

(Author unknown; found in a church in Somerset, England)

I attempt to ascertain, through the expressive therapies, if and when the client learned to "live with" criticism, hostility, and ridicule and which of the client's ego states (parent and/or child) were contaminated by the accompanying cognitive and behavioral injunctions. The goal is to use appropriate modalities to redirect those cognitive and behavioral energies into ego-syntonic and socially acceptable functional behavior.

Selecting Techniques

In selecting the appropriate tools and techniques for assessment and treatment, it is necessary to draw upon the existing general knowledge of the profile of the sexual offender against children while being alert to possible additional and unique characterological disorders (Groth 1982). Descriptions of this population often include poor communication skills; seeking affection and romantic gratification by acting out fantasy relationships (such as Cinderella and Prince Charming); identifying with the victim and construing the victim as a pseudoadult substitute or assuming the role of a pseudoparent. The offender often has problems with reality, stress, and the control of impulses; suffers from a sense of isolation, guilt, anger, and depression; has a need for power and control; prefers to maintain the status quo in interpersonal relationships; and may have various rationalizations for behaviors (e.g., "Better she should learn it from someone who loves her rather than some bum."). The offender is described as characterologically immature and selects maladaptive methods of resolution of life issues. Therefore, the tools and techniques we select should facilitate the expression of these qualities and enhance the offender's capacity to recognize and verbalize them. At the same time, the arts therapy interventions also should offer the offender an opportunity to explore alternative behaviors and risk taking in the safety of the therapeutic environment.

Before introducing the expressive therapies to clients, I find it essential to have tried them out, experientially, myself. This is necessary to (1) comprehend the remarkable speed with which these techniques can bring emotional content to the surface, (2) have a sense of the amount of time needed to complete such activity, and (3) be familiar with the properties of materials necessary for the execution of the project (Naitove 1979). Since the vast majority of those working with this population may well suffer from the same sense of ineptness and lack of skill in the arts as their clients, and have similar reservations concerning self-revelation, the reader may want to explore these exercises with a friend, coworker, or local arts therapist. Under any circumstances, be prepared for surprises.

Eliciting and Evaluating Data

Many inferences can and have been drawn from the manifest content of arts expressions. Usually these assumptions are derived from a constellation of cultural, professional, and personal opinions that do not belong to the creator of the work. This should be avoided assiduously. The primary consideration should be what the creator of the work has to say about it. The rest of us are likely to approach the work from an array of preconceptions arising from our own experiences and aesthetic biases derived from cultural, environmental, and educationally acquired standards that may not be shared by the client. Therefore, it is incumbent upon the therapist to listen and to look for recurrent themes and symbols that may have been variously described but that generally seem to conform to characterological descriptions of obsession, regression, egocentricity, manipulation, aggression, and realistic or unrealistic preoccupation.

The illustrations accompanying this chapter were created during the first arts therapy session with a group of paroled offenders who had been remanded to therapy by the court and had already been meeting together in an open-ended group for a year and a half. Most of the illustrations are photographs of collages produced by the offenders during a two-hour meeting. Two of the illustrations are photographs of drawings made by one member.

The offenders made the collages after they looked through a collection of old magazines, cut and tore out selected pictures and words, and affixed them to a blank piece of paper by means of glue or double-stick tape. There are no photographs of the men themselves in the collages.

The illustrations consistently contain elements of isolation, conflicting emotions, sadness, and bravado. In the discussions that followed the exercises, clients were able to recognize and share these commonalities, many for the first time. Commonalities in feeling states, rather than differences in practices, can provide a solid basis for effective group psychodynamics. In succeeding sessions, the group can focus on these elements, literally and figuratively drawing on the self-awareness of individual members.

In eliciting information, the therapist must be particularly guarded in his or her manner of asking questions about the clients' work, to avoid what Carl Rogers called "leakage" (betrayal of the questioner's bias, goals, and perspective) (Rogers 1961). Questions should be framed in an open-ended manner, such as "Tell me about that red area." or "Could you say something about those forms (lines or spaces) over there on the right?" or "What do those words you put in your picture mean to the forms (people, objects, animals) you have there?"

Changes in this manifest content of the work are the best indicator of the quality and degree of the client's therapeutic progress. Some examples of specific things to look for are changes in physical movements (relative positioning of the limbs to torso or qualities of freedom and control, such as balance, flexibility, or tension), the use of the general space in which the action takes place (as in breaking the pattern of "going around in circles"), and flexibility in personal space (e.g., proximity changes from six to fifteen inches). In arts expressions, one looks for changes in the use of space on the page, along with changes in qualities of order and symmetry, color, and form. Many of the elements of arts expressions can be found on the multi-modal evaluation form called the CENDEX (available free of charge from the National Educational Council of Creative Arts Therapies, Inc., listed in the Resources section). Commonly, these changes in arts expressions will corroborate changes in attitudes and behaviors seen outside the therapeutic environment. These may be reflected in reports from staff and individuals with whom the client comes in contact and might include observations such as improvements in socialization, work behaviors, sleeping habits, carriage, and general appearance.

Materials for Use in Expressive Therapy

Materials for arts therapy activities are inexpensive and can usually be scrounged from a variety of sources; many are recycled waste products. A variety of magazines containing numerous photographs (e.g., *Life, People, Sports Illustrated, Ebony,* and *National Geographic*) are used for collages. White and colored papers, approximately 12 by 18 inches, glue sticks, transparent tape, scissors, and marking pens in at least eight colors are among the basic graphics art media. A cassette or record player is useful for background music for movement activities, guided imagery, and recording orations. Homemade playdough is an inexpensive and useful substitute for clay. Packing materials, carpet and fabric scraps, and cartons are useful for environmental constructions and puppet making.

Poetry collections, such as those mentioned in the Resources section appended to this chapter, can be obtained from interlibrary loan. Eastman Kodak and Polaroid have provided grants, equipment, and materials for photographic and video projects for educational and therapeutic purposes. Such projects can provide insight into the perspectives of this population and provide visual records and source materials for activities in other media.

Introducing the Arts Activities
and Designing Sessions

Within a given session, arts activities follow a common progression, beginning with a warm-up exercise designed to orient the participants to activities, the therapist, and the group; continuing with a core activity designed to meet therapeutic goals; and concluding with an experience intended to restore clients to the reality of here and now. This last experience may involve cleaning up the room and returning materials to their storage place, a general discussion concerning the session, or a relaxation exercise.

When approaching individuals and groups unfamiliar with these types of activities, it is simplest to use the direct approach, saying something like, "Today we are going to use a different approach to working on the issues we have been discussing. We are going to use some arts materials. The reason is that it is often easier to talk about a picture than some of the feelings that went into making that picture. Also, sometimes it is hard to trust words. Before we begin, there are a few simple rules that we will follow:

1. These activities can be fun.

2. Most of the activities will be conducted without any talking (although laughter is definitely okay).

3. Anything and everything that is created or expressed will be accepted on its own merit, without judgment as to skill or talent. You are not expected to be artists, poets, or photographers any more than I am.

4. Only the person who created the expression can validate its meaning. Others can comment only on their own reactions and the source of those reactions.

5. If you create something meaningful and important to you but you are not quite ready to talk about it or share it with the rest of us, you may, for the moment, have the option to 'pass,' but you should know that you will be asked to share it eventually.

6. There are no right or wrong ways to do these activities. Within the rules, everything you do is right.

7. Anything and everything expressed will be kept in confidence as long as it does not violate the law or the regulations of the institution.

8. Violence against the person, property, or product of another will not be tolerated. These are the only rules. Everything else you do is right and perfectly acceptable.

Warm-up Activity

One way to begin the session is with a physical warm-up. The purpose of this activity is to release tensions and focus energy and attention on the goals of the session. In one group, a member had been a trainer of oxen. I asked him to demonstrate the whip-cracking motions necessary to get the oxen moving, then we all duplicated the motion. Having done this several times, we then pretended to be the oxen, straining at the yoke, trying to get the heavy sledge moving. We would take turns being oxen and trainer, putting all our energies into the activity. (There could even have been competitions, such as which team of "oxen" could move the weights farthest, if there had been enough time and if the group had been large enough and ready to handle this element.)

This activity served three purposes. First, it lent importance to the trade of a group member. Second, it focused on the reality of life outside the therapeutic environment. Third, it gave the various members an opportunity to experience the power and control elements inherent in the man's profession. This last issue was familiar emotionally to the group but not readily verbalized. It set the scene for the focus of the day's session.

On other occasions, we have used the motions of a carpenter and progressed to building a house as a mimed dramatic activity designed to enhance concentration and motivate the group to work together. Simple activities, such as laying a large, heavy carpet, also can be used for this purpose.

Core Activity

From the warm-up, we progress to the core activity designed to focus on a particular therapeutic objective. An initial objective might be to ascertain individual perceptions of self, how others may perceive us, and, if the two subjective perceptions differ, how to reconcile these images. It would be foolhardy to assume that all this could be accomplished in one session, but having introduced the subject, the initial session can deal with the first two concepts.

Making Drawings or Collages. One technique that relates to this topic is to have the group make drawings or collages depicting "Me as I See Me" and "Me as Others See Me." Offering the option of making a collage permits the client to bypass issues of talent and skill in making a drawing and provides a quick and easy means of successful rendition. Ease, success, and immediate gratification facilitate cooperation in exploring expressive activities, in which the risk of failure may previously have been a deterrent.

The group is informed that they may tear out pictures in order to have rough edges to equate with "rough" subjects or cut out pictures they perceive to be "clear-cut" statements. It is not usually necessary to add that pictures may be combined to present the desired image or that words may be cut out or written on the pictures as well. Those who prefer to draw should be allowed to do so, although making a collage is usually preferred initially.

Clients are requested to make two separate pictures, which they should title on the back "Me as I See Me" and "Me as Others See Me." They also should add their initials and the date, as this will facilitate demonstrating change, or the lack of it, if the exercise is repeated periodically during the course of treatment. Having the identification on the back maintains the anonymity of the creator, should the therapist wish to make a photographic record of the work for educational purposes. After everyone has completed both pictures (the therapist also should participate to validate his or her own image as perceived by the group), members may share and discuss their pictures.

This exercise is frequently quite informative. One group of paroled child molesters, who had been in verbal therapy for more than a year and a half, commented that they had learned more about each other from this one exercise than in all the preceding months of therapy. The group comprised eight men, most with minimal education, varying in age from the early thirties to the late fifties or sixties, and living in rural New England. Although they would ask questions for clarification, they rarely commented on the artist's perceptions. The men were amused, however, when the psychologist leading the group said that he presented himself to others as a "sphinx" but was actually "as soft as a puppy dog" (Figure 10–1). Perhaps the men were amused because child molesters have been known to refer to the penis as a "puppy dog's nose" when exposing themselves to very young children.

After the sharing is complete, and the works and statements about them have been accepted at face value, the therapist may then lead the discussion in such a manner as to facilitate insight and feedback from the group. It was evident from one set of pictures (Figures 10–2 and 10–3) that the artist, Al, felt that others had a negative image of him, while he perceived himself to be a lonely, foolish individual without much hope for the future. Since he did not say this in so many words, I chose to comment on the positive elements. There are two potentially positive statements in each picture, and I pointed these out to him. In the collage titled "Me as Others See Me," Al suggested that the others were able to see another side of him and that he wanted one more chance to prove them right. When I asked him about this, he confirmed this impression.

One way to proceed might have been to have Al pretend to be walking "along the edge . . . of the crumbling cliff . . . of disaster" that he had depicted in his collage. We then might have asked the group how he could be saved from that disaster. What options might be available? Could he leap the chasm to safer ground? Could he anchor a rope and lower himself to

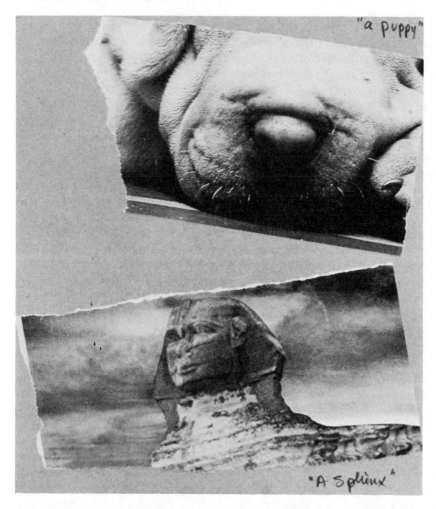

Figure 10–1. Collage by group leader (a psychologist): The Sphinx is actually "as soft as a puppy dog" inside

Credit: Pierre Bastianeli, Biomedical Communications, Dartmouth Medical School.

safety? Having explored Al's options with the group and encouraged the appropriate actions to ensure Al's safety, we then might have asked Al whether he knew what real-life difficulty the "crumbling cliff" represented. The metaphors could be taken a step further to ascertain what options Al might have to rescue himself from his solitude and his precarious relationship with society. Strengthening Al's self-image and social skills by providing him with

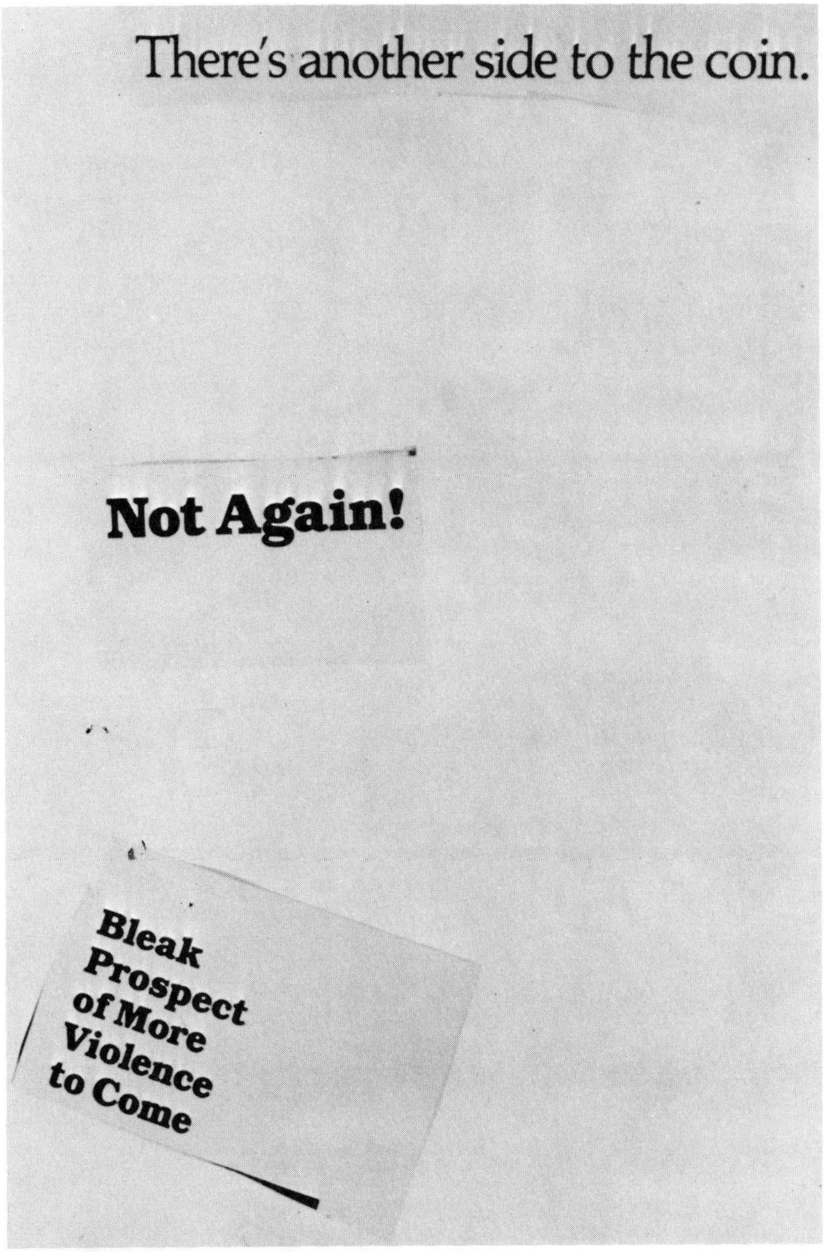

Figure 10–2. Collage by Al (a parolee): "As others see me"

Credit: Pierre Bastianeli, Biomedical Communications, Dartmouth Medical School.

Figure 10–3. Collage by Al: "Me as I see me"

Credit: Pierre Bastianeli, Biomedical Communications, Dartmouth Medical School.

a sense of efficacy in altering his pattern of behavior, as well as the group's stated support of such actions, might provide him with the courage to make the leap to social conformity and alter the bleak prospect of his future. This would become one of the goals of his treatment. The success or failure of this treatment might be evident in Al's interactions with the group, development of relationships outside of the group, and a more positive attitude expressed in future portraits.

Bob, on the other hand, felt compelled to express his anger before he could even approach the subject of self with any degree of rationality (Figure 10–4). It has been my experience that Caucasian clients will often select photos depicting blacks because they identify with various aspects of the social image of blacks: oppression, aggression, and sexuality. Whether one or all of these elements were inspirational to Bob's selection of this magazine photo was the focus of future sessions. Bob's next picture (Figure 10–5) demonstrated, according to his statements about it, an awareness of pretense/bravado (he smiled sheepishly when describing the left side of the illustration). He then soberly described the goals of his therapy as he perceived them and the fears he still harbored, which are depicted on the right side of the same collage. Of Figure 10–6, Bob said that others had expectations of him that he found burdensome. He said that he had tried to make it clear that maintaining the facade of playboy, lover, and "man of steel" was no less difficult than trying to meet the demands of therapy, and that was why he made this additional picture. His response to all these demands was anger, he said, returning to his first depiction.

Until Bob can assume responsibility for both the inner and outer images he projects and alter them to conform to an ego-syntonic, socially acceptable image, he will remain at risk. The fact that Bob perceives himself as someone willing to "try hard" to conform provides the motivational element necessary to redirect his energies into behaviors more constructive than anger.

Carl was a newcomer to the group. Although his two pictures (Figures 10–7 and 10–8) are similar in some ways (for example, in the words used to project his current image), they also are quite different. He spoke in therapeutic jargon but seemed to believe that others saw him as younger (no mustache), more flexible (mouth), and more in control (relationship of eyebrows to eyes). These are no accidents of the pen. He has drawn five different portraits of himself in his self-image picture, each employing different artistic license to make his point. Carl has clearly tried to bury some of his feelings (e.g., anger and confusion) along with his past. His picture tells us that he is both scared and optimistic. He has tried to show us how much self-awareness and control he has by describing past and present emotions in terms of behaviors. From both his verbal statements and those written on his picture, he appears to be operating on the theory that if he can control the behaviors, he has contained the emotions. He was the only one in the group to draw rather than use pictures from magazines. Doing so allowed him to stay aloof

Figure 10–4. Collage by Bob (a parolee): "Anger out of control"

Credit: Pierre Bastianeli, Biomedical Communications, Dartmouth Medical School.

Figure 10–5. Collage by Bob: (left side) "As others see me"; (right side) "As I see me"

Credit: Pierre Bastianeli, Biomedical Communications, Dartmouth Medical School.

Figure 10–6. Collage by Bob: "I can't do it all!"

Credit: Pierre Bastianeli, Biomedical Communications, Dartmouth Medical School.

Figure 10–7. Drawing by Carl (a parolee): "As others see me"

Credit: Pierre Bastianeli, Biomedical Communications, Dartmouth Medical School.

from the group gathered around the magazines and to demonstrate his artistic abilities. When he talked about his pictures, he spoke loudly and assertively, almost daring us to doubt his word. I suspected that Carl was still very angry and very much at risk.

Don, on the other hand, had the realistic awareness that others perceived him as a comfortably settled married man and devoted father (Figure 10–9). He couldn't resist tweaking others for their complacency with such an image ("maybe a little too comfortable"). Don searched until he found two prints of the same illustration, which he used in two collages (Figures 10–9 and 10–10). According to Don's statements, Figure 10–9 was intended to indicate how others perceived him, while the one without the comment (Figure 10–10) expressed his desire to return to that lifestyle. Yet he also expressed, both verbally and graphically, his desire to be one of the boys, perhaps even a "Marlboro man," albeit a rural New England version (Figure 10–11). Don said that the old woman reminded him of his mother and that

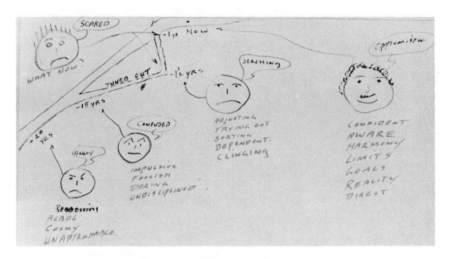

Figure 10–8. Drawing by Carl: Me as I see me"

Credit: Pierre Bastianeli, Biomedical Communications, Dartmouth Medical School.

he had grown up "on the far side of Lonesome Mountain." He said that he still felt as though he were living in isolation and that no one really cared about him.

One of the benefits the group saw in this exercise was that it gave them something new to talk about. They would look at their sense of isolation, which is enhanced by the long New England winters, in another light. They were isolated not only by their feelings of guilt and secrecy and by the poverty and marital problems that many of them shared, but also by the physical situation of their rural farm lives. They could now see that being housebound during the winter months presented an opportunity for sexual intimacy with children and thus a violation of social mores. Identifying these contributing elements provided subjects for therapeutic activities that offered alternatives to impulsive, antisocial, and illegal behaviors.

New Englanders are famous for, and proud of, their succinct speech, but these men could now acknowledge that this characteristic had led them to suppress communication of disturbing emotions. Clearly, they had no difficulty finding words in magazines that closely approximated their feelings. Although they spoke about their pictures sparingly, it was evident that they felt that the words and pictures included in their collages said as much as they deemed necessary and more than they had previously cared to vocalize. This presented an opportunity to discuss other aspects of communication, including the interpretations and effects of silence.

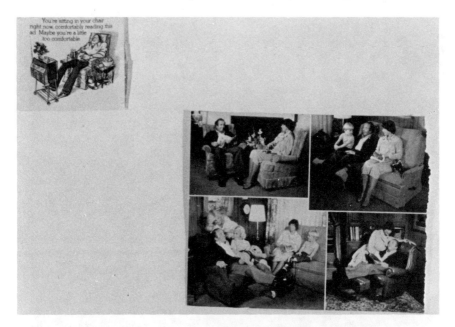

**Figure 10–9. Collage by Don (a parolee): "As others see me" and
"Maybe you're a little too comfortable"**

Credit: Pierre Bastianeli, Biomedical Communications, Dartmouth Medical School.

This led to a discussion of other types of nonverbal communication, such as body language. Each group member was asked to demonstrate a gesture of common body language, such as the signals of a coach or referee, policeman, or cheerleader. The group was then involved in a series of mime exercises, such as playing a game of catch, eventually leading to a brief game of baseball involving all the group members. This activity requires the utmost concentration and attention to detail, as well as mutual cooperation. On occasion, it may be desirable to have a catcher or umpire, as well as a pitcher, to reduce conflict and validate the batter's perception of where the ball went. When the group members work to resolve these differences in perception among themselves, the activity can improve the social cohesiveness of the group and the behavioral patterns of individual members.

Using Photo Cards. Another core activity that can be very revealing may evolve from the warm-up exercise in body language. It involves the use of "photo cards," which are simply file cards of various sizes with a wide selection of photos. Included in the constantly growing collection of cards are individuals and groups of both sexes and all ages; portraits and full

Figure 10–10. Collage by Don: "This is the way I'd *like* it to be"

Credit: Pierre Bastianeli, Biomedical Communications, Dartmouth Medical School.

figures, both resting and active; animals of all sizes, both aggressive and playful, domestic and wild; reproductions of paintings, abstract and representational; and objects and environments. As an introduction, the leader selects several photos of people and passes them around the group. Each member is asked to select and comment on two body parts from which he has drawn an impression of the individual in the picture. The cards are passed again, and this time each member is asked to select one card about which he or she will be asked to tell a brief story.

What usually happens is that people select photo cards of people who either remind them of someone they have known and regard negatively or positively or of someone they idealize, abhor, or identify with. The stories commonly involve projections as to economic and social status, as well as generalizations relative to feeling states. When this information is not forthcoming, the leader may ask judiciously phrased questions, such as "Would he or she be likely to come to a fair, and if so, would he or she be likely to come and watch your ox-pulling event? If this person lived in your town, where would that be? What kind of house? Have you ever worked or been

Figure 10–11. Collage by Don: "As I see me"

Credit: Pierre Bastianeli, Biomedical Communications, Dartmouth Medical School.

in such a house? What are some of the things the individual might do that would annoy or please you?" These stories might be developed further in collages, murals (depicting the town these people populate, including services, and employment), and dramatizations involving encounters, incidents, crises, and solutions.

Another activity in which these photo cards may be used is to have the members select several cards around a theme, such as grief, anger, heroes, or adversaries. In one session, the group was asked to select photos that reminded them of some occasion or someone who had been outstanding in their lives. One client (Evan) began by selecting photos that he said reminded him of his wife. Among these was a photo of a reclining nude female. As he was telling us about his photo selection, he would pick up this photo and slap it down, saying nothing about it but moving quickly on to another, about which it was easier for him to talk. His agitation increased as he began to run out of photos to describe. Finally, he threw the nude photo back into the original pile of photo cards in the center of the floor, around which we were all seated. Hissing angrily, he said, "That bitch was my mother! She ruined everything for me." He then told us about her sexual abuse of him as a child.

Another member of the group, a minister named Frank, selected photos of boys who reminded him of the lads in his church choir whom he had molested. He seemed quite sensitive to his ability to identify boys who could be coerced into participating in his perversion. He said that he had selected a group of photos of children to illustrate what he perceived to be the most important attributes (loneliness, vulnerability, eagerness to please, poverty), qualities that seemed to describe this small, soft-spoken man himself.

Therapeutic Goals and Techniques

Specific Applications of Theories and Suggested Approaches

Al was clearly depressed. His artwork and body language told us as much. His difficulty seemed to lie in his inability to reconcile his negative self-image with "another side" of himself, which he could neither illustrate nor describe. We would have to ascertain whether Al was not only willing but able to ascribe to himself and then reconcile the possibility that he had the capacity for both positive and negative feelings simultaneously directed at the same target. Currently, his own *internal authoritarian,* or conscience, was being supported by the verdict of society and was unlikely to broach any controversy. His internal and basically optimistic "child" was depressed by this but not crushed. It wanted one more chance. Activities that would allow Al an opportunity for immediate gratification, creativity, and achievement might help counterbalance the oppressive reality of his crime. Activities that emphasized cause-and-effect relationships and provided for ascending levels of decision making would be most likely to enhance his ability to moderate his behaviors in socially acceptable ways. The expressive arts modalities most likely to facilitate these goals would be those that accommodated his preferred learning and communication modes. Since it is unlikely that he is aware of these attributes, we can best ascertain them by providing him with a variety of expressive tools until he finds the ones that are most satisfying to him and in which he achieves the greatest "success" (defined as clarity and consistency with intent).

Bob had difficulty reconciling his desire for a positive self-image with his outward-directed anger. It has been my experience that many who have a strong internal authoritarian influencing their domineering behaviors are actually fearful that they will lose all joy in life through social conformity. In other words, there is a fine line between the bully and the child. Bob assumed the macho roles of his culture lest others perceive him as anything less than a man of steel, a superman. If he gave up this facade, he might be sacrificing the only fantasy that ever gave him satisfaction, as well as the only positive self-image he had going for him. Before relinquishing this self-image, he would have to recognize and acknowledge the source of his anger. He would have to be able to accept that he could have simultaneous feelings of a positive as well as a negative nature and learn how to direct those energies appropriately. Activities that allowed him to explore other, more socially acceptable leadership roles (e.g., through drama exercises in which group members try every role in a court scene—prosecutor, defendant, judge, and jury) could be insightful and helpful for him.

Carl must learn that understanding his emotions and their source within himself can help him control them. Arts activities could offer him a safe and acceptable opportunity to express even his angriest feelings. Once objectified in this manner, these feelings would probably become less threatening, and Carl might learn that there are socially appropriate tension-reducing outlets for his negative emotions. Drama activities might enhance his socialization, while art and writing activities could provide expressive and ego-syntonic approaches to insight and control.

Art and Mime

Don, a very reserved and quiet man, expressed a desire for more social interaction, particularly among his peers. I would offer him the opportunity to explore this nonverbally through activities in art and mime. For example, one technique involves two people creating a cartoon together. A large piece of paper is scored into a dozen or more units; one of the partners draws the first frame, and the other draws in the next. They continue, without talking, taking turns until the work is mutually conceded to be complete. Results often include written dialogue. Commonly, one partner will lead the action by risk taking, while the other may prove to be a rescuer or parenting influence. Humor often emerges, and the activity is generally regarded as pleasurable and nonthreatening, even though the injunction not to talk makes the outcome a mystery until the end.

Similarly, mimed improvisations involving themes of morality and ethics can provide opportunities for humor, insight, and alternative modes of communication. I have found that offering small groups of four or five an opportunity to explore a concept (such as one involving ethics or morality) nonverbally in clay or on a mural-size sheet of paper can be a successful way to introduce this activity. For example, the suggestion is made that the group deal with the issue of right and wrong. They are given five minutes to discuss and decide how they will express this dichotomy. They may choose to make a mural showing a car going through a red light, causing an accident and resulting in the driver's going to prison. Objectifying an amorphous concept makes it concrete and meaningful, facilitating its transformation into human interaction. Therefore, I usually have clients follow the clay activity with a brief nonverbal dramatization. The therapist may note whether or not the group dealt with the question of why the driver went through the red light (was he drunk or late to work?) and how each might relate these motivations and events to his own sexual behaviors. Such activities facilitate the recognition of symbolic metaphors and illustrate how we transpose experience into metaphor and back into responses to stimulae.

Movement

Evan seemed to have ambiguous feelings about the women in his life. His trust of women was minimal, but he retained an ideal of what the male-female relationship could be. It was this fantasy that he acted out with children, yet it did not satisfy his needs. He seemed to cling to a concept that could not accommodate conflicting feelings directed at a single target. As long as this persisted, he would not be able to build a lasting relationship. In addition, as long as he held on to negative feelings toward others, based on his childhood experiences and corroborated by society through his own incarceration for similar acts, he could not begin to develop a sense of his own self-worth. His internal authoritarian or conscience was his own worst enemy because it had so much negative experience and self-awareness of antisocial urges to support it.

We needed to help him develop a positive self-image, along with an acceptance and understanding of emotional dichotomies. Exercises emphasizing trust relationships, such as taking turns being blindfolded and led about, over and under real and imaginary obstacles in the environment (and sharing the experience of each role with partners), or physical support exercises in which there is mutual dependence and support to realize these objectives (such as partners squatting, back to back, linking arms, and trying to get up and down) might be useful.

Music and Poetry

Exercises involving self-awareness, self-image improvement, and socialization might help Frank, as would finding new ways to develop peer respect and acceptance. He would have to develop satisfying ways of combating his loneliness and sense of isolation that are in accord with our social mores. Through the literary arts and music, he could explore his religious convictions and develop a means of expressing his emotional needs.

Frank's intellectual acumen and emotional complexity would provide a considerable challenge to any therapeutic approach. After almost two years of verbal group therapy, his preoccupation remained steadfast. The simple group and individual exercises outlined in this chapter would not help him accomplish his therapeutic goals. In his case, it would be worthwhile to explore whether interrelating arts activities with verbal therapies and behavioral extinction would help him. Using music therapy in conjunction with verbal and behavioral therapies probably would be most helpful. According to his own statements, music and poetry were two of his favorite modes of learning and expression, and his religious convictions were bound up in them. Liturgical music, hymns, and folk songs might be useful in helping him identify and express his own emotional needs. It is plausible that they might provide a motivational force and a therapeutic tool in his recovery.

One approach to using poetry might be to have the group make spontaneous scribbles called "gesture drawings." These are marks made on three 8½-by-11 pieces of paper in less than two seconds each. The instructions are to cover as much of the paper as possible within the time allowed. Each scribble is numbered in order, and after three are completed, the individual goes back and writes a title on each one. Both the titles and the gestures give an inkling as to what was on the artist's mind at the moment. Although the first drawing is made spontaneously, the artist attempts to exert increased control over the expression with each succeeding drawing. The titles reflect that process of control, as well as the underlying concept.

The group is then directed to write something based on the concepts revealed in the gesture drawings and their titles. The members then share their work, and the discussion is directed toward finding a relationship between what was expressed and what had been on their minds before beginning the exercise. This technique can be repeated throughout the treatment process and can be indicative of change and progress.

Other writing exercises involve envisioning oneself as an object in the room (or an animal, plant, or other object) and writing a brief paragraph describing that object. The choice of object and the characteristics used to describe it can be very revealing of self-image. Another technique might involve having the leader bring in poetry selections relating to issues concerning the group or having members share pieces that are meaningful to them. Each would then write something on the topic. This approach also can be used for sharing musical selections on tape or record as well.

One technique that I have used involves the use of what I call the "choral poem." In introducing the exercise, I usually offer an open line that contains a metaphoric challenge—e.g., "The trees chattered" or "The sky winked." Each member is asked to contribute a line, which is written down. Each participant is then asked to select words or lines in the poem that are most meaningful. A tape recorder is turned on. Someone is asked to begin by saying out loud, in an appropriate tone and pitch, the line or word he has selected. Others jump in whenever they choose. Words and phrases can be repeated over and over, and there can be brief pauses. Nonverbal sounds that seem appropriate also may be interjected. The choral poem is allowed to run its course.

Because of inhibitions, the recitation usually begins slowly. The leader can help by interjecting his or her own selections. Soon the group gets involved and the piece reaches a climax, then gradually subsides. The tape is then replayed. Although it has been my experience that the initial recitation is usually the best and most satisfying, occasionally the group may feel that it has created something worthy of polishing and presenting publicly. This should be encouraged, as it not only improves the status of the members among their peers (this can be very important in prison), but it also encourages others to try their hand or voice at creative expression.

The Missing Piece

Grover presents the classic image of a Down-Easter: tall, slim, weathered, and reserved. The magazine photos he selected for his collage of how others perceive him show a lobsterman and pillar of the community (Figure 10–12). His self-image collage includes elements both consistent and conflicting with that perception (Figure 10–13). Relocated from his place of birth and trade, Grover said that he still loves water, fishing, and seasonal pleasures (the landscape photo), but the change has been traumatic (the car wreck).

Grover could have cut apart the two paintings of flowers to fit them in vertically, but the thought did not occur to him. Why not? He had cut them out initially, why not carry the act one step further? Lying on their sides, the paintings are distracting and ineffectual, and they invite correction. What is missing? What part of himself remains obscure in Grover's self-awareness?

Grover could have found other pictures of flowers or other reproductions of paintings to express his concepts, but he chose classical European arrangements focusing on mass and color. Mass and color are also found in the group portrait seen in Figure 10–12. Grover included a piece of the caption from the magazine, indicating that this is a photograph of physicians. Is this a comment on the authoritarian role of psychotherapists? It is certainly different from the image one might have of a group of lobstermen.

Native New Englanders take deep pride in their European heritage. I suspect that part of what is missing in Grover's life is being a member of a group sharing his cultural background. Indeed, he may well be homesick, for although the inland mountain regions have numerous lakes and ponds, life here is different from that on the coast. Another element of northern New England fishing village life, not familiar to the casual visitor or as common inland, is the habit of keeping diaries and writing poetry. One such village I visited had an entire section of its library devoted to the writings of the children and adult members of the community dating back to the late 1700s. This personal, often private, but communally accepted form of self-

Figure 10–12. Collage by Grover (a parolee): "As others see me"

Credit: Pierre Bastianeli, Biomedical Communications, Dartmouth Medical School.

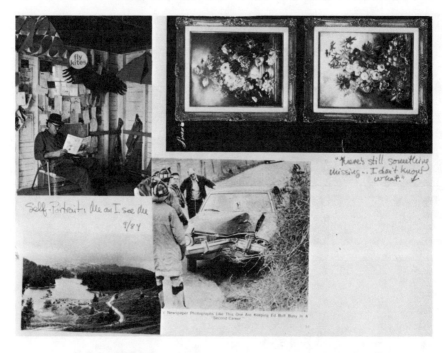

**Figure 10–13. Collage by Grover: "As I see me . . . there's still
      something missing."**

Credit: Pierre Bastianeli, Biomedical Communications, Dartmouth Medical School.

expression and catharsis is difficult to maintain in an environment in which
it is foreign. Grover pictures himself reading (most rural people with seasonal
trades are avid readers). He is sitting in a shed full of kites. Kites are for
flying, for dreaming, for escaping the bonds of gravity.

I worry about Grover. Partly because of the long, severe winters and
sense of isolation, New Englanders have a particularly high suicide rate.
Retired and dislocated men also have a high risk of suicide. The car wreck
and the paintings on their sides imply a sense of depression and an incapacity
to thwart disaster. The kites imply flight, escape. What may soon be "missing" from this picture may be Grover.

What is the likelihood that a clinician will recognize these qualities in a
client's self-portrait? What is the likelihood that the clinician will support a
possible need on Grover's part to express himself literally? I believe that
understanding and support of clients' nonverbal and metaphoric representations are essential therapeutic interventions. What relationship is there between the fundamental changes in Grover's life and his molestation of
children? And what can be done about it? And if we have these answers but

do not offer Grover an ego-syntonic method of exploring or expressing his feelings about them, we will have accomplished little.

Arts Therapist as Consultant

The main obstacle to using the skills of an arts therapist in working with this population is a lack of understanding of the techniques and knowledge the therapist can contribute to the treatment objectives. This chapter is intended to help remove that obstacle. It is essential that we recognize that no one individual or therapeutic discipline has proved successful in all circumstances and with all populations and individuals. We must work together and share our knowledge and skills.

I am reminded of a child with several severe learning disabilities with whom I had been asked to work. Operating academically several years below his chronological peers, this bright, attractive lad had no athletic prowess to fall back on for peer status and self-esteem. Both his physical and cognitive functions were affected by his mixed right and left brain dominance. Together we discovered that he had developed remarkable tactile skills to compensate for his learning disabilities. Blindfolded, he could distinguish between types of grass, grades of sandpaper, and the blossoms and leaves of various plants. He could barely read, write, or do mathematics, but he could repair a motor, build a model vehicle without plans (although he could not tell you how he did it), and teach himself Morse code. We used Morse code to improve his math skills and a tape recorder to help him meet his writing requirements. Reading presented another problem. I gave him one of those braille cards that says something about being blind and has a modest braille alphabet. In moments, he had deciphered the entire message. I tried to get braille materials for him to enhance his reading skills, but he was declared ineligible because he was not legally blind. (The concept of limiting an educational or therapeutic tool to the population for which it had been originally designed, regardless of its applicability to others, presents some real problems to therapists and clients.) Eventually the boy recovered some vision in his nondominant eye which enabled him to read without functional conflict. What he had learned about his other cognitive skills during therapy enabled him to graduate from high school. Followup has shown, however, that he has never reached his full intellectual potential.

This example illustrates that having access to professional arts therapists can increase the number of techniques available to the primary therapist. An arts therapist can provide diagnostic consultation or supplemental treatment in some cases or even become the primary therapist when the situation warrants. The arts therapist's training and experience embrace psychological, developmental, and metaphorical issues, as well as a familiarity with the media and techniques needed to implement, direct, and conclude treatment. He or she often offers both skill and economy within tight fiscal and time constraints.

How can arts therapy consultants best be used in the treatment of sexual offenders? First, they can facilitate the collection of diagnostic, treatment, and evaluative data. They also can facilitate group and individual therapeutic progress. If you are developing a new program, I would recommend including an arts therapist in the team protocol. If budgetary constraints prohibit this expense, arts therapists might be useful on a periodic basis, alternating with or serving as adjuncts to verbal treatment. In this situation, I would recommend that an arts therapist consultant be written into the protocol to work with groups and individuals on a biweekly, weekly, or bimonthly basis. Arrangements allowing the arts therapist to work individually with particular offenders who are less comfortable with or more resistant to the traditional verbal modes of treatment could enhance and clarify diagnostic and treatment objectives and, perhaps, even expedite them.

In my work with offenders, victims, and survivors of sexual abuse, I have found arts therapy to be an invaluable asset in accessing data, providing a sense of self-awareness, and enhancing self-image, learning, and development, while providing an alternative outlet for disruptive ideation and behavior.

References

Berne, Eric. 1975. *Transactional Analysis in Psychotherapy*. New York: Ballantine Books.

Groth, A. Nicholas. 1982. "The Incest Offender." In Suzanne M. Sgroi, ed. *Handbook of Clinical Interventions in Child Sexual Abuse*. Lexington, MA: Lexington Books, 216–40.

Harter, Susan. 1983. "Cognitive-Developmental Considerations in the Conduct of Play Therapy." In Chas. E. Shaefer and Kevin J. O'Connor, eds. *Handbook of Play Therapy*. New York: John Wiley & Sons, 100–04.

Law Alert 200. 7 Lawyers Weekly, Inc., Boston. April 1986, 5.

Naitove, Connie E. 1979. "Art Therapist: An Ambiguous Figure." *American Artist Magazine*, September, 46–49.

Rogers, Carl M. 1961. *On Becoming a Person*. Boston: Houghton-Mifflin.

Resources

You can locate arts therapy consultants in your area by writing to the national organizations of art, dance, drama, poetry, and music therapy or by contacting the National Educational Council of Creative Therapies, Inc. (24

Rip Road, Hanover, NH 03755, 603-643-2651). Additional resources and references are listed below.

American Art Ther. Assoc.: 505 E. Hawley St.; Mondelein, IL 60060

Amer. Dance Ther. Assoc.: 2000 Century Plaza; Columbia, MD 21044

Nat'l Assoc. for Drama Ther.: 19 Edwards St.; New Haven, CT 06511

Nat'l Assoc. for Poetry Ther.: 225 Williams St.; Huron, OH 44839

Nat'l Assoc. for Music Ther.: 1133 15th St. N.W., Suite 1000; Wash., DC 20005

Amer. Assoc. for Music Ther.: 66 Morris Ave., P.O.B. 359; Springfield, NJ 07081

Art

Berensohn, P. *Finding One's Way with Clay*. New York: Simon & Schuster, 1972.
Rubin, Judith R. *The Art of Art Therapy*. New York: Brunner/Mazel, 1984.

Dance/Movement

H'Doubler, Margaret N. *Dance: A Creative Art Experience*. Madison: University of Wisconsin Press, 1977.
Wethered, Audrey G. *Drama and Movement in Therapy*. London: MacDonald & Evans, Ltd., 1973.

Drama

Schattner, G., and R. Courtney. *Drama in Therapy*. Vols. 1 and 2. New York: Drama Book Specialists, 1981.

Music

Gaston, E. Thayer. *Music in Therapy: Progress in Psychotherapy*. New York: Grune & Stratton, 1958.
Gray, V., and R. Percival. *Music, Movement and Mime for Children*. Oxford: Oxford University Press, 1962.

Poetry

Koch, Kenneth. *Wishes, Lies, and Dreams*. New York: Vantage, 1970.
Leedy, Jack. *Poetry the Healer*. New York: J.B. Lippincott, 1973.

Interdisciplinary

Naitove, Connie E. "The Creative Arts Therapist: Jack-of-all-Trades or Master-of-None?" *The Arts in Psychotherapy* 7 (no. 4):253–259.

11

Child Sexual Abuse Redefined: Impact of Modern Culture on the Sexual Mores of the Yuit Eskimo

Sheila J. Thompson

Editor's Note

In the 1970s we became aware that children who had gonorrhea infections beyond the neonatal period were children who had acquired these infections as a result of sexual contact with an infected adult or with another infected child. Persons who wished to explain the presence of a gonorrhea infection in a child by postulating that nonsexual transmission could occur frequently quoted the 1971 study by Shore and Winkelstein described in this chapter.

I believe that Sheila Thompson's description of the conditions that existed when the study was performed is both enlightening and helpful. This chapter allows us to appreciate those conditions more fully and places in proper perspective the impression of Shore and Winkelstein that nonvenereal transmission of gonococcal infections to children might have occurred in the Yuit Eskimo. In fact, the infected children had been sexually active, and some had been victims of sexual abuse. Ms. Thompson has provided us with a cultural context that enables us to understand how the study was performed; it is, therefore, a valuable contribution to our knowledge about child sexual abuse.

Introduction

The following chapter is based on information obtained and observations made by the author while living for a period of ten years in a Yuit Eskimo village in Alaska. Additional information is presented from interviews and anthropological sources. Its primary purpose is to present data supporting the observation that modern American sexual mores have profoundly affected those of the Eskimo and have led to a modern redefinition of preexisting Eskimo cultural patterns such as sexual abuse. At the same time, a lack of awareness of contemporary sexual mores has led some researchers to conclude that Eskimo children were acquiring gonorrhea infections via nonsexual methods of transmission.

To provide a context for the cultural changes, it is necessary to describe the relative isolation of the community and its surrounding area in regard to location, communication and transportation resources, language, and education. I will then present information to document the degree to which each type of isolation diminished as Caucasian influence increased and became more prevalent.

It must be stressed that the observations presented here pertain only to the Yuit Eskimo residing in the Kuskokwim River delta area of Alaska and should not be generalized to apply to the Inuit Eskimo of northern Alaska or the Canadian or Iberian Eskimo.

General Background
of the Yuit Community

In 1965, as a federal employee, I was sent to live and work among the people of a large Eskimo village (population 1,000) located in southwestern Alaska. At that time, the population of the village was 95 percent Yuit (Yup'ik-speaking) Eskimo, with the balance of the population composed of Aleut, Athabascan Indian, Caucasian, and interracial mixtures. The Caucasian segment was primarily comprised of clergy, store owners, teachers, Public Health officials, and personnel from the Bureau of Indian Affairs, the Federal Aviation Agency, and the State Division of Family and Children Services. In the mid-1950s, a DEW line station (Distant Early Warning radar defense system) had been established near the village. Abandoned by the time I reached the area, it was still a subject of controversy in regard to the problems it had created concerning alcohol abuse and relationships with the native people.

Over the next ten years, the population rose to 3,200, and the percentage of Eskimo inhabitants decreased to 85 percent, with a greater influx of Caucasians caused by expansion and inception of agencies such as Alaska Legal Services, educational systems such as Kuskokwim Community College, and the Yukon–Kuskokwim Health Corporation.

According to 1986 figures from the *Alaska Geographic Almanac,* the population was by then approaching 3,700, with the percentage of Eskimo reduced to approximately 67.6 percent.

The village itself, a hub of transportation, commerce, and education for a 56-village area encompassing 60,000 square miles, is located 420 air miles west of Anchorage and 80 miles inland from the Bering Sea along the Kuskokwim River. Travel to and from the village is by air, with commodities either flown in or brought in by barge in the summer. Travel to and from other villages is by boat or airplane, with winter travel also aided by dogsled or snowmobile. The means of transportation have remained constant over the years, although air transportation has increased to accommodate the greater need to travel to villages and large cities.

In 1965, transportation was an isolating factor. The community also had limited access to telephone and radio communication with the continental United States and the rest of the world. The three primary radio stations received in the village were Armed Forces Radio, Radio Moscow, and a church-affiliated station. There was no local newspaper until the advent of the *Tundra Drums,* a weekly publication begun in the early 1970s. Television, through the Public Broadcasting Network, was introduced in 1973, bringing noncommercial and educational broadcasting to nearby villages by satellite. Broadcasting hours were limited, however, as were the number of television sets and variety of programs presented. At this time, a local radio station was put into operation, presenting programming in both English and Yup'ik, the local Eskimo dialect. Movies were prevalent and very popular, offering people glimpses of life elsewhere. Families would attend movies nightly, regardless of what was showing. In 1965, teenagers especially enjoyed the "beach party" and Elvis Presley films.

Language itself was a barrier to communication. The Eskimo elderly primarily spoke the native dialect, while children and young and middle-aged adults were bilingual. Because many of the children had been educated by Caucasian teachers, English had become their first language. Thus, a language barrier, or communication gap, existed between the generations.

The language barrier did not persist, however, as an educational movement to teach the native language uniformly to the Eskimo people resulted in bilingual education in the schools. By 1975, the primary grades were taught bilingually, with the assistance of native teacher's aides, and the higher grades received instruction in Yup'ik, which for the first time in history became a written as well as a spoken language. With the expansion of the native language to written form, the *Tundra Drums* was able to publish in both languages and disseminate information to a broader base of people.

Thus, due to its location, limited transportation and communication systems, language barriers, and limited educational opportunities, the community was still in a state of isolation in 1965. Greater influx of modern technology and educational advancement tended to decrease this isolation after 1965, and in time, it began to change the native people's concept of themselves in relation to other cultures, particularly that of modern America.

The Eskimo people, especially the children and adolescents, began to emulate the "heroes" they read and heard about and saw in the movies and on television. The use of American slang increased, leather jackets and miniskirts were popular, and rock and roll was the current fad. They began to question their native cultural patterns as they visualized and experienced other lifestyles. Use of snowmobiles increased, causing a decrease in the use of dogsleds, and teenagers earned money from commercial fishing to buy motorcycles so they could "cruise" the three miles of paved road in the town.

I arrived during this period to work with the native people, particularly the youth. My first task was to learn the Yup'ik language as best I could, with the assistance (and persistence) of my young Eskimo friends, who immersed me in the language by limiting our conversations to Yup'ik. They were excellent and patient teachers, not only of the language, but also of their customs, traditions, and heritage.

I lived, not as an "agency" person in government-built housing, but with the Eskimo people in a house similar to theirs—approximately 15 by 20-feet, made of a tarpaper-covered plywood-and-frame construction with little insulation. There was no running water or sewage system. Water was delivered to the home and stored in covered fifty-gallon oil drums. "Honey buckets" (chemical toilets) were used for human waste and were collected by sanitarians twice weekly. Although there was no means of refrigeration in my house, many of the native people had refrigerators or freezers. Good hygiene was difficult to maintain under these conditions, but without exception it was a goal of every household.

Homes such as these were typically inhabited by five to ten persons, often including grandparents, parents, and their children and stepchildren. In addition, families often cared for children of relatives by informal adoptions. Privacy was at a premium, and it had been that way for many years prior to my arrival, especially in the smaller villages.

Writing about Eskimo community life in the 1880s, Wendell Oswalt stated, "A nuclear family was small and consisted of a couple and two or three children who would survive into adult life. Under these conditions there must have been a wide variety of individuals attached to the core nuclear families for household units to be composed of up to twenty individuals. These units might include one or more parents or siblings of the couple, stepchildren, more distantly related persons, adopted children, orphans and nonrelatives" (Oswalt 1967, 188).

In 1956, Oswalt studied the community of Napaskiak, a small village located upstream from the village in which I lived. At that time, he noted that most households had the same makeup as in the 1880s but fewer occupants—from three to nine (Oswalt 1963, 55).

Perhaps this pattern of living closely together contributed to the development of certain sexual mores in the Eskimo culture. Living in close proximity to others in a small space that shut out a harsh external environment made physical familiarity a necessary part of life, and all aspects of that familiarity became acceptable and natural.

In this regard, Oswalt noted, "Sexual differences and bodily functions are regarded casually from early childhood" (Oswalt 1963, 44). In summer, small children would wear little more than a shirt when playing in or around the house with friends. Children of both sexes played together without adult supervision from toddler to marriage age. He noted that children often would play "hide and seek," which included talk about sexual organs and activities, as well as experimentation. "Sexual interests are further manifested in close body contact during some play. Boys and girls lounge on the beds or bump against each other and giggle. They may also grab at each other's pubic region" (Oswalt 1963, 44).

Up to the late 1940s, girls were expected to marry prior to the onset of their first menses. Gradually, the age of marriage was delayed until fourteen or fifteen. Because territorial law precluded this, legal marriage took place at age sixteen, but often couples lived as mates prior to the legal ceremony. Marriages were arranged by parents, with the bride and groom having little say. Sexual intercourse between unmarried adolescents and other adolescents or adults was accepted as normal and a matter of little concern (Oswalt 1967, 202). Pregnancy out of wedlock did not necessarily mean that the girl would marry the father of the child. In the old culture, what might have been viewed as promiscuity by modern American culture was an accepted way of life among the Eskimo. Public displays of sexuality were regarded as taboo, however, as people valued their privacy and dissuaded public displays of emotion.

Working with children, adolescents, and their families in the mid- to late 1960s allowed me to see that this way of life was still very prevalent. Because of the scarcity of beds in households (especially in the smaller villages), it was not uncommon for young children to sleep with parents or older siblings of the same or opposite sex. Neither was it uncommon for adolescents to sleep in the same bed with adolescent siblings of the same or opposite sex. In these close quarters, sexual experimentation was a natural progression, for children had been introduced early to their parents' sexual activity, either by watching or by being in the same bed. In addition, older siblings would sexually "tease" or play games with younger children, just as they would in the context of other childhood games. In much the same way, older relatives also were known to engage in playful sexual acts with young children and adolescents. Mutual masturbation and digital penetration were natural eventualities, and by adolescence, so was intercourse. This activity was considered a natural and occasional process of maturation. The activities were engaged in privately, usually in the home or away from the home in secluded areas. Open promiscuity was discouraged, perhaps as a carry-over of the taboo of the old culture.

A few adolescent girls occasionally complained about older "cousins" or "uncles" who would "take them" forcibly after overindulging in alcohol. Others had the same complaint about peer group boys who would try to seduce them after having too much to drink. The complaints, however, seemed halfhearted, for the girls themselves usually were drinking at the time and seemed to use this as an excuse for their victimization. This was done with a certain degree of naiveté and flirtation. The introduction of alcohol into the scenario tended to add an element of physical force that had not existed in the childhood "games." Alcohol allowed the old taboos to be broken.

The boys, on the other hand, had the attitude that "that's what people do," and this was their excuse when questioned as to their actions. Some had learned sexual aggressiveness from hearing about escapades of older boys or men, and part of that learning process involved alcohol as a precursor to the sexual act—"to make me feel good like a man."

By this time, the historical and cultural role of the Eskimo male as a proficient, conscientious provider for the needs of his family and village through hunting, fishing, and trapping had been usurped by state and federal laws that limited the extent to which he was allowed to perform the very tasks that provided him with a major source of self-esteem. For some, this loss of self-esteem could not be replaced by a job, for very often training and education were lacking. Consequently, some chose to obtain a false and temporary sense of power and esteem through the use of alcohol.

Likewise, the historical and cultural role of the female had changed. Under the old ways, a woman might gain a major source of self-esteem through her skills as a skin sewer, clothing maker, and food preparer and preserver. Now, however, her skills were replaced by manufactured clothing, canned and frozen foods, and sewing machines. The family no longer relied totally on her skills for its well-being. She, too, could find a job—if one were available and if she possessed the necessary training or education. But as was the case with her male counterpart, her role and a source of her self-esteem had changed primarily to that of keeping her family together by helping them, as well as herself, adjust to the new cultural changes. In some cases, the use of alcohol was a quick route to a false sense of importance, taking the place of a prior source of self-esteem and also offering temporary relief from having to deal with these changes.

With these cultural changes and with the increased consumption of alcohol, which resulted in a loss of inhibition, the sexual scenario changed to include occasional acts of violence. It should be mentioned that young people rarely used obscene language publicly to describe sexual acts or sexual organs. Boys and girls may have traded stories in private, but derogatory comments about others' sexuality did not become prevalent until the early to mid-1970s, as Caucasian influence increased even more.

In the 1960s, there was a certain naiveté among young people about birth control and reproduction in general. If a girl became pregnant, she bore no burden of shame. After the baby was born, it was raised in the same family as a sibling. Here is one example: In 1970, a fifteen-year-old girl who was attending a summer program at the University of Alaska in Fairbanks complained one morning of a stomachache and later that same day gave birth to a baby boy. She had not realized that she was pregnant, and neither had the physician who had examined her that morning! After the birth, she and her baby stayed with my family while she finished her summer on campus. In addition to showing her how to care for her newborn, I instructed her in reproduction. She had no idea how she had conceived and borne a baby. At the end of the summer, she and her baby returned to her family, who welcomed her and "baby brother" warmly. The whole event, to her and to her family, was very natural.

In 1964, homosexuality and transvestism were accepted in the Yuit Eskimo culture, to the extent that in one family, the two teenage girls would style their older brother's hair, manicure his nails, and lend him their perfume. The three of them were included in all teenage activities, and their brother was rarely excluded or ostracized in any way.

In the early 1970s, however, homosexuality among the Caucasians in the community was less accepted by both Caucasians and Eskimos. By that time, Caucasian values had a bigger influence on attitudes toward sexual mores, and it was generally felt that the Caucasians should "know better." Therefore, Caucasian homosexuality remained closeted.

In the past, transvestism had been practiced occasionally in the smaller villages by raising young boys as girls and having them perform the tasks of girls. A rare occurrence was observed as late as 1973, when a twelve-year-old girl from a small village was sent away to boarding school and, shortly after her arrival, was found to be a boy. According to information at the time, the child eventually underwent a sex-change operation, as it was felt that the child, after being raised as a girl, had psychologically become a girl. Fewer still were the cases of females raised as males, for the onset of menses brought the deception into the open. As Caucasian influence, through religion, education, and health services, increased, this practice ceased to exist.

Evolution of Community Awareness of Sexual Abuse

The term *sexual molestation* to describe the sexual acts that had been occurring between adults and children and adolescents and children did not come into general public use until the early 1970s, and then largely because of Caucasian influence. It was at this time that two incidents occurred.

In the first, a Caucasian father was arrested and charged with incest with both his male and female children. The Caucasians in the community were aghast, and the Eskimos became more aware that certain behaviors against children were wrong and punishable by law. In the past, wrongdoers had only been chastised by the family or village elders.

In the second case, a Caucasian social worker was arrested for molesting young Eskimo boys. Because this incident was a direct threat to the Eskimo people, they were incensed, and the social worker had to be placed in protective custody. As is common in the "lower 48," the boys involved were treated more as witnesses than as victims by law enforcement officials. Little assistance was given to them in the form of counseling or medical care, other than that required to obtain evidence for the prosecution. The emphasis was on punishing the transgressor rather than helping the victim.

Upon observation and reflection, it seemed that these incidents and the publicity surrounding them sparked a new awareness in the Eskimo people, and along with the rise of reported cases of venereal disease, they were the major forces that led to a self-redefinition of the Eskimo's sexual mores.

In the 1960s, venereal disease, becoming more widespread throughout the villages, seemed to hold little or no stigma among the native people and was thought of as no more serious than streptococcal infections or otitis media, the two prevalent maladies of that area. Penicillin and other antibiotics were readily available through the Public Health Service, and the people had no qualms about seeking treatment. Anthropologist Norman Chance, in his 1966 study of the northern Alaskan Eskimo, indicated that these people readily accepted modern medicine because they had few preconceived medical practices to unlearn. Perhaps this also was true for the Yuit Eskimo. Although they seemed to understand about the transmission of the disease, that understanding did not prevent them from continuing to engage in the sexual practices that caused them to contract it. Perhaps the future consequences of venereal disease did not seem important because it was easily treated with antibiotics, as were other bacterial infections.

Oddly enough, these diseases, which were introduced to the native population by the Euro-American influx, became prime targets for eradication by that same group. In the early 1970s, throughout the state, clinics and hot lines were established to attempt to halt the spread of the disease. Because of this concerted effort by the Public Health Service, more awareness was generated, and a stigma was gradually placed on those who were unfortunate enough to contract the disease. Venereal disease became differentiated from other bacterial infections because it made private activities public—again, a breaking of the old taboo.

Even more attention was called to the growing epidemic as native health aides uncovered cases of pediatric venereal disease. Trained by Caucasian physicians to recognize symptoms, the native aides became the primary referral agents to the Public Health Service, because the Eskimos trusted their own, who could communicate in their language and shared their cultural background. In addition, they educated their people as to the spread of venereal disease and the dangers if left untreated. As more pediatric cases were discovered, the Eskimos came to realize that their sexual practices, although natural to them, resulted in negative effects. Gradually, this reeducation developed into a rethinking of the sexual morality.

During the time I resided in the area, an article published by two Public Health Service physicians (Shore and Winkelstein 1971) attempted to reflect the growing incidence of pediatric gonorrhea. Their findings seem to be grossly misleading, however, in that the doctors purported to show evidence of nonsexual transmission of gonorrhea in Eskimo children, paying little or no attention to the sexual mores of the native people on whom the study was based. Neither physician spoke the language of the people or was closely acquainted with their cultural patterns. Both dealt with the people primarily on a medical basis and did not have the inherent trust of the native people, as did the health aides.

Their study took examples from villages in the Kuskokwim area and involved 15 cases of gonorrhea in 14 native children ranging in age from 21 months to 12 and a half years. (One child was infected twice.) They indicated that seven contracted gonorrhea by indirect contact, three by sexual contact, and five from unknown causes. In each of the seven "indirect contact" cases, it was noted that the children slept with parents, one or both of whom had gonorrhea. If the physicians had made themselves aware of the sexual practices of the people, they would not have surmised that no sexual contact took place between parent and child. If careful investigation of the five "unknown" cases had been made by persons who spoke the language and who had the trust of the native people, a history of sexual contact with parents, other adults, adolescents, or siblings—any of whom could have been infected—would have been elicited.

By neglecting to take into account the preexisting sexual mores of the people on whom the study was based, the physicians presented data out of context, ignoring clues that would have invalidated their hypothesis. It is disturbing to note that this study was accepted as valid by other medical professionals not versed in Eskimo culture.

At the time the study was being conducted, however, its existence was unknown to the community. What was known and widely communicated were the dangers of venereal disease. Religious leaders echoed the words of the medical staff, and school personnel were alert to rumors and ready to report possible cases. The newspaper printed information about venereal disease in both languages and promoted the idea of establishing centers where sexually and physically abused women could find refuge and receive medical treatment and counseling.

Today, with the influence of the National Organization for Women, government support for women's shelters, increase in education, and more concerted efforts in combating venereal disease, child sexual abuse is recognized as a statewide problem. Information has been disseminated to even the smallest village. Law enforcement has increased its area of influence, and more perpetrators have been brought to justice. Women's groups have been formed to counsel families and children who are victims of physical and sexual abuse. Children are being taught to have respect for themselves and their bodies. Although violence and alcohol abuse still accompany some sexual acts, sexual abuse is now recognized as being unjust, immoral, and unlawful.

The "old ways" still exist to some extent, but to a greater degree, acculturation of the Eskimo to modern American sexual mores has redefined their cultural practices. Just as acculturation has affected native language, religion, customs, education, and subsistence patterns, so too will the effects of the cultural impact on sexual mores continue to reveal themselves over time.

References

Alaska Geographic Almanac. 1986. Edmond, WA: Northwest Publishing Co.

Chance, Norman A. 1966. *The Eskimo of North Alaska.* New York: Holt, Rinehart and Winston, 62.

Oswalt, Wendell H. 1963. *Napaskiak.* Tucson: The University of Arizona Press.

Oswalt, Wendell H. 1967. *Alaskan Eskimos.* San Francisco: Chandler Publishing Company.

Shore, William, M.D., and Jerry Winkelstein, M.D. 1971. "Non-Venereal Transmission of Gonococcal Infections to Children." *Journal of Pediatrics* 79:661–63.

Index

About the Contributors

Daniel Abrahamson, Ph.D., is Codirector of the Center for Adult and Adolescent Psychotherapy in South Windsor, Connecticut. Through the Traumatic Stress Treatment Program at the Center, he specializes in working with people who have been victimized and traumatized. Dr. Abrahamson received his Ph.D. in clinical psychology from the State University of New York at Albany.

Carolyn Agosta, ACSW, is a cofounder and Codirector of Ending Violence Effectively, a Denver-based treatment center for victims of violence (especially rape, incest, and other forms of family violence). She holds a Masters of Social Work degree and has been working with victims since 1974. Ms. Agosta is the founding chairperson of the Denver Victim Services Center and the founder of the Self-Protection Instruction Team, a Colorado-based program that teaches personal safety and techniques to prevent or reduce violence in one's life.

Barbara S. Bunk, Ph.D., has been a clinical psychologist on the Staff of New England Clinical Associates, a private office in West Hartford, Connecticut, that is devoted to the treatment of sexual abuse, since 1984. Dr. Bunk specializes in the treatment of child sexual abuse victims, offenders and their families, and has extensive experience in working with adult survivors as well. A faculty member of the Saint Joseph College Institute for Child Sexual Abuse Intervention, Dr. Bunk holds a Ph.D. in clinical psychology from the University of Toledo. She was formerly a children's therapist at the Children's Resource Center in Bowling Green, Ohio.

Richard L. Cage, M.A., has been a member of the Montgomery County Maryland Police Department since 1971. For the past eleven years, he has been a detective in the Youth Division and a member of the Child Abuse–Sexual Offense Unit. During this time he has conducted more than one thousand child sexual abuse investigations and has interviewed more than three thousand children. Detective Cage holds a Bachelor of Science degree in criminology from the University of Maryland and a Master of Criminal Justice degree from George Washington University. He has lectured throughout the United States on the role of law enforcement in investigating cases of child sexual abuse and has been a consultant to The Chesapeake Institute for the past four years. In 1987, Detective Cage served on the Surgeon General's planning committee for the development of protocol for cases of child sexual abuse and received the Governor's Certificate of Merit from the State of Maryland in recognition of his outstanding contributions in the field of victims' rights and services.

Jan Marie DeLipsey, M.Ed., is Executive Director of Treatment and Evaluating Services, a sexual assault treatment clinic for victims and perpetrators located in Dallas, Texas. She frequently serves as an expert witness in sexual assault cases and has been appointed by the Governor of Texas to serve on the Inter-Agency Council on Sex Offender Treatment. Ms. DeLipsey is currently a doctoral student of psychology at Texas Woman's University.

Denise J. Gelinas, Ph.D., received her doctorate in clinical psychology from the University of Massachusetts. She is the cofounder and former Codirector of The Incest Treatment Program at Baystate Medical Center in Springfield, Massachusetts. Dr. Gelinas is now a part-time faculty member of the Smith College School of Social Work and the Saint Joseph College Institute for Child Sexual Abuse Intervention. She has written extensively about treatment for child sexual abuse and provides consultation and training to agencies and practitioners. She also maintains a private psychotherapy practice in Northampton and Springfield, Massachusetts.

Sue Kelly James, M.S., has been the coordinator of the Dallas County Rape Crisis and Child Sexual Abuse Center since 1978. Along with her coauthor, Jan DeLipsey, Ms. James developed an evaluation and treatment program for child sexual assault victims as well as a program for videotaping the testimony of child witnesses. She received a Master of Science degree in rehabilitation counseling from the University of Texas Health Science Center in 1976. Ms. James does both consulting and teaching on child sexual abuse in Texas and in other states. Her current research and training focus is on effective interviewing of child victims and identification of false allegations of sexual abuse.

Michael F. Johanek, M.D., is a division psychiatrist for the First Marine Division and heads the Alcohol Rehabilitation Department at the United States Naval Hospital, Camp Pendleton, California. He is also the Director of Mental Health for the Base Brig at Camp Pendleton. Dr. Johanek was elected to Phi Beta Kappa as an undergraduate at the University of California at Berkeley in 1973. He also graduated from the University of California School of Medicine in San Francisco in 1977 and then completed a residency in psychiatry at the Naval Hospital in Oakland. Dr. Johanek currently serves as a volunteer therapist for the Oceanside Chapter of Parents United in San Diego County.

Mary Loring is a cofounder and Codirector of Ending Violence Effectively, a Denver-based treatment center for victims of violence (especially rape, incest, and other forms of family violence). She has been working with victims of sexual assault since 1980 and is the cofounder of Project Challenge, a statewide effort to enable victim services to become integrated and accessible to persons with disabilities. She was also the founding chairperson of the Colorado Coalition Against Sexual Assault.

Lisa McCann, Ph.D., received her doctorate in clinical psychology from the University of Kansas and a Master of Social Work Degree from Columbia University. She is Codirector of the Center for Adult and Adolescent Psychotherapy in South Windsor, Connecticut and founded the Center's Traumatic Stress Treatment Program. Dr. McCann is a member of the American Psychological Association and the Society for Traumatic Stress Studies. She currently specializes in treatment and research with victimized populations.

Connie E. Naitove, A.T.R., holds a M.A.L.S. *degree* from Dartmouth College and is a registered arts therapist, a registered drama therapist, a certified poetry therapist, a professional drama therapist, a recreational therapy specialist and has completed her training as a clinical transactional analyst. Ms. Naitove is a Diplomate of the American Board of Psychotherapy, a Clinical Associate of the American Board of Medical Psychotherapists and a fellow of the American Orthopsychiatric Association. A staff member of the St. Francis Center for Personal Growth, Inc., in Vermont, she also conducts a private practice in Hanover, New Hampshire.

Laurie Anne Pearlman, Ph.D., received her doctorate in clinical psychology from the University of Connecticut. She is a psychotherapist as well as the Research Director at the Center for Adult and Adolescent Psychotherapy in South Windsor, Connecticut. Dr. Pearlman is a member of the American Orthopsychiatric Association, the American Psychological Association, and the Connecticut Psychological Association. She is currently engaged in research about the epidemiology and treatment of trauma victims.

David K. Sakheim, Ph.D., is a clinical psychologist on the staff of the Center for Adult and Adolescent Psychotherapy in South Windsor, Connecticut. Dr. Sakheim received his training at Brown University and the State University of New York at Albany. He currently specializes in the treatment of abusers and victims and has a special interest in the treatment of multiple personality disorders.

Sheila Thompson, M.C.W., holds a Masters degree in Child Welfare from

Saint Joseph College in West Hartford, Connecticut, where she is also a part-time instructor. Ms. Thompson is also a certified alcohol counselor in Connecticut and a reality therapist with the Northeast Association for Reality Therapy, serving both on the Board of Directors and as a faculty member and trainer for that organization. For the past eight years, she has been a case worker for a municipal social services agency, specializing in services to individuals, families, and groups. Prior to moving to Connecticut, she lived, worked, and completed her undergraduate studies in Alaska.

Carolyn J. Wabrek, M.Ed, is Director of the Sexual Therapy Program at Hartford Hospital in Hartford, Connecticut. She received her sexual therapy training at the University of Pennsylvania School of Medicine in the Department of Psychiatry and her Masters degree from the University of Hartford. A former president of the Connecticut Association for Marriage and Family Therapy, Ms. Wabrek is also a charter member of the Society for Sex Therapy and Research and a full member of Sigma Xi Scientific Research Society. She is the coauthor of numerous publications on human behavior and sexual therapy and has lectured extensively, both nationally and internationally, on these topics.

About the Author

Suzanne M. Sgroi, M.D., is Executive Director of New England Clinical Associates, a private treatment center for child sexual abuse. She is Director of the Saint Joseph College Institute for Child Sexual Abuse Intervention in West Hartford, Connecticut. Dr. Sgroi served as program developer of The Connecticut Department of Children and Youth Services' Sexual Trauma Treatment Program from 1977 to 1979 and is a teacher and consultant on child sexual abuse for child protective services and the Municipal Police Training Council.

A physician in private practice in Suffield, Connecticut, Dr. Sgroi is also actively involved in teaching and consulting on child sexual abuse. She is the author of *A Handbook of Clinical Intervention in Child Sexual Abuse* (Lexington Books, 1982), which received the American Journal of Nursing Book of the Year Award in 1983.

A native of Fulton, New York, Dr. Sgroi received her A.B. in Liberal Arts from Syracuse University, and her M.D. from the State University of New York at Buffalo. Her internship was served at the Millard Fillmore Hospital, Buffalo, New York, and residency in internal medicine at the Rochester General Hospital, Rochester, New York. Before moving to Connecticut in 1972, she served as a Rotating Physician, Internal Medicine, on the Hospital Ship Hope mission to Natal, Brazil.